TASTE THE STATE GEORGIA

Elberta peaches, once the most popular variety in the United States, but now an increasingly rare sight in Georgia given their vulnerability to disease. Photograph © David S. Shields.

TASTE THE STATE
GEORGIA

DISTINCTIVE FOODS AND STORIES
FROM WHERE EATING LOCAL BEGAN

KEVIN MITCHELL AND DAVID S. SHIELDS

FOREWORD BY MASHAMA BAILEY

© 2025 University of South Carolina
Foreword © 2025 Mashama Bailey

Published by the University of South Carolina Press
Columbia, South Carolina 29208

uscpress.com

Printed in Canada

Library of Congress Cataloging-in-Publication Data can be found at http://catalog.loc.gov/.

ISBN: 978-1-64336-544-2 (hardcover)
ISBN: 978-1-64336-602-9 (ebook)

The authors have made every effort to identify the copyright holders of the historical recipes in this book and to obtain permission to reproduce them. We would be pleased to rectify any omissions in subsequent printings.

CONTENTS

Foreword vii

Preface ix

Apples 1

Barbecue 5

Benne 8

Biscuits 10

Brunswick Stew 15

Butter Beans 18

Cane Syrup 20

Catfish 24

Chatham Artillery Punch 29

Cheese Straws 32

Chicken Pie 35

Coca-Cola Cake 37

Coleslaw 40

Collards 43

Condiments 45

Corn Bread 51

Country Captain 54

Country Ham 57

Crab 59

Crowder Peas 64

Deviled Eggs 67

Doves 70

Duck 72

Figs 75

Fried Bologna 78

Fried Pie 80

Green Tomatoes 83

Grits 87

Grouper 90

Guinea Fowl 92

Guinea Squash 98

Honey 101

Lard 103

Mull 106	Roast Turkey 164
Mullet 111	Rutabagas 167
Mustard Greens 114	Savannah Red Rice 170
Ogeechee Limes 117	Sea Island Red Peas 174
Oils 119	Shrimp 177
Okra 122	Snap Beans 182
Oysters 126	Squash Casserole 185
Peaches 129	Sweet Potatoes 188
Peanuts 132	Sweet Potato Fries 196
Pears 136	Trout 198
Pecans 139	Turnips and Turnip Sallet 201
Persimmon Beer 142	Vidalia Onions 206
Pickles 145	
Pimento Cheese 148	*Menus of the 1913 Georgia Products Feasts* 211
Poke Salad 151	*Sources* 259
Possum and Taters 153	*General Index* 273
Rattlesnake Watermelon 158	*Recipe Index* 283
Rice and Gravy 161	*Menu Index* 285

FOREWORD

I'm a New Yorker, born and raised. My mother is from Georgia, where she was born and raised. When she moved to New York with my father, for school, work, and to start a family, the essence of her upbringing was often on full display through the meals that she cooked for us. We could tell when my mom was missing her hometown because on Sundays the house would fill with the smells of cornbread, butterbeans, and smothered turkey. She loved the South, and for a moment she returned with us, her family, to live in Savannah for several years. Most of my formative memories are about food, family, and the South, even while growing up in New York City. From that watchful child's eye of mine I would listen to stories of my mother's youth while we ate. My parents, siblings, and I spent many summer vacations and holidays traveling back and forth between the Bronx or Queens or Savannah and Waynesboro, Georgia.

Ten years ago, when I returned to the Hostess City to take the helm at The Grey restaurant, I began to refer to myself as a second-generation Southerner removed. I felt the need to ground myself in my family's Georgian history. This was my way of staying connected to those stories of the rural South my family talked about while I was growing up. My mother's parents, the West family, created a safe place for many folks growing up in Waynesboro for decades. These stories focus on generosity, community, and food. When developing the menu for The Grey, I would reminisce about the long summer days and the cold winter nights during our frequent visits to formulate my thoughts around the ingredients from my grandmother's kitchen.

Taste the State Georgia is a book that has justified the significance of those experiences. With the discovery of the menus from the 1913 Georgia Products feasts held throughout the state to promote eating local, Kevin Mitchell and David S. Shields have researched the contributions Georgia has added to the landscape of Southern food. Researching ingredients like oysters, Vidalia onions, apples, and cane syrup this book is full of discoveries from the cultural traditions of the Native Americans, enslaved Africans, and colonial settlers. We learn about trade routes and migration patterns that helped shape the economics of the

Peach State. We learn about food production and the businesses built to distribute them.

Modern dishes are a result of centuries of cultural exchange and adaptation, but Mitchell and Shields choose not to focus on that. This book helps us to understand the true nuances of the South and Southern food, dish by dish, ingredient by ingredient. It explores the interpersonal relationships that Georgians have with the land and the sea. We can relive, through foodways, the popularity of different areas in the state and gain better understanding on how and why certain areas were favored over others. They explore the successes and failures around building a food culture and what was discovered along the way. Mitchell and Shields show us the receipts on how some Georgia foods went in and out of vogue. They explore the effects of politics and economics within Georgia's food culture, and how they have affected the health and nutritional value associated with Southern foods. It's fascinating to discover why Georgians eat what they eat.

I have never come across a book so clear with its intentions to dispel the myths of how iconic Southern ingredients and recipes came to be. The importance of *Taste the State Georgia* and the regional foods within it can be a source of pride for people and communities. Knowing the origins of a dish can strengthen personal and communal connections to heritage, allowing people to preserve and pass down traditions. My mother did for her children, allowing me to gain perspective around the significance of dishes like stewed collards, Savannah red rice, squash casserole, boiled peanuts, and chestnut dressing. This book will prepare you for your next Georgian culinary adventure and give you a bit of history on why Southerners eat what they eat.

Chef Mashama Bailey
Savannah, Georgia

PREFACE

This book celebrates Georgia's distinctive foods. It highlights the dishes and ingredients that have bolstered Georgia's reputation as a place for superlative eating. It tells the stories of how now-famous preparations for pimento cheese, chicken pie, and sweet potato fries came to be. You will find recipes here, classic formulations drawn from historical sources, and Chef Kevin Mitchell's updating of revered Georgia dishes, but this is much more than a cookbook. This book shows how and why Georgia food matters, both as a kind of southern cookery and as American cuisine. It charts how Native American, European, and African food cultures mingled to form something distinctive and compelling.

This is the second food portrait of a particular state that we have presented. The success of *Taste the State: South Carolina's Signature Foods, Recipes, and Their Stories* showed us that in-depth explorations of geographic food culture—past and present—has an audience. Yet in certain respects, Georgia should have been the state that launched our culinary historical explorations of a southern state's foods, not South Carolina. Georgia, after all, was the first state in the United States that made a concerted effort to define its distinctive culinary culture. That happened more than a century ago, when the Georgia Chamber of Commerce challenged the state's hotels and counties to hold dinners featuring local products and preparations. Ideally the hosts would source their foods from within the county, but if items had to be sourced from farther afield, they had to be Georgian at minimum. On November 18, 1913, seventy-five towns and cities in Georgia staged these Georgia Products Feasts. Thousands sat down to meals at which "Georgia raised food alone was served." The success and seriousness of the endeavor was registered in the state's newspapers, which printed descriptions, highlights of the day's oratory, and most revealing of all—menus.

What prompted Georgians to emphasize their local productions? The very same reason the localities stress their cookery today—a sense that a cosmopolitan commercially driven type of eating is being imposed from "outside." In the first decade of the twentieth century groceries across the South began stocking canned goods, processed foods, and packaged grains from national suppliers. Northern and western food companies began to dominate the offerings. This invasion of nonlocal products set the Georgia Chamber of Commerce advocating for "food from here." The response exceeded the organizers' expectations in its enthusiasm, ingenuity, and thoroughness, with localities managing to produce out-of-season items, because they were such signatures of a place that it was unthinkable not to include them. Every region of the state responded, and the surviving menus, which we have reproduced as a coda to this study, supply a detailed, highly specific picture of what Georgians identified as their food in the Sea Islands and Lowcountry, Midlands, and in North Georgia. These menus have instructed our table of contents here.

Some of the menu items—country ham, collard greens, corn bread, sweet potato pone, barbecue—were not peculiar to Georgia but belonged to the southern larder generally. Nevertheless, the hosts reckoned there was a way they prepared the dishes that made them "ours." They knew enough about dishes claimed as signatures by other states—Virginia's fried chicken, Alabama's Lane cake, Florida's pompano, Texas's chili con carne, South Carolina's broiled rice birds, Louisiana's crawfish—to exclude them from the menus. Nonetheless their cultural consciousness was such that they grasped that southern food differed from the foods of the North and West, and that Georgia food belonged to a regional set of foodways.

Everyone in 1913 Georgia knew, and in 2025 presumes, that southern food stands somewhat apart from American cookery. In the country at large beef has long been the most important meat; in the South, pork rules. In the United States wheat is the most important grain; in the South, corn. The potato—boiled, mashed, baked, or fried—ranks number one among tubers; in the South, the sweet potato reigns. In most of America if you mention the word "peas," the green garden pea comes to mind. In the South, you may be speaking of field peas, black-eyed peas, or crowder peas. In the United States California-grown almonds lead sales among nuts; in the South it is the pecan. And then of course we have the nut that isn't really a nut but a subterranean legume—the peanut—which we boil as well as roast. Favorite greens nationally? Lettuce. In the South? Collards, turnip, and mustard. And the South has grown since colonial times the foods of Africa—okra, watermelon, sorghum, eggplant. These commonplaces of understanding have operated as a background in Georgia's food sensibility.

Southern food does have some common regional elements. Yet as any southerner will tell you, it is your state that matters in football, in property law, in politics—and in food. Some I am sure will deplore this as the afterlife of the South's old civil religion of states' rights. But there is no denying the persistence of state mystique. When it comes to food, "states' rights" means "states' bragging rights." Every southerner knows the throw-down dishes—the key creations upon which a state's claim to culinary fame rests. Let's just think of sweet things: Texas pecan pie, Florida key lime pie, Louisiana pralines, Arkansas black apple cake, Kentucky bourbon bread pudding, Tennessee blackberry jam cake, North Carolina Moravian sugar cake, Mississippi mud pie, Alabama Lane cake, South Carolina rice pudding, Virginia chess pie. Georgians don't even have to fire up their brain cells to put forth their candidate for the southern states throw down: peach cobbler.

Yet it is a misrepresentation on some level to insist that some essential "Georgia-ness" defines all the ingredients and dishes here. Indeed, some were shaped before the colony was settled or the state was constituted. Cherokee and Muskogee maize, beans, squash, bird peppers, chestnuts, groundnuts, persimmons, mayhaws, plums, and mulberries remained a food constant before, during, and after the European settlement of the state's territory. European livestock, garden vegetables, grains, and fruits filled pastures, gardens, fields, and orchards. Consider the Austrian religious refugees, the Salzburgers, who settled in Ebenezer, Georgia, in the 1740s and quickly became the foremost millers in the South during the colonial era. Using networks of coreligionists in Europe, they secured seed for Timilia durum wheat, a distinguished old pasta and bread wheat grown in Sicily. The first macaroni and cheese, served in the 1790s in Charleston, South Carolina, and Savannah, Georgia, by Angelo Santi, employed this classic hard wheat. African ingredients that crossed from Madagascar and West Africa—okra, benne, guinea squash, watermelon, field peas, guinea corn (grain sorghum), finger millet—and the cooking knowledge that shaped the many one-pot stews and fried items are central to what would become Georgia cooking. Then there are items brought in from the West Indies during the colonial period including sweet potatoes, sugar cane, and arrowroot. In the later twentieth century Latin migrant laborers worked harvests and sometimes plantings in Georgia. Tiendas (stores) were established to service the workers. Gradually Mexican and Central American foodways entered Georgia. Because this cultural incursion came in farming areas and small towns, it operated as an additional vernacular of cooking out in the country, not cosmopolitan ethnic fare found in the big cities. The complex mixture of ingredients and culinary knowledge produced something unprecedented, distinctive, and creative. And this mixture was to some degree beyond Georgian.

Within Georgia various regional identities have become entrenched and associated with certain products and dishes. These regional identities were foregrounded in the 1913 Georgia Products Feasts menus, and they endure as hallmarks—Fort Valley pecans, Ocmulgee catfish, Sapelo Island clams, Elijay apples. There are other kinds of regionality at work as well. The Gullah Geechee cookery of the Sea Islands may share more with Lowcountry cooking of South Carolina in terms of African cooking aesthetics, ingredients, and dishes than north Georgia cooking. Yet it is a kind of nonsense to suggest that it does not belong in this collection.

If the 1913 Georgia Products campaign serves as a point of departure for our overview of Georgia's food, providing a core repertoire of ingredients and dishes that Georgians themselves put forward as their food, it cannot be the entire frame for *Taste the State Georgia*. Tastes change. Some items once broadly loved are now cherished by a select few: Ogeechee lime pickles, possum and taters. Georgia's most distinctive stew—mull—didn't appear on a single menu from 1913. It emerged as an important camp dish, then restaurant special, and then home preparation (in the case of shrimp mull and chicken mull) over the course of the twentieth century. Creativity is a constant in food history—and new pleasures are created every decade: the pimento burger, the Vidalia onion tart, sweet potato fries. The twentieth century greatly enriched the range of dining in Georgia, and we have made an effort to show how tradition changed in the past century. Not every change will be discussed here. Georgia has been a significant player in the national and international beverage and candy industries. Since these stories have been told extensively elsewhere, we will not make them central to this book. However, we hope you like seeing Coca-Cola Cake included.

Getting the tradition right is important. Tracking the exact trajectory of change in taste and consumption patterns of the past century is informative and amusing. So this treatment of Georgia cooking is more historical than others you may have encountered—those by our talented friends Nathalie Dupree, Matthew Raiford, or Damon Fowler for instance. How do we present the past? We have taken care to locate and reproduce early classic forms of recipes. These often appeared in newspapers and agricultural magazines rather than in cookbooks. You can verify this for yourself by counting your grandmother's clippings in her recipe box. We have searched manuscript collections, church cookbooks, reports from travelers, historical hotel menus, ingredient profiles from early agricultural journals or classic horticultural books such as *Gardening from the South* (1856) by William N. White. There are certain pre-1975 cookbooks that are regarded as Georgia classics and we examined them all. Kevin at times updates a traditional dish to suggest how it might be made more conveniently, or with more impactful flavors. These are set off from the other recipes reproduced here. We combine historical illustrations and contemporary photographs to provide you with an interesting visual representation of the items we discuss.

Our approach was to divide the entries between us, each selecting those we were most enthusiastic to compose. And when our enthusiasm matched, we collaborated. If you would like to dig deeper into a particular recipe, our sources are noted so you can consult the primary sources grounding our presentations. To help ensure accuracy in crafting this food landscape, it was not unusual that we shared our entries with those with special knowledge of the subject for correction and or supplementation. It is not surprising that the number of people who study the history of southern food has grown in the past decades. While a generation ago the emphasis would have been on the labor of production and processing and the race dynamics surrounding it, that work has discovered so much already that we can turn to matters of horticultural history, ethnobotany, cultural anthropology, and market history. The plentitude of catalogs produced by Georgia seed companies and nurseries, such as N. L. Willet of Augusta, Thomasville Nurseries, Rood Pecan Groves of Albany, Wight Nurseries of Cairo, Milledgeville Nursery Company, B. W. Stone of Thomasville, Piedmont Plant Company of Albany, G. M. Bacon Pecan Co. of DeWitt, P. D. Fulwood of Tifton, Omega Plant Farms, H. G. Hastings of Atlanta, Alexander Seed Company of Augusta, Curry-Arrington Seed Company of Rome, and L. M. E. Berckmans's nationally famous Fruitlands nursery in Augusta, ensured that we had a rich paper trail of the fruits and vegetables whose seed was sold as "Georgia-grown."

Our ambition is to supply food profiles that will be informative to all, with each containing some information that will be novel to even the expert cooks and gardeners of Georgia. We devote a few entries to lost items—foods that were once central but became either functionally extinct or passed out of fashion. There is a peculiar pleasure that attaches to reviving old dishes, and these lost food entries are an invitation to you to have a hand in redeeming something special from culinary purgatory.

Kevin: My intrigue with Georgia food first began when I moved to the state in the early part of the 2000s. It was then when I experienced my first sweet Georgia peach, a flavor that completely eclipsed the peaches I grew up eating in New Jersey. I have had other rarer connections to the flavors of Georgia, such as the Ossabaw pig from our friend Tank Johnson and when David generously gifted me a prized bottle of the Sapelo Island Purple Ribbon Sugar Cane Syrup. With these few experiences my heart, mind, and tastebuds were opened to the greatness of this large state. As implied above, at times I take some culinary liberty with some of the historical recipes. I do this to show how the flavors and tastes of diners have changed over time. Do not fret though, in my effort to update, I still give a nod to history while giving you something new to ponder. Writing this book with David has allowed me to explore my tastes as well. You are now invited to explore yours.

David: My involvement in Georgia food is multifaceted. As chair of the Carolina Gold Rice Foundation, I had the privilege to contribute to the restoration of rice planting in Georgia a decade ago. I also had the unique opportunity to assist the late Cornelia Bailey, matriarch of Sapelo Island, in restoring purple ribbon sugar cane to its ancestral growing area. I've contributed heirloom seed to numbers of farming operations across the state—to Hickory Hill in Thomson, to Comfort Farms in Milledgeville, to Gilliard Farms in Brunswick, to Wormsloe outside of Savannah. As chair of the Ark of Taste for the South, I have aided Georgia growers in ensuring some of the states' most endangered and historical ingredients—rattlesnake watermelon, pumpkin yam, Ogeechee lime, Kleckley sweet watermelon, Ossabaw pig, Yates apple—were entered onto Slow Food's register of the world's most imperiled and flavorful foods. And I have published biographies for many of the most important professional chefs in Georgia in my book, *The Culinarians* (2017) and wrote the history of the rise of Lowcountry cookery, *Southern Provisions* (2015). Writing *Taste the State Georgia* with Kevin has enabled me to explore in depth the history of this greatly significant place in the story of southern and American food.

More than two centuries ago Jean Anthelme Brillat-Savarin, the founder of the field of gastronomy, made a distinction between feeding—ingestion inspired by the desire to quell hunger—and dining—consumption moved by pleasure and thought more than biology. To appreciate the glory of good food, one must understand what one is eating. This book provides a rich understanding of more than sixty ingredients and dishes associated with Georgia. It does so with the hope that your table experiences will be richer, more insightful, and more enduring in memory. Each entry offers a path by which you can connect personal experience with a broader cultural practice and deeper local history. The tradition of Georgia's food continues to change and develop. What the future will bring we cannot know precisely. But with the state's wealth of plants and animals, we do not doubt that it will continue to be an enviably sumptuous cuisine strongly evocative of place and Georgia's people.

Apples

On the hills outside of Blairsville, the classic apples that delighted generations of Georgians stand in tidy rows. These are not apples that you now find in the grocery store, the commodity fruits grown in the Pacific Northwest. These are varieties bred or discovered as seedlings by southerners that were long adapted to the growing conditions and culinary needs of our region. Their names are resonant—the Nickajack, the Disharoom, the Horse, the Rabun, the Cranberry of north Georgia, the Yates, and the Black Limbertwig. Some were cider apples, some were for drying, some were for saucing, some were for fresh eating. Different varieties ripened at different times. Early season apples, such as the Carolina Red June, the American Permain, and the Early Strawberry, announced a new yearly cycle of fruit. Many of the apples in the Blairsville orchard came to light after long neglect during the great recovery of southern apple heritage that took place in the last thirty years. The nationalization of the produce market during the twentieth century nearly eradicated many splendid old varieties as modern all-purpose apples such as the Honeycrisp, the Fuji, the Pink Lady, the Red Delicious took over the produce section. Under the auspices of the University of Georgia, Josh Fuder, Ray Covington, and Stephen Mihm have planted the Heritage Apple Orchard to ensure that the classic flavors remain available, and Georgians can secure scion wood to grow their own trees of their old favorite types.

The apple (*Malus domestica*) is an edible fruit grown from trees now cultivated all over the world. First cultivated in central Asia eighty-five hundred years ago, ancestral forms of the apple still grow in Kazakhstan. Apple trees spread into Europe during the Iron Age. Rome cultivated it as early as 300 BCE. Romans brought it to the British Isles and in 1622, Britons carried apple trees to Virginia for planting. In North America apples spread westward and southward with settlement. Today there are nearly eight thousand varieties, and of these, hundreds of southern varieties remain in cultivation. Creighton Lee Calhoun's *Southern Apples* (1995, expanded 2010) documented the profusion of types and uses. But many historical varieties now survive in only a handful of trees.

When one speaks about the apple today, one thinks about Washington state produce shipped from the Pacific Northwest. Within this book, we pay homage to the extraordinary apples that come from the South, and Georgia particularly. For years the state of Georgia has been touted as the Peach State. Yet commercial-scale apple growing has gone on in the territory around Ellijay for more than century, and orchards of Red Delicious cover Habersham County, providing a local source for a common commodity fruit, fresher than any shipped from Northwestern apple states. Georgia began projecting a presence in the national sales scene in the first decade of the twentieth century. Ambitious farmers began expanding the scale of their orchards. Porter Orchards in Essom, Georgia, was the largest in the South in the period between the two world wars. As early as 1908, Georgia apples were displayed conspicuously at the National Apple Growers Show in Washington state. Out of fifteen hundred exhibits Georgia apples received second place, establishing themselves as some of the best in the country. In 1914 growers formed the Georgia Apple Association.

In the first part of the twentieth century the orchards grew a greater variety of apples than they do now. In 1927 Georgia State College recommended the following varieties by month:

> July: Yellow Transparent and Early Harvest
> August: Regal and Brilliant
> September: Grimes Golden
> October: Red Delicious, Grimes Golden, and Kinnard
> November: Red Delicious, Kinnard, and Jonathan
> December: Kinnard, Stayman Winesap, Jonathan, and York
> January: Stayman Winesap, Limbertwig, Arkansas Black, and York
> February: Stayman Winesap, Terry, and Yates
> March: Terry and Yates

In the middle of the twentieth century the Red and Golden Delicious Apples dominated plantings, but recently the tides of taste have turned against the Red Delicious. Nowadays the recommended varieties for cultivation are Anna and Dorsett in the southern counties. In the upper part of the state, Ginger Gold, Gala, Mollie's Delicious, Ozark Gold, Golden Delicious, Mutzu, Yates, and Granny Smith dominate new plantings.

The Grimes Golden (parent of the Golden Delicious) and the Yellow Transparent were revered as sauce apples, the best sort to boil down to a rich dark sauce to go with pork chops, gingerbread, or further cooked into apple butter, applesauce pie, or eggless applesauce cake. The process for making homemade apple sauce is covered in the following recipe for Apple Sauce Pie. We treat Fried Apple Pie in our entry on Fried Pies.

Apple Sauce Pie

Sunny South (December 29, 1879)

Take mellow, tart apples; pare, core and stew till the pulp is free from lumps and mash fine. To every pint of the sauce add a teaspoonful of butter, one teaspoonful of ground cinnamon, and beat all together. Line a pie-tin with crust and fill in the sauce. Cut strips of pastry and decorate the pie. Bake in a moderately hot oven. When the crust is done the pie will be ready to remove from the oven. To be eaten warm with a dressing of sweetened cream dipped over it.

The pectin in apples acts as a prebiotic, which could aid in digestive issues. For those who suffer from allergic reactions to dairy or eggs, applesauce is an excellent substitute when baking cakes, waffles, and pancakes. That comes in handy in my (Kevin's) household, as my daughter is allergic to eggs. Additionally, apples provide a good source of fiber.

A more distinctly flavored and pungent apple is called for when making fried apples or apple compote. The peppermint gush of the Honeycrisp doesn't quite serve. Older classics such as the Arkansas Black (a good choice for apple cakes) and the Black Limbertwig are ideal if you can source them.

Compote of Apples

Savannah Tribune (December 25, 1911)

One pound of apples, one quarter pound of lump sugar, one capful of water, the juice of half a lemon, a few drops of red coloring. Put the sugar, water, and lemon juice into a clean enameled saucepan and let them boil quickly for ten minutes. Peel the apples, core them, and cut them into quarters. Throw the pieces into the boiling sirup. And let them cook slowly until clear and tender but not broken. Then remove the apples, reduce the sirup, and add a few drops of coloring. Arrange the apples in a glass dish and pour the sirup over. A little cream of custard served with them is a great improvement.

In 2000 an estimated 360,000 apple trees were growing in the state, producing twenty-seven million pounds of apples. The state has five growing zones, three dedicated to conventional varieties. Though apples grow throughout the state, most are grown in north Georgia. Ellijay in Gilmer County is considered the apple-growing capital of Georgia. In 2021 Gilmer County produced $3,948,750 in sales. Outside of Gilmer County, the following counties produce the most apples: Fannin, Taylor, Habersham, Haralson, Hall, Macon, Polk, Walker, and Murray. Fourteen varieties dominate plantings in those counties, the most popular being Red and Golden Delicious, Granny

Maestro, a young Boykin spaniel, admires a bowl of Albemarle Pippin apples, one of the South's standard cider apples. Photograph © David S. Shields.

Smith, and Fuji. Though not bred in Georgia, these apples dominate its orchards because of an enduring national demand for the varieties.

Growers throughout the state face daunting challenges. Soil chemistry must be balanced, or the trees will not grow. Trees are susceptible to many diseases such as black rot, fire blight, scab, bitter rot, and Alternaria. Insects—apple tree borers, scales, aphids, fruit worms, and red spider mites—invade the orchards. Growers have to be current with the latest science on pest and pathogen control. Fortunately, the apple industry has a strong grower association, robust support from universities, and powerful advocates in the state's department of agriculture.

The most recent development in the Georgia apple industry has been the revival of hard cider in the state. Mirroring the burgeoning of artisanal cideries in New England and Virginia, Georgia has looked to old apples: the Yates, the Hewes Crab, the Stayman Winesap to renew its affection for hard cider. Mercier Orchards, Reece's Cider, Treehorn Cider, Urban Tree Hard Cider, and North 2 South Cider Works are in the vanguard of this movement with new cideries planned and coming on line. Georgia is fortunate in having its own cider apple. The Yates apple dates to 1844, discovered as a seedling in Fayette County by Matthew Yates. It has two virtues: It produces a great deal of juice and it has a distinctive flavor with a good amount of sugar. Its pale red skin with dark streaks is visually striking. One of the best things, however, about the Yates is that it stores exceptionally well, allowing it to be enjoyed year-round. It is also heat tolerant, a must for a Georgia apple. Many southern cideries outside of Georgia have adopted the Yates as a component of their cider mixtures. At the time of publication, it is the Georgia heirloom variety most in demand regionally.

Barbecue

As I (Kevin) sit in front of my laptop, I ask myself, what is Georgia barbecue? Is there such a thing? In the barbecue world, one rarely hears of Georgia having its' own distinct style. When you look at the map of the United States, you will see that the state of Georgia borders four central states known for barbecue. These states are North and South Carolina, Tennessee, and Alabama. You would need to drive far through Mississippi and Louisiana to get to another famous state for barbecue, Texas. When you sample barbecue made from across Georgia, you encounter sauces borrowed from several styles. Mostly you will find the sweet tomato-based sauce from Tennessee, the tangy flavors of mustard-based sauce from South Carolina, the tartness from vinegar-based sauce from North Carolina (my favorite), and the mayonnaise-based sauce from Alabama. No matter the style, barbeque in Georgia is accompanied by one side in particular, Brunswick Stew.

When discussing barbecue, you must consider two things: barbecue as food and barbecue as event. Barbecue as food relates to the type of meat being cooked. Since the 1880s, pork has been the meat of choice, and prior to that time, beef shared the pit with pork. Pigs are barbecued before they have fully matured. Old cookbooks tell you that it is a young pig—a shoat—that makes for the best roasting or barbecuing. The breed of the hog influences the ideal age for barbecuing, since some kinds set meat quicker than others (the Georgia Ossabaw being the slowest). Often the pig is fed barley, apples, peanuts, or mulberries in its final weeks of life to sweeten the flesh. There have also always been a few local specialists in goat barbecues, a tradition that has undergone revival in the past decade with the influx of Latinos into the state. Still, the hog rules. And on the pig, Georgians prefer the rib, shoulder, and the ham. Cooking techniques include smoking, grilling, and pit cooking. The meat must be heated low and slow to achieve the ideal tenderness. Regular mopping of the meat with sauce ensures that it will be saturated with flavor.

Barbecue is a serious business in Georgia. Even in the wake of restaurant closures due to the COVID-19 pandemic, there must be more than four hundred eateries that feature barbecue, not that many fewer than the 474 visited by Steve Story in the 1990s when he compiled *The Peach State Glove Box Guide to Bar-B-Que*. It is not surprising that barbecue is now featured on the menus of fast-food chains and is a fixture in stadium concessions. Food trucks have been fixed on it as a dependable sell. A roll call of Atlanta's most popular food trucks features Willie B's Sisters Southern Cuisine, C-BO's BBQ, Gotta Have It, Biggum's BBQ, Crave Hot Dogs & BBQ, Greedyman's Bar B Que & Grill, Smokin' Mo's, The Royal Pig, Carson's, Pappy 2's, Memphis Diva Queen, and Sweet Auburn BBQ. It is the food of choice for tailgates at sporting events. The pulled pork sandwich must be the most cherished use of bread known in our region.

Before barbecue became linked to football tailgates as a ritual food of communal celebration, it was tied to politics. In 1794 the state legislature stipulated that barbecue would be served as the celebratory meal for the anniversary of Independence Day. Fourth of July barbecues became crowded occasions for feasting, political oratory, and shooting contests. Soon any politician or would-be politician who wished to set a campaign in motion staged a barbecue to attract the people. Indeed, the ability to prepare barbecue became at times a requisite for office. This was the case for John W. Callaway. Callaway, a 300-pound man from Wilkes County, Georgia, earned the title "King of Barbeque" early in the twentieth century. He was also the sheriff of Wilkes County. According to the *Atlanta Constitution*, since Callaway hosted his first barbecue, he never lost an election. The pinnacle of the political barbecue was the Slaton Barbecue, an annual event staged over several decades in the beginning of the twentieth century. Begun during the Hon. John M. Slaton's days as a state legislator, the yearly feasts brought together the principal officials and representatives of the state, for friendly revelry. Partisan rancor was forbidden, though witty banter with a party edge was expected. It continued long after he served as governor and into the 1930s.

Political barbecues were outdoor occasions, sometimes attracting thousands of attendees. When and under what circumstances did barbecue come inside? When and where did it debut as restaurant fare? Robert Moss, contributing barbecue editor for *Southern Living* magazine and author of *Barbecue: The History of an American Institution*, writes about Augusta's two most famous African American barbecue cooks, Augustus Ferguson and Pickens Wells. Ferguson's journey into barbecue was by happenstance. Born in Pickens County, South Carolina, in 1856, he found his way into Georgia in 1875 after a minor run-in with the law. Once in Augusta, he began to work with J. A. Bohler, a cotton farmer. Bohler was known for hosting large barbecues on the farm to raise money. Ferguson cooked. He did that for several years until he decided to go out alone. Once he started freelancing in 1898, his name became synonymous with barbecue, including hen barbecue. Soon after, he was advertised as the barbecue cook at Jansen's Restaurant on Ellis Street in downtown Augusta. This would be the Georgia restaurant that turned barbecue into a dining experience.

Pickens Wells's foray into barbecue began near the end of Augustus Ferguson's stint cooking for J. A. Bohler. After apprenticing under Ferguson, Wells took over cooking for Bohler and became well known for barbecue in his own right. He prepared a barbecue for President William Howard Taft during his famous tour of Georgia in 1909. Unfortunately, soon thereafter Wells ruptured a blood vessel in his brain. Though his reign was short-lived, he secured his place in barbecue royalty with his specialty—pulled pork.

During the twentieth century every sort of civic association, club, military unit, church group, community, and school held barbecues in every part of the state. People did distinguish between "old fashioned" barbecues—outdoors, cooked in pits, with more than simply pork on the menu, and the "barbecue dinner," a meal of pork and sides served to people in a meeting or dining room. Three of the Georgia Products Feasts in 1913 were barbecue dinners sponsored by rural counties. The dinners were catered by specialists in "cue." Pork would be the focus if not the exclusive item on the protein menu.

The automobile was the single greatest force driving change in barbecue during this time. The roadside barbecue pit or shack sprung up like mushrooms along Georgia's highways in the 1920s. The pioneers of this form were caterers who decided that itinerant cooking was too much a bother. J. L. Glawson of Myrtle Springs supplied the model of this kind of eatery. They were open Thursdays, Fridays, and Saturdays, and for dinner on Sundays. They served pulled pork sandwiches as well as plates of barbecued pork and sides. Others of the first-generation shacks included the Dixie Barbecue Stand in Fitzgerald, Bowens Barbecue Stand in Cordele, and the Georgia Barbecue Stand in Decatur. There were also many barbecue stands in Georgia's cities, often run by Black people. The rural roadside stands tended to have white proprietors until at least World War II.

Contests have been another force in shaping barbecue in the twentieth century. The first took place in 1963, sponsored by the 4-H in connection with regional and county fairs. For budget reasons, the subject was chicken. In 1966, The National Cookout Contest was organized with a major cash prize of $10,000. The contest was shaped by James Beard's vision of male outdoor pit cookery of meats and was by no means restricted to barbecue. Georgia's first national finalist, Stanley W. Brown of Decatur, advanced submitting barbecued beefsteak. Memphis began the serious organization of southern pork barbecue in 1977. In the early 1980s a Georgia Championship BBQ Pork Cookoff launched at Stone Mountain. From 1984 to the present day, barbecue crews using mobile propane gas cooking rigs have refined sauces and smoking regimens on a contest circuit. A curiosity is that contests now employ the same industrial pink pig for contestants (no distinctively flavored heirloom guinea hogs can be employed). Barbecue contests are now all about sauce, smoke, and cooking temperature.

So what is a serviceable sauce that could be used by a home cook for a broad spectrum of meats, not just pork? Try this.

Barbecue Sauce

2 cups catsup
1 small Coca-Cola
1 bay leaf
1 tablespoon Worcestershire sauce
1 teaspoon mustard
2 teaspoons vinegar
1 package dry onion soup
1 teaspoon garlic powder
Salt and pepper

Mix all ingredients and simmer for one hour, stirring occasionally.

Benne

Sometime late in the colonial period, planters and settlers adopted the name used by enslaved Africans for sesame—the Mende name "benne." Planted by Africans in their huck patches, benne had many uses. The leaves steeped in cold water could soothe stomach troubles. The pods in which the famous seeds form, when harvested before they hardened, could be sliced, sautéed, and consumed as a green vegetable. The parched seeds sprinkled over rice or grits or greens imparted a deep earthy flavor. They were an excellent adornment to biscuits and rolls. The benne seed's composition was 45 percent oil and when pressed provided a fine-tasting salad oil or frying medium. The benne seed cake (mash) left over from oil pressing could be used like a roux in stews, or could be fed to fowl, hogs, and cattle.

Benne oil, because it cost less than lard, enjoyed extensive use during the nineteenth century, particularly after failures to create a large-scale olive oil manufactory in Georgia. Benne could be grown easily, was an annual plant, and entailed no great delay from planting to harvesting, unlike nut trees and the olive. Benne oil tasted much better than cottonseed oil and did not spoil like canola. Georgia Governor John Milledge sent a bottle of benne oil to Thomas Jefferson in 1809 stimulating the ex-president's interest in the plant and its products.

J. McCormack sold the first benne oil in the state in Augusta in 1809, having received bottles from Col. Few in New York. Darien storekeeper O. Legriel would become the oil's first in-state manufacturer, offering "Darien Cold Press Castor & Benne Oil" in spring of 1823. One bushel of benne seed could produce two gallons of oil. Manufacturers retailed their oil in both drugstores and groceries. Because benne grew readily, and because a mortar and pestle could release the oil if the mashed seeds were afterwards tossed into a simmering pot of water and the lipids on the surface skimmed, benne oil became an item of homestead manufacture.

One factor prevented benne oil from becoming a commodity scale product—the difficulty of harvesting the seed. At the end of summer, the pods ripen on the plant at different times, from bottom to top. When

Heirloom benne seed is typically used without hulling. Its cooking characteristics and plant morphology differ from twenty-first century sesame. It can be roasted (parched), virgin pressed for oil or used raw as a condiment. Here roasted benne is being employed as part of the mash for beer. Photograph © David S. Shields.

ripe, benne pods shatter, spraying seed in every direction. The usual method of harvest is to chop the plant off at the ground when the first pods ripen and hang the plant upside down along with other benne plants in a tote until they dry down. When the plants desiccate the totes are beaten, the pods burst, and the seed is collected from the bottom of the bag.

When chemist David Wesson at the end of the nineteenth century learned how to refine the stink out of cottonseed oil, farmers turned away from benne and turned their trash cottonseed into cash by generating gallons of odorless, colorless, and tasteless Wesson Oil. By 1900 most Georgians who had grown benne had suspended cultivation, and a widely syndicated article appeared in Georgia newspapers touting "Sesame Culture in the South," hailing the plant as a "New and Lucrative Crop for the Planters." Agricultural memory is short.

Truth be told, the failure of the benne oil manufactory in the late 1880s did not wipe the plant from the countryside. Its great liability—the tendency of seed pods to shatter—proved a benefit if you intended benne seed to be fowl food in a farmyard. Florida in the late nineteenth and early twentieth century found benne the easiest to grow source of nutrition for chickens, guinea hens, turkeys, and geese. Children were the other great constituents for the seed. Benne seed candy—made with pulled molasses, cane syrup, or honey became a favorite homemade confection prior to the Civil War. Benne patties, benne cakes, and benne brittle became standard Georgian candies. The M. Sharon Candy Company in Augusta made benne candy their headline attraction. They made batches daily at twenty cents a pound in 1907. Small regional candy companies spanned the twentieth century—Harry Litman's Savannah Benne Candy Company in mid-century occupied 239 E. Broughton Street from the end of World War II until 1970.

Biscuits

In England a biscuit is any sort of baked good using dough made without yeast. In the American South biscuits are hand-sized, quick-baked savory cakes. In Georgia all biscuits nowadays are quick breads using chemical rising agents, either baking powder or some mixture of baking soda and an acid (buttermilk, cream of tartar). Whether scratch made or preprepared (think Pillsbury Grands!), the biscuit enjoys a prominent place in the breadbasket at breakfast and at dinner. Only corn bread rivals it for popularity.

When the Georgia Products Feasts were held in 1913, two types of biscuits were widely popular in the state. The oldest form of biscuit, the beaten biscuit, did not use a chemical leaven to get the dough to rise in the oven. This biscuit was universally prepared in the South during the colonial period and the first half of the nineteenth century. By beating the unleavened dough and shortening hundreds of times with an axe handle, it created a unique uniform texture. It was a solid, compact biscuit—not the fluffy style now preferred. The beaten biscuit remains a local foodway in Maryland and Kentucky but has passed from favor in most parts of the South because of the extended exertion needed to pummel the dough into the proper consistency. The Beaten Biscuit is listed twice in the menus from the Georgia Products Feasts, Quick Rise Biscuits three times, and Corn Biscuits once. Because there have always been a minority of cooks who revered the "old ways" and reckoned the beaten biscuit an ancestral food, we've supplied a descriptive recipe detailing its manufacture.

Beaten Biscuit

Macon Telegram-Herald
(September 30, 1889)

To a quart of good flour add a teaspoonful of salt and a heaping spoonful of lard (a piece about the size of a duck's egg). Rub the lard well into the flour until it is all thoroughly incorporated; then mix into a stiff dough with cold or warm water as you choose. I always use warm water in cold weather for comfort's sake. It requires very little water, for the dough must be as stiff as it well can be to be thoroughly mixed. Then transfer it from the mixing tray to a clean kneading board or table, and knead with all your heart, holding first one end of the dough and then the other until it is flexible and perfectly satin-smooth to touch, and will peel in flakes like tissue paper. Really well-kneaded dough will 'pop, pop' under the pressure of the hands like miniature champagne corks. It is very tiresome to knead, though it is good exercise for the muscles of the breast, shoulders and arms. . . . Many cooks who object to kneading beat the dough with the end of a rolling pin, but it is not so nice as kneading with the hands.

I always make twenty-four biscuit[s] out of a quart. Mold them into shapely balls, roll them out about as thick as your finger, say half an inch, or as much less as you choose, stick them through several times with a fork (a three-tined fork is *de rigueur* down South) and put them, just not touching, in the pan and set in a well-heated oven. They will require from twenty minutes to half an hour to bake according to the heat of the stove.

We don't have to spend much time considering the corn biscuit; it was an outgrowth of a period of milling experimentation that attempted to make corn flour and corn starch commodities as well as cornmeal and grits. The problem was that corn flour had no ready-built clientele clamoring for it. So millers added it to wheat flour as an adulterant while charging the 100 percent wheat flour price. Corn flour developed a shady reputation that became fully negative during World War I. In 1918 in a set of directives for restricting consumption in conjunction with the war effort the US government mandated corn flour/wheat flour mixtures. Predictably the contrarian spirit of the public rose up against the mixture, against corn flour. RIP corn biscuit 1918.

And the other three biscuits at the feasts? What exactly were they? The knowledgeable Mrs. S. R. Dull provides the answer: "In the south, where quick hot bread is a daily affair, it is buttermilk biscuits we want." Behind her observation was kitchen knowledge. She knew that two schools prevailed in scratch-baking quick-rise biscuits. The users of baking powder (a chemical combination of acid and soda that releases gas when heated in an oven, puffing up a disk of dough) preferred whole milk in their mixture. This produced a dry, somewhat hard biscuit that did not go stale quickly. The users of baking soda needed to employ an acid, and the lactic acid in buttermilk not only enabled the gas expansion in the oven, but also produced a softer, moister biscuit. Worrying whether the buttermilk biscuit went stale was rarely a problem, since most were gobbled while the biscuits were still warm. Here is Mrs. Dull's recipe.

Buttermilk Biscuit

Mr. S. R. Dull, *Atlanta Journal*
(June 20, 1926)

2 cups flour (before sifting)
1 cup buttermilk
1 teaspoon salt
½ teaspoon soda

Into the flour put salt and soda and sift into a bowl, chop shortening into flour or mix quickly with fingers. Pour in the buttermilk and mix into a dough using a spoon. Flour well the board and turn dough on; with the hands knead quickly until smooth enough to handle, using flour as necessary. Roll out dough half inch thick, cut, place on a baking sheet, bake in a hot oven about ten minutes, or until done.

Baking powder biscuits were made with the same proportions, except that whole milk substituted for buttermilk, and one used 3 teaspoons of baking powder instead of ½ teaspoon of baking soda. By a hot oven, 450°F was meant. The 10 minutes would probably be too short a time by current standards. Twelve to fourteen would probably be optimal. Though no specification of flour type is made by Mrs. Dull, any soft white winter wheat flour that has not been enriched would serve. All old recipes for baking presumed you preheated the oven before putting in the dough.

Among cooks there is a fundamental distinction made between scratch biscuits and those baked from mixes. Scratch biscuits follow the recipes like those given above. The first biscuit mixes appeared in 1939. The Fixt brand had all of the dry components of the biscuit formula in a pound-sized box for 17 cents. Food processors realized that even this level of kitchen labor was too much for some. They aspired to the ultimate in convenience—premixed and preformed biscuits that one only had to heat and serve. These would have to be either frozen or refrigerated to work. Ballards Foods inaugurated Ballard's Oven Ready Biscuits in 1949. They were sold in cans. Pillsbury bought Ballards in 1951. They introduced Ballard's Biscuits to the big cities in Georgia in 1953. Later that decade the famous cardboard tube was created—just peel off the label, smack the middle of the tube on the edge of the counter, and biscuit dough would bust free ready for the oven. As if confirming Mrs. Dull's dictum of 1926, Pillsbury's Grands!, the best-selling preformed biscuit, is buttermilk, moist and fluffy.

While the buttermilk biscuit and the baking powder biscuit stand at the center of southern cuisine, several developments became consequential over the years—the cheese biscuit, the sweet potato biscuit, the benne biscuit, and the cream biscuit have expanded the sorts of pleasures one can have with quick breads. The oldest of the tweaked forms is actually the English sweet biscuit made with sugar and an egg incorporated into the dough. This was called the "party biscuit" in Georgia in the period before World War II. The cream biscuit is also old, using sour cream instead of buttermilk as the acid and moisture in the mix. It is a denser type of moist biscuit than a buttermilk biscuit, with a similar "tang."

The cheese biscuit became a significant renovation of the classic baking powder biscuit. The harder, denser baking powder biscuit needed something extra to compete with its popular cousin the buttermilk biscuit. In Georgia the Snowdrift shortening company promoted the concept of the cheese biscuit in the 1920s. Because lard has

Buttermilk biscuits on the sideboard, ready for serving. Photograph © David S. Shields.

flavor, there was not much need for supplementing the taste of the biscuit when it was used. Hydrogenated cottonseed oil products such as Snowdrift, Cottonlene, and Crisco had been designed not to have flavor. These oil producers, perhaps to distract consumers from a sense that "something was missing" began printing recipes for Cheese Biscuits in their print advertising. Here is Snowdrift's from 1926.

Cheese Biscuits

Snowdrift ad, *Atlanta Journal*
(November 2, 1926)

2 Cups Flour
4 Teaspoons Baking Powder
½ Teaspoon Salt
2 Tablespoons Snowdrift
¾ Cup Milk
¾ Cup Grated Cheese

Sift flour, baking powder and salt together, cut in Snowdrift and mix with liquid. Toss onto floured board and roll to 1/4 inch thick. Sprinkle with grated cheese and fold once. Cut and bake on greased baking sheet at 450 degrees F.

Note that the variety of cheese was not specified. It can be said without equivocation that at that time the mediocre quality of cheese available in much of the United States hindered the popularity of the cheese biscuit. It wasn't until after World War II and after the popularization of biscuit mixes that the cheese biscuit boomed. Perhaps home cooks began feeling guilty about using mixes in the post-World War II period and felt that adding something uncalled for in the box directions took their baking one step closer to what their mothers did. In a 1950 blurb featured in the *Dallas Morning News*, the home section editor recommended, "Vary hot biscuits made from packaged mix by adding a half cup of grated yellow cheese or a half cup of chopped cooked ham to the standard recipe." By "yellow cheese" the editor was suggesting that grocery store American cheese was fine as a flavor additive. In a 1960s newspaper recipe, editors took to recommending Cheddar and tweaking the dough further by adding a "suspicion of dry mustard" to fashion "Spicy Cheese Biscuits." When urban gourmet shops and grocery stores with fancy food sections spread in the later decades of the twentieth century, the range of cheese varieties available in Georgia grew. The Parmesan biscuit, goat cheese biscuit, Gouda biscuit and the like began appearing on party trays.

All of these biscuits are not particular to Georgia, but given this state's central role in the early development of the sweet potato, a special connection has existed between this place and the sweet potato biscuit. Two forms emerged in the state. We have included the savory style in our entry on sweet potatoes. Here is the sweet style, which became popular about the time of the Georgia Products Feasts in 1913. This early recipe is an example of the double-rise baked good—that is, a preparation that employs both yeast *and* baking soda with buttermilk to make the biscuits fluff. The cook no doubt felt that adding mashed cooked sweet potato to dough would inhibit the gas expansion during cooking. Almost invariably sweet potato biscuits come out denser than any baking powder biscuit.

Sweet Potato Biscuit

Jeffersonian (February 6, 1913)

One pint of mashed sweet potatoes
1 cup sugar
2 eggs
1 kitchen spoon of lard
1 pint buttermilk
1 teaspoon soda dissolved in the buttermilk
2 teaspoons of salt
1 yeast cake dissolve in 1 cup of luke-warm water

Mix all the ingredients, add enough flour to make a stiff dough, roll and cut for biscuits. Put in greased pans; let rise over night.

Does the double-rise method produce better results than simply using soda and buttermilk? Some. More if you use a sweet potato without much fibrousness to the tuber. The flavor of the sweet biscuit, however, is totally winning.

Brunswick Stew

There has always been a fascination with the way the history of a dish is told. Several dishes have many origin stories, and Brunswick stew is one of them. If you are a resident of Georgia, it originated in the county of Brunswick in the city of Brunswick in the state of Georgia. If you are from the state of Virginia, it originated in the county of Brunswick in the city of Brunswick in the state of Virginia as well. When you travel Highway 46 in Brunswick, Virginia, you will find a historical marker that states that the stew was created by Jimmy Matthews. Jimmy, an African American chef, first took a spoon to this stew with a foundation of tomatoes and chicken in 1828. Like with many of these dishes we may never truly know the origin, however they are delicious nonetheless. The story we uncovered is very interesting and offers several points of debate.

The first appearance of Brunswick stew in print occurred not in Virginia and not in Georgia, but in the *Charleston Southern Patriot* newspaper of August 13, 1845. It presented a recipe in the form of a poem.

How to Make a Brunswick Stew

Charleston Southern Patriot
(August 13, 1845)

Take two dozen good potatoes,
As many of the best tomatoes,
Of butter take a full weight pound,
Pour in water and stir them round;
Then take a good fat chicken,
And flour just enough to thicken,
Put them on the fire and let them stew,
And when they're done you'll eat 'a few.'

First off, we should note that the stew has often been called a "hunter stew." It has been made with whatever one had available. Early recipes contained squirrel, which is not used as much today. Other proteins were rabbit, chicken, and pork, which are commonly used today. In some versions the protein gets put through a grinder, but most cooks prefer it cooked in whole pieces long enough for the meat to shred. The stew also contains chunks of potato that thicken the stew. In most hunter stews, cooks use an array of vegetables such as corn, okra, carrots, and onions. Recipes are left up to the creativity of any camp cook.

The dish's catch-as-catch-can character was explored in the first written meditation on the origin of Brunswick stew, an article that appeared in the *Alexandria Gazette* of June 26, 1855. According to the author, the residents of Brunswick County, Virginia, would gather at shady springs during the hot summers. "For the entertainment inwarldly [*sic*] of the company a sufficient number of squirrels were shot, and in the absence of a supply of them, chickens were to do duty and often were used in combination. These articles were placed in a pot with a sufficient quantity of water and set to stewing over a slow fire. In due time were added tomatoes, corn, butterbeans, potatoes, with the requisite condiments of salt and Cayenne pepper, all of which, when properly cooked, furnished to the participators a feast which Apicius might have envied." Every pre–Civil War mention of Brunswick stew, except for the first, the Charleston recipe, locates the dish in the Old Dominion.

When in 1871 Brunswick stew first appears on the bill of fare at a Georgia restaurant, Med Henderson's in Savannah, it was identified as "Virginia Brunswick Stew." In the 1880s the "Virginia" designation disappeared and the phrase "chicken Brunswick stew" emerged to indicate that what was served was no country concoction full of squirrel meat. Its appearance can be taken as an indication of just how miscellaneous the makeup of a Brunswick stew might be. A reporter in 1894, in a general description of a "Georgia Barbecue" spent a moment describing Brunswick stew, that "delicacy for which no recipe ever existed except in the fertile brain of those who create it by intuition. The pot is filled to the brim with a thick pottage in which red and yellow are the predominant colors, the tomato, and mustard being two of the chief ingredients. It is served in saucers and nothing, but beer will relieve the heat which its preponderance of cayenne pepper leaves on the tongue."

In the 1890s, the stew's popularity exploded during the barbecue boom around Atlanta, Macon, and Augusta. A menu of shrimp salad in green peppers, Brunswick stew, and barbecued meats (mutton, beef, and chicken as well as pork) became standard at outdoor events, saloons, and eating houses where barbecue specials were held on certain nights. Potato salad and macaroni and cheese were the other sides. In 1895 Atlanta's Midway's Saloon at 11 South Broad pioneered barbecue specials. Brunswick stew was its accompaniment.

The Midway inspired immediate imitation by other Atlanta eateries scheduling barbecue and Brunswick stew specials: Tom Ware's Cafeteria and The Kindergarten Restaurant. Yet outdoor event cookery was where most encountered the pairing. The phrase "barbecue and Brunswick stew" became something of a culinary slogan in the 1890s. It was Brunswick stew's participation in the Georgia barbecue bill of fare during this decade that vested the stew with state identity, not any origin in Brunswick, Georgia. The slogan holds true today. If you patronize many barbeque restaurants throughout both states today, you will see a version of Brunswick stew on the menu.

The Real Brunswick Stew

Atlanta Journal (May 29, 1938)

1 pigs head, feet, liver and heart.
2 quarts of peeled and diced tomatoes.
4 quarts of peeled, diced Irish potatoes.
1 quart finely cut okra.
13 ears of finely cut corn (or two cans).
2 large onions, cut fine.
6 garlic buttons, tied in a cheese cloth.
1 tablespoon dry mustard.
Juice of lemon.
½ lemon, put in whole, seed removed.
1 bottle Worcestershire sauce.
1 medium bottle chili sauce.
1 pint bottle tomato catsup.
½ pound butter.
Salt, black and red pepper to taste.
Sweet peppers, both green and red, may be used if desired.

Thoroughly clean pig's head and feet. From the head remove the teeth and gums, upper and lower. Place head, feet, liver and heart into boiling water and cook slowly until meat falls from the bones and will come to pieces. Remove from the liquor, remove all bone and every tough part, pull to pieces and mash and chop until fine. From the liquor remove scum and replace the meat. If not much liquor, add hot water. Add vegetables and season; cook slowly and for several hours. If too thick, add hot water; if thin, add light breadcrumbs, one large loaf. When ready to serve, add half pound of butter. Stir almost constantly during the cooking. If it should stick or scorch, change the vessel, as any scorch will ruin the entire stew. Fresh vegetables are always preferable, canned ones may be used. Cut fine and fry the okra in a little grease. This prevents being slick. Brunswick stew must be served hot. Note: Other meat besides the pig head and feet may be used—chicken, veal or both.

One of the strange monuments to the fantasy that Brunswick stew originated in Georgia was a "pot mounted on a concrete podium carved with the statement, 'In this pot the first Brunswick Stew was made on St. Simon Isle, July 2, 1898,'" displayed at the Highway 17 Welcome Center at the entrance of the causeway to St. Simons Island. Someone perhaps should inform the chamber of commerce that restaurants on the other side of the state were featuring Brunswick stew on their menus well before the summer of 1898. A second monument to the Georgia nativity of Brunswick stew also has been constructed on the Sea Islands.

In 1987 Brunswick inaugurated a Main Street Jubilee Festival with a stew contest as its centerpiece. In 1988 the contest included a delegation from Brunswick County, Virginia, participated. While St. Simons caterers Lisa Cook and Fran Kelly won, the dispute was sufficiently lively that a rematch was scheduled for the following year.

In 2006 the Brunswick stew champion was Henry Hicks, a Virginian tobacco farmer, trained by Theo Matthews. Matthews was the great-grandson of Jimmy Matthews, who is said to have created the popular stew in the antebellum era.

Butter Beans

Since the 1690s when the Sewee-Siouan people conveyed the small lunette-shaped beans to settlers living on the lower Santee River, the sieva (pronounced *sivvy* and named after the Sewee nation) or butterbean had taken up a central place in Lowcountry cookery. Its cultivation spread from Florida to Maryland and westward to Louisiana. They were modest sized, not like the huge fat limas from Peru—the big white lima and the speckled or Christmas lima, both imported into North America during the antebellum period. The big limas, favored by northern consumers, could taste chalky and have the texture of an undercooked chestnut. The sieva beans had a tender texture; indeed, so creamy that in the 1860s southerners began referring to them as "butterbeans." Because the Butter bean plants grew as vines, keeping them from tangling into mats on the ground became growers' priority. They would erect poles into frames or tepees and train the bean vines to twine around; from this growing habit they were categorized as "pole beans." Butter beans were "largely grown in the South and Immensely popular" (*Willet's Catalog*, 1917). The forms favored by the Creek, Cherokee, and Siouan people had willow leaves. The settlers favored the "bean leaf" butter beans of which there were several strains, distinguished by color: pale green–white, reddish purple, speckled red, mottled brown. Native American cooks boiled, mashed, and mixed the mash with cornmeal which was then baked to make bean bread.

Sometime in the 1880s farmers began to find pole-grown beans less convenient to harvest than bush grown. The demand set the major American seed companies breeding. Within a brief span, three important strains emerged: two from northern breeders—Henderson's Dwarf small lima and Burpee's Large Bush Lima. (It should be noted that northern seed companies opted for "lima" as the market category for these lunette-shaped beans of whatever size. Southern seed companies kept the old nomenclature—sieva, butterbean, butterpea). The third important bush lima, the Jackson Wonder Bean, was bred by Thomas Jackson of Cobb County, Georgia. The Jackson Wonder Bean would be Georgia's great contribution to the American butter beans and limas.

N. L. Willet of Augusta, an agricultural writer popular a century ago, described the Jackson Wonder bean thusly, "A flat brown bean, mottled with deep brown spots: size is somewhat larger than Sieva. Most prolific Bush Lima grown. Originated in Cobb County, Georgia, and is fully adapted to all the South. Flourishes in the driest weather, and is almost drought proof. Flavor is rich

Butter beans and eggplant, a southern marriage of native beans and African eggplant. Originally eggplant was called "guinea squash" in Georgia. Photograph © David S. Shields.

and delicious. A perfect bush butter bean, growing 18 inches to 2 feet high. Begins blooming early and if kept closely picked continues to bear until frost kills the plants. Good for summer use or as a winter shelled bean. One of the most valuable introductions for Southern home gardens ever made."

Thomas Jackson introduced the bean in 1891 in a national campaign. He made seed available to several seed companies and its widespread adoption was nearly immediate. The most astute assessment of the variety was given by W. Atlee Burpee, himself greatly concerned with breeding bush limas: "Thoroughly tested at Fordhook Farm, we would pronounce it a prolific strain of the Speckled Sieva, or small Lima, of established bush character and real merit, resembling Henderson's Bush Lima, but larger in size of beans, with better filled pods; it is also more easily shelled than the Henderson Lima." All three bush lima beans remain in cultivation in 2025 as befits American classics. All have been steady sellers for seed companies and found at the produce stand for at least 130 years.

Jackson, when introducing his creation, voiced the standard southern objection to the lima beans being promoted by northern companies: They tasted bland and rather chalky. His wonder bean was "rich, marrowy, and fine flavored, nutritious and healthful, and superior in all these qualities to the lima." Furthermore, Jackson had been reading the recent scientific literature on nutrition and realized that bean flour made from Wonder Beans was well suited to a range of culinary uses. In this regard he was well in advance of popular taste. Each pod contains three or four variegated beans. The colors—ranging from reds and browns to purples—cooked dark. This was a point of objection among those fastidious souls who only consumed pale whitish–green sievas or lima beans. But among diners who rated flavor above pallid appearance, the Jackson Wonder Bean ruled supreme.

There are foodways associated with the butterbean, foremost among them the rite of shelling the beans into a bowl. The expert sheller knew how to pop the beans clean from the pod with her thumb and by the end of the season could shoot a bean halfway across the porch to hit a brother or a sleeping dog.

Eight varieties of heirloom butter bean still grow in Georgia. Kitchens around Thomson, Washington, and Crawfordville abound in mottled pole butter beans. Because the older varieties have a diverting array of colors and markings, bean fanciers display them dried in jars as a kind of kitchen décor. Red, black mottled, speckled, black-eyed, pink-eyed, white, pale green, yellow—they all taste splendid.

Butter beans are cooked low and slow in salted water or stock with a piece of fatback or bacon. When tender, butter and pepper are added. If you wished to fancy up the dish, you added a dollop of cream before serving and perhaps a scattering of shelled pecans. In the late twentieth century, a preference for preparing the beans without cured pork or butter arose. With remarkable rapidity the butterbean became a first-call salad ingredient to be dressed with vinegar and herbs. (Mayonnaise appeared in very few Georgia bean salads.) Tomatoes, Vidalia onions, dill, and sometimes mint found their way into the bowl. Butterbean salads are now standard in new southern vegetable cookbooks but rarely does one encounter an Italian treatment such as combining butter beans with pasta. More often a Latino take, with citrus and lime juice, finds its way to the Georgia table.

Cane Syrup

A ribbon of sunshine trickling on the crown of a breakfast biscuit, a golden pool of sweetness in which you dip corn bread or crispy fried chicken—cane syrup remains a splendor of Georgia cookery. It has been with us for more than two centuries.

After the Portuguese made Brazil into a sugar factory in the 1530s, Europe's colonial powers dreamed of turning territories in the Western Hemisphere into wealth engines by planting cane. Regardless of culture, anyone who tasted the fine crystals of refined sugar craved more. The demand for cane sugar quickly became nearly unlimited. England wished to cash in on this sweet commodity and found in the 1660s that some of the West Indian colonies—Barbados, St. Kitts, Jamaica—could grow and process cane if it expanded the labor force of enslaved Africans. Sugar wealth drove England's industrial revolution, and the Lords of Trade and Plantations wished to plant more. Yet England did not consider any of its thirteen North American colonies capable of growing it. Because this perennial grass came into being in the tropical regions in South Asia, it does not thrive where temperatures fall much below freezing. Cane will die from cold. Not until the English gained control of East Florida after the Seven Years' War in 1763, did they experiment with cane culture on the North American mainland. Would-be colonists received land grants along the St. Johns River if they would plant cane. Some did, using the creole cane in common use in Barbados. Whatever cane was grown in North America was crushed and boiled to syrup, not refined to sugar.

Planters made money on commodity crops in the South—tobacco, rice, indigo, cotton, pine trees. Once a staple was established, every planter jumped on the bandwagon. So it was with cotton in Georgia. It is difficult to make a fortune if every neighbor plants the same thing you do, increasing the product's availability and driving down the price. In 1809 Thomas Spaulding of Georgia, irked with the low price being paid for cotton, decided to plant three acres of sugar cane on his plantation on Sapelo Island. The cane variety he grew was Otaheiti, a green cane, the ancestor of "Home cane" now grown in Florida syrup patches. It was juicier than creole cane, and had stems with thicker walls, good for using as fuel in the fires beneath evaporation vats. From 1809 to 1812 Spaulding planted cane to build up his acreage. He did not attempt processing the cane to sugar until 1812. Growing and processing sugar demanded much labor, and Spaulding expanded the numbers of enslaved people billeted on Sapelo Island where his plantation stood. Then too, cold killed portions of his plantings. But the losses weren't so dire to daunt Spaulding from constructing a sugar mill on Sapelo Island to boil syrup and refine granulated sugar. He paid attention to the sugar experiments in Louisiana, newly annexed to the United States, and noted how damaging cold temperatures disrupted the industry.

In 1814 a remedy appeared. An American schooner from St. Eustatius dispatched a load of purple ribbon cane to Roswell King on St. Simon's Island. This purple-striped

Sapelo Island Geechee Cane Syrup using the rediscovered and restored Purple Ribbon Sugar Cane, a variety used on the Spaulding plantation during the antebellum period when the ancestors of the current residents of Sapelo labored as enslaved field hands. Now the descendants grow the old cane for their own profit. Photograph © David S. Shields.

cane had thick walls and could withstand nighttime temperatures down to 22°F. Spaulding secured some and built his sugar enterprise on it. In 1817 Louisiana planter Joseph Coiron secured canes and planted them near New Orleans. Both Georgia and Louisiana's sugar culture exploded because of Purple Ribbon Cane. Acreage expanded, and sugar refiners sprung into being. By 1825 the price for raw sugar had dropped so low that it became affordable to middling households. The great age of jams, jellies, preserves began— and also cane syrup.

Georgians made a calculated decision in the antebellum period not to manufacture white granulated sugar for reasons of economy. It could not compete nationally with the efficient Louisiana manufacturers or internationally with the West Indian sugar factories that had been up and running since the 1680s. Some raw sugar (brown sugar) came from Spaulding's and other early Georgia mills, but Louisiana quickly seized the initiative and became the American center for refining sugar. Cones of Louisiana sugar sat on grocery shelves, and barrels of New Orleans molasses traversed the continent. Georgia opted for cane syrup. It required less time, fuel, and care when boiling sap. If one controlled the heat and prevented the liquid from scorching (flat evaporation pans proved best for this), if one skimmed the foams of starch that collected on the surface, if one kept the wood steadily filling the firebox, if one stirred, if one could judge when the proper viscosity and color had been achieved, one could produce cane syrup without great difficulty.

As early as 1819, merchants J. G. Collins and Franklin & Minturn offered hogshead barrels of Georgia syrup for sale in Manhattan, New York. Shipped by schooner from the coastal port at Darien, Georgia, syrup found regular buyers in Savannah, Charleston, Alexandria, Virginia, and Baltimore. At first, shipments were small; thirty hogsheads were the largest quantity noted in any mercantile advertisement of the 1820s. It came in two grades: "Superior" was ready to be bottled and retailed for "family use." The plain grade made up the bulk of wholesale transactions. This would be used for anything from rum manufacture to being a preservative. After the Civil War, because the canes were perennial, syrup was one of the first commodities available for export and sale. But the industrial-scale production of cane syrup did not take place until the twentieth century, when Grady County became Georgia's center for sugar.

The growers, processors, and merchants of Grady County had a simple goal—to provide to American households a table syrup that would rival maple syrup. In 1921 a promoter wrote, "You purveyors . . . know that the North and West sorely need a high-standard, rich, pure table syrup to displace the unnutritive, watery, artificially colored imitations of maple and the mucilage like glucose preparations which, jointly, are in almost complete control of the consumption demand in the nation's Markets." Grady's sugar entrepreneurs had some sound reasons: Pure maple syrup was scarce and expensive; its imitations legion and full of adulterations. The glucose alternatives—think Karo Corn Syrup—tended to be strongly flavored and greatly viscous. Georgia cane syrup began appearing on grocery shelves in the 1920s and competed with maple syrup in terms of price and availability. One curious irony was that jobbers began using Georgia cane syrup as a base for making fake maple syrup.

Georgia syrup prospered because the farmers and processors cooperated in overcoming difficulties. The universal adoption of a two-phase evaporation method employing invertase enabled the Grady County producers to make syrup that did not crystalize or ferment. Repeated efforts at fine-tuning the branding of the syrup enabled in the later 1920s the product to stand more clearly distinct from the syrup mixtures that flooded grocery shelves. In the 1930s, concerted lobbying efforts enabled those with sugar interests to prevent the boosting of the processing tax per gallon on syrup to 4 cents.

There were also efforts at diversification that did not quite have the same success, such as the initiative to manufacture cane sugar vinegar.

There would be, however, one regular purchaser of their product for much of the mid-twentieth century: soft drink manufacturers. Coca-Cola used cane syrup until 1980 when as a cost-cutting strategy they switched to high fructose corn syrup. The decline of Georgia cane syrup can be tied to this shift and to the rise of cheaper sugar beet sugar in the United States generally. While Robinson Georgia Syrup and Cane Patch Cane Syrup remained common retail brands into the 1970s, after 1980 cane syrup became a specialty item.

Since the 1970s the production of backyard cane syrup by farmers has become something of a cult. The autumn ritual of crushing the cane and boiling down the juice in backyard cauldrons or pans has become an occasion of sociability. Neighbors and friends take turns skimming and getting their hair sticky from the fumes of the evaporating cane juice. Experienced boilers can tell by the drip of the liquid when it has reached the optimum viscosity for syrup.

Perhaps the most important development in cane syrup in the twenty-first century has been Cornelia Bailey's rematriation of sugar cane to Sapelo Island in 2016. The sole residents of Sapelo Island are descendants of those enslaved who worked on Spaulding's plantation. Developers had their eyes on Sapelo Island, a maritime forest preserve off the coast of Georgia. The island is as large as Manhattan Island, and it remained a largely undisturbed semitropical enclave, owned and maintained by the State of Georgia, except for old private holdings by the saltwater Geechee inhabitants of the Hog Hammock community. These African American islanders numbered less than a hundred. But they were disinclined to sell their holdings to the developers. So the developers engineered an increase in the property taxes that islanders had to pay. Bailey, Sapelo Island's matriarch, realized the islanders needed a source of revenue to pay their taxes. She looked to Sapelo's agricultural heritage, growing and selling the famous sea island red peas grown there. With the aid of the Carolina Gold Rice Foundation and Dr. Steve Kresovich of Clemson University, Bailey secured cuttings of virtually extinct Purple Ribbon Sugar Cane. Syrup was brewed by Dr. William Thomas and Jerome Dixon Senior of Townsend, Georgia, and by Maurice Bailey on Sapelo Island. Its restoration generated national news stories—and splendid cane syrup, most of which has been secured by restaurateurs.

Catfish

The catfish is Georgia's fish of legends. Around the whiskered "fish with no scales" a trove of country lore has risen from every part of the state. Tales of monstrously large catfish slumbering in the mud of slow rivers or big lakes—mammoth "blue cats" exceeding 100 lbs. deep in Lake Eufaula or five-foot-long flatheads lurking in the Altamaha or Ocmulgee Rivers. Almost as numerous are tales of the appetite of catfish: like feral hogs, wild catfish are enthusiastic omnivores. Fishermen vie to tell the tallest tale of who landed a cat on the most outlandish bait: "I put a chunk of ivory soap on a hook." "It bit on a cherry tomato." "A piece of rancid fatback—can't miss." "Got him on a wad of foil from a chewing gum wrapper." These stories meld into another kind of tale, concerning what is found in the stomach of a landed catfish when gutted and prepped for cooking. An *Atlanta Journal* article of 1930 collected accounts of live water moccasins, diamond rings, and petrified mammoth teeth emerging from catfish bellies. More fanciful are the angler stories about multiple catches. "Caught an eel. Then a 20 lb. cat swallowed the snagged eel. Eel wriggled around in the cat and pushed his way out its gills. Another cat sees the eel, lunges. Two cats & one eel on one line!" These multiple-catch tales were favorites in country newspapers. Another species of legend concerned farm fields being invaded by catfish. Well before the invasive "walking catfish" escaped into the drainage ditches and canals in Florida in the twentieth century, settlements in Georgia related tales of entire populations of catfish leaving rivers. Most of the time a spell of rain and an overflowing riverbank filled the plow furrows with fish. But sometimes the opposite happened. In 1887, when the Flint River fell low, catfish crawled out the banks and spread through woodlots and cornfields for miles along the river. "The noise they make in pulling the corn would be equal to a hundred head of hungry cattle."

There has always been a contingent in the population that balked at eating catfish. Observant Jews did not partake because of the scriptural ban on consuming sea creatures without scales. A contingent of Christians became obsessed with issues of unclean and adulterated food in the nineteenth century, so the catfish became a suspect item among urbane members of "polite society" because it was a "bottom feeder" and "mud dweller." At the dawn of the twentieth century the US Fish Commission felt it had to become an advocate on behalf of the catfish as a food fish. "The Fish Commission is of the opinion that the catfish is much underrated also by those who gauge its commercial value. They say that it is one of the very best pan fishes. Its meat is white, crisp and juicy, and of excellent flavor. The experts consider the flesh of the channel catfish superior to that of the black bass, the wall eye, the yellow perch, or any other percoids. Among fresh water fish they say it is inferior only to the white fish and the trout."

The Georgia Products Feasts featured two catfish dishes: Dublin's menu listed Oconee Channel Catfish fried in Cottonseed

Oil and Macon's menu offered Catfish Chowder. We readily grasp why the channel cat was singled out for the Dublin menu, because of all the catfish varieties, it was particularly commended by the Fish Commission. Before you wrinkle your nose in distaste at the thought of frying the Oconee channel catfish in cottonseed oil, be aware that in 1913 this oil was the miracle of the age (see the entry on Benne to learn more).

First about the frying. Vegetable-based cooking oils (cottonseed, benne oil, canola oil, sunflower seed oil, refined peanut oil) have the benefit of being cheap and renewable. Lard, the favored frying medium of the nineteenth century, because it is derived from an animal that must be fed and raised was relatively expensive. Hydrogenated cottonseed oil had been created in the 1880s as a lard adulterant. Mixed with lard it performed just as well as all-lard cooking fat, and cost less. So, you now know what to fry catfish in (not butter, not low smoke point oils such as olive oil or unrefined peanut oil).

If prepping the fish yourself, fillet the catfish into portions suitable to be laid on a plate and consumed by one person. If the "mud dwelling" habit of the fish bothers you, soak the fillets in fresh water. If you are cavalier about such matters, simply sprinkle them with salt and let them sit for at least a half hour. Prepare a bowl of egg wash—beating three or more raw eggs—yolks and whites—to a froth. Dip filets into the egg wash and then into a dry plate of cracker crumbs or seasoned cornmeal. There are various approaches to the coating. Here is an instruction from the dawn of the twentieth century.

Fried Catfish

Savannah Morning News
(March 20, 1904)

Soak in cold water for a half an hour before cooking, to draw out the blood and any suspicion of earthy taste. Then roll in fine Indian meal or a mixture of meal and flour, and fry in fat salt pork drippings or olive oil until brown and crisp on the outside, and white, delicate, and sweet within. Served with baked or stuffed potatoes and cabbage and celery salad.

"Indian meal" was an old designation for cornmeal. If the meal was too grainy and lard the frying medium, the result could be crude. Country caterers—specialists in barbecues, fish fries, and open air Brunswick stews—sometimes used corn flour instead of cornmeal for a finer crust. In the twenty-first century some Lowcountry cooks began using a rice flour and beer batter for dipping, taking Japanese tempura as a model. There was also an old warrant for doing this, since rice flour fritters (puffs) were a classic element of Gullah Geechee fish camp cooking. The cabbage and celery salad said to accompany the fish was, of course, coleslaw. The acid tang of a good slaw is the ideal complement to fried fish.

Much of the South has been caught up in a war over white catfish stew (no ketchup) versus red catfish stew (ketchup and Worcestershire sauce). Georgia had its own dish: catfish chowder, a decidedly thinner soup than the standard deep South stew. The *Atlanta Journal* published a classic rendition in 1905.

Catfish Chowder

Atlanta Journal (August 13, 1905)

Skin, clean and cut off the heads. Cut the fish into pieces two inches long and put into a pot with some fat pork cut into shreds—a pound to a dozen medium-sized fish, two chopped onions, or half a dozen shallots, a bunch of sweet herbs and pepper. The pork will salt it sufficiently. Stew slowly for three-quarters of an hour. Then stir in a cup of milk, thickened with a tablespoonful of flour; take up a cupful of the hot liquor and stir, a little at a time, into two-well-beaten eggs. Return this to the pot, throw in half a dozen Boston or butter crackers, split in half; let all boil up once and turn into a tureen. Pass sliced lemon or cucumber pickles, also sliced, with it. Take out the backbones of the fish before serving.

Catfish have collected a wide variety of names—bullhead, bull pout, or channel catfish. It is a large family of fish, all possessing barbels (the famous catfish whiskers). The primary saltwater catfish, the hardhead, is found in coastal waters with soft mud bottoms. Of the catfish found in brackish and fresh water the blue catfish is the largest, followed by the flathead, channel, white catfish, and bullhead. Weights of these fishes range from five to 150 pounds. There are thirty species all told in the United States and the season for cat fishing differs by geographic region. In southern waters, the season may begin as early as March or April and continue through the depths of winter.

Catfish have always been one of the fixtures in a farm fishpond. In 1962 Roy Mann and Ernest All of Floyd County began the first catfish farm in Georgia, supplying fish to the local food economy. He stocked his ponds with channel cats, the variety that has been the choice for most fish farming operations that grow catfish rather than tilapia. The difficulties of controlling algae and keeping ponds free of disease hindered the development of the farms, but in 1969, Atlanta Food Processors Cagle Inc. started buying up catfish farms. Georgia government threw its backing behind the idea, underwriting the opening of a farm at Mayfield that would serve as the hatchery for regional fish farming operations. The steady supply of catfish enabled it to become a regular menu item on fast-food restaurant menus. Since the late 1970s farmed catfish has been the primary source of catfish available at fish counters and restaurants. Aquaculture is a challenging business that entails a good bit of capital outlay, but it is buoyed by a public demand that has proven to be inexhaustible.

Fried Catfish

KEVIN MITCHELL

What more can be said about a beautiful piece of fried catfish? Nothing! Enjoy.
Serves 4

- 2 cups buttermilk
- 1 tablespoon hot sauce
- ¼ teaspoon granulated garlic
- ¼ teaspoon granulated onion
- 4 teaspoons kosher salt
- 1½ teaspoons freshly cracked black pepper
- Zest of 1 lemon
- 1½ pound catfish filets, cut into 2-inch pieces
- 2 cups plain yellow cornmeal
- ¼ teaspoon cayenne pepper
- 4 cups or more vegetable oil

(continued)

Fried catfish by Kevin Mitchell. Photograph © Rhonda Mitchell.

Combine the buttermilk, hot sauce, granulated garlic, granulated onion, 1 teaspoon of each salt and pepper, and lemon zest in a large bowl or zip-top plastic bag. Add catfish, cover, seal, and refrigerate for 2 to 4 hours.

Combine the cornmeal, cayenne, and remaining 3 teaspoons salt and ½ teaspoon black pepper in a shallow dish. Dredge catfish in cornmeal mixture and refrigerate for 8 to 10 minutes (see Note).

Heat oil in a Dutch oven or cast-iron skillet.

Fry the fish in batches until golden brown, 5 to 7 minutes per side. Drain on a paper towel-lined baking sheet. Serve with your favorite coleslaw or collard green slaw.

Note: Storing the catfish in the refrigerator once breaded allows the breading to adhere to the fish and not fall off during frying.

Chatham Artillery Punch

Before New Orleans invented the cocktail in the antebellum period, the dominant mixed alcoholic drink was punch. The theory of punch was simple: Combine as many potent liquid elements as one could manage in a bowl. If we define a drug as anything that triggers a non-nutritive response in the body while also inspiring a desire for it, punches were experiments in multiplying drugs: sucrose, caffeine, alcohol, spice, even capsicum (hot pepper). In the colonial era the punch bowl became the center of sociability, the object at the center of the table that drew the worship of the tavern club, the shared delight of attendees at the ball. All of the big early American cities had their signature punches. Philadelphia had its Fish House Punch, Boston its Meeting House Punch, Charleston its St. Cecilia Punch, New Orleans its Hurricane. Savannah did not lack in this regard. It had its Chatham Artillery Punch, as described by A. R. Watson in an 1873 ode.

> Dews of Hybia ne'er were sweeter,
> Wine of Bacchus ne'er completer;
> Very stupid is Clicquot
> Krug, at best, is but so-so;
> Peiper Heidsick very flat;
> Poor the yield of every vat
> Put beside thee, in a bunch,
> Mine-my own Artillery Punch.

The Chatham Artillery was a provincial company of artillerymen commissioned by the State of Georgia in 1776 under the command of Joseph Woodruff for the defense of Savannah during the American Revolution. They remain an active unit, last mobilized in Operation Enduring Freedom in Afghanistan. During President George Washington's visit to Savannah during his first term, in 1791, the Chatham Artillery saluted his entry into the city by boat with twenty-six volleys from their field guns. Legend held that President Washington imbibed of the Artillery's punch on the fourth day of his Savannah stay on May 14, 1791, during the public dinner in the grove. The recipe for what the president was served, who concocted the punch, or whether it differed in any respect from the punch served to the visiting president four days earlier at Brown's Coffee House are questions now unanswerable. When Charles C. Jones Jr., wrote his *Historical Sketch of the Chatham Artillery* in 1867 no particular emphasis was made of serving President Washington punch during his 1791 visit, but he did indicate that the artillerymen favored "champagne punch."

What can be said without doubt is that the public reputation of Chatham Artillery Punch as the most alluring and dangerously potent of refreshments began about the time Jones wrote his *Historical Sketch*. At the artillery's headquarters in Savannah, a punch began being served regularly by "Mike, the ne plus ultra of Barkeepers." In April of 1868 when Mike returned to public hospitality, he offered Artillery Punch to the public at The Awning Post Saloon on the corner of Bryan and Whitaker Streets in Savannah. There can be little doubt that Mike (Michael T. Quinan) supplied a professional's refinement to the company's original formulation, mixed in a horse bucket by A. B. Luce from the booze supplied by William Davidson to honor the Republican Blues' return from Macon [actually Milledgeville] in 1859. The Blues were founded in January 1852 as a subsidiary force defending Savannah. This bucket was filled with ice. Into the ice was poured "A quart of good brandy, whisky and rum, each . . . and sugar and lemon added. The bucket was filled to the brim with champagne" (1885). There was no finesse to this mixture. What Mike supplied was a classicist's sense of balance drawn from a century of classic punches. The formula that has come down is classic mid-nineteenth century—with sparkling Catawba wine (America's home-grown substitute for champagne) and green tea rather than black in the mixture. The formula survived the legal suppression of Artillery Punch in Savannah in 1907 and the national prohibition in 1919. The classic recipe was printed in the *Christ Church Savannah Cook Book*.

Chatham Artillery Punch

(12 Gallons—Serves 200)
Christ Church Savannah Cook Book
(1933)

1 lb. green tea
3 gals Catawba Wine or Rhine
1 gal. St. Croix rum
1 gal. Brandy
1 gal. Rye whisky
1 gal. gin
5 lbs. brown sugar
2 qts. maraschino cherries
3 doz. oranges
3 doz. lemons
2 or 3 large stone or glass crocks

Put tea in 2 gals cold water. Allow to stand over night. Strain and add juice of the oranges and lemons. Add: Brown sugar, cherries, and all of the liquor. Cover lightly. Allow to stand (ferment) for two to six weeks. Strain off cherries and put liquid in gallon or quart bottles. Mix 1 gallon of this stock with 1 quart of champagne [sparkling Catawba] (charged water may be substituted for champagne). Pour over large piece of ice in a punch bowl and serve.

Once Mike Quinan took Artillery Punch public it quickly became an object of imitation. The first tale of its power to humble adult human beings came in a notice of the Mayor's Court in August 11, 1868. "A well dressed young man, who had been tasting [. . .] of artillery punch, was found by Policeman McGuire, on Sunday night, lying the street in a perfectly oblivious condition. . . . It appeared that this unsophisticated young gentleman was not aware of the intoxicating power of artillery punch and furthermore, that this was his first appearance in the Mayor's Court, and therefore he went scot-free."

In 1870 an event occurred that etched Artillery Punch in the minds of newspapermen throughout Georgia. A convention of editors convened in Savannah and during a reception the influence of a "huge bowl" spread across the room. The whole company got deliriously drunk. Some danced, some sang, some orated, some stood gazing heavenwards in rapt meditation. "Some told me that this powerful liquid that caused all these demonstrations was known in Savannah as 'Chatham Artillery Punch,' but I am sure it was nothing more than river water mixed with sea breeze." Henceforward the heralds of Georgia's world of print knew from experience the power of the punch. Perhaps the newspaperman with the greatest love of Artillery Punch was Joel Chandler Harris, author of the Br'er Rabbit stories, who labored at the *Savannah Morning News*.

The tale of the "unsophisticated young gentleman" was the first of a rich newspaper lore of victims felled by a fusillade of Artillery Punch. President Chester A. Arthur, visiting Savannah in 1883 on the recommendation of his physicians to undertake recreation, was visited by a contingent of Chatham Artillerymen on his yacht. The *Savannah Daily Times* described their alternative to Savannah's noxious water:

> It is the mildest and most innocent looking liquid one ever saw. To the eye Sunday school picnic lemonade is a wild delirious intoxicant beside it. Of a pale straw color, and just the slightest suggestiveness in flavor of lemon and rum, it is seemingly the least pretentious of all the beverages that claim Bacchus as godfather. But, great Allah! How it does belie its looks and taste! The President hid his disgust the best he could as he drank of the seductive punch to his own health. Mr. Arthur is a connoisseur in liquors, and there was a fine, almost aesthetic something about that punch that immediately captivated the President.

He became so ill his entourage feared for his life. It took several days of medical ministration to bring the president fully into the realm of the living.

The next to be laid low was Admiral of the Navy George Dewey, visiting the city in 1900. In the debate afterwards whether it was chicken salad or Artillery Punch that knocked out the hero of the Battle of Manilla Bay, the prevailing opinion sided with the latter. In 1909 President William Howard Taft stared it eye to eye without falling during his visit to Savannah. The new leader of the United States earned almost as much respect for that as he did for enthusing about possum and taters at the banquet held in Atlanta.

Georgia was the first southern state to surrender to the forces of temperance, legislating a ban on the production, sale, and transportation of alcohol in 1907. Lurid tales of Artillery Punch's effects were in the temperance propaganda arsenal. Even when the nationwide experiment in prohibition collapsed in 1933, it took Georgia an additional two years to repeal its ban on the business of alcohol. Harriet Colquitt was banking on that repeal taking place, for in 1933 she published in *The Savannah Cook Book* a recipe for Chatham Artillery Punch, paving the way for its revival. In the nine decades since its resuscitation, Chatham Artillery Punch has been the single most famous and beloved Georgian punch.

Cheese Straws

Sometimes a food thrives because its champions find the best occasion to feature its qualities: French toast as breakfast fare, roasted peanuts as spectator refreshment, bean dip as home entertainment fare for watching football. The cheese straw took nearly a half century to find its proper occasion—the beverage party.

In 1934 University of Georgia classics professor W. D. Hooper published the Loeb Library translation of *De Re Rustica*, a collection of observations on agriculture and rural life composed in ancient Rome by Cato. It included a recipe for "libum," a digestive cake made from goat milk cheese and flour, ancestor of our modern cheese straw. The modern version was created by French restaurant chefs in the wake of the French Revolution as a puff pastry cheese entrée to provide variety to the cheese course toward the end of a meal. Its recipe first came into American hands in Louis Eustache Ude's *The French Cook* (Philadelphia, 1828). After the Civil War, American home cooks determined that the dry cheese biscuit was an ideal accompaniment for salads, thinking of it as a form of a crouton. In October of 1865 *Godey's Lady's Book* featured three recipes, the first of which resembles the cheese straw we now know. Recipes began appearing in newspapers in 1876.

Cheese Straws

Baltimore Bulletin (January 22, 1876)

Sift one cupful of flour upon a pastry board, make a well in the center and put into this two tablespoonfuls of cream, three ounces of grated cheese, two tablespoonfuls of butter, the yolks of two eggs and half a teaspoonful of salt, a dust of pepper and a little nutmeg; if the paste is too stiff use a little milk until you can work it without breaking; roll out thin, cut in narrow strips, lay them on a buttered tin and bake to pale yellow; serve as a relish, hot or cold.

Nutmeg was entirely optional. One important matter was ignored in this early instruction—what kind of cheese? There were two traditional schools of thought. The majority employed Cheddar. Cosmopolitans employed Parmesan. When commercial bakeries began manufacturing cheese straws in the 1890s, they cut costs by using cheap industrial cheese, the ancestor of "American cheese." The quality of the cheese employed directly influenced the sumptuousness of the flavor of the straw. It did not pay to stint.

Cheese straws were national, not regional in the nineteenth century. But in the South at the end of the nineteenth century, hospitable women discovered that because of the dryness of the biscuit, cheese straws were the ideal item to serve on occasions of beverage-centered hospitality.

There was, of course, a culture war over beverages at the turn of the twentieth century between the partisans of temperance and lovers of alcohol. In southern states, newspapers depended on public favor, and the larger part of the readership tended to be religious and abstainers from spirits, wine, and beer. Yet in the larger cities a strongly entrenched, predominantly male drinking culture had existed since the founding of the republic, with the tavern as its central institution. The cheese straw was not bar food. It was associated with home entertainment. In 1910—nine years before Prohibition—the *Jeffersonian* newspaper directed, "Serve Cheese Straws with afternoon Tea." And it resided at the tea table until Prohibition's repeal in 1933 when the cocktail party exploded into popularity in urban centers. At that point the cheese straw and its companion the benne wafer migrated from the tea table to the cocktail table. When playing bridge boomed in the 1950s, cheese straws became a bridge snack, rivaling the licorice candy bridge mix in popularity.

A spirit of contest sometimes moves home entertainment. A host or hostess strives to appear the most fashionable, elegant, well equipped, and novel. The plate of hors d'oeuvres became one place where making things fancy took place. Cheese straws that had spent most of their existence as long, thin baked rectangles or sometimes tubes, in the early 1960s developed a ruffled edge. Cecily Brownstone, the Associated Press's food editor, published widely syndicated instructions on how to make Extra Special Cheese Straws using a fine grater to reduce the size of

Note the feathered edges, hallmark of fancy cheese straws. Photograph © David S. Shields.

cheese particles so it formed smoother dough and a crimping pastry nozzle on a pastry bag through which to extrude the dough and give the straw a feathered edge.

After the shape went fancy, hosts and hostesses began tweaking flavor. Often experiments went in the direction of upping the pungency of the straws. Dry mustard powder might be added to the basic dough, or cayenne dusted over the top before baking. Some added celery seed or benne to the surface for a textural and flavor enhancement. In the latter half of the twentieth century and into the twenty-first, recipes for cheese straws have been one of the most frequently published in Georgia newspapers—an essential adornment of hospitality.

Pimento Cheese Straws

KEVIN MITCHELL

When I moved to Charleston, I was introduced to cheese straws and pimento cheese and became hooked. Here is a great way to combine the two. The addition of smoked Gouda takes this to another level.

Yields 25 to 30 straws

- 1½ cups unsalted butter, softened
- 1 cup freshly shredded yellow sharp Cheddar
- 1 cup freshly shredded smoked Gouda cheese
- 1½ teaspoons salt
- ½ teaspoon cayenne pepper
- 1 tablespoon chopped pimento peppers
- 1 tablespoon flat-leaf parsley, chopped
- 4 cups all-purpose flour

Preheat the oven to 350°F and line baking sheet with parchment paper.

Beat all ingredients except the flour at medium speed in a stand mixer until blended. Gradually add flour, beating just until combined.

Use a cookie press with a star-shaped disk, or a pastry bag with a star tip, to shape the mixture into long ribbons on prepared baking sheets. Cut ribbons into 2-inch pieces.

Bake for 12 minutes or until lightly browned. Remove to a wire rack to cool.

Chicken Pie

In the decades after the Civil War a temple to chicken pie emerged in the small railroad town of Smithville in Lee County, Georgia. Built of wood, three stories tall, with a veranda and dining room, the McAfee Hotel arose across the street from the depot of the Central of Georgia Railroad. Smithville served as the central transfer point for passengers going from Atlanta to Montgomery, Alabama, and the timing of the various trains permitted taking a meal during the layover period. The meal at the McAfee consisted of smoking hot chicken pie and scuppernong wine. The pie became so famous that the hotel became known as "The Chicken Pie House." And savoring a forkful of gravy-laden chicken and piecrust formed a memorable feature of the culinary experience of nearly every traveler through southwest Georgia. The McAfee remained a shrine until the rise of the automobile, when train travel declined in importance. The hotel fell victim to fire in 1933.

But memories of chicken pie die hard. And small Georgia towns hold firm to recollections of past glories. So in 1996 Smithville organized a Chicken Pie Festival to honor the dish that made three generations of Georgians smile when they thought of the town. Each year since then, on a weekend in late October or early November, thousands of people fill Main Street, witness the Chicken Pie Contest, enjoy the classic car show, feast at vendors' tables, and revel in the afternoon of entertainment.

Classic chicken pie is not the same as chicken pot pie. The former is a much purer and simpler thing: cooked chicken, chicken gravy, and pie pastry (usually lattice topped, but sometimes a full top crust). There are no green peas, celery, or carrot cubes. There are no vegetables at all to distract one from the sumptuous savor of yardbird in yardbird sauce.

Mrs. S. R. Dull, the matriarch of early twentieth-century Georgia cookery, provided a classic instruction on how to make the true chicken pie. Pay close attention.

Chicken Pie

Mrs. S. R. Dull, *Atlanta Journal*
(June 30, 1929)

The chicken is boiled in a small amount of water, just enough to cook it tender, about two cups. Salt, just a little, is added to this and when done there is not more than a cup or less of the water or liquid, and this is used in the pie along with butter and milk. When making a pie my rule is to line only the sides of the pan with pastry, leaving the bottom free, which method makes it less apt to scorch. A layer of chicken, salt (if needed), pepper and butter is added, then a layer of pastry, which is rolled thin, cut in strips about an inch wide or little more and placed criss-cross over the chicken. Another layer of chicken and pastry is added until all is used. Then the liquid from boiling, with sufficient milk, is added and should come about three-fourths of the depth of the pie. When all of this is in, the top crust is placed over the entire top. Many punctures with a fork over the pastry are made and generous cross cut in the center, and the pie is ready for the oven.

The pie is cooked in a moderate oven until the top crust is crisp and brown. The venting of the top crust or the use of a lattice top releases the steam and prevents the contents from boiling over the sides of the pie pan.

Mrs. Dull was a classicist when it came to flavoring the filling of the pie. Nutmeg or mace, Worcestershire sauce, bay leaf, and powdered ginger have entered in the formulae of the winners of the Smithville contest. There is a sect of chicken pie makers that incorporate sliced hard-boiled egg into the fabric of the pie, arguing the egg is rightly a component of the chicken. This verges on specious reasoning. But since we haven't tasted the end result, we will not render a final judgment yay or nay.

One element of the classic chicken pie has altered over the years—the crust. In the heyday of the McAfee Hotel, lard supplied the shortening in a classic crust and soft white winter wheat the flour. The rise of vegetable-based shortenings (Cottonlene, Crisco, margarine, et cetera) in the 1920s changed the fabric and flavor of crust. Not everyone liked the change, so a strong contingent of home cooks continued to use lard in making piecrust. The rise of the magazine and newspaper cooking columns introduced two novelties: biscuit crust chicken pie and puff pastry chicken pie. The former became popular after World War II, and quickly led to variations including the incorporation of grated cheese and parsley into the crust. Puffed pastry crust for chicken pie began appearing in the 1990s, particularly after frozen puffed pastry began appearing in grocery story freezer sections.

Coca-Cola Cake

In the late nineteenth century, John Pemberton, a pharmacist from Atlanta, decided to develop a tonic. At that time, it was common for pharmacists to create nonalcoholic tonics, as alcohol consumption was frowned upon. In 1886 he succeeded in formulating the recipe for Coca-Cola, combining the active ingredients of the coca leaf (cocaine) and kola nut (caffeine). Asa Candler acquired the Coke formula in 1888 and under his leadership the company discontinued the use of the coca leaf and implemented marketing strategies that would transform Coca-Cola into a widely recognized brand. Sadly, Pemberton passed away before witnessing the full success of his creation.

Later, Coke would find its way into recipes. A recipe for Coca-Cola Cake, based on the Texas sheet cake, would first appear in 1959 in Galveston, Texas. Some have said that the first recipe for Coca-Cola cake appeared in Charleston, West Virginia; we have not seen evidence for that. The cake would become one of the most celebrated southern desserts. Unfortunately, there is no history of the cake's creator. Based on several recipes, Coke does double duty, as it is used in the frosting as well as the batter.

In the 1990s the popularity of the Coca-Cola cake grew and eventually recipes would leap from the pages of community cookbooks into the pages of professional cookbooks. Anne Byrn offers a version of the cake in her *American Cakes* cookbook (2016). During this time the popular chain Cracker Barrel added it to their menu on a seasonal basis, however it was permanently added to the menu in 2012.

One thing to also note is that the cake is not for the faint of stomach. Though Coca-Cola is a main ingredient as a sweetener, the addition of marshmallows further adds to the sweetness of the cake. In an article in 2018 by the *Daytona Daily Times*, the writer jokes "Leave it to the Southerners to take a chocolate cake and figure out how to add more sugar to it."

Bourbon and Cherry Coca-Cola Cake

KEVIN MITCHELL

Like many southerners, I love a good Coca-Cola Cake. I wanted to do something different for this recipe, using Cherry Coca-Cola instead of regular Coca-Cola. The addition of bourbon or whiskey gives you the feeling of enjoying a cocktail. I used Uncle Nearest whiskey.

Makes one 9 × 13 cake

For the Cake

- ½ cup Cherry Coca-Cola
- ½ cup ginger beer
- 2 tablespoons good quality whiskey or bourbon
- 16 tablespoons (2 sticks) unsalted butter, cubed
- ¼ cup cocoa powder
- 2 cups all-purpose flour
- ¾ cup light brown sugar, firmly packed
- ¾ cup granulated sugar
- 1 teaspoon baking soda
- ½ teaspoon salt
- ½ cup sour cream
- 2 eggs
- 1 teaspoon vanilla
- ½ cup chopped cherries

For the Icing

- 14 tablespoons (1¾ sticks) unsalted butter
- ¼ cup Cherry Coca-Cola
- ¼ cup ginger beer
- ¼ cup good quality whiskey or bourbon
- ¼ cup cocoa powder
- 4 cups confectioners' sugar, sifted

FOR THE CAKE: Preheat oven to 350°F. Spray a 9 × 13 × 2 cake pan with baking spray.

Pour the Cola, ginger beer, and whiskey into a large saucepan and add the butter and the cocoa powder. Cook over medium heat, stirring frequently until the butter is melted and the mixture is smooth. Remove from the heat.

Whisk the flour, sugars, baking soda, and salt in a large bowl until well combined. Stir the Cola mixture into the dry ingredients until thoroughly blended and smooth. Put the sour cream into a 2-cup jug or liquid measuring cup, then break in the eggs and add the vanilla. Beat the eggs with the sour cream and vanilla, then add this to the batter and stir until thoroughly combined. Stir in cherries.

Spread the batter into the prepared pan in an even layer to the corners. Bake for 15 to 20 minutes, until a tester inserted in the center comes out clean.

FOR THE ICING: Make the icing while the cake is in the oven. In a 2-quart saucepan, melt the butter with the Cola, ginger beer, whiskey, and cocoa powder over medium heat, stirring until combined. Beat in the confectioners' sugar, about a cup at a time, until the icing is smooth and combined.

Take the cake from the oven and pour the icing over it, covering as much cake as possible. Tilt the cake pan or use an offset spatula to cover the entire surface, working quickly before the icing begins to set. Leave the cake to cool in its pan. The cake can be made up to 2 days ahead and kept covered in a cool place.

Coleslaw

The ideal partner of fried fish, barbecue's faithful sidekick, the picnic salad upon which the vegetarian and the carnivore can agree, coleslaw is an old Georgia favorite. Georgians in the 1800s took to calling it "cold slaw" and that's how it appears on six of the Georgia Products menus of 1913. "Cole" derives from the German name for vegetables in the brassica family—turnips, cabbages, collards, kohlrabies. One reason that "coleslaw" became "cold slaw" is because slaw, like potato salad, is a dish that can be anointed with a hot dressing or a cold dressing. When one said, "cold slaw," one indicated what form of slaw was being served. As Elizabeth Wood, a USDA home demonstration agent, indicated in the *Jackson Progress-Argus* in 1945, "Cabbage salad may be hot dressed or cold dressed, depending on whether a wilted or a crisp slaw is wanted. Hot dressing wilts shredded cabbage somewhat, and this limpness is preferred by some cold slaw epicures. Those who want their cabbage crisp, add cold dressing just before serving. For cold slaw many people like a sweet-sour cooked dressing, well seasoned with mustard and celery seed."

Coleslaw, like sanitation, companionate marriage, and the public debt, is a Dutch contribution to American culture. In its earliest manifestations it did not employ mayonnaise. Oil, salt, pepper, and vinegar were the original dressings. The variety of cabbage was important, with conical-headed filderkraut and old large red Dutch cabbages being the original choices, but drumheads and Charleston Wakefield cabbages became later favorites. Any cabbage that tastes sweet and fresh raw will do.

Restaurants pioneered coleslaw dressed with mayonnaise, and no restaurant more than Folsom's Reading Room Restaurant on Marietta Street in Atlanta. From 1885 to 1909 Folsom's served a free side dish of coleslaw with every order on their menu except the ice cream dessert. Many people tasted the Reading Room's slaw, because every day at closing the city's poor would congregate at Folsom's back entrance to collect the freely dispensed overage of the day's food preparations.

One of the odder items one encounters on early Georgia menus is hot cold slaw, a contradiction in the form of a salad. Here is a recipe dating from 1910 in which the cabbage and dressing are cooked, then cooled to room temperature.

Cold Slaw

Atlanta Golden Age
(December 29, 1910)

Cut the cabbage very fine. For a quart of cabbage take the yolks of three eggs, beat them well, 1 ½ cups of vinegar, two large spoonfuls of sugar, one cup of thick cream, a teaspoonful of mustard, salt and pepper. Mix this with the eggs. When hot, add the cabbage, cover and stew until it is thoroughly hot. Let it cool before bringing to the table. Some add olive oil, but we like butter.

The riddle of this sweet-and-sour recipe is whether the mustard is powdered or prepared. A turn-of-the-century cold slaw could be quite yellow because of the mustard content. Indeed, it was so yellow that the bachelor dandies of the period slang named the large yellow chrysanthemum they wore as a boutonniere "cold slaw with mustard."

A century ago coleslaws that did not cook the cabbage inspired fear in that segment of the population that feared dyspepsia, a gastric disorder thought to arise from eating raw vegetables and fruits. Despite not being cooked, the original formulae called for the shredded cabbage to sit in vinegar and salt for a good while before serving. The first vegetable to be added to the cabbage was usually onion. The addition of pickles, peppers, and a multitude of herbs was a later nineteenth century development. Sour cream was the first emulsifying addition. Mayonnaise came at the very end of the nineteenth century. An 1893 recipe from Athens lays out the formula for uncooked slaw.

Cold Slaw

Woman's Work (October 1, 1893)

Chop or shred fine, half a head of crisp, white cabbage. Rub the yolks of two hard boiled eggs to a powder; add a pinch of salt, a teaspoonful of sugar, half as much mustard, and a tablespoonful of olive oil or butter; then beat in two-thirds of a cupful of vinegar, and pour over the chopped cabbage.

In some parts of the South a spirit of substitution reigned when it came to the vegetable at the heart of the dish. Collard slaw is found in places in North Carolina, South Carolina, and Georgia. Celery slaw is the preparation that enjoyed a heyday in New York and the upper Midwest in the twentieth century. In 2010 kale slaw began appearing on Atlanta menus. Yet shredded cabbage remained the favorite green at the heart of the slaw. Where creativity most manifested itself was in dressing the shredded cabbage or supplementing it with other ingredients. Consider this "Household Hint" from the *Griffin Daily News* in 1925: "In preparing coleslaw an excellent substitute for vinegar is the juice from sweet pickles, and the addition of a cup of black walnuts." In tweaks such as these we see Georgians making an old American dish into a new peculiarly local preparation. When Georgia became the country's prime producer of pimento peppers in the mid-twentieth century, sliced pimentos found their way into the mix, as in Louise Doak's Dutch Slaw recipe in *Gems from Georgia Kitchens* (1963). In the 1970s the availability of garlic powder in groceries led to a vogue for garlic slaw. A classic formulation appears in the Newnan Junior Service League's *A Taste of Georgia* cookbook.

In the 2020s the great debate is how much sugar, if any, you put in coleslaw. Historically it has been administered with a liberal hand. But the oversugaring of American food that began in the latter part of the twentieth century has elevated the risk for diabetes in Georgians. Using Duke's Mayonnaise in a slaw dressing is a step toward moderation, since it does not employ sugar. We don't recommend using artificial sweetener as a sugar substitute in your family recipe.

Collard Green and Cabbage Slaw

KEVIN MITCHELL

Usually, when you have fried fish, it is served with a mayonnaise-based cabbage and carrot coleslaw. The slight bitterness and crunch of raw collards goes well with the sweetness of the carrots and cabbage. To keep it light, I use an oil and vinegar-based dressing along with the smokey notes of smoked paprika.

4 to 6 servings

- 1 tablespoon extra virgin olive oil
- 5 cups of collard greens with thick stems removed, leaves halved lengthwise and cut crosswise into ¼-inch strips
- ½ cup apple cider vinegar
- ½ tablespoon fresh lemon juice
- 2 teaspoons sugar
- 1 teaspoon creole mustard
- ½ teaspoon celery seed
- ½ teaspoon smoked paprika
- Salt, to taste
- Freshly ground black pepper, to taste
- 3 cups green cabbage, cored, cut in half, then cut into thin slices
- 2 cups shaved carrots (using a vegetable peeler)
- ½ small Vidalia onion, thinly sliced

Mix the oil and collard greens in a stainless-steel bowl and massage with your hands for approximately 5 minutes.

FOR THE DRESSING: Whisk together the vinegar, lemon juice, sugar, mustard, celery seeds, and paprika in a small bowl. Season to taste with salt and pepper.

FOR THE SLAW: Combine the collard greens, cabbage, carrots, and onions in a very large bowl. Add the dressing, stirring to coat well and season generously with salt and pepper. Refrigerate until the collard greens soften and wilt slightly, stirring occasionally, for at least 1 hour and up to 3 hours.

Note: For convenience, you can purchase prewashed and precut collards from your local grocery store.

Collards

Georgia blue stem, white cabbage, Vates, and glazed, the collard reigns as the king of winter greens. Simmered with jowl or side meat, in water seasoned with salt and maybe a spoonful of sugar, collards cook until the leaves get slippery and swap flavors with the pork. Collards and their cooking liquid (potlikker) marry perfectly with corn bread. As a side, collards work with a range of dishes from fried chicken to pork chops to fried fish. Reckoned among the most nutritious and tonic of southern vegetables, they appear on home tables, in barbecue joints, and in fine-dining restaurants. There are rules for preparation: Wash thoroughly, cut out the stalks and thickest ribs (unless you have a tender cabbage collard, in which case leave them be), cover in salted water, add a ham hock, jowl, or chunk of fatback, and cook until tender. If the smell of cooking collards bothers your family members, toss a few pecan meats into the liquid while it is cooking. They will temper the aroma.

In our grandparents' time collards were invariably boiled with a piece of cured pork. Now chefs and adventurous cooks have taken to simmering them in vegetable stock or substituting a smoked turkey leg for a hock, braising them in oil, or shredding them and making collard kraut. One particularly tasty innovation is creamy collard soup, made with pureed greens.

Much has been made of the nutrition found in collards: the calcium, vitamins A and C, the iron. But Georgians knew that collards were "tonic" long before nutrition scientists identified the first vitamin (B_1) in 1910.

In southern lore, Georgia was the collard's home. But well before the "old Georgia blue" [blue-stem collard] became the standard green in the cookpot, collards had a history. Collards, or "coleworts" as they were sometimes called in Great Britain and in New England, come from a plant family that was originally acclimatized to north Europe, a colder clime than in the American South. So their first appearance in seed catalogs, from the second quarter of the nineteenth century, tend to be from northern seed brokers. Both names—coleworts and collards—appear. Colworts were brassicas that did not head; they formed splayed or flat leaves. Collards were not originally distinguished by varieties. There were "long collards," a term that meant collards that formed large fulsome leaves; these were contrasted with cabbage sprouts, the immature form of cabbage that set separate leaves before forming a head.

Southerners attempted to grow heading cabbage, usually from seed imported from England, the continent, or from northern US companies such as Hovey Seed in Boston or Landreth Seeds in Philadelphia. When Georgians saved seeds from the drumhead or savoy or green glazed cabbages that they grew, the epigenetics of the plant would turn off the chemical triggers that activated incurved leaf growth. Instead of forming heads, they sprouted into a splay of large leaves. So cabbage varieties such as green glazed became the green glazed collard. Collards that derived from heading cabbage types received the name "cabbage collards."

North Carolina boasts a famous yellow cabbage collard, celebrated in an annual festival at Ayden. Georgia produced the white cabbage collard, probably derived from the old sugarloaf cabbage (English Wakefield) first imported into the Lowcountry by gardener Robert Squibb in 1786.

Most collards were grown as annual plants. They became standard garden patch plants among Black and white farmers. Because collards drew salt out of soil, growers with saltwater inundation problems or mineralization problems along the coast grew it extensively to clean up fields. Hence the scale of growth became massive and collards became installed in foodways throughout the region. Certain strains of collard lent themselves to perennialization. By cropping off the flowerheads the plant became a "tree collard," the longest of the long collards. Some grew fifteen feet tall. There are still farmers in the region who cultivate collard trees bearing leaves large enough to fill the contents of a greens pot. A single leaf might serve as a dinner portion.

By the 1870s the various strains of collard were stabilizing in the South—the blue stem, the green glazed, the white cabbage collard, the yellow cabbage collard, the flat leafed collard. Seeds were segregated for each type and sold as such. In the North, however, the collard remained a kind of generalized southern plant and was sold without attention to variety. By the 1920s, Grady County, Georgia, became the principal source of collard seed for the United States, with the Georgia blue stem variety predominating and the white cabbage as a secondary production. Grady's version of the white cabbage collard was a cross between the Georgia blue and the Charleston Wakefield cabbage performed by the Georgia Agricultural Experimental Station at Griffin. This version of the white cabbage collard now predominates in the South; the older landrace from the 1830s survives in the South as the Stony Mountain collard.

White cabbage collards grown by Sarah Ross, director emeritus at the University of Georgia Center at Wormsloe Historic Site. Photograph © David S. Shields.

Once the collards have been lifted from the pot, one still has a sumptuous treasure: pot likker. Dunking corn bread into the unctuous broth has long been standard practice. But expert home cooks have used it as the liquid to flavor gravy, particularly for mashed potatoes, ham (if you wish an alternative to red eye gravy), and rice.

Condiments

Sometimes regional cookery makes use of ingredients or preparations originating from elsewhere. When curry powder began being imported by southern coastal merchants in the 1790s, cooks in Charleston and Savannah began incorporating it into local dishes. Condiments are special cases. These accompaniments to dishes can operate as a complementary flavor, a sauce, or a constituent. There are three items found ubiquitously in usage in Georgia food that came from without but became embraced as necessities at the Georgia table: Tomato Catsup, Worcestershire sauce, and Pepper Vinegar. We thought sketches of this trio had to appear here.

TOMATO CATSUP

What was the most important southern recipe to emerge between the American Revolution and the Civil War? A few candidates came immediately to mind: the baking soda biscuit, the mint julep, and southern fried chicken. But in terms of mass sales, there is one preparation that eclipses even fried chicken in national sales: tomato catsup, a condiment that did not exist when the United States was born but was greatly popular at the time of the American centennial. At the millennium it stood as the most important condiment in the country. The rise of salsa since 2000 split the tomato following, and mayonnaise became foremost in 2020 in terms of aggregate sales.

Before tomato catsup there was a panoply of catsups using ingredients other than tomatoes—fermented sauces that concentrated amino acids and supplied that earthy umami depth to dishes. In the pages of early nineteenth-century southern newspapers, you encounter notices for anchovy catsup, cucumber catsup, gooseberry catsup, grape catsup, lemon catsup, mushroom catsup, oyster catsup, pepper catsup, and green walnut catsup. In the early 1820s, in Maryland, tomato catsup was added to the repertoire. The first recipe appears in an 1823 issue of the *Easton Gazette*.

Homemade "ketchup" made by June Taylor, a nationally known canner and maker of preserves. "Catsup" was the preferred spelling of noncommercial makers of the condiment; "ketchup" became the preferred name among commercial producers in the nineteenth century. Photograph © David S. Shields.

Tomata Catsup

Easton Gazette (October 4, 1823)

Wipe the tomatas clean, and slice them in a deep pan, to every layer sprinkle a handful of salt, let them lie for twelve hours, put them in a skillet and let them boil four or five minutes, then strain them through a coarse cloth, to get all the juice, pour it in the skillet again and boil it briskly thirty minutes: to one quart of liquor add a quarter of an ounce of mace, ginger, and half a quarter of an ounce of white pepper, strain it through a thin cloth, and when cold bottle it, and cork it tight; put four or five blades of mace, and six cloves in each bottle, and some nutmeg. Shake the bottle when used.

The thin texture of this first form of catsup resembled the contemporary liquid anchovy catsup, a preparation that with the addition of tamarind in the 1830s would morph into Worcestershire Sauce. There were other ways of going about making catsup, resulting in thicker texture. The Baltimore-based *American Farmer*, the United States' first national agricultural periodical, offered in 1827 the recipe for a version with the thick texture of tomato ketchup that we now recognize.

These first recipes for tomato catsup were formulated before sugar became cheap and widely available in the country. (The tipping-point year when refined sugar prices fell because of output from Georgia and Louisiana refineries becoming productive was 1825.) The original savory form of tomato catsup would always put heat and spice forward.

Most of the early experimentation about the culinary preparation of tomato catsup took place in the South, largely because it was only in that region that tomatoes were popular. It took a medical campaign in the late 1830s that asserted the hygienic salubriousness of the tomato to make it loved in other regions. In manuscript recipe collections from the antebellum period, tomato catsup rivaled black cake as the most frequently encountered formula.

Bottled tomato catsup was a grocery fixture in the late antebellum period—and the question is whether the earliest commercial forms of this catsup were imported from England or were American-made produced by northern manufacturers. The Civil War forced local manufacture, and J. L. Mims of Augusta pioneered the sale of local homemade catsup.

Columbus, Georgia, offered a sweeter version of tomato catsup during the 1860s. As the recipe below indicates, brown sugar mellowed out the acid in the tomatoes. We should recall that it wasn't until the Livingston Acme tomato of the 1870s that the sometimes-sharp acidity and inconsistent ripening (centers green, flesh beneath the skin ripe and red) were overcome in a reliable cultivar.

Tomato Catsup

Columbus Sun (May 23, 1862)

To a half bushel of skinned Tomatoes, add 1 quart of good Vinegar; 1 pound of Salt; ¼ pound of black Pepper; 2 oz. of African Cayenne; ¼ pound of allspice, 1 oz. of Cloves, 6 good Onions; 2 pounds Brown Sugar; and 1 handful of Peach Leaves.

This sweeter catsup would be a portent of ketchup to come. Yet it would be a mistake to claim that a standard tomato catsup existed in the nineteenth and early twentieth century in Georgia. Indeed, it was one preparation that everyone staked a claim to, when producing it at home, by adjusting ingredients and proportions to personal taste. The preponderance of allspice in the Columbus recipe is unmatched among southern catsup recipes of that century. Homemade catsup remains an honored local food among gardener cooks with lots of tomato plants. Nowadays the use of certain tomatoes with superior flavor (the Cherokee purple, the yellow German, the Brandywine) can make homemade catsup a fine-dining experience, particularly if one avoids a Heinz-level of sweetening.

WORCESTERSHIRE SAUCE

For nearly 170 years, any Lowcountry seafood recipe with a sauce or liquid component almost invariably included Worcestershire sauce. How did this fermented brew of smashed anchovy, tamarind, barley malt vinegar, and molasses become the master additive after salt and pepper? What was the flavor theory behind its universal adoption? How did it get introduced into the southern pantry?

The commercial history has been told on countless occasions, particularly by the Lea & Perrins company of Worcestershire, United Kingdom. It was the creation of the Lea & Perrins apothecary in the 1830s, no doubt one of the liquid condiments fashioned as digestive aids (bitters, digestifs, etc.) popular since the mid-eighteenth century. The early ads indicated that it was "prepared from the Recipe of a Nobleman in the County." And much speculation about who this nobleman was, and whether the sauce derived from India has been published in the previous twenty-five years. Culinary historians, however, are on more solid ground when they observe that this appears a latter-day attempt to fashion an equivalent of the classical Roman garum, a salty pungent fish sauce.

Worcestershire sauce began to be imported in substantial quantity in the United States in early 1843 by John Duncan & Son in New York City. In November 1843 it appears in a list of "rich fish and meat sauces" imported by Dickson & Mills, of Charleston, South Carolina. Shortly thereafter Hone and Connery made it available at Harris' wharf in Savannah and J. A. Millen & Company at Metcalf Range in Augusta. It headed a group of imported sauces that also included Reading, John Bull, Quin's Camp, Carice, India Soy, and Harvey sauces. Its primacy in early ad listings suggests that from the first it was esteemed the most useful and flavorsome of the sauces. Only John Bull's sauce of the others would last a decade. Indeed, Worcestershire sauce dominated a category of sauces that vied with pepper sauces (supplying heat) and catsups (a category that emphasized a sweet-savory mixture). Worcestershire sauce had an acidulous sour note, supplied by tamarind, with a more pronounced salt and earthy taste (supplied by the anchovy), along with the sweetness of molasses. It has a surprisingly sharp tang.

The sauce more than any other available to nineteenth-century Americans supplied that earthy quality that twenty-first century culinarians call umami. This is not so much an issue with meat, which has its own quality of umami. It is more needful for fish and seafood. Southerners had little notion about the ingredients that made up this deep flavor. They didn't associate the taste of anchovy sauce with the fermented anchovy component in Lea & Perrins. They suspected that the astringency derived from ginger. When the Civil War blockade prevented importation of Lea & Perrin's sauce, southerners concocted their own "Worcester." The formula was not even close—and verged on tomato catsup—but this version printed in Augusta just after the Civil War gives an idea of the culinary imagination of apothecaries in the South.

Worcester Sauce

Augusta Daily Constitutionalist
(July 14, 1866)

Take one gallon of ripe tomatos, wash them in three quarts of water, boil it half down and strain it through a sieve. When all is drained, add two table spoonfuls of ginger, two of mace, two of whole black pepper, two of salt, one of cloves, one of cayenne; let them simmer in the juice until reduced to one quart, pour in half a pint of best vinegar, then pour the whole through a hair sieve, bottle in half pint bottles, cork down, tightly seal, and keep in a cool place.

Experimenting with exotic ingredients as condiments became somewhat common in Great Britain and Anglo-America in the 1790s, when British and American trading vessels began adding curry powder to the other spices from South Asia and India. Tamarind, native to Africa and long cultivated in India, was the exotic, global component of Worcestershire. The South embraced these elements more readily than New England. And southern fish stews—which tended to be less milk based than northern chowders—began expanding their constituent ingredients, in large measure because of the influence of African American household cooks. The hot pepper came into play before the turn of the nineteenth century. The tomato became a standard ingredient in the 1830s (tomato ketchup and tomato paste would become late-nineteenth century equivalents). Using roux as a thickener became commonplace in Charleston and Savannah in the later 1840s. The adding of sherry or Madeira as a finisher to a fish stew can be attributed to the influence of green turtle stews and terrapin à la Maryland which skyrocketed in repute during the first half of the nineteenth century. Worcestershire sauce appeared on the scene just as roux, tomatoes, and sherry had transformed the character of seafood soups and stews. It supplied an astringent, salty bass note that harmonized with the sweet and caramel dimensions that had come into the dishes. By 1860 it was standard in red chowders (those incorporating tomatoes), crab stews, shrimp gravies, shrimp pie, and the entire range of deviled seafood dishes. It did not appear in early gumbos, but by the 1880s the sauce's associations with seafood was such that you couldn't make a shrimp mull, crab soup, cooter stew, or okra soup without at least a tablespoon of Lea & Perrins. In 1899 John Duncan & Son expanded from being the importer of Worcestershire sauce to its American manufacturer. Consequently, Worcestershire sauce became more widely available and less expensive, thus installing itself as a pillar of one-pot cookery in Georgia and the South in general.

PEPPER VINEGAR

What gives a bracing acid and heat counter to the mellowness of long-cooked greens? What supplies sass to a plate of chitterlings? What bestows bite to fresh sliced tomatoes when a rainy season has robbed them of intrinsic acid? What cuts the fat when pork belly carries too much flab? Pepper vinegar!

Adding red peppers to the handful of black peppercorns in pickling vinegar was common practice in eighteenth-century Atlantic cookery. Toward the end of that century the production of spice and herb vinegars began in earnest. It was the great age of popular faith in vinegar as a tonic tuning up one's health. Flavored vinegars—shrubs—vied with beer and ale in city beverage consumption. Bottled pepper vinegar became an import item at the outset of the nineteenth century. Charles McKenna the high-end Savannah grocer in Market Square carried both tarragon and chili vinegar among his assortment of imported sauces.

One of course did not need to buy a British bottle; you could always whip up something at home. The first and cheapest "pepper vinegar" employed black pepper exclusively, something available at every Georgia grocer. Among the poor, black pepper vinegar became a medicine and, during the Civil War when patent medicines were in short supply, it became a camp cure countering chills, diarrhea, and camp fever if we are to trust the "Every Soldier His Own Physician" column in the *Southern Recorder* on June 10, 1862.

The imported form of pepper vinegar used cayenne or chili peppers. One problem of reconstructing the history about pepper vinegar is the imprecision of names used by southerners in the eighteenth and nineteenth centuries. Hot peppers were generically called "guinea peppers." Cayenne peppers were used for any red pepper that grew pointing downward (the name derived from the Cayenne River region in French Guiana). Cayenne is first documented in English in Nicholas Culpepper's 1654 herbal. They would also be called "red peppers." Peppers that grew upwards tended to be called "bird peppers." The Tabasco pepper did not become significant until the mid-nineteenth century. Its fruits grow heavenward as well. The jalapeño, habanero, hatch, and serrano hot peppers only came to be known in Georgia in the twentieth century. Cayenne had become a significant article of import in Georgia in the 1790s when grocers Peter Catonnet, James Belcher, and John I. Sluyter brought it into Savannah. African American cooks became drawn to it in the nineteenth century. Some of the best early recipes for pepper vinegar appear in Black newspapers.

Pepper Vinegar

Afro-American American Advance
(October 7, 1899)

Take the seeds from six red peppers, cover these and six whole ones with cold salt water and let stand until next morning. Wash in clear water, simmer until tender and drain. Put one pint of vinegar into the preserving kettle with one-third of a cupful of sugar, one tablespoonful of grated horseradish, one medium-sized onion sliced, and one teaspoonful of white mustard seed; add the peppers, simmer 15 minutes, strain, and when cool, bottle.

The sweet element is noteworthy in this preparation. Opinions diverged about putting sugar in many recipes: in corn bread, in cooked greens, and in pepper vinegar. Some have argued an ethnic proclivity to sweetening foods; that is fantasy. We can supply an archive of sugar in the corn bread/green/vinegar recipes from Anglo-American cooks from the 1800 to 2000. Perhaps the most widely read pepper vinegar recipe of the nineteenth century was the sweetened formula published in Virginian Marion Harland's *Common Sense in the Kitchen*—as canonical a work of Anglo-American southern cookery as exists from the late nineteenth century. Rather there were communities of taste preference that emerged. And in the purist camp of pepper vinegar creators, the foremost was Annabella P. Hill.

Pepper Vinegar

Annabella P. Hill, *Southern Practical Cookery and Receipt Book* (1872)

Put into a quart bottle thirty small pods of green or red pepper (make of both kinds separately),. Set the bottles in an oven in water; make the water boil. When the peppers are thoroughly hot, pour in good vinegar to fill the bottle; cork tight.

Several things stand out about this recipe: the absence of salt, the awareness that immature green peppers and mature red peppers cook and behave differently and should be separated, the controlling of the baking of peppers by having the quart bottle in a water bath. This remains an excellent method to follow if (1) the peppers you are using have great intrinsic flavor and (2) the vinegar you are using has a distinctive quality.

By 1890 pepper vinegar became an essential kitchen preparation in Georgia. It was made with cayenne peppers, bird peppers, or tabasco peppers; it was sweet or plain; it was pungent. Experienced cooks knew how to use it in ways other than as a condiment. Combine it with tomato sauce and you had sauce picante. Combine it with green walnut catsup, you had Cherokee sauce. Add it to barbecue sauce and its fiery flavor deepened.

Corn Bread

Are you on team corn bread? Or team biscuits? The contest between corn bread and biscuits in the Georgia breadbasket is long standing. The state, except for a brief period in the colonial era, did not grow hard bread wheat—it grew soft winter wheats, such as purple straw, that were good for biscuits, cake flour, and flavoring whiskey. Georgians also grew lots of corn—the white flint corn favored for grits and corn bread in the Lowcountry, white and yellow dent corn in the Midlands and Uplands. Wheat flour was often more expensive, so corn bread dominated the breadbasket. But in 1901 the corn crop failed, and corn became expensive. Biscuits held sway until World War I, when the US government reserved wheat flour and bread for the use of the troops and urged southerners to revive their old love for cornbread. They responded well. Corn bread would establish a foothold on the Georgia table that would continue to the present day.

Georgia grows several varieties of corn. Hard flint corns such as Sea Island White Flint corn, Guinea Flint, and Creek Indian Flint were long preferred for hominy grits and making old-style corn bread. Densely packed with starch, the kernels often shattered to chunks under the stones, rather than grind fine. They made grist rather than meal or corn flour. Dent corn was softer than flints and became favored for finer grinds of meal and flour. Hastings prolific, Cocke's prolific, Hickory King, golden dent, Neal's Paymaster vied at local mills to become the local favorite meal corn.

Corn bread was the central baked good in an array of items employing cornmeal or corn flour prepared in ovens. Some of the oldest items, corn pone, the corn dodger, and hoe/ash cake, dated from the era (pre-1850) when cooks worked at hearths rather than stoves. The recipes were Native American in origin and typically employed nixtamalized corn (hominy). All of these first-period corn preparations use minimal ingredients, salt is the sole seasoning, and the preparation uses embers as a heat source.

An 1899 article in the *Augusta Chronicle* entitled "Decline and Fall of Corn Bread" (an old-school click-bait title), spoke not about the unfashionability of corn bread, but of these older baked-corn preparations. The popularization of the cookstove, the invention of chemical leavens, the cheapening of sugar and molasses, and the growing culture of print enabled more complex treatments of cornmeal and corn flour. Corn bread and its soufflé-like cousin spoonbread (more eggs more butter) would never fall from favor, even during that fraught period when the American medical establishment identified the cause of the vitamin-deficiency disease Pellagra with a southern corn-centric diet in 1909.

We should take a moment to recall these old baked cornmeal preparations. Corn dodgers were made of meal, water, and salt worked into a dough, shaped into long tubes, laid on a griddle and baked. They were cooked brown and did not rise. A similar dough makes up hoe cake, though milk is sometimes substituted for water and the dough is somewhat wetter. On a preheated griddle (or hoe blade) you pour out a round cake of dough and let it cook, turning it over when the underside browns. Some cooks preferred to salt hoe cake intensely. Corn pone uses the same dough as the hoe cake but fries it in lard or bacon grease in a skillet. All of these early Georgia preparations use no sugar. Only salt, water or milk, and meal.

But corn bread is entirely more lavish a thing. Its quality depends on the meal, of course, and those who like rustic skillet corn bread prefer a coarse, almost grits like, grind or use a combination of grits and meal. Those who favor a cake-like texture, go for a smooth meal, and some even combine meal with corn flour if they are attempting to make a fine crumb in the bread. Corn bread is leavened with baking powder or with buttermilk and baking soda. Geechee bakers add a spoonful of sugar to their dough. There is a purist element using white meal with no sweetener. Yet the real innovation of the generation of cooks who used stoves rather than hearths was to mix wheat flour with cornmeal to create a more even textured loaf. The old contest between corn and wheat was resolved by "both please!" in this tradition of corn bread baking. The earliest Georgia recipe we can find of this middle path of corn bread cookery comes from the year after the Civil War. Here we supply a later, clearer recipe.

Best Corn Bread

Daily Constitutionalist
(September 21, 1886)

Make a thick batter of 1 quart of sweet milk, and one quart of buttermilk, 2 tablespoonsful of saleratus [baking soda] and one of salt, 1 teacup molasses, 2 teacupsful of wheat flour, (or shorts) and corn meal enough to thicken it. Bake two hours in an over a little hotter than for wheat bread.

The bake time seems excessive, but today we have little concept about how efficient cookstoves of the mid-nineteenth-century were.

The twentieth century saw the industrialization of milling nationally and in Georgia particularly. When Midwestern yellow dent corn began to be grown at enormous scale and national milling companies provided yellow cornmeal at a low price point to grocers everywhere, Georgians began buying yellow meal in quantity, particularly between the two world wars. This meal was degerminated—largely starch—and so did not possess the robust flavor of stone-ground local corn produced by local mills. People became aware of the loss of flavor in the 1920s and local operators of grist mills using old mill stones sensed an opportunity. Birdsey's Mill in Augusta was the first to make "stone ground" cornmeal an advertising point in 1930. For nearly a century now, local mills have provided to corn lovers in the state an alternative to mass-production cornmeal. The mills had a difficult task combating the buying public's inclination for convenience and low cost. Matters became particularly difficult during World War II when American culture became obsessed with foods that could be prepared speedily. The war brought us Minute Rice and instant mashed potatoes. The first corn bread mixes appeared on Georgia's retail shelves. Miss Chambers and Clinch Corn Bread Mix were the first, then Jiffy, Martha White, Marie

Callender's, Betty Crocker, and Krusteaz. There were generations of Georgia cooks who never made corn bread from scratch.

The heroic millers who held out against industrial Midwestern meal saw their perseverance rewarded at the end of the twentieth century when the southern food revival placed a particular premium on open pollinated heirloom corns ground by water powered stone mills. These include Nora Mill in Sautee, Logan Turnpike Mill in Blairsville, Perkerson's Mill in Cobb County, John's Mill outside of Jasper, and Barker's Creek Mill in Rabun Gap. Truth be told, the public turned to these mills seeking grits more than cornmeal. The culinary revival of interest in good grits had begun in the late 1980s when Craig Claiborne, food writer for the *New York Times*, celebrated chef Bill Neal's shrimp and grits at Crook's Corner restaurant in Chapel Hill, North Carolina. Southern chefs realized that grits operated as a starch base other than rice and potatoes. But southern chefs asked the suppliers of their grits to supply a finer grind for use in baking corn bread. The 1990s saw corn bread become a standard offering in a wide range of restaurants, from barbecue shacks to American fine-dining venues. It had always been on the Thanksgiving menu and Christmas, often in the form of corn bread dressing for the turkey, but now it was a bread-basket fixture, a barbecue joint side, and a roadside breakfast staple.

Today excellent heirloom cornmeal is readily available from the web. You can watch a YouTube video on how to enliven your corn bread with Parmesan or jalapeño peppers. An archive of recipes is available with a few strokes of your fingers on the keyboard. Corn bread remains one of Georgia's traditional foods with a broad and enthusiastic following that includes both professional chefs and home bakers who will not let corn bread become stale.

Country Captain

When North America belonged to the British Empire in the 1700s, that empire girdled the globe. Its protected trade network circulated exotic products from South Asia—tea, spices, jalap, coconut, ginger—to ports in North America and the West Indies. It sometimes communicated foodways and dishes as well. Curried chicken originated in India. The chicken was indigenous to South Asia, the spices that made up curry—cumin, fenugreek, cardamom, curry leaf, turmeric, corianders, galangal—were South Asian as well. When curried chicken began being served in the port cities of the South at the end of the eighteenth century, local cooks tweaked the formula. They added New World peppers. Or tomatoes. Or pineapple. One version of chicken curry took root in the Lowcountry and sometimes bore the picturesque name, "Country Captain."

Curry powder begins appearing in advertisements in southern newspapers in the 1790s. Grocer Henry Ellison of Coates Row in Charleston imports it from London in 1797—part of his stock of spices, confections, teas, and alcohol (drugs all). In Savannah John J. Sluyter, a grocer on Whitaker Street, offered a similar stock in 1800. The English-speaking sections of the South, because of their British colonial legacies, adopted the spice mixture well before French Louisiana did. Indeed curry was only popularized in New Orleans in the late 1830s and 1840s by chef Auguste Broué, proprietor of the restaurant Le Pellerin.

India generates many spice mixtures that fall under the name "curry." So exactly what combination of ingredients is meant when we encounter "curry powder" in a recipe or an advertisement? Did it have fenugreek in it? Was turmeric a necessity? How much? English speaking users of the spice mixture scarcely knew that a range of styles existed, or that Indian cooks prepared their own from fresh ingredients, not premade, until a recipe for an "imitation of India Curry Powder" appeared in the London *Magazine of Domestic Economy* in 1836. Only after this time did the suggestion that one could make one's own begin to spread among domestic cooks in the South.

Early 1800s Lowcountry recipes for curry powder are rare, but do exist. Here is one from 1844, housed in the South Carolina Historical Society manuscript collections. It indicated that curry was a composite powder—with a base that you preprepared and bottled—and then added the pepper element at the time of cooking. Heed the instruction: "Grind them into an impalpable powder"—that means literally that you cannot feel the grain of any ingredient between your fingertips.

Curry Powder

Maria Louisa Poyas Gibbs, *Recipe Book* (ca. 1844)

Dry well a quarter of a pound of cardamom seeds and the same quantity of coriander seeds. Beat or grind them into an impalpable power. Dry and reduce also into an impalpable powder, an ounce of caraway seeds, an ounce and a half of turmeric, and two ounces of black pepper. Mix this latter powder with the former both having been first carefully sifted, and all that does not pass, being again ground. Now add half an ounce of the best powdered ginger and a large nutmeg grated. Put the powder into a closely stopped bottle for use. When you make a curry, add either of green chili bruised with salt, or of cayenne pepper, the first in preference, as much as you think requisite to impart to the curry the heat you desire. The mild curry should be made with the powder alone, quite free from any addition of either chili or cayenne peppers.

Country captain is novel in combining two cooking methods. The jointed chicken is floured and fried before being slow cooked in a liquid curry sauce incorporating bell peppers, tomatoes, and raisins. It is garnished with slivered almonds and served over steamed rice. The name is borrowed from the Anglo-Indian name employed for a particular way of preparing chicken with curry. It is first described in the United States in the *Boston Commercial Bulletin* of March 17, 1877, in one of the serial installments of Hadji Nicka Bauker Khan's "Indian Sketches" written expressly for that paper. "There is a way of broiling split chickens, peculiar, I fancy, to India, immediately after death, by which the flesh remains tender. If kept ten minutes, the flesh would become as tough as saddle leather. 'Country Captain' is the same broil, with a bilious-looking sauce of curry-powder, turmeric, melted butter, fried onions, cloves, almonds, cardamoms, &c. sprinkled over it, a compound which added to plain boiled rice makes the famous Bengal kedgeree rice" (1). This method of prepping chicken first appears in print in the United States in Mary Randolph's *The Virginia Housewife* (1824) as "To Make a Dish of Curry in the East-Indian Manner." (Note this is three decades before the frequently cited Chicken Curry recipe in Eliza Leslie's *New Cookery Book* of 1857.)

The Americanization of the dish dates from the last quarter of the nineteenth century when tomatoes and raisins were added. Mary J. Lincoln, matron of the Boston Cooking School, published a recipe in 1900 with the two-step frying and stewing method. It adds the tomatoes and raisins, but not garlic or bell peppers (the conjunction of green peppers and tomatoes made a dish "à la creole" in the 1880s). So Lincoln's recipe had one further elaboration before it became standard southern country captain. There has been also one subtraction. Lincoln added sugar to her dish. Southern cooks do not.

Several cooks in mid-twentieth century Georgia—from the Columbus area—made the dish nationally significant. In Columbus African American cook Aire Mullen (born 1888) catered many events at Fort Benning. She made General George S. Patton a devotee. Martha Johnson, an army nurse from Columbus, popularized the dish on the Mississippi gulf coast. Daisy Bonner, cook at President Franklin Delano Roosevelt's summer retreat at Warm Springs, north of Columbus, prepared a version so sumptuous it became FDR's favorite dish. The following is Aire Mullen's version from Columbus.

Country Captain

Aire Mullen via Mrs. H. F. Crecelius, *Dallas Morning News* (March 9, 1958)

Cut into 12 pieces a 3-pound chicken or 1 large guinea fowl. Skin, and fry to a golden brown in olive oil. In the meantime, brown for 10 minutes in more olive oil 1 onion, peeled and finely chopped, 1 green pepper, seeded and chopped, and 1 clove of garlic, minced. Stir them as they cook, and moisten with 8 ounces of water. Then season with 1 teaspoon of salt, ½ teaspoon of pepper and 1 ½ teaspoons of curry powder. Again stir well, and add 6 large red tomatoes, peeled and crushed, ½ teaspoon of chopped parsley, and ½ teaspoon of powdered thyme, and stir well.

Now put the fried chicken in a casserole, cover with the foregoing mixture, and add about ½ of the oil in which the chicken was fried. Cover the casserole and bake for 45 minutes. Have blanched a roasted to a light brown ½ pound of almonds, and add these to the chicken along with 3 tablespoons of dried currants. Arrange cooked rice on a platter, place the chicken in the center, and pour the sauce over all. Serve each person a helping of the chicken and the rice and the sauce, accompanying each portion with a piece of crisp bacon.

Country Ham

Dotted across the Georgia countryside stand small temples to the southern tongue. Some look rather shabby, a ramshackle shack in a back pasture. In the hill country one can come across sturdy stone outbuildings, venerable with age and dark with use. And among young farmers, one can find trim state-of-the art sheds with drafting systems that they learned to construct from YouTube videos. The owners of these buildings are the latest generation of an old priesthood—the devotees of cured and smoked meat. In their smokehouses they perform the magic rites with smoke and salt.

While numbers of different meats might find their way into the dark recesses of these smokey cells, the one that inspires the most reverence goes by several names: country ham, smoked ham, dry-cured ham. Whether made from the hind leg of a piney woods shoat, a fatty Ossabaw from the coast, a deep-flavored guinea hog, or an imported Iberian black pig, the ham that endures the long seclusion in the smokehouse emerges the finest of all home-processed proteins. "The greatest Christmas present I ever received was a home cured country ham from my uncle in Butts County." Perhaps you don't have an uncle from the area around Jackson—no worry—you can buy a holiday dry-cured ham from one of a number of processors in the state: Exotic Jamon Iberico from White Oak Pastures near Bluffton, or classic whole leg from Dillard House in Dillard. If you need an organic ham, you would order from Gum Creek Farm in Roopville.

Country ham differs from the wet-cured city hams that dominate the grocery shelves. The wet-cured ham processes more quickly. In former days it pickled in pork barrels at those stores where local politics got hashed. Now it is wet packed twenty-first-century pork processing factories. The true country ham is "brick-red, momentously salty, packed with flavor. A top-quality ham is so fine-grained it appears dry, but when a knife glides through, peeling off a parchment-thin slice, it beads with moisture" (December 8, 1985). This is the soul of a ham biscuit, the star of a holiday side table, the engine for increased beverage consumption at a cocktail party or tailgate.

Prior to the last half of the twentieth century, when refrigeration was introduced to the curing process to diminish bacterial infestation, the country ham was cured according to a set regimen. The hog slaughter took place in one of the winter months. The back legs were trimmed; salted (either buried in salt or deposited in a brine so salty an egg could float on it); dressed with saltpeter (sodium nitrate, a preservative) and sometime molasses or brown sugar; coated in pepper, red pepper, and/or brown sugar; bagged in burlap; and hung up for flavoring in cold smoke. Georgia smokers used either green hickory wood (expensive) or corn cobs (cheap) for smoking. The burlap bag was introduced late in the nineteenth century to inhibit skippers, an insect that could reduce a ham to mush if allowed access to the meat. The introduction of pepper and hot pepper into the ham's coating also served as a deterrent to pests and pathogens.

After it has been smoked and aged for some months, the ham is ready for use. A well-cured ham can be sliced paper thin and eaten as Georgia's equivalent of prosciutto. But the more traditional way to eat ham is to boil and then bake it in a glaze (Coca-Cola or peach). Before cooking, you must soak the ham to leach some of the salt out of it. Old cookbooks recommend an overnight soak at least. Because too much salt has ill effects on older people, a 24- to 36-hour soak better serves consumers. Some cooks made the imparting of flavor as much a function of the soak as diminishing the saltiness. In *The Savannah Cook Book* of 1933, Harriet Ross Colquitt doused the ham in sweet tea and molasses. Some used ginger ale and brown sugar. Two generations of women in the late twentieth century soaked country ham in Coca-Cola. Not all hams are so "momentously salty" that they require prolonged soaking. One must sample the fresh ham to determine what you should do. Every ham, however, benefits from flavor enhancement.

Boiled ham is soaked, scrubbed, and covered in liquid that is brought to a boil then reduced to a simmer. It cooks at moderate heat for 20 minutes per pound. The heat is turned off and the water allowed to return to room temperature. After the ham has been extracted from its bath, one trims the rind and much of the fat layer off, leaving less than a quarter inch. Score this with a sharp knife and into the fat rub brown sugar and black pepper and punch cloves into the surface. Then you brown the ham in a hot oven—usually not too long. If you want a rich glaze, there are several traditional paths you can follow. Quick peach glaze can be made with a jar of peach jam, a quarter cup of brown sugar, a quarter cup of peach brandy, and some dry mustard powder for additional kick. But every creative chef has her or his own take, from Dr. Pepper and pickle juice (Alton Brown) to sorghum and apple cider vinegar.

Crab

Blue crabs have been part of the coastal Georgia diet for thousands of years. The delicate flavor of fresh steamed crab, with its modest fattiness, its hint of salt, its flakey texture have proved so tempting that multitudes willingly undertake the labor of cracking claws, dismantling shells, and picking backfin meat from their snug receptacles of cartilage. For eating the blue crab takes pride of place among the crab species that live along the hundred miles of Georgia coast—Atlantic horseshoe, calico, ghost, spider, fiddler, hermit, mole, and purse crabs. Only three types of crab serve as regular food sources: the blue crab, stone crab, and oyster crab.

Stone crabs first appeared in Georgia seafood stores in 1961, the claws, shipped in from Florida, quickly established themselves as a dining novelty. Now steamed claws of stone crab appear on the menus of Georgia Sea Island restaurants and climatic shifts have brought breeding populations of the stone crab along the Georgia coast. The miniature oyster crabs (*Zaops ostreus*) are soft body mini crustaceans that live in bivalves and, fried, make up the secret crunchy ingredient in island omelets.

The blue crab, however, stands foremost in the hearts of eaters. The Native Guale, Yamasee, and Timucua Peoples ate them roasted and boiled. The Georgia colonists favored serving them in milk-based soups and stews. In the 1800s, baked dishes such as crab pie came into fashion. Among the saltwater Geechee, crab pilau (now called "crab rice") became a key dish. After 1935 crab salad became a favorite entertainment dish in Georgia, the inevitable fixture at a summer party or wedding reception.

Crab rice, the classic Gullah Geechee seafood pilau, has several methods of preparation. Usually the crabmeat is not boiled with the rice, but the crab flavoring is imparted to the grain by including chunks of fried crab shell in the rice pot. Often fresh crabmeat is mixed with steamed crab flavored rice and finished in an oven. Photograph © David S. Shields.

The harvest and processing of blue crabs so that crab meat could be enjoyed by people across the state did not begin until Sam Lewis organized Lewis's Crab Factory in 1935. Located on Bay Street in Brunswick, it had the size and staff to pick and pack crabmeat from every trap brought to the factory by crabbers in Glynn County. It operated its own vessels for shrimping and crabbing and, in addition to crab, processed conch, oysters, clams, and shrimp. It employed numbers of pickers and packers, entire families for multiple generations—many of them African American—until its closure in 1998. Its cans of pasteurized crabmeat graced the shelves of the Giant Food grocery chain and enjoyed sales from Jacksonville to Boston. Its closure at the end of the twentieth century occurred because of declines in the crab population in Georgia's coastal waters and the undercutting of domestic prices by imported Asian crabmeat. The crab population crashed from 1998 to 2005. In 2003 the Georgia Commercial Blue Crab Fishery collapsed. Only in 2019, through the COVID-19 era, did the population replenish to levels seen in the early 1990s. Much of the fresh Georgia crab enjoyed by residents in the past two decades has been harvested by recreational crabbers or has been shipped in from other southern states.

Lewis Crab Factory made crab salad a summertime signature of late twentieth-century hospitality. Even with the factory's demise, canned blue crabmeat from other sources remains available. Let us say this: The substitutions of cheaper Alaskan king crab meat in classic Georgia seafood recipes just doesn't work. Different, stringier texture. Less fattiness. Relative lack of flavor. So get blue crabs or the meat by hook or by crook.

While Georgia residents in the latter decades of the twentieth century borrowed ideas from other places, such as the crab boil from Maryland, it never had the significance of a shrimp boil, a catfish fry, a barbecue or a Brunswick stew fest as an outdoor food event. So we will concentrate on dishes that grew up natively, or had long histories: crab soup/stew, deviled crab, crab pie, and crab salad. We will also celebrate the seasonal splendor of the soft-shelled crab.

There exists a way of seasoning crabmeat in Georgia dishes. They are not heavily spiced with cayenne or pepper. This said, the popularity of Zatarain's rather peppery seafood boil products from Louisiana upped the Scovil heat rating of boiled crab after the 1960s. mace or nutmeg is frequently a flavoring agent, Worcestershire sauce supplies umami, and rice is often served with the dish. This general path of preparation preserves the delicacy and intrinsic flavor of crabmeat.

CRAB STEW

At the beginning of the twentieth century the Pickens Café at 122 Wentworth in Savannah served the thick milk and cream-based crab stew that became the standard in the oldest of Georgia's cities. When Harriet Ross Colquitt published *The Savannah Cook Book* in 1933, the stew she presented stripped down the classic Lowcountry dairy stew.

Crab Stew

Harriet Ross Colquitt,
The Savannah Cook Book (1933)

Make a roux of two large tablespoons of butter and two scant tablespoons of flour, and when smooth, add one pint of milk and season with salt. When this comes to a boil, stir in one lemon, chopped fine (skin and all), plenty of pepper and paprika, and cook well. Just before removing from fire, add the meat from one dozen crabs. Heat well, but do not boil. Add one tablespoon of Worcestershire Sauce, one tablespoon of wine, and serve.

Several observations. The original Pickens Café stew mixed a stock made from simmered crab shells with the milk. It had mace as well as paprika. It specified Madeira as the wine to brace the stew before serving. Colquitt in 1933 was publishing just as Prohibition was repealed. The supplies of wine in Savannah were inconsistent, so she chose not to specify which to use, on the off chance only sherry might be available. This stew was not a chowder, lacking bacon as a flavoring and potatoes or crackers to add body. In the post-World War II period, diced celery began appearing in the stew. The stew was also not a mull in that it had a roux base.

The incorporation of tomatoes, peppers, and onions into a crab soup made with crab shell stock in which milk is later added has long been recognized by Georgians as Crab Soup a la creole, a creation of Louisiana. The *Atlanta Journal* published an iconic recipe for this dish in its November 23, 1902, issue. It is one of those dishes (shrimp creole is another) that Georgians have borrowed to lend variety to the table.

DEVILED CRAB

Perfected by African American caterers in Philadelphia at the dawn of the nineteenth century, deviled crab became a favorite restaurant menu dish in Georgia during the years 1882 and 1883. The New Hotel in Brunswick, Leake & McCrea Restaurant in Marietta, and Kaufmann's Restaurant in Savannah built the public taste for the cayenne-laced baked mélange of crabmeat and bread crumbs served in a crab shell. Mrs. Grant Wilkins provided the first recipe published in Georgia in 1891. It showed an up-to-date kitchen savvy by calling for the use of canned crabmeat, an innovation in marketing that enabled crab to be served in inland cities without spoilage.

Deviled Crabs

Mrs. Grant Wilkins, *Atlanta Journal*
(April 4, 1891)

For one dozen persons, use one large can of crab, taking care to first remove all the hard particles which may be in it. Take three eggs, beaten separately, mix them, and then stir in the crab one tablespoonful at a time until all of the crab is used. Then add the juice of half a lemon, three tablespoonfuls of melted butter, a little salt and red pepper, and two tablespoonfuls of cracker crumbs. Put in the shells, and cover with cracker crumbs mixed with a little butter. Bake in a hot oven for a few minutes.

Some have preferred using dried mustard powder to cayenne, but the spicing is never volcanic. Only just enough to tingle your lips.

SOFT-SHELLED CRAB

Periodically adult crabs molt their shell in order to grow larger. During the first two days after molting, the exterior of the crab has not solidified into a hard carapace. When soft the body of the crab is tender and succulent. Soft-shell crabs command a premium at the market, so crabbers make an effort to segregate those jimmies and sooks in their catch on the verge of molting their shells. They are isolated into salt water holding impoundments and harvested when just soft. In the era before widespread freezer technology, "softies" were strictly a seasonal treat, beginning in April and extending into September, though becoming scarce after June. Packed alive in seaweed, they were shipped from the coast to inland cities to be consumed.

A national fad for consuming fried soft-shell crabs blew up in the eastern coastal cities during the 1880s—becoming with lobster one of the must-have seafood items of the Gilded Age. Hicks's Restaurant in Savannah made it the great spring draw through the 1890s. Augusta's fine-dining resort of the 1890s, The Delmonico (the name an homage to the temple of Gilded Age dining, Delmonico's Restaurant in Manhattan), featured it on its September 1890 menu along with pompano, lobsters, oysters (three types), Spanish mackerel, Langley bream, and fresh water trout. The Delmonico was not supplied by soft-shell crab from Brunswick or Savannah. No harvesting operations existed there for these sumptuous creatures. Instead they were shipped from New York, Baltimore, or Charleston where the African American fishmonger Charles C. Leslie maintained a soft-shell impoundment at Mount Pleasant. The Chesapeake Bay however landed and shipped the most soft-shell crabs from the 1890s to the 1990s.

Throughout the twentieth century there were two classic ways of preparing them: broiling and skillet frying. In the 1990s the Miki Restaurant in Atlanta introduced soft-shell tempura to Georgians and they embraced it avidly, securing an enduring place in eaters' hearts alongside the broiled and fried soft-shell crabs.

Broiled Soft-Shell Crabs

Savannah Morning News (June 12, 1904)

No method of cooking the crabs is more delicate. Choose large, fine crabs, dip in melted butter and season lightly with salt and pepper. Arrange on a gridiron and broil until they take a delicate brown color, turning from side to side very few minutes. Arrange on rounds of toast and pour over them hot melted butter, flavored with a little lemon juice and chopped parsley.

Fried Crabs, Maryland Style

Savannah Morning News
(June 12, 1904)

To be at their best, fried crabs must be simply cooked. Any thick coating of butter or flour serves only to spoil the delicate flavor. The East[ern] Shore Marylander, who knows crabs at their finest, chooses large ones that are absolutely soft, a condition which lasts only a few hours. Then he fries them carefully, seasons lightly with salt and pepper, fries in liquefied butter to a rich brown, and serves them on a hot platter garnished with parsley and quarters of lemon.

CRAB SALAD

The earliest forms of crab salad recorded in Georgia were simple: a lump of fresh crabmeat served on lettuce leaves and drizzled with vinaigrette dressing. This form appears in the "From Mary's Cook Book" column in the *Atlanta Journal* in September of 1909. The familiar form in which crab is accompanied by diced celery and hard-boiled eggs and dressed with mayonnaise became popular as a home preparation between the two world wars. Georgia's greatest newspaper cooking oracle, Mrs. H. S. Dull, supplied the measurements in 1935: two cups of crab meat, one cup of diced celery, four diced hard-boiled eggs, and one half cup of mayonnaise. By 1935 Duke's Mayonnaise, the sugarless southern favorite, had become widely available in Georgia. Dull observed that frequent amendments to the basic salad include tarragon vinegar, pimento, and capers.

Since the first importation of curry powders into Savannah at the end of the eighteenth century, British mixtures of fenugreek, cardamom, pepper, and turmeric have been used to gussy up flavors in chicken dishes (Country Captain, featured in this book) and steamed shrimp (curried shrimp). It became an element of crab salad in the 1970s. Both a hot curry crab salad, on the model of curried shrimp, and a cold salad became popular. The cold salad simply added a teaspoon of curry powder to the mayonnaise in a standard crab salad.

Crowder Peas

Field peas (*Vigna unguiculata*), those earthy-flavored, long-podded peas whose dried stalks and seeds so delighted cattle that they were called "cowpeas," rivaled beans on the Georgia's plates as the favored legume. Field peas came from Africa, one of the foods transported across the Atlantic, on ships freighted with enslaved African people. Beans were grown in the Western Hemisphere, having been domesticated by Native Americans. Many different varieties of field peas came over from Africa: the delicate white lady peas (favorite varieties include the white acre, ladyfinger, rice pea, Texas cream, and conch peas); the black-eyed pea; the speckled whippoorwill peas loved by Virginians; the deep chalky-flavored iron, class, red ripper, and Indian peas; the black pea; and Georgia's favorite peas, the sea island red pea and the brown sugar crowder pea. (Sea island red peas are featured in a separate entry.)

What is a crowder pea? It is a pea whose seeds grow so thickly within the pod that they mash against each other, and so have flat ends. The peas look a little boxy when shelled. There are other peas you can get of course—the pink-eyed purple hull from the gulf coast, the Knuckle hull pea, even the mottled hog brain pea.

Fresh peas taste livelier than dried, so summer is the season to prep them. Field peas are easily grown and are a fixture on many farms, as a rotation or co-crop because the roots fix nitrogen in the soil, countering the extraction of the chemical by field crops such as cotton or corn. Produce stands often sell fresh peas, either in the pod (you grab how many you want to take home and shell), or already shelled in plastic bags. Only very delicate fields peas, such as the rice pea, can have the immature pods harvested as green beans. Most other varieties are cultivated only for their hulled seeds. Stripping seeds from the pods was a common home task for farm children. Because the fresh peas undergo fermentation almost immediately, shelled peas should be used or frozen within twenty-four hours after processing. Elsewise they will sour and become inedible.

How do you know when you are confronting an authentic crowder pea pod? Here

Nowadays the colorful pinkeye purple hull pea has eclipsed the brown sugar crowder as most popular crowder field pea. Crowders have seeds with flattened ends from being crowded by their fellow seeds in the pods. Photograph © David S. Shields.

is a brief visual description extracted from the *Augusta Chronicle* in 1859: "It is found in a curved bumpy pod.... The outside of this pod is a little rough, resembling green velvet, and the inside is lined with white vegetable satin. In this sumptuous bed of the interior repose a half dozen or so of the blessed globules."

The brown sugar crowder was grown in the Midlands and the Upcountry. Indeed the sugar crowder was deemed a poor soil crop that would only set a profusion of pea pods if the soil was not greatly fertile. Good sandy loam would set plants producing foliage instead of pods. If one prefers eating a "mess" of field peas as a side dish, the horticulturists at the Georgia Agricultural Experimental Station who tested the varieties had decided opinions about culinary quality. Hugh N. Starnes of the Griffin Station observed: "The best table peas are Sugar Crowder, White Crowder, Mush, Large Lady Pea, Small Lady and Rice."

So, what, exactly, was a sugar crowder? "Brown (Sugar) Crowder," Starnes continued, "is a widely used, all-purpose variety. The plant is dark green, thick-stemmed and branches. The pods are round, plump, medium green and are filled with brownish peas crowded tightly together. The seeds are smooth, buff brown with darker brown eyes. It produces green peas in 80 to 85 days" (1951). When shelled and eaten fresh the peas are green; only when allowed to dry in the pod on the vines do they turn buff brown. These dried peas are kept in mason jars in dry storage and reconstituted by soaking and boiling months later. Field peas were year-round eats.

PEA LIKKER

Much attention has been paid to the old southern pot likker, that cooked down collection of greens and hog flesh that stands at the heart of African American traditional food. Not much attention has been paid to its cousin, pea likker. Macon mayor Smith Bridges proposed an elaborate Georgia Products Feasts in 1913. The soup course alone was impressive: "Vegetable, mixed; potlicker, pealicker; diamond-backed Savannah Terrapin, Brunswick stew, and Catfish chowder." Macon, Georgia, loved pea likker so much that it had a hotel in the 1880s whose unofficial name was the pea likker hotel. The folks there knew how to make it too: First of all they had no confusion about what was meant by peas: cow peas. In Macon the brown crowder was preferred. On the coast the sea island red—and the black-eyed pea was popular everywhere, provided one had a strain of eyed pea that didn't taste too chalky. What pea likker wasn't was the juice from canned garden peas, an item that began appearing in recipes in the 1910s as "pea liquor." Abomination.

Recipes varied for pea likker, depending on locale, availability of ingredients, and the cook's creativity. But most followed the five flavors template found in nineteenth-century Gullah Geechee cooking: fat (hog trotter, maw, or side meat; or sardine grease), sweet (onion or teaspoon of sugar), salt, sour (horsemint or citrus leaf), heat (cayenne, bird pepper). Water was the medium in which it was cooked. There is no Georgia mull tradition of cooking it in milk that we've located. How thin or thick one cooked it depended on the cook's sense of how much nutrition was needed; some cooked the peas until they broke apart; some strained the liquid off after simmering and ate the peas separately, serving the liquor in a mug.

Hugh Gibson, in an interesting article on St. Helena Island Gullah cures published in 1962 in the Charleston *News and Courier*, wrote that pea liquor made with sardine fat was administered to children with mumps and adults with smallpox to diminish the effects of the disease. But by the 1870s it was something more than invalid food for the saltwater Geechee. It had become a general "country dish" enjoyed for its unpretentious wholesomeness by every sort of inhabitant of the region.

Deviled Eggs

Devilment. In some small towns there is only one question: Who makes the best damned deviled eggs in the city limits? By some odd communal alchemy, a shift occurred with the turn of the millennium. Cakes no longer stood at the apex of preparations by which one judged the boss cook in the local pecking order. They had been supplanted by deviled eggs. Every cook worth the name had a "family recipe." What they actually had was a tweak—bacon crumbles, chives, shallot, special mustard, sherry vinegar, caviar—designed to elevate one's plate above those on the buffet table at the Wednesday night church manna feast or at the neighborhood holiday party.

There are several schools of thought about the "finish" of the eggs. There are those who believe a liberal shake of paprika, dusting the yolky filling with a scatter of pungent particles is classic. Others eschew the red pepper and trust to their skills at piping, or their management of the color of the filling—tints that range from French's mustard yellow to orangey Aztec gold.

The perpetual contest for supremacy does at times bring out the worst instinct in cooks and so a company is served deviled ostrich eggs—"bigger is way, way better"—or the sadistic Carolina Reaper-tinged deviled eggs. There are over-creative eggs: the ones with avocado, lobster, chicken liver, or sriracha added (See "Why Don't You Bring the Deviled Eggs" in the June 6, 1973, *Atlanta Journal* for a roadmap to deviled egg excess and damnation.) Today you will encounter deviled duck eggs, pheasant eggs, and supersized Leghorn hen eggs. You'll find the yolky filling supplemented by salmon roe "caviar," by miniature edible flowers, and dried miniature Asian shrimp.

Culinary historians agree that the ancestor of our current deviled eggs sprung up in Spain during the 1200s. The mashing of the yolks of hard-boiled eggs and mixing them with soft butter, spices, and seasonings, then filling into the cavity of the halved boiled eggs with the mixture has occurred for nearly eight hundred years. The American craze for deviled eggs dates from the 1870s when recipe writers concurred that mustard, butter, and pepper of some sort had to be admixed into the mashed yolks. Touching that mixture up with a dash of vinegar was the early point of controversy. For 150 years deviled eggs has been the staple recipe in newspaper food sections—the formula most likely to be printed during the course of a year. Here is classic formula from the *Savannah Morning News* in 1886.

Deviled Eggs

Savannah Morning News
(July 26, 1886)

Boil six eggs hard and throw them into cold water. Divide into halves, cut crosswise, take out the yolks and rub to a paste with a generous teaspoon of butter. Season with pepper, salt, and a suspicion of mustard. Mold into balls the size and shape of the abstracted yolks, put back into the hollowed whites, fit the halves neatly together and roll each egg up in tissue paper, as you would a bon-bon, twisting the paper at the ends.

While the creation of bon-bon deviled eggs is charming, it made the wrapper not the filling the star of the presentation. In the twentieth century creating the most alluring yolk center became the aim of cooks concerned with eye appeal. Whether by intensifying the color or using pastry tube nozzles to fancy up the texture, the fillings became the star of the buffet or picnic platter.

Because the deviled egg became so popular, it became a matter of contest. So some of Georgia's greatest urban food legends tell of the struggle to become the foremost master of devilment. There is one from the late 1920s, during the height of Prohibition, about a scuffle in the big Methodist church in a GA town. (Mulberry Street in Macon?) The supremacy of the boss cook—an "old bachelor" from an "old family"—was being challenged by an ambitious young beauty from Atlanta who had married into the church. The beauty learned through her housekeeper that Mr. Q had a cellar of Madeira. She bribed Mr. Q's housekeeper to photograph the extensive collection of bottles. Then she secured a bottle of Madeira herself to use as a new flavoring for

Deviled eggs prepared by Kevin Mitchell. Photograph © Rhonda Mitchell.

her superlative deviled eggs. At the fellowship dinner Mr. Q sampled one of his rival's eggs, instantly knew the secret of the much-praised new flavor, and announced that his rival had used contraband alcohol to achieve it. Mrs. A smiled and replied that she wondered how Mr. Q could be so familiar with the flavor of Madeira. Could it be that he is a devotee of the bottle—at which point she produced the photograph of the cellar where Q's coat of arms is conspicuously displayed stenciled on a cask near the banks of bottles. Parishioners had to intervene to prevent physical mayhem.

Deviled eggs can be served hot or cold. What is most important is that the whites of the eggs are not overcooked or tattered. The time-honored method for hard boiling eggs for deviled eggs is to puncture the shell of the fat end of the egg with a needle, cover the eggs with cold water and bring the pan to a rapid boil. Once boiling, turn off the heat and set the pan off the burner, letting the covered pan sit in the hot water for 15 minutes. Then plunge the eggs into cold water. The inner sheath of the egg should not adhere to the white albumin and the shells peel easily away. The eggs should be refrigerated immediately.

If one were to look for an admirable recent improvement of the deviled egg, it would have to be the use of mayonnaise and butter in equal proportions in making the yolk paste. While some home cooks had done this since the 1920s, it did not become general practice until Julia Child recommended it in her 2000 book, *Julia's Kitchen Wisdom*. The result is a more flavorful and creamy filling.

There was one regrettable moment in the history of deviled eggs in Georgia. In that era of questionable taste in so many areas, the early 1970s (men's fashion, interior décor, car design), the Georgia Egg Commission decided to promote deviled eggs casserole. Yes, it was as bad as it sounds—a can of cream of mushroom soup, stewed celery swimming there among the deviled eggs in a baking dish, potato chips as a topping. Why adulterate something so simple and splendid as a classic deviled egg? Fortunately, that moment passed.

Doves

Many a young hunter has gone into the field yearning to kill the first deer and been disappointed, but a sixteen-year-old with a shotgun, hunting license, migratory bird stamp, and good eyes can almost be insured of the satisfaction on that first day in a dove field at the beginning of September. With three shells loaded, one usually finds the mark, and the unforgettable sight of a mourning dove tumbling off trajectory onto the ground. Perhaps the family has an experienced retriever, an eager Boykin, a sturdy golden, a springer, or a Brittany. It tears off into the stubble at the margin of a cornfield and with unerring precision, clamps the bird and trots back. An older voice will call out, "That's your bird, Corey." Is it little wonder that dove hunting has become the most popular field sport in the American South.

Though the mournful call of the dove sounds above many Georgia farmsteads over the warm months, it does not reside here year-round. It migrates, and as a migratory bird, it cannot be hunted over a baited field—that is a field strewn with cracked corn, rice, millet, or other grains. Such fields attract attention from doves on the wing. Their memory is such that they will return to grain laden fields they've seen for ten days, so regulations prohibit hunting over fields that had been baited yet cleared for ten days. A per-person bag limit of fifteen is now in effect. Some of the doves have been banded for population monitoring, and conservation-minded hunters have long logged into the US Fish and Wildlife Service website to report.

A newly harvested agricultural field (corn or millet in early September; peanuts in October) does not count under the law as a baited range, so it stands as the most desirable location for a dove shoot. Getting access can be a challenge to city dwellers—but kinship networks, school and business friendships can result in invitations. If you have money, there are always catered hunts where one can be assured of good hunting in picturesque surroundings. If one lives in the country, a dove hunt serves one of the great rites of sociability where a neighborhood reknits its connections. Tales of great shots, great retrieves, and great dove pies blossom in the wake of a great hunt. There is also a dark lore of dove hunting concerning illegal hunts on restricted land regardless of bag limits and posted no trespassing signs. Fortunately, there is no great market for dove meat at the crossroads gas stations.

Doves can be dressed easily; many do so in the field. Game laws usually require a fully-fledged wing attached to any meat taken from the field. Breasting the dove requires you to pinch away the skin and feathers from the breast, exposing the length of the keel bone. Wearing sanitary gloves, you insert your thumb under the keel bone, pulling up while using the other hand to pull down on the legs. This will extricate the breast meat in one large lump. The entrails will fall away with the legs. With a knife or kitchen scissors, cut off one wing, leaving the other attached until getting home. As a rule, smart hunters examine the entrails of the bird for telltale spots on the liver indicating fungal issues with the food sources. A capable hunter always disposes of the remains of the birds neatly.

My (David's) favorite dove pie recipe appeared in Christ Church Savannah's *From Savannah Kitchens*, the contribution of W. W. Sprague. This spiral bound volume bears no date, but was published in 1962. An interesting regional cookbook, it contains numbers of recipes of more than usual interest: Charleston Rice Wine, Chatham Artillery Punch, White Turtle Stew, Sweet Potato Puffs, Broilers Basted with Orange Wine, and of course Dove Pie (with Madeira!).

Dove Pie

W. W. Sprague,
From Savannah Kitchens (1962)

Line a 2 quart casserole with short pie crust. Use 6 to 8 doves for 4 people. Sear the birds over high heat until brown, in 2/4 block butter in large iron skillet. Salt and pepper them. Remove birds to casserole. In the same skillet put 2 cloves garlic and 1 medium sized onion, both finely chopped. Cook a few minutes. Add 1 bay leaf and 1 can chicken broth to sauce and heat. Add one 4 oz. can mushrooms and 2/4 cup good Madeira wine. Stir, and pour this sauce over doves in casserole. Cover with pie crust. Bake in 350-degree oven for 45 minutes or until the crust is brown. Serve with a glass of good Burgundy wine at room temperature.

Another classic preparation that is simpler and part of the repertoire of most capable camp cooks is smothered dove. It requires your dove breasts, a stick or so of butter, salt, water, flour, and Worcestershire sauce. The breasts are first browned in the butter in your skillet. Then you fill the skillet with water until you cover the breasts, simmer, remove the birds, and make a gravy with the remaining liquid. Put birds back in and simmer until meat falls from the bone. Besides Worcestershire as a flavoring, some add lemon juice, some red pepper, and some vinegar. The cooking works better if your skillet is covered during simmering.

Duck

In the romantic history of Georgia food, the roast duck in the Dutch oven was gunned down in the half-light of early morning with a twelve-gauge shotgun from a blind of switch cane and cattails. Whether a wood duck, a redhead, a black duck or a teal, even a scaup or a widgeon, they would be retrieved by your water dog and would be processed quickly—gutted, the feathers pulled off, the head and feat chopped away. The hunter or the cook made an effort to extract the shot. Then the carcass would be hung to age for a few days in a cool if not cold place. Georgian camp cooks and home cooks knew what to roast the duck with—turnips if you liked French style—sweet potatoes if you had a sweet tooth—oranges if you wished to do in Cumberland Island style. If you were

Duck with turnips is a classic autumn dish. Usually prepared in a Dutch oven, it is a preparation with French antecedents. The duck fat caramelizes the roasted turnips. Photograph © David S. Shields.

cooking camp style, turning it on a spit before an open fire, then stuffing the bird with Vidalia Onion and Sage stuffing proved simple and satisfying.

Most of the ducks that migrate into the state and challenge Georgia hunters originate in the extraordinary part of the upper Midwest and Canada known as the Prairie Pothole Region—North and South Dakota, Iowa, Minnesota, Montana, Manitoba, Alberta, British Columbia, and Saskatchewan. The surviving grasslands there are the great nursery for Georgia's ducks, so the Ducks Unlimited chapters in the state contribute large percentages of their proceeds to preserving the ecosystem there.

Truth be told, farmers became smitten with raising ducks in the first decades of the twentieth century, both for eggs and meat. In 1900 a farmer made the following observation and posed a question in a Savannah newspaper: "The best esteemed of all flesh foods is duck, and yet there are 100 chickens marketed to one duck. . . . Why not grow more of them?" Intelligent farmers took the hint. The majority of duck consumed in the state for the past century has been domestic farm ducks—mallards, American Pekins, Muscovys, and Cayuga. Hotel demand for ducks had exploded in the 1890s. Hence every hotel dining room with any ambition for much of the twentieth century featured duck seasonally and frequently. Those farmers who adopted ducks in their fowl yards tended to be rewarded, particularly when they realized that they were nearly fully matured by the time they were three months old. Most duck operations disposed of most of the drakes when they reached this age. Females that did not lay energetically joined them.

In the mid-twentieth century Mrs. Darwood Holm of Atlanta became the hostess cook who provided model recipes for preparing both wild and domestic ducks. In the classic 1963 *Gems from Georgia Kitchens* cookbook, besides supplying a generic recipe for roast duck, she provided special instructions for wild canvasback and domestic mallard.

Mallard or French Duck

Mrs. Darwood Holm,
Gems from Georgia Kitchens (1963)

Clean duck without scalding. Wipe, then rub with salt and pepper. Place a lump of butter inside duck; truss and put into pan at 450 degrees for 20 minutes. Use its own gravy to pour over duck when placed on platter before serving. Or try 3 tablespoons currant or plum jelly mixed in gravy before pouring over duck. Garnish with parsley.

By gravy Mrs. Holm meant the pan juices and melted duck fat pooled in the roasting pan. This should put us in mind of the extraordinary flavor and utility of duck fat. If you wanted to boost the flavor of pastry, you could substitute duck fat for lard or Crisco. It made particularly memorably puff pastry if you could keep the fat cold enough. It also served as a preservative. Anything suspended in duck fat would keep until the fat turned rancid, something that would not take place in a refrigerator. Finally, peanuts roasted in duck fat supply rich umami to a humble snack.

Mrs. Holm's inclusion of a canvasback duck recipe was a nod to culinary history. In the nineteenth century the rare roasted breast of the canvasback stood foremost in the hearts of epicures and clubmen. They were hunted to scarcity, and by 1900 many a menu boasting canvasback duck actually served a redhead or wood duck in its place. The distinctive flavor of the canvasback, derived from its diet of water celery, became less and less known. Now that the habitat for water celery in eastern rivers and bays has been degraded, the canvasback duck of today is not the fabled canvasback of yore, the most distinctive tasting duck to have every come to the table.

Still, there are plenty of wild ducks and several domestic ducks worth the effort to prepare. One of the greatest dishes is hunters duck stew with lots of root vegetables. My favorite version of this Georgia classic is contained in the mysterious *The Unrivaled Cook-Book*, one of the greatest southern cookbooks of the last half of the nineteenth century, by Mrs. Washington (a pseudonym) in 1886.

Wild Ducks (Stewed)

The Unrivaled Cook-Book (1886)

Clean, draw, wash, wipe; put in a raw carrot or onion and boil ten minutes. Then lay in very cold water half an hour; they cut up pepper, salt, flour them, and fry to a light brown; put them in a saucepan and cover with a gravy made of the giblets, necks, and some bits of lean veal; add a minced shallot, a bunch of sweet herbs, salt, and pepper; cover closely and stew until tender; take out the duck, skim and strain the gravy, return to the fire, and put in a cup of rich cream in which an egg has been beaten, thicken with browned flour, add a tablespoonful of wine and the juice of half a lemon, beaten in gradually, boil up, and pour over the ducks.

Certain ducks are better suited particularly for grilling rather than baking, roasting, or stewing. The teal, for instance, performs best when split, seasoned, and set on a hot grill over coals. The smell of melting duck fat flaring on the coals is one of the great patio smells of the South.

Figs

Draw a line from Augusta to Macon and Macon to Columbus. To the east and south of that line, you can plant any fig variety available in American nurseries and see it thrive. Indeed, half of Georgia is a paradise for figs. Since the colonial period, in city yards and farmsteads certain long-cherished varieties—the brown turkey, the little sugar fig (celestial), the white Adriatic fig (or Smyrna fig), and the lemon fig—have flourished, sometimes growing into vast rangy trees. To the west and north of that line you have to choose your fig variety with some care, for many varieties die back when exposed to a hard freeze. The hardy Chicago fig is perhaps the only widely available variety that can endure the temperature extremes of the state's northernmost counties.

What we call the fruit of the fig is an involuted cluster of flower heads. Because fig trees are native to an area in the Middle East extending from Iraq to Afghanistan and were pollinated by wasps that flourished there, but cannot survive in the American South, most varieties of fig do not produce seeds. The "fruit" goes unpollinated and the tree must be propagated by rooting cuttings. But that is easily done, and in parts of the state the fig is the most popular fruit tree grown. In some regions the trees grow so vigorously the grower has to decide whether to prune and shape the fig to a size compact enough to enable easy harvest of the fruit.

While a portion of the yearly fig crop appears at the produce stand, much is grown for home or local use. Fig lovers tend to grow several varieties, knowing that certain types ripen early, others late in the season; and that certain are best suited to certain kinds of preparation or consumption: the brown turkey and sugar fig were fine for fresh eating and preserving, the white for drying, and the Kadota for preserving, not fresh eating.

A century ago an Augusta orchardist described the sequence of ripening:

> *End of June:* "The Brown Turkey fig gives us its first ripe fruit. The little figs have been forming since the last cool mornings of April left us, and stealthily they have grown until they have reached the size of a small egg. Then suddenly without any warning they swell up, turn

Late-season lemon figs ripening on the tree, a common sight in all but the northernmost counties in Georgia. Photograph © David S. Shields.

brown and then begin to take on a withered appearance. When it looks like it could not stay on the bush another minute without falling to the ground and bursting with its sweetness, pull it off, it's ripe."

Early July: "The White fig comes a little earlier than the sugar fig, but not quite so soon as the brown Turkey, and is a profuse bearer of a fairly good fig for eating, but rather soft and watery, and with an abundance of seeds. It is not a good preserving fig, because when boiled in syrup becomes mushy." But when dried it is the variety that most closely resembles the classic dried Smyrna fig.

Middle July: "The Celestial—or as we call it down here—the little sugar fig, is just mouthful of toothsome daintiness. It bears a heavy crop, comes a little later than the brown Turkey and is fine for table use. Unlike the former fig, which begins to ripen its second crop in the early days of August, and gives you a continuous feast until frost, the sugar fig bears a big first crop, and a big second crop, but both are over in a few days."

August: "The favorite of the ladies for preserving, is the Lemon Fig. This fig is the latest of the varieties ripening with us, and its last crop, while fairly larges, is made up of fine large figs. It makes its name both from its color which is light lemon yellow, and its shape—which is different from the others of the fig family. It represents a rude semblance to the lemon. This is a fine large fig, and is very firm even when ripe; and it retains this firmness after cooking to a most remarkable degree. When preserved, it is almost transparent, and is a beautiful and tempting dainty." (1910)

From 1910 to 1915 extensive plantings of figs took place in Georgia anticipating the emergence of a national market for fresh figs. That market never quite took off. But fresh figs became a seasonal item on southern produce stalls. Invariably the harvest outstripped the demand, leaving an overage every August. Hence the enormous popularity of the favorite home fig preparation, fig preserves. Here is Mrs. Dull's instruction from 1924.

Fig Preserves

Mrs. S. R. Dull, *Atlanta Journal*
(September 7, 1924)

5 pounds figs.
2 pounds sugar.

Put just enough water to sugar to wet. Put on fire and melt; boil until rather thick syrup. Put in half the figs. Boil slowly until pink, and the syrup is thick; stir to prevent sticking. When figs look pink and clear, lift out on a platter and place in sun or air. Put in the other half and cook the same way. When the second lot of figs is done, and the syrup thick, pack in jar, fill with the boiling syrup and seal. Place the first lot cooked back into the boiling syrup, which is left, and bring to boil long enough to heat through. Fill jars and cover with syrup and seal. If lemon or ginger is liked, cook with the fruit. Add one lemon or more cut into thin strips. For the ginger, four or five pieces an inch long.

The nod in this recipe toward the combination of fig and citrus points to another favorite Georgia fig preparation. This recipe from Augusta dates from 1911.

Fig Marmalade

Augusta Chronicle (December 29, 1911)

Two pounds of figs, two oranges, two lemons. Use juice of oranges and lemons and shred only the orange peel. Boil figs, juice, and rind for one half an hour: then add one pound of sugar to two pounds of figs. Boil another half hour and cover while hot.

By "cover while hot," the author means can while ingredients are still boiling in sterile lidded glass jars.

In the 1920s the Vienna Bakery in Brunswick introduced Georgians to fig cake, creating a popularity that prompted home bakers to take it up. Instead of using the fresh figs in the original, bakers began opening up their jars of preserved figs and chopping them up to create the confection.

Fig Preserve Cake

Atlanta Journal and Atlanta Constitution (November 27, 1976)

2 cups flour
1 teaspoon salt
1 teaspoon nutmeg
1 ½ cups sugar
1 cup vegetable oil
1 cup chopped fig preserves
1 tablespoon vanilla
1 teaspoon cinnamon
3 eggs
1 teaspoon [baking] soda
1 cup buttermilk
½ cup chopped nuts

Sift flour, salt, soda, and sugar together. Add oil, beat well. Add eggs, beat well. Add milk, beat well. Add figs, nuts and spices and beat well. Pour into tube pan and bake 1 hour and 15 minutes at 325 degrees F.

This was served with a buttermilk sauce combined with sugar, thickened with cornstarch, and flavored with vanilla.

Fried Bologna

In Georgia, as in most of the South, pork matters more than beef or lamb. So was it any wonder that the most pork intensive of all old-world sausages, the Mortadella di Bologna, inspired immediate and deep devotion when it was first imported in the 1820s? Bologna was sold in two forms: a fat cylinder or a loop of sausage. In 1827 bologna was advertised as the headline attraction of the store at 159 Broad Street in Augusta. That same year merchants Bradley, Claghorn, and Wood of Savannah announced a bushel of bologna for sale. It would never fall out of favor thereafter. Town butchers such as J. J. Joyce of Savannah and Thomas Keany of Brunswick began adding Georgia-made bologna to their line of offerings. In the early twentieth century Swift and Company of Atlanta and W. W. Rawlins Sausage Company of Albany began producing quantities on a commercial scale.

The glory of the hog is the fat—that's where the flavor dwells. But Americans have listened to so much propaganda about fat being the cause of all evil regarding weight, obesity (the true culprit is sugar), and health that other beloved European products such as cured lardo have failed to find an American following. But there is a place where that splendid pork fat can go and receive a hearty welcome: bologna. Indeed, in the classic Mortadella di Bologna small white chunks of pure cured pork fat sit intermingled with the fine-grained amalgam of mashed pork meat. (Mortadella was named after the mortar in which pork was mashed in Italy in the fourteenth century.) In effect any time we have a bologna sandwich, we taste morsels of lardo.

Yet the flavor of pork fat amplifies when fried or roasted. (Think of bacon.) Inevitably some cook somewhere decided to slap a round slice of bologna on the griddle. How bologna was fried had no set formula. *The Wayne County News* on December 7, 1904, suggests that slices be "dipped first in cracker crumbs. All of the slices are to be cooked in 'deep fat,' and then lifted out. Next put them in a shallow frying pan and scrumbled up beaten eggs with them." This is the first glimpse of a classic Georgia breakfast dish, bologna scramble. An evolved version of this recipe was offered in the August 22, 1930, issue of the *Atlanta Journal*.

Bologna Scramble

Atlanta Journal (1930)

¼ pound bologna, chopped
6 eggs
1 tablespoon mustard
2 tablespoons milk

Beat eggs lightly with milk and mustard, add bologna and scramble.

But as the twentieth century wore on, the open-faced bologna sandwich outpaced the scramble in popularity. Because bologna's edges tend to curl when subjected to heat, the experienced bologna fryer cuts slits around the perimeter, enabling the fried bo-

While some prepare this classic dish with presliced lunchmeat bologna, serious devotees of fried bologna buy a whole chub and thick slice it. A recent wrinkle in its preparation has cooks using air fryers to cook it rather than frying it in oil or fat in a skillet. Photograph © David S. Shields.

logna to lie flat—something desirable when it is nested on some toasted rye bread and a smear of Duke's Mayonnaise.

One cultural development of the last half of the twentieth century was the prominence of fried bologna on menus of food served to prison inmates in Georgia. This and "baloney's" decidedly down-market associations caused it to fall out of favor with the increasing numbers of suburban Georgians interested in food. The year 2000 can be identified as the year of its greatest disfavor. In 2003, Glynn Moore questioned in the *Augusta Chronicle*, "What ever happened to bologna? It was popular when I was a boy, particularly in the form of fried bologna sandwiches. Nowadays bologna is scarcely mentioned in polite company." But that exile from favor would end shortly thereafter, for circa 2010 the chefs of the lardcore movement, intent on reviving southern food in all its humble glory, rehabilitated bologna as part of their renovation of southern tradition. Places such as Five and Ten in Athens became celebrants of that fatty splendor of pork and the Georgia bologna tradition. And in a host of country meat markets (We think of Pinetucky Country Meats in Swainsboro.), the display cases of the butcher counters foreground chubs of bologna. "Thick cut, or thin?"

Inattentive cooks sometimes fry bologna at too high a heat, causing the surface to char and blister. If sliced too thin, the heated slice will warp its edges. Photograph © David S. Shields.

FRIED BOLOGNA

Fried Pie

The fried pie is old southern cooking. Its daddy was the Cornish pasty and its momma was the apple fritter. German-Americans and Franco-Americans believed it was a turnover that accidently fell in the skillet rather than baking in an oven. It had the handy size of its parents. Like all of its relations that went through baptism in boiling lard, the fried pie had a rough reputation and a cheap price. A South Carolinian in 1852 observed in the pages of the *Edgefield Advertiser*, "The cheapest diet in the world, we think, is a fried pie. We tried fourpence worth the other day, and for forty hours we were so crammed that our eyes stuck like a lobster." The general fear that fried foods led to dyspepsia and that dyspepsia led to insanity and physical ruin caused many to fear fried pie. Its critics alerted readers to a host of ill effects. A week after the Carolinian offered his comments above, a Philadelphian offered a recipe "to make a nightmare:" "Just before going to bed, eat two pig's feet and a fried pie. In less than an hour you will see a snake larger than a hawser, devouring eight blue-haired children, who have just escaped from a monster with sorrel eyes and a red-hot overcoat." Philadelphia was the northernmost outpost of southern cooking, and the city claims rather arrogantly to have created the fried hand pie. But Georgia, Tennessee, South Carolina, Virginia, and Kentucky can document early instances (as early as the 1780s in some case) of sweet fried hand pies.

While savory fried pies existed, particularly hand pies of chicken and peas, the apple fried pie became the most commonly consumed. It differed from an apple fritter—a preparation in which chunks of raw or partially cooked apple are mingled with batter and spoonfuls fried in bubbling fat—by having a prepared crust crimped around an apple sauce or cooked apple filling and then deep fried. In Georgia peaches rivaled apples as the fruit filling of choice. The great question in fried pie preparation was the optimum dough for frying. Those who cherished simplicity and convenience opted for biscuit dough. But one could do better and tastier. Caroline Coe's recipe for a Christmas fried pie published in the *Augusta Chronicle* during the holiday season in 1913 provides a detailed formula for making an ideal fry crust.

Fried Pie Crust

Caroline Coe, *Augusta Chronicle*
(November 30, 1913)

In one cupful of scalded milk melt two tablespoonfuls of butter and add a quarter of a cup of sugar and a little salt. When cool add half a yeast cake and soften in two teaspoonfuls of water. Stir in a pint of flour and let rise until it is all foamy. After this has risen beat in one egg and beat all very thoroughly. Now add one scant cupful of sugar and a half teaspoonful, each, of nutmeg and cinnamon. Add enough flour to kneed and let rise again. Now roll out the mixture and add a little flour until it is as thin as possible without danger of breaking. (For if a hole comes in the crust the fried pies will be ruined.) Cut this round about the size of a tea saucer and put in the center a large tablespoon of spiced apple sauce. Fold over the edges and pinch together and fry in deep fat as you do fried cakes.

Coe's was a sweet crust. Biscuit dough was not. Preparation required either the filling or the exterior to provide the pie's excitement. A common way of dressing the pies fresh from the fry skillet was to shake sugar and cinnamon over the surface. This supplied a confectionery finish to the dish.

Locally made fried pies are the pinnacle of southern cuisine. Peach and apple pies have been made throughout the South—with famous creators such as Hubig's in New Orleans and Barnett's Tender Fry of Charlotte, North Carolina. Barnett's even tried its hand at a Georgia signature, the sweet potato fried pie, which can be found in west Georgia at Carrollton. The Mulberry Baptist Church in Hoschton was rebuilt on proceeds from the sale of sweet potato and apple fried pies. The fried sweet potato pie calls for the filling—the sweet potatoes—to be baked soft, cooled, sweetened, and spiced. An egg is often mixed in, sometimes coconut. Chefs might add bourbon. Good sweet potatoes do not really need much additional sweetening if one chooses a good pie potato—the heirloom Porto Rico or the modern garnet. Cane syrup rather than white or brown sugar imparts an additional dimension of flavor.

The apple fried pie, not surprisingly, has had a strong following in Ellijay. At the annual Georgia Apple Festival, fried apple pies are a mainstay. Now it is rarer to see there the old-style pie made from dried apples. Yet the desire to keep the texture and flavor of the old style of apple preparation in the face of change and the demand for convenience can be seen in the practices of home cooks. A recipe from 2004 by Lucille Kirk from Pickens County shows the adaptations of the old to the new. Keeping the old-style apple preparation, Lucille rendered every other part of the recipe kitchen easy.

Lucile Kirk's Fried Pies

Lucile Kirk (September 23, 2004)

2 quarts died apples
1 ½ Cups sugar
2 tsp allspice
1 stick butter
Water to cover apple mixture
2 cans Texas Style Biscuits
Flour (for rolling out biscuits)
Shortening

The night before: combine dried apples, sugar, allspice, and butter in a saucepan. Cover with water. Cook on low heat until the water is cooked out. Be careful to watch during this process as the apples have a tendency to stick. Refrigerate the apple mixture overnight.

The next day: The fruit mixture should be very cold. Roll out the canned biscuits on a floured surface. Get them as big (thin) as possible. Add the cold fruit mixture to one half of the rolled out biscuit leaving room along the edge. Fold over. Using a fork crimp the edges to keep the apple mixture from escaping. Melt enough shortening (about ½ inch) to cover the bottom of an electric skillet set to 350–400 degrees. When the shortening reaches the 350–400-degree temperature, add your pies. Fry each side to a golden brown. Drain on paper towels and enjoy.

Most home cooks who prepare fried apple pies now use fresh Honeycrisp and Granny Smith. Fried pear pie is a fixture around Perry, Georgia, using the hard "sand pears" grown in backyards throughout the state.

Georgia has several local masters of the fried pie. Over the years the Jasper Farmer's Market hosted several of the greatest—Mary Anders Vinson, whose fried apple pie was a draw until her death in 2019, Irene Neal of Burnt Mountain and Antonia Guerra of Ellijay. The sale of homemade jams and fried pies at farmers markets and church fundraisers was illegal until 2006 when House Bill 1380 gave legal sanction to this practice, which had gone on under the table for decades. From 1968 to 1992 McDonald's offered a fried apple pie on their menu. Bowing to nutritionists who argued that baked apples were "better for you" than fried, it ceased to be offered in most restaurants in 1993.

The stigmatizing of fried foods to some extent preserves the ancient prejudices of the nineteenth century when fried pies were reckoned an invitation to delirium. The public does not fret at McDonald's fries or KFC's chicken. But when sugar and frying converge the "snake larger than a hawser" crawls into the imaginations of the monitors of American health and the directive "thou shalt not" issues from on high.

Green Tomatoes

Gardeners know that every growing season will be punctuated by a basket of green tomatoes—the October beefsteaks forestalled from ripening by a dip in temperatures. Throughout the season the plants produce a scatter of "ever-youngs"—tomatoes prevented from turning red by the too-abundant foliage of your tomato patch. Green tomatoes were inevitable. The question was the best way to make use of the unripe "berries." After tomatoes became nationally popular as a garden plant in the 1840s, Georgia's gardeners confronted the challenge of the green crop. The initial response was to pickle them. *The Augusta Daily Constitutionalist* in winter 1863 published the usual method of first-generation green tomato growers: cutting the tomato into transverse slices, salting them, and then heating them in seasoned vinegar until the green flesh begins turning translucent.

Green Tomato Pickle

Augusta Daily Constitutionalist
(February 1, 1863)

Cut one peck [¼ bushel] green tomatoes in very thin slices—sprinkle with salt, and let them remain a day or two.

12 onions
1 ounce black ground pepper,
1 ounce Allspice
¼ lb. white mustard seed,
3 pods green pepper

If wanted very sharp, add ½ tea-cup of ground mustard. Cover with vinegar, and let them simmer until the tomatoes look clear.

The tomatoes of the 1860s were not as broad, nor as uniform in shape, nor as classically red as tomatoes of the 1870s and 1880s when A. W. Livingston bred his line of classic tomatoes and the beefsteak class of tomato came into existence to service the sandwich trade. The green tomato slice pickle also became a favorite sandwich element, cherished particularly in ham sandwiches.

Marietta, shortly after the Civil War, noted the utility of green tomato vines in clearing out infestations of bedbugs: "Take green tomato vines, put them into a basin or tray, pound them to pieces as fine as possible, then stain the bedsteads, where they inhabit with the juice, fill the crevices with the pieces of vine: lay leaves under the ends of the slats." Though we have never known anyone in our lifetimes that resorted to this method of pest control, it comes to mind whenever we hear anyone puzzled with what to do with old tomato vines.

Perhaps the most important development in tomato cookery taking place during the years before and after the Civil War was the development of tomato catsup, discussed in detail in an earlier entry. Catsups had long existed in Georgia cookery before the tomato became the focus of a catsup preparation. When tomato catsup joined the ranks in the 1850s, it employed ripe tomatoes, cooked down, strained, and cooked again with vinegar, back and red pepper, and spices. In classic tomato catsup, there was no sugar. Green tomato catsup did not join the pantry until the 1880s. The usual preparation appeared in print in Emma Paddock Telford's 1904 newspaper primer, "Home Made Catsups and Chilis," supplying recipes for every traditional form of catsup made in the United States since its founding, including the definitive sugarless tomato formula.

Green Tomato Catsup

Emma Paddock Telford, *Augusta Chronicle* (September 18, 1904)

Chop fine seven pounds of green tomatoes, with four red peppers; add one quart of vinegar and cook an hour and a half. Then add one pound of brown sugar, two tablespoonfuls each of salt and mustard, one tablespoonful each of cinnamon and allspice and one teaspoonful of ground cloves. Cook three hours more, bottle and seal.

Note that the natural acidity of green tomato required sugar as a counterbalance. Was the absence of salt intentional?

At the turn of the twentieth century, Georgians began sampling a dish pioneered by gardeners of the upper Midwest, fried green tomatoes. No doubt you are saying to yourself, Midwest? But this is an iconic southern dish! A moment of reflection should lead to understanding. Where are there more green tomatoes than any place else? In those northern regions where the growing season is woefully short and substantial percentages of the tomatoes do not ripen. Necessity breeds invention. With a plentitude of hard green tomatoes on hand, they cast about for a palatable solution. The recipes that begin showing up in Midwestern newspapers in the latter 1870s called for thick slices, egg wash, and bread crumbs. It was a dish served at breakfast or lunch. When the first southern recipes appeared at the turn of the twentieth century, the slices were thinner (a quarter to a third of an inch) and the dish was served at dinner.

Fried Green Tomatoes

Atlanta Journal (October 4, 1903)

Wash six large tomatoes and cut into slices one-half inch long. Beat the yolk of one egg with a tablespoonful of cold water. Sprinkle over the tomatoes a little salt and pepper, dip each slice into the beaten egg and then into fine bread crumbs. Fry a nice brown on both sides in butter and serve on a hot dish with the following sauce: Cream together two tablespoonfuls of butter with one of flour, and when thoroughly blended brown in the frypan; add to this one cup of scalded milk, stirring constantly until it thicken; cook for three minutes, add one tablespoonful of salt and pour round the tomatoes which have been nicely arranged on a chop platter.

The one element that underwent the greatest alteration in the recipe once it had been installed in southern cookery was the breading. While bread crumbs may have been the first coating, it would be quickly superseded by seasoned flour and, later, seasoned cornmeal. A bareback thick-sliced fried green tomato also existed. A Charlestonian in 1899 observed that these unbreaded green tomatoes "are a new accompaniment to steak, and are said by those who have tried them to form a particularly happy combination."

Another Green Tomato specialty that became popular at the turn of the twentieth century was green tomato pies. Instead of the sugared slicer pies with their fans of flat cut disks of apples that became an Appalachian fixture, Georgia embraced a holiday mince pie in which diced apples and chopped green tomatoes intermingle with syrup amid two crusts. Mrs. C. G. M. offered her recipe to the readers of the *Atlanta Journal* in December of 1904, in time for it to be incorporated in that season's yuletide sideboard.

Green Tomato Mince Pie

Mrs. C. G. M, *Atlanta Journal* (1904)

For two pies take one pint of finely chopped green tomatoes, three large apples chopped fine, two cupfuls of brown sugar, three tablespoonfuls of flour, a saltspoonful of salt, a heaping teaspoonful of mixed spices ground and one-half cupful of sharp cider.

Mix in the order named and dot the surface with a tablespoonful of butter. Bake between two crusts. One-half cup of seeded raisins is a nice addition.

The 1992 movie *Fried Green Tomatoes*, while successfully implanting the idea of a fried green tomato in the national imagination, did little to convey its look, flavor, or behavior in the skillet. Indeed, the dish is not discussed in the movie's dialog or given visual shape beyond the notice that it was available at the Whistle Stop Café. Perhaps the mystery of what it was bears responsibility for the explosion of menus throughout the South offering the dish in the late 1990s.

The mystique of the green tomato was further enhanced by the appearance of the Central American tomatillo, a hard green mini-tomato, in produce sections of groceries, buoyed by the increasing popularity of Mexican cuisine. So green tomato catsup morphed into green tomato salsa.

Green Tomato and Peach Salad

KEVIN MITCHELL

This is a great summer salad. The acidic flavor of the green tomatoes goes well with the sweetness of the peaches. The addition of tarragon gives an anise flavor, making this a refreshing salad on a hot summer day paired with grilled chicken or fish.
Serves 8

- 1 pound English cucumbers, diced
- 1 pound green tomatoes, quartered
- ½ pound grape tomatoes, cut in half
- 2 large peaches, pits removed and sliced into wedges
- Zest (grated or microplaned) and juice of 1 orange
- 1 tablespoon benne seed oil (can substitute extra virgin olive oil)
- 2 tablespoons fresh tarragon, chopped
- Pinch of red pepper flakes
- Salt and pepper to taste
- Benne seeds for garnish, optional

Mix everything except the benne seeds in a bowl. Serve on a platter, sprinkled with benne seeds if using benne seed oil. For an extra kick, add more red pepper flakes if you wish.

Green tomato and peach salad by Kevin Mitchell. Photograph © Rhonda Mitchell.

Grits

How fortunes change! In 1995 an Athens newspaper columnist complained about the low regard that foodies had for grits. "Grits are the underdog. Modern, trendy cookbooks heap lavish praise on Italian polenta without a mention of grits, even though polenta is really just a posh, fashionable, distant, foreign cousin of grits." Now, twenty years later, grits rule! Every southern restaurant, whether high style or road food, has grits conspicuously on the menu, and one dish, shrimp and grits, featured as a "sure sell." Grits are now southern culinary royalty. Numbers of artisan mills offer stone-ground grits using flavorful heirloom corn with names such as Jimmy Red, Guinea Flint, Hickory King, Blue Clarage, Virginia Gourdseed, and Pencil Cob.

We can understand why grits had lost its reputation in the last half of the twentieth century. Most southerners were eating Quaker or Martha White Instant Grits. They ate them with sugar, or cheese, or gravy, or butter. Breakfast grits were fuel, not fine dining. The intrinsic flavor of the corn was not greatly apparent because the white dent corn being milled for the grits had been degermed (for shelf life). The modest intrinsic flavor was attested by the tendency of cooks to add flavor to the grits. There were a few generally available high-quality brands available—Adluh Stone-Ground White Grits foremost among them. But the convenience of "instant grits" marginalized them. Today the grits featured in restaurants are stone-ground whole-kernel heirloom strains. That said, the vast majority of grits being served today are not traditional hominy grits, but simply grits. Grits are dried corn kernels rough ground—the name grits scramble the spelling of the name for rough ground corn, grist. Hominy grits are lye-processed dried corn kernels ground into rough grist.

Hominy grits predominated on the Georgia table until after the Civil War. Early settlers followed the native preference for white flint corn for grits in eighteenth and nineteenth centuries using the round-kernelled sea island white flint corn. The Muskogee preferred green hickory wood ashes when making lye water for corn processing but would also use certain oak varieties. They left the ears to dry on the stalk, harvested them, then stripped off kernels into a bath of lye water. The kernels soaked until the skin could be slipped off.

Bathing kernels in a lye solution (nixtamalizing) alters their chemistry. The change enables niacin, a vitamin crucial to good health, to be released and ingested. No lye processing, no niacin. If you have a deficiency of niacin in your diet, you suffer a painful, sometimes fatal disease, pellagra. Though they did not know about vitamins, Native Americans discovered in antiquity that using ashes and water to change the corn made it more wholesome as well as better tasting. They ate the processed kernels—big hominy, Muscogee *osofki*, Hispanic *posole*—and they ground it into hominy grits. Many early Georgians adopted this practice, particularly with white flint and white dent corns. Many flint corns grew only one ear per stalk, so when the prolific southern white dent corns such as Carswell, Hickory King, or Cocke's Prolific became available, they were grown instead, because they invariable grew two or more ears per stalk.

Yellow corn became popular because of the rise in the American Midwest of two dent corns: Leaming (a southern Ohio yellow dent) and Reid's yellow dent (ancestor of the Midwestern yellow dents). Massive plantings took place on the Great Plains, so cheap yellow meal flooded eastern and southern groceries. Some families couldn't afford to choose the more expensive white meal. Its use in corn bread caused some to try it for grits. The carotene imparts a flavor, an oily unctuousness, that some like.

In the 1990s Elizabeth Terry, executive chef at Elizabeth on 37th in Savannah, and Nathalie Dupree began advocating for the use of stone-ground grits from one of the surviving small grist mills in the South. Georgia had Fielder's Old Fashioned Water Ground White Grits ground in Junction City and Georgia Agrirama Country Store Grits milled in Tifton.

Stone-ground grits feel a bit chunky. They absorb a fair amount of water when cooked. If you use a Instapot, a proportion of three cups of water to one cup grits will produce excellent grits. On the stove cooking with an open pot, four cups of water to one cup of grits and constant stirring should produce an excellent result. You always want to add butter or fat of some sort to the cooking pot. The degree of salt is a matter of personal preference. If you are serving the grits with gravy, use less salt.

Georgians began cooking cheese grits during World War II, encountering the dish in the wildly popular *Cross Creek Cookery* by Marjorie Kinnan Rawlings. The Pulitzer-Prize winning writer from Central Florida collected recipes from her neighborhood in the orange belt of Florida and captivated readers and cooks with vignettes of domestic life and rural foodways. Rawlings in her account of cheese grits identified the dish as a Baskin, Alabama, specialty. She does not specify a kind of cheese beyond saying that "one cup medium strong shaved cheese" gets added to the cooked grits when finished. Cooks in the *White Trash Cooking* tradition use American Cheese. Restaurant cooks prefer Cheddar.

Cheese grits stimulated experimentation among Georgia cooks. Cheese grits soufflé became a company dish among city hostesses. Grace Hartley's recipe in the March 28, 1963, issue of the *Atlanta Journal* provides a template of a hospitality staple. Garlic cheese grits also had a vogue in the latter half of the twentieth century. But the most curious evolution of cheese grits was introduced from North Carolina, when the *New York Times* writer Craig Claiborne popularized chef Bill Neal's shrimp and grits served at Crook's Corner Restaurant in Chapel Hill. Neal had adapted the old Charleston breakfast dish shrimp and hominy into a dinner "main." One alteration from the Charleston original was to use yellow cheese grits instead of white hominy grits as the grain base for the dish. Many Georgians took up this version of the Lowcountry classic as their version.

Day-old cooked grits have become another area of Georgian experimentation. Cooked grits once cooled will gelatinize into a solid. So cooks often spread the leftover grits into a sheet in a container, refrigerate it, and cut it into shapes to either bake or fry. In the antebellum period the fried hominy cake was deemed the ideal accompaniment of canvasback duck. But later in

Deep-fried grits cakes made of Guinea Flint corn, a flavorful old variety grown along the Georgia coast. This is the splendid fate of day-old grits. Photograph © David S. Shields.

the nineteenth century, fried grits became decidedly lower class in its associations. In part because the fried grits were formed into a patty, dunked in egg and coated with bread crumbs before being sautéed in a skillet. Prepared thusly it was the cousin of a potato pancake. The Maryland method was to spread the leftover grits into a thin sheet, cut them into fanciful geometric shapes, and deep fry them crisp and golden brown. The famous New Orleans eatery Tujaque's deep-fried their grits, preparing them with egg and breadcrumbs like the sautéed version, but flash frying them in a bath of hot oil. Elizabeth Terry experimented with both the sautéed cake and the deep-fried crisp grits shapes. Indeed, she is largely responsible for popularizing the fried grits cake and chip in fine-dining restaurants. She used the patty as an appetizer, adorning it with black-eyed pea relish or pepper jelly. She used the chip as an accompaniment to seafood dishes.

Grouper

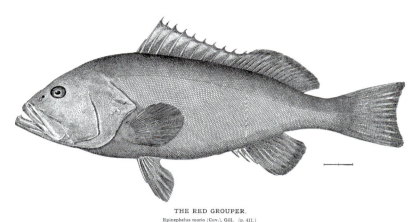

THE RED GROUPER.
Epinephelus morio (Cuv.), Gill. (p. 411.)
Drawing by H. L. Todd, from No. 22129, U. S. National Museum, obtained in the Washington Market, District of Columbia, by G. Brown Goode.

Red grouper (Epinephelus morio). Overfishing has pushed the population to near threatened status. Drawing and engraving by H. L. Todd. From Vol 1 [illustrations] of George Brown Goode, The Fishes and Fishery Industries of the United States (Washington, DC: GPO, 1887).

The coastal waters off Georgia host several members of the vast sea bass family called "grouper." Most possess a sturdy body covered in small scales, a broad mouth with a projecting lower jaw, rows of spikey depressible teeth, and a few large, fixed canines. They vary widely in coloration from gaudy to drab and can alter coloration to match the sea bottom. Groupers as a family are protogynous hermaphrodites. They begin life as females, and after producing eggs, their endocrine systems turn them into males. The most popular are from heaviest to lightest, largest to smallest, the Warsaw, the speckled hind, the Jewfish, the gag, the black, the red, the snowy, the scamp, and the yellow mouth. Primarily a game fish landed for local consumption until the mid-twentieth century, they became an important component of the commercial fishery, along with snapper and blackfish, in the 1950s. The standard bait tends to be live shrimp or eels. Some grouper are deepwater varieties caught at depths of 150 feet or more, usually around reefs. The Warsaw, the speckled hind, and the snow grouper belong to this group. Others are landed at more moderate depth, from twenty to 150 feet—the black, scamp, gag, red, and Jewfish. They congregate at isolated rocky outcrops on the ocean bottom of the Atlantic coastal shelf. Often caught by commercial vessels registered in Florida and landed at Brunswick or Savannah, the catch peaked in the 1970s at seven hundred thousand pounds. Overfishing throughout the 1980s occasioned a decline in both catch and the size of the average grouper landed by the end of the 1990s.

In classic Georgia coastal cooking grouper has a rather restricted range of treatments: It is baked; pan sautéed; battered and deep-fried, fish camp style; barbecued in a vinegar pepper sauce; or filleted, poached, and served with a sauce. In the last preparation the variety of sauce chosen reflects the ambition of a cook with lemon juice and capers or tartar sauce on the normal end and financière being on the ambitious. During the nineteenth century, grouper was a common component of fish stews. Later, the firm texture and lack of fat made grouper a favorite ingredient for restaurant chefs, particularly at the island resorts and clubs. Since 1970 a number of restaurants won reputation for their grouper dishes: The Crab Trap in Kennesaw in the 1970s, the Café de la Paix at the Atlanta Hilton and also George's Restaurant in Atlanta in the 1980s, the Holiday Inn Beach Resort at Jekyll Island in the 1980s and 1990s. Its favored place on menus was supplanted by snapper in the twenty-first century. With the catch declining, some disreputable restaurants have taken to calling fried tilapia or Asian carp "grouper" on their menus. Caveat emptor!

More flavorful than catfish, but with an agreeable meaty clean texture, pan-fried grouper is an ideal fish sandwich filler. Because of the large size of filets, using a roll or bun rather than a sandwich slice of bread better serves an eater. The standard batter for pan-fried grouper, detailed in a March 31, 1996, recipe in the *Augusta Chronicle*, calls for buttermilk and flour in equal proportions, paprika, and salt. A lighter crust can be had with rice flour, ice-cold beer, and an egg.

Baked stuffed grouper has been a standard company dish and restaurant fish course. In restaurants the luxe preparation stuffs the fish with crabmeat, at home corn bread and herbs has enjoyed particular favor. Because the size of groupers varies greatly with age and variety, offering a template amount of stuffing makes little sense. In Florida—particularly in Daytona Beach and Sarasota—large groupers are barbecued in a tomato sauce. While some eateries on the islands experimented with barbecued grouper, it has never become a fixture of coastal Georgia cuisine. Frying, boiling, and baking remain the chief ways of cooking this sumptuous group of fishes.

Guinea Fowl

Of all the edible things that crossed from West Africa to the West Indies and American South, the cookery of guinea fowl is perhaps the least discussed. They came to Georgia in the colonial period as a yard fowl. In the West Indies they naturalized. On the Cape Verde Islands, some of the Lesser Antilles, and in Jamaica they were hunted as game birds. While known to the ancients, the guinea fowl was not cultivated in Europe from the fall of the eastern Roman Empire to the seventeenth century when they were reintroduced.

You will hear the guinea fowl before you see them. The males shriek, the females quarrel, warn, and announce their presence with a raucous butt-CRACK! They operate as an early warning system announcing intruders on a farm. When you see them, you'll note immediately the naked head crowned by a bony helmet, the paired wattles at the angle of the gap, and the black plumage speckled white. You may occasionally see a southern flock bearing crowns of feathers on the head. The farm birds in the South have yellow or reddish legs. wild guinea fowl have grey legs.

There is something about the guinea fowl that is always striving to be wild. If given some liberty on the farm, they will roost in trees and roam far to find obscure places to nest, hidden from the eyes of hawks (and now coyotes). Mother birds will abandon their nest if a human touches it, whether in the wild or in a poultry house. You have to build niches so they can pretend they're hiding, and you have to have high perches in the house to suggest tree roosts. In the Lowcountry Gullah farmers removed eggs with a long stick with a scooped end. The hen knows if too many eggs are missing from the nest and will abandon it if there are fewer than five eggs beneath her. They are impatient too when the chicks are hatching and will leave sometimes after three or four have worked their way free. You have to intervene and take the rest of the pipping eggs into an incubator.

The flavor of the meat recalls game birds—with more piquant flavor than chicken. All guinea fowl that come to market are from five to ten months old. The flesh of a year-old bird tends to be too dry, too tough, and too musky flavored for enjoyable eating. But a bird eight or nine months of age will taste much like a game bird. The first recipes appear in print after the Civil War—for instance a Virginia recipe from Marian Harland's *Common Sense in the Household* (1871). Since that time they've enjoyed ebbs and flows of favor. In the 1910s they became a favorite banquet dish. There was a 1950s push for guinea fowl as consumer meat. But the bird will not endure the factory-style production that today's meat chickens suffer. So it has pretty much disappeared from the meat section of chain grocery stores in the United States. It is a specialty item, a resource for the restaurant trade, and an enduring feature of southern farms because it is a great forager of insects with a particular zest for fire ants. (In earlier ages it was held out as a possible devourer of boll weevils.) If you have a good connection with your local custom meat processors, you can get guinea fowl meat without too much difficulty.

In 1906 C. F. Langworthy summarized the common southern approach to cooking guinea hens.

Cooking of Guinea Fowl

C. F. Langworthy, *The Guinea Fowl and Its Use as Food* (1906)

Very young birds are best broiled and should be trussed and served like chickens. The older birds are sometimes roasted, boiled, fricasseed, or cooked with a little onion and bacon in a casserole. A homely but excellent southern substitute for the latter method is obtained by covering the bottom of a skillet with sliced onions slightly browned, laying on it the guinea fowl nicely cut as for a fricassee, putting thin strips of bacon over the meat, adding a little water, and finally closing the skillet tightly, by means of paper tied over the top, and cooking in the oven until well done. Another favorite was to half roast the birds and then finished the cooking by broiling. The giblets may be used in gravy or otherwise like those of chickens.

Classic guinea hen fricassee is also a rather simple dish. Boiling giblets, wing tips, and neck, you simmer a guinea hen stock. You pour it over the jointed fowl and cook at moderate temperature for an hour. In a separate skillet you make a béchamel sauce with cream, flour, butter, and stock. The seasoning traditionally makes use of some of the following—salt, pepper, grated orange peel, mace, clove, and parsley. The bird is served over a bed of rice and the sauce poured over the cooked pieces of fowl. See for instance "Fricassee of Guinea, You Asked for It," *The Atlanta Journal* (September 15, 1960).

Guinea hen was the chief ingredient in a classic Georgia stew that went by several names—guinea gumbo, guinea and okra stew, and Carolina gumbo (though never called this in South Carolina). This recipe appeared in *The Atlanta Journal* in 1944.

Carolina Gumbo [Guinea Gumbo]

The Atlanta Journal (June 22, 1944)

Slice 2 onions; fry; cut up a good-sized guinea hen . . . put in with the onions and fry brown; slice a quart of okra and 4 tomatoes; put all with the fowl in a stew pan, and pour hot water over it. Let boil until thick; season with salt and pepper. Eaten with rice if so desired.

This recipe works better if you use a brown roux as a base upon which to build the other ingredients.

Guinea hen eggs enjoyed particular repute among southern bakers who reckoned them superior to chicken eggs in making cakes because "the white is thought to be lighter when whipped than that of hens' eggs" (1905). Smaller in size than a hen's egg, it inspired spirited debate among those who thought the flavor of the yolk piquant and useful, particularly when boiled and employed in sauces, and the economists who couldn't see beyond the small size of the eggs. They should notice that a guinea hen begins laying in March and will continue uninterrupted until the first frost, eclipsing any brooding chicken in the yard. The eggs remain in demand.

Roasted Guinea Hen

KEVIN MITCHELL

I love to serve guinea hen during the holidays as an excellent replacement for turkey or chicken. It has great flavor; just be careful as it does have a low-fat content. The addition of butter and Madeira not only adds flavor but moisture as well. There are good sources to procure the guinea hen, such as Joyce Farms in North Carolina and D'Artagnan in New York. Next time you are looking for something new to serve for your holiday feast or for a quick dinner, pick up a hen and enjoy.

Serves 4 to 6

- 1 guinea hen, about 4 pounds, rinsed and patted dry
- 6 teaspoons unsalted butter, melted
- ½ cup good-quality Madeira
- 1 bunch fresh thyme, 2 tablespoons leaves chopped
- 1 bunch flat-leaf parsley, 2 tablespoons leaves chopped
- 1 bunch fresh tarragon, 2 tablespoons leaves chopped
- ¾ teaspoon kosher salt, plus more to season bird
- ½ teaspoon coarsely ground black pepper, plus more to season bird
- Madeira Gravy to serve (recipe follows)

One day before cooking, place the hen uncovered in the refrigerator to allow the skin to dry.

Preheat the oven to 400°F.

Mix the butter, Madeira, chopped herbs, salt, and pepper in a stainless steel bowl. Rub the hen with this mixture inside and out. Stuff the bird with the herb bunches. Season all over with salt and pepper.

Place the hen in a roasting pan with a holding rack. Roast in the oven for 20 minutes. After 20 minutes, baste the hen, in ten-minute intervals, with any juices that have collected at the bottom of the pan. Roast until the hen reaches an internal temperature of 160°F, approximately 1 hour.

Remove from the oven and rest for 10 minutes to allow juices inside the bird to settle. Remove herbs from the cavity. Place the bird on a cutting board and carve as you like. Place the hen pieces on a serving platter. Serve with Madeira Gravy.

(continued)

For the Stock

3 pounds turkey or chicken necks, drumsticks, or wings
4 tablespoons olive oil, divided
2 cups peeled and chopped carrots
4 cups chopped yellow onions
2 cups chopped celery
1 cup chopped shallots
1 cup chopped cremini mushrooms
1 cup chopped maitake mushrooms
1⅓ cups good-quality Madeira
4 sprigs thyme
2 sprigs sage
1 sprig rosemary
5 quarts plus 2 cups water

For the Gravy

1 quart stock
10 tablespoons cold unsalted butter, diced and divided
¾ cup all-purpose flour
1 cup good-quality Madeira
Fine sea salt and freshly ground white pepper to taste

Madeira Gravy

Makes 2½ quarts stock and gravy to serve 8

For the Stock:

Place an oven rack in the middle of the oven. Preheat the oven to 425°F. Rub the turkey parts in two tablespoons of olive oil. Arrange them in a single layer in a roasting pan and roast until brown and crisp, about three hours. Reserve the pan drippings.

When the turkey is finished, heat the remaining two tablespoons of olive oil in a large heavy-bottomed stockpot over medium heat. Add the carrots and cook, stirring occasionally, until golden brown, about 10 minutes. Add the onions and cook, stirring occasionally, until golden brown, an additional 10 minutes. Add the celery and cook, stirring occasionally, until golden brown, about 8 minutes. Add the shallots and mushrooms and cook, stirring occasionally, until golden brown, about 10 minutes.

Add the Madeira, scraping the bottom of the stockpot to release any browned bits, and simmer for 5 minutes to burn off the alcohol.

Add the roasted turkey bones to the stockpot. Add two cups of water to the roasting pan, scrape the bottom to release the browned bits, and add all to the stockpot. Add the remaining five quarts of water and bring to a simmer. Reduce the heat to low and simmer the stock uncovered until rich in flavor, about three hours.

Strain the stock through a fine-mesh sieve. Discard the bones and vegetables. You should have 2½ quarts of stock. Cool to room temperature. Cover and refrigerate until ready to use. The fat will rise to the top as it chills.

For the Gravy:

Skim the fat off the top of the stock. Transfer one quart of stock to a medium heavy-bottomed saucepan and simmer over low heat. Turn the heat off, cover the saucepan, and leave it on the stove.

Heat 6 tablespoons of the butter in a separate saucepan over medium heat. Add the flour and stir with a whisk to form a thick, smooth paste. Cook, stirring constantly, until golden brown, about 8 minutes. Stir in the Madeira and cook, stirring constantly, for 5 minutes to burn off the alcohol.

Pour the warm stock into the butter mixture and vigorously whisk until it is incorporated. Cook over medium heat, stirring frequently, until a sauce consistency is achieved, 20 to 25 minutes. Season to taste with salt and pepper. Stir in the remaining 4 tablespoons of cold butter, one piece at a time. Strain through a fine-mesh sieve. Add more stock if too thick. Serve with Roasted Guinea Hen.

Note: The remaining stock can be refrigerated for three days or frozen in a tightly covered container for up to three months.

Guinea Squash

Eggplant

Like many ingredients that made it to the New World from Africa, such as okra, the guinea squash crossed the Atlantic with a set of growing practices and preparations attached. Many of these diaspora products bore the common English prefix "guinea" a geographic designation for the Gold Coast and Slave Coast territories in West Africa. Botanically, the eggplant (*Solanum melongena*) is considered a fruit, since it consists of seeds, however it is cooked and eaten as a vegetable. There are several varieties of eggplant, ranging in color and shape. When the eggplant was first introduced in Europe and America, it was not received with much fanfare. As time passed the popularity of the eggplant grew and now it is considered one of the great vegetables in the culinary world.

It came to England in 1597, yet the name eggplant first appeared in 1763 because an oval, white-fruited variety became a popular show plant in display gardens. Other varieties, less novel in appearance, spread out of Africa and won places in gardens because they were insect and drought resistant. Today you can find the white variety of eggplant, however they are considered an heirloom variety. While records exist of eggplants being grown in the British American colonies, they possessed a strange variety of names and designations. Susanna Wright of Pennsylvania referred to hers as "the roast beef plant."

Georgia horticulturist William White in his antebellum classic, *Gardening for the South*, observed that "the varieties of purple eggplant are the only ones used in cooking, the white variety being raised for ornament." He had not encountered the red oblate shaped *Salonum aethiopicum* variety kept in Geechee gardens, a deeper flavored, more bitter variety reputed by its growers to have great medical efficacy. In 1857 White noted that the eggplant "is now rapidly working its way upward in general esteem" as a vegetable. He noted that the favorite mode of preparation in the South was frying and offered this recipe as guide.

To Fry Eggplant

William White, *Gardening for the South* (1857)

Cut the egg-plant in slices a quarter of an inch thick. To remove the acrid taste, pile the slices on a plate with alternate layers of salt; raise one side of the plate, that the juice may run off. In half an hour wash them well in fresh water, and fry them quite brown in batter.

Since those pioneering days of guinea squash cookery, the number of eggplant varieties has expanded. The old market staples—the Florida high bush eggplant and the black beauty, dominated produce sales over the twentieth century. The American globe varietal is now the most common and will be found in any grocery store.

This eggplant has a deep purple color and is short and stubby. The Chinese eggplant, often confused with the Japanese eggplant, is a mild, purple-toned variety that has fewer seeds and is sweeter compared to the globe eggplant. The fairytale eggplant, with its purple and white color, has a sweet flavor and a tender flesh that does well on your backyard grill. The graffiti eggplant is very similar to the fairytale varietal. This is a great eggplant that can be eaten whole when cooked. The Indian eggplant, which is slightly larger than a golf ball, with a deep reddish-purple skin is used in many Indian curry dishes. The Italian eggplant is very similar to the American globe; however, it is slightly smaller and is most famous for the Italian dish caponata. Japanese eggplant is a long slender variety that cooks extremely quickly and is good stir-fried with vegetables. The little green eggplant variety has a beautiful pale green skin and is light and

A field of black beauty eggplant growing near the coast. This cultivar, favored in 2025 for its heat tolerance and disease resistance, retains many qualities of its West African ancestor, the purple guinea squash. Photograph © David S. Shields.

smooth flavor. The rosa bianca eggplant varietal unlike the others has no bitter flavor and the skin is a purplish-white color. Finally, Thai eggplant is extremely bitter, due to the great number of seeds; it is similar in size to the Indian eggplant but has an olive-green skin.

When growing eggplant, you must know that they love to grow in hot climates and thrive in manure and compost-rich soil. They love water but only until the plant is well established; after that overwatering the plant could ruin them.

The repertoire of eggplant dishes has expanded from the days when guinea squash was either sliced and fried or baked like a squash. The most African of the old recipes required the eggplants to be boiled, then mashed, seasoned, and formed into cakes for deep frying. The seasonings were personal, sometimes elaborate, and rarely recorded in recipes. Here is an old, minimalist recipe for fritters. Practiced cooks elaborated the flavor extensively.

Eggplant Fritters

Evening News (August 9, 1914)

Boil the eggplant in water with a tablespoonful of lemon juice or vinegar, then mush and drain. To a pint of eggplant add two beaten eggs, a half cupful of flour, and salt and pepper to taste. Form into cakes and brown on both sides in hot fat.

Egg Plant Salad

Jules Arthur Harder,
Physiology of Taste (1885)

Peel two middle-sized Egg Plants, cut them in slices a quarter of an inch thick, sprinkle each slice with a little salt, and put them together again. After half an hour press them gently, to extract the moisture. Then dry them on a napkin. Fry them lightly in clarified butter, then drain them on a napkin. When cold cut them in small pieces, put them in a salad bowl, with some scalloped pickled sturgeon, a spoonful of grated horseradish mixed with mustard, a clove of fine chopped garlic, a little fine chopped parsley, and a handful of water cress. Season them with salt, pepper, olive oil, and vinegar. Mix the whole well together, then arrange them properly, and garnish them with stoned olives and hard-boiled eggs cut into quarters.

Honey

Georgia produces two monofloral honeys that command international respect and premium prices: sourwood honey, from the mountains of north Georgia, and tupelo honey, from the estuary banks of south and east Georgia. Each derives from the nectar of a flowering tree. The sourwood tree grows in the East only in the Blue Ridge and Appalachian Mountain areas and in Georgia only in the northern tier of counties. And in these regions, honey is produced only in the higher elevations. The honey season runs for just five to six weeks from late June to early August. Tupelo honey derives from nectar on the blossoms of the white tupelo (*Nyssa ogeche*) a tree that loves warmth and moisture, growing on river and stream banks from the Apalachicola River to the Ogeechee River. The blossoms of the white tupelo, besides honey, produce the Ogeechee lime, a sour fruit famously made into pickles (see entry).

The demand for sourwood honey exceeds supply. Some years the sourwood (*Oxydendron arboretum*) doesn't bloom. While north Georgia boasts a substantial community of beekeepers, in the past three decades they have had to struggle with all of the pathological and environmental afflictions that have imperiled honeybees. The summer roadside stands that sell honey in mountain country have earned a bad reputation for selling "sourwood honey," when locals know that the Sourwood trees did not blossom. Fortunately, sourwood honey has several qualities that can't easily be counterfeited: Its chemistry prevents crystallization; its flavor combines a buttery caramel with a subtle bite of ginger and clove; the fragrance is that of pie spice—cinnamon, clove, a touch of nutmeg.

Tupelo honey production also cannot meet demand. The seductive flavor of the honey accounts largely for the demand. Rose, vanilla, citrus, spice, and cooked apple combine in an alluring amalgam. Chemist Samantha Rachelle Gardiner revealed the basis for the unique flavor of tupelo honey: fructose, rose-scented phenylacetaldehye, citrusy nonanal, vanillin, eugenol (clove), and (E)-β-damascenone (the cooked apple flavor).

Often regarded as the model for all monofloral honeys, tupelo honey came to be because of the labor of Floridian Sidney Smith Alderman (1835–1922). An orange grower, Alderman nurtured bees to pollinate his groves. He noticed the extraordinary forest of wild white tupelo that grew in the wetlands along the Chipola River, a tributary of the Apalachicola. The hives closest to this stand of flowering trees produced honey remarkable in its flavor, lack of granulation, and white-green color. In 1872 he determined to produce honey exclusively from this tupelo forest. Honey fanciers noticed the extraordinary quality immediately. Demand exploded and Alderman tried to meet it, expanding his operation to fourteen hundred hives at six sites by 1892. Through the 1890s he shipped eighty-four thousand pounds of tupelo honey to New York and Boston. Georgia beekeepers took notice, since the white tupelo grew extensively in the state. The initial centers of tupelo honey production were along the banks of the Georgia rivers that fed into Silver Lake and the Apalachicola River: the Flint to the east,

Spring Creek and the Chattahoochee to the west. In the 1920s Decatur County exported substantial quantities of tupelo honey from hives along the Flint River to Europe. In the 1930s J. J. Wilder of Cordele, Georgia, became one of the largest tupelo honey producers in North America, tending approximately five thousand hives. For a century tupelo honey has remained a fixture of Georgia food. One of the classic preparations is cantaloupe balls sweetened with tupelo honey and mint.

Sourwood honey was reckoned the ideal sweetener for a breakfast biscuit, a hunk of corn bread, and a pancake (if you didn't favor maple or cane syrup). In the 1970s it began to be added to barbecue sauce mixes for chicken and duck. It also performed well in baking. Both sourwood and tupelo contributed to the pleasure in the classic confection, honey cake.

Honey Cake

Augusta Chronicle (May 28, 1952)

2 cups sifted cake flour
3 teaspoons baking powder
¼ teaspoon salt
½ cup shortening
2 egg yolks
1 cup honey
½ cup milk
2 egg whites
1 teaspoon vanilla

Sift flour, baking powder, and salt. Cream shortening until light. Beat egg yolks until lemon colored, gradually adding ½ cup of the honey while beating. Add the egg-honey mixture slowly to the creamed shortening, creaming while adding. Add sifted dry ingredients alternately with milk, mixing well after each addition. Beat egg whites until stiff; gradually beat in remaining ½ cup honey until mixture stands in stiff peaks. Fold into cake batter until well blended. Bake in 2 greased 9-inch layer cake pans in a moderate oven (375 degrees F.) for 30 minutes. Cool and frost as desired.

Honey cake is one of the more ancient European baked confections. Some Georgians felt that the traditional formula might be improved by soaking the honey cake in either rum (coastal preference) or bourbon (north Georgia preference).

While sourwood and tupelo honey stand foremost in demand of Georgia's honey varieties, the state's beekeepers do produce other varieties, including gallberry and orange blossom. Some areas of the state produce "wildflower honey" from the region's native blossoms. All monofloral production is artisanal, requiring strict attention in its preparation. Keepers harvest hives weekly and process honey in small batches instead of seasonally. Because the application of heat or pressure can alter the flavor of honey during its extraction from the comb, most producers of monofloral honey use gravity extraction, a slower technique. Many do not filter the honey, or do so minimally, offering it "raw." Numbers of beekeepers offer honey in the comb and pollen in addition to jars of extracted honey. If you wish to support your local honey producers, consult the "Honey" page of the Georgia Beekeepers Association website: https://gabeekeeping.com/honey.

Lard

For much of Georgia history the chief question concerning frying had to do with whether bacon fat or lard best suited making something flavorful, crispy, and golden brown. The turn in the twentieth century to vegetable oils—Wesson Oil (originally cottonseed oil), peanut oil, and finally canola oil—was driven by economics, not taste preference. Indeed the seed oils were engineered not to have taste. David Wesson in the 1890s had opted not to give cottonseed oil a flavor after he figured out how to steam and blow the stink out of it. Consumers opted for cheapness not superior flavor. It costs money to raise a pig, so lard and bacon fat cost more than pressed seed oil.

The cotton growers, and there were many of them in Georgia, were all for the change. They even publicized the claims of physical culturists and food purists, persons with whom they had little ideological affinity, that animal-based products were unhealthy. The vegetarian wing of the physical culture movement spent much of the 1890s trying to convince Americans that butter was dangerous and that milk was responsible for the American tuberculosis outbreak of 1892. If anything drove the adoption of Wesson Oil, hydrogenated Cottonlene, and Crisco in Georgia it was the interest of the cotton industry. There was a moment in 1890 when the power and desire of the cotton interest became baldly visible. The Conger Compound Lard Bill was introduced to quash the efforts of the cotton interest to create a lard substitute from hydrogenated cottonseed oil and beef tallow. Unscrupulous lard manufacturers had already added admixed hydrogenated cottonseed lipids with lard and sold it as pure lard. The cotton interest was adulterating lard and offering an ersatz substitute under the lard name. (They would be compelled by law to sell their mixtures under the designation "compound lard.") Would it surprise you to learn that they underwrote the publicity campaign that suggested that lard was old-fashioned and unhealthful—not the sort of thing a twentieth-century Georgian should be ingesting? Here's a taste of 1908 anti-lard propaganda: "Cottonlene Biscuits are light and flaky. They have none of that heavy-as-lead suggestion, that greasy taste, and that after-heaviness of lard biscuit." Nevertheless, lard remained the gold standard of lipids in the early twentieth century. Witness the branding of hydrogenated cottonseed products: "Snowdrift Hogless Lard." But friends, there is no lard without the hog.

What is lard? It is the rendered fat that clusters round the kidneys of pigs. At the time of a pig's slaughter, the leaf fat gets stripped from the kidneys and deposited in a cauldron. Sometimes it is ground before being subjected to heat, to ensure greater rapidity and consistency in the melting of the fat. The whiteness and purity of the re-congealed fat (lard) mattered greatly, and tricks of the trade distinguished the accomplished renderer from the DIY home butcher. Here are wise words: "Grind the fat or chop it as you would sausage meat. . . . The object is to get the fat into such a condition that the tissue and fibrine will separate quickly from the clear fat. Now, by the mild heat and constant stirring, melt to the consistency of thin gruel, then scatter salt enough over the surface to carry down all the scraps. Salt does not melt in pure lard, and therefore will not give it a saline taste. Then allow it to settle and dip the clear fat out into a vessel" (1889). The semisolid portion left after the extraction of the pure melted fat is left to fry—these will become the famous "cracklings" that lend texture to corn bread.

Lard's decline into retro status, and the public perception that users were practicing a form of perverse rural recalcitrance ensured its increasing marginalization with each passing decade in the twentieth century. Its rivals played up liabilities: its tendency to spoil when not refrigerated, its difficulty blending with certain kinds of flour in baking. In 1947 Armour premiered its "Pastry Blend" pure lard. Armour had hydrogenated the lard to make it shelf stable and lighter in texture. Those people who purchased it had two purposes for it: incorporating into baked goods, particularly piecrusts and biscuits, or using it to fry fish or french fries. Lard's high smoke point was appreciated by traditional fry houses.

The classic piecrust required only four ingredients: flour, lard, salt, and water. The quality of each ingredient influenced the final product. The flour should be soft white winter wheat. Here is a basic instruction of the sort followed by the home bakers who kept lard on groceries shelves for the last century. One matter not discussed here is that lard should be employed cold. And the water should be ice water. Since hydrogenated lard does not require refrigeration and is stored at room temperature, it must be chilled if it is to have the best results. What is the desired end product? "Pastry made with lard is not only tender and flaky, but also has a nut-like flavor" (1958).

Plain Pastry

Anne Kingsley, *Augusta Chronicle*
(January 28, 1934)

Lard is the ideal shortening for pastry as many tests have proved. It is a soft fat and is pliable over a wide range of temperature. Moreover it is easily digested and its food value is high.

1 ½ cups flour
6 to 8 tablespoons lard
½ teaspoon salt
3 tablespoons ice water

Have the ingredients, room and hands cool in making pastry. Handle the mixture quickly and lightly. Mix salt with flour. Chop in lard with a pastry cutter or work in with the fingers until the mixture is coarse and granular in appearance. Work in water lightly and rapidly with a fork, stirring until the dough just holds together in a ball. Roll to about 1/8 inch in thickness and transfer to the pie pan without stretching the dough.

Nutritionists examining hydrogenated seed oils in the 1990s discovered they were full of risky trans fats, and were, consequently, more deleterious to one's health than nonhydrogenated lard! Lard's 45 percent monounsaturated fat, and its 40 percent saturated fat offer a healthier profile than butter. While not as healthy as olive oil as a lipid, traditional lard was substantially more beneficial than margarine, Crisco, Snowdrift, and even hydrogenated lard. The true danger food was the hydrogenated trans fats found in Crisco, the shortening many households had embraced in place of traditional lard. In 2010 a group of southern chefs declared, "Enough!" They made lard the focus of a movement—the lardcore revolution. They jettisoned the hydrogenated lard that food processors had created to make it more like Crisco and reverted to traditional rendering processes. Its standard bearer was Sean Brock in Charleston. Its Georgia adherents included Hugh Acheson, Linton Hopkins, and Kevin Gillespie. In the early 2010s the lardcore movement grabbed public attention and notoriety, but it lacked a coherent philosophy beyond, nonhydrogenated lard is good. Its emphasis on creating flavored lard-based smears for bread was a mistake—too much entrenched competition from butter.

The chief shortcoming of the artisanal lard movement was its inadequate consideration of the flavor of lard. No one had researched whether the meat and fat of different breeds of hog produced different flavors—until Bob Perry, resident chef of the University of Kentucky conducted his landmark 2014 comparative study. It turns out that most don't. Lard from the industrial pink pig of American industry tastes much the same as that from a Tamworth hog, if you render it in the classical manner. But there are a few important exceptions. The most famous traditional lard pig of the South, the guinea hog, produces lard with deep umami resonance. The Ossabaw pig, the "most efficient fat producing mammal on the planet," also has a distinctive fat flavor profile. Where varietal distinction emerges is when pork meat and fat are cured. In lardo—the cured form of lard cherished in Europe—each breed of pig takes on a distinct flavor. In Europe the Mangalitsa pig is particularly valued for its flavor. There are people in Georgia who are trying to do the same with the Ossabaw pig.

The Ossabaw Island pig descended from a pair of Canary Island hogs left on the coastal island by Spanish mariners in the sixteenth century. Because Spanish vessels had to sail up the Florida and Georgia coasts to catch the gulf stream where it approaches the Western Hemisphere most, and because these fleets encountered hurricanes and risked wrecking on these coasts, they would populate islands with pigs to serve as a meat source for marooned sailors. Those on Ossabaw Island survived until our time. The island proved a difficult environment for the hogs: hot, humid, with periods of food scarcity. They evolved to store enough fat to tide them over periods of scant food. So in the twentieth century biologists recognized it as the most efficient fat-producing mammal in the world, and researchers on obesity found them the ideal experimental subject. The Ossabaw's extraordinary fat drew the attention of the lardcore movement, and the pig became a Georgia signature.

Today the average person will most quickly understand the glories of lard when tasting french fries cooked in boiling lard. The difference in quality can be astounding. But we think the long-term future of guinea hog lard lies in baking. If you want the taste of your place in baking, using the most flavorful of ingredients, employ guinea hog lard instead of butter when making puff pastry (like the *sfogliatella* of Naples or the *salasnjaci* of Serbia). Use flour made from soft white purple straw winter wheat, the South's original biscuit and cake wheat.

Mull

The signature autumnal stew of Georgia has milk as its principal liquid, crackers for a thickener, a good deal of pepper as a seasoning, and chicken, game, wildfowl, turtles, or snakes as a protein. A quartet of vegetables often appears in the mix: onions, bell peppers, celery, and carrots. Potatoes also might appear. Streak-o-lean bacon provides the fat. A mull is usually prepared by a man, either outdoors, or in a rural restaurant. Like South Carolina's pine bark stew, Kentucky's burgoo, or Virginia's Brunswick stew, it appears as the principle communal meal dish of an event—a fair, a political stump meeting, a revival, a hunting party, a church social. According to the *New Georgia Encyclopedia*, "Mull is traditionally a cold-weather dish. Northeast Georgians speak of the 'mull season.' Chicken Mull is an occasional side at Georgia BBQ stands."

The term "mull" is thought to come from the word "muddle," meaning to mash together ingredients in liquid. Yet there is no firm date for when the word comes into general usage. What we do know is that the popularity of the dish arose in the state during the second quarter of the twentieth century. (No mulls are mentioned in the many menus for the Georgia Products Feasts in 1913 or the subsequent decade.) Jim Christian of the University of Georgia in the 1980s laid out the norms for the dish: "Mull is very popular in the rural South and can be made with goat meat, catfish, chicken, squirrel, rabbit or dove. They cook the meat until it comes off the bone and put it back in the broth they cooked it in. Then it's seasoned and most people put soda crackers, and it's seasoned with flour and starch. Some people fry bacon and put that in there. They also use onions and bell peppers, celery, and carrots."

While availability often dictated which protein went into the Dutch oven, certain cooks and certain venues became famous for particular forms of mull. Roscoe's Kountry Kitchen in Crawford, Georgia, in the late 1960s and through the 1970s became locally famous for turtle mull. Which kind of turtle? "Well, this here one is a mud turtle, and this is a snapper, and rest is just pure old turtles." A native of Social Circle, Georgia, Roscoe Long learned his culinary art there. "The mull is served in big bowls with plenty of crackers. It contains ground-up turtle meat, potatoes, onions, red pepper, juice of garlic, and milk. It sticks to the ribs." Long realized that even in 1970 he was the conservator of a waning tradition: "I'm the only restaurant around that serves turtle mull or soup or stew—call it whatever you want. Not a lot of people make it, and in the old days most everyone made it, but now they don't."

In the mid-1960s the Athens Bowhunters Club devoted its annual game dinner to the making of snake mull. At the Oconee National Forest campgrounds, the club set up a cauldron and stewed the chopped meat of copperheads and rattlesnakes. The newspapers annually reported the event, repeating the same tired joke, "Everyone ate copperhead mull but the cook."

If chicken mull constituted the commonest and plainest version of this hearty stew, perhaps the most piquant and beloved hunt season mull featured another bird, dove.

Louise Thrash, food editor of the *Augusta Chronicle*, transcribed Bobby Neely's recipe for Dove Mull in 1979.

Dove Mull

Bobby Neely, *Augusta Chronicle*
(May 24, 1979)

In a heavy iron pot with top, line bottom and lower sides of pot with sliced streak-o-lean bacon. Add 3 stalks of celery. 1 medium bell pepper chopped fine, cover this with more streak-o-lean. Salt and pepper birds then make a layer of birds in pot, then a layer of diced potatoes, then chopped onions. Another layer of birds, potatoes and onions. Be sure to salt and pepper the potatoes and onions as you put them in. Place top on pot tightly. Bring heat up until you hear the contents bubble. Cook for about one hour, bubbling, not on high. Then add ½ small bottle of Worcestershire sauce and a stick of butter. Cover and cook ½ hour, then add about a cup of milk. Never stir the pot. Cook about 15 more minutes, take top off and serve in soup plates, since the mull makes its own juices.

Every family of mull has its own territory in Georgia. Chicken mull developed in the area around Athens and turtle mull in that region transected by Interstate 20 from Augusta to Atlanta. Shrimp mull was the creation and glory of the Sea Islands. The two most popular forms of mull—forms that have migrated from the world of outdoor male cookery to indoor kitchen offerings prepared by men or women have been shrimp mull and chicken mull. Each deserves a detailed treatment.

SHRIMP MULL

The gulf coast has its shrimp creole. South Carolina has its shrimp and grits. The Georgia Sea Islands has shrimp mull. This dish was created by the saltwater Geechee sometime in the last half of the nineteenth century in the Lowcountry. It was the favorite dish of the famous African American pilot, agronomist, and US Congressman Robert Smalls (1839–1915) at Beaufort, South Carolina. It became an open-air event dish in the early twentieth century, prepared outdoors in kettles by men for hunt clubs, holidays, and seaside excursions on St. Simons, Sapelo, and Jekyll Island. In the 1950s restaurants, such as the Forward Deck in Brunswick, began adopting it as a local signature dish.

Shrimp mull feasts began to be announced in east Georgia papers in the early 1930s. But national awareness of the dish only occurred when eminent food writer Clementine Paddleford featured the dish in her account of a picnic on Sea Island in Georgia during her southern trip of 1951. Saltwater Geechee cook Ben McIntosh prepared the meal, which included barbecued chicken and hush puppies as well as the Mull. Paddleford printed a recipe in a widely syndicated article entitled "Sea Island Picnic."

Shrimp Mull

Clementine Paddleford,
Chicago Tribune (March 10, 1951)

3 bacon slices
1 ½ cups diced onion
1 green pepper, diced
2 stalks celery, finely chopped
1 quart uncooked, cleaned shrimp
1 quart water
1 cup ketchup
Black pepper to taste
1 teaspoon Worcestershire Sauce
Salt to taste
Tabasco to taste

Fry bacon slices until cooked. Add onion and sauté until golden, add pepper and celery; simmer, lid on pan, 5 minutes. Add shrimp, then water to cover; add ketchup, black pepper, Worcestershire, salt and Tabasco. Simmer until thickened, 30 minutes. Yields four portions.

The recipe scaled down the kettle-sized proportions that McIntosh used. Anyone familiar with pine bark stew or red catfish stew will note similarities: the ketchup (no whole tomatoes), the Worcestershire sauce, the bacon, the onion. Since tomato ketchup and Worcestershire sauce are both creations of the later part of the second quarter of the nineteenth century, this standard formulation found in event kettle dishes must have evolved in the latter half of the century. The green peppers are novel, as is the tobacco. Shrimp mull had to have had an edge to it.

The second important saltwater Geechee cook who influenced the development of shrimp mull was Ceola Johnson, head cook of the Forward Deck restaurant in Brunswick. Johnson refashioned a version used on Blythe Island by Judge J. C. Butts. Again, she included no milk. She intensified the tomato and celery flavor while amplying the spicing with allspice and curry powder.

One of the more curious episodes I (David) have had in Lowcountry eating was ordering shrimp mull and being served a dish that looked like shrimp chowder—all white in thickened milk. Some northern hotel cook's idea no doubt. The real deal lives on in many Lowcountry households and appears in important Gullah Geechee cookbooks such as Sallie Ann Robinson's *Gullah Home Cooking the Daufuskie Way* (2003).

CHICKEN MULL

In 1986 real estate developers bought out the land leased by the Chase Street Café in Athens, forcing it to close after four decades of existence. The temple of chicken mull went dark. It was the featured dish on Thursdays and Fridays, its name standing at the top of the blackboard in big chalk letters. Sarah Hansford, the matriarch of the family that owned the café, cooked the stew, which one reporter described as "a gray mush made of chicken, crackers, and milk, but whose exact ingredients are something of a family secret." The last bowl was served in late October of 1986.

Local variations emerged in terms of its preparation and local masters of its preparation. In Clarke County the African American barbecue cook Harry "Squab" Jones served a stew made up of "a quantity of minced chicken and half as much of turtle meat in an old-fashioned pot . . . when the stock was ready, a dozen quarts of whole milk and some butter are added. After this has been thoroughly merged, Worcester sauce, salt and pepper are added. Finally a half bushel of cracker crumbs are stirred in and it is ready to serve" (1945). Jones prepared large quantities in an iron kettle for outdoor events from the 1930s through the 1950s.

The oldest chicken mull recipes lacked vegetables. But over the course of the twentieth century devotees of the tomato began insinuating chopped tomatoes into the mix. In the latter decades of the century this pink tinged version seemed to be more au courant than the classic to newspaper food editors. We reproduce one such formulation from the 1990s published in *The Atlanta Journal*. The closing note that rabbit can be substituted for chicken points to the adaptability of mull. Duck mull was probably the most prevalent substitution and was a favorite camp dish. But rabbit meat more closely tasted like chicken.

Chicken Mull

Nancy Roquemore, *The Atlanta Journal* (February 8, 1996)

1 4-pound roasting hen or fryer
2 small onions, chopped
½ pound butter
1 quart milk
1 28-ounce can plum tomatoes, drained and chopped
½ cup cider vinegar
1 red pepper (optional)
½ pound saltine crackers, crushed

In a large kettle or Dutch oven, cover the chicken with water. Bring to boil over high heat. Reduce heat to low and simmer till done, about 1 hour. Remove from heat and set aside to cool. When cool enough to handle, remove meat from bones. Grind meat and put into large, heavy-bottomed sauce-pan. Add onion, butter, milk, tomatoes, vinegar and red pepper if using. Bring to boil over medium-high heat. Reduce heat to low and simmer until onion is tender. 10 to 15 minutes. Thicken with crushed crackers. Season to taste with salt and pepper.

Variations: Rabbit can be substituted for Chicken.

Chicken mull. While most mull recipes were intended for outdoor cooking, chicken mull and shrimp mull became household preparations. Crumbling saltine crackers over the cooked mull and stirring them in is regarded as classic finishing. Photograph © David S. Shields.

Though chicken mull was more an inland than a coastal dish for much of the twentieth century, restaurateurs along the coast began adding it to the bill of fare after the closure of the Chase Street Café. Booty's Fish House in Royston, Georgia, of Route 17, became the place that a roadside consumer could get chicken mull on a nightly basis in the 1990s. Athens stills boasts a number of eateries that offer Chicken mull.

In terms of home cooking, chicken mull country extends from Athens to Anderson, South Carolina, then skips much of that state and resumes again in parts of North Carolina. Indeed Bear Grass North Carolina holds an annual Chicken Mull festival. When it began to be served there is something of a mystery, since there is not much of a paper trail. A subject for more research. . . .

Mullet

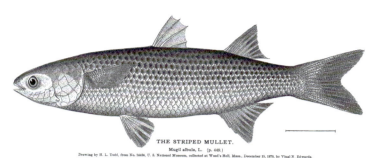

Striped mullet, or pop-eyed mullet, or jumping mullet (Mugil albula) was fried, smoked, pickled, and poached. The roes were cured and enjoyed great popularity. Drawing and engraving by H. L. Todd. From Vol 1 [illustrations] of George Bown Goode, The Fishes and Fishery Industries of the United States (Washington, DC: GPO, 1887).

During the first decade of the twentieth century the Florida legislature started fretting about the extent of the harvest of mullet in its coastal waters and began limiting the fishing season. The representatives feared that the uninhibited harvest of this tasty saltwater fish would destroy the population, preventing posterity from enjoying fried mullet, mullet stew, and salt cured mullet roe. There were two seasons—one began in late February and lasted until May, the second and most important began in late August and ended in mid-November or on December 1. Georgia's fish lovers fretted. One writer to the *Cairo Messenger* in 1925 groaned, "So here we are! Raised largely on salt mullet, and there is no finer sea food, only to be deprived of them at this late time, after December 1st each year, by a Florida law!"

Mullet congregate in schools and are caught in the coastal shallows by men hauling gill nets, or "stop nets" that close off the entrance of a creek or bayou. While they were caught on the islands, the majority of mullet consumed in Georgia came from catch landed in the gulf states. Latinx did much of the netting in the gulf, saltwater Geechee manned the fishery in the Georgia islands. The men processed the fish as well as catching them, extracting roe sacks from the females, and salting the roe sacks and the male and female fishes in barrels. Different parts of Georgia stocked their mullet from different waters. Counties on the Florida border (Decatur and west) got gulf mullet and those on the coast from Geechee fishermen on the sea islands.

In the early twentieth century many African Americans engaged in cotton picking in south Georgia would be paid at the end of the week from September well into November. The tradition of pooling some of that money to hold a "hot supper" and a frolic became a weekend rite: "The 'hot suppers' consisting chiefly of fish and mostly of mullet, are usually held on Saturday night, hence the heavy shipments Friday. Yesterday the Southern Express Company shipped four solid cars of mullet out of Savannah. They were consigned to smaller towns in Georgia where cotton is being picked" (1908). Invariably the fish were fried in these celebrations. The same lard would be used to fry a multitude of fish and would take on a rather pungent smell. When cottonseed oil began being sold throughout the South one quality in its favor was an absence of intrinsic odor and a tendency not to be an amplifier of fish smell. The primary question concerning frying mullet is whether the cook uses cornmeal or flour to dredge the mullet fillets before tossing them into the fry kettle. If cornmeal, cooks had a decided preference for white meal to go with the body of the fish. If flour, the fried fish would often be served with corn bread, hominy grits, or baked sweet potatoes. We've tried mullet both ways and determined that a combination of cornmeal (or even corn flour) and wheat flour provides the pleasures of both methods. Here is a recipe geared for family consumption that comes from the Lowcountry.

Fried Mullet

Jim Rooney,
Jim Rooney's Edisto Eatin' (1996)

6 skinned mullet fillets
3 c. milk
½ c. corn meal
½ c. flour
1 tsp. salt
1 tsp. pepper
1 tsp. garlic powder
Peanut Oil-Olive Oil

Soak fillets in milk for 20 minutes, then roll them in mix of corn meal, flour, salt and pepper, and garlic powder. Fry fish in hot oil at least 3 inches deep. Turn a couple of times until golden brown. Remove and dry on paper towels. 350 degrees is proper temperature for any fried fish.

Not all mullet was fried. It might be stewed or baked and stuffed. On the coastal islands it would be poached and served with a bacon or fatback pilau using Carolina Gold rice.

> Pop Eye Mullet and Greasy Rice
> Make a Po' Man lose his Wife

So sang one of Charleston's last hucksters, a single-name street celebrity known universally as "Wilson" in the 1940s and 1950s. He sold striped mullet out of a gaudy cart, painted red and yellow, and crowned with a carving of a cat. The pop-eyed mullet he sold was striped mullet, the jumping fish of southeastern waters. The dish that Wilson celebrated was a mullet and bacon pilau. Pork fat dissolved in cooking the rice turned the dish slippery. Chopped onion, salt, and pepper were the other permissible ingredients in the pot. The mullet was fried or poached island style ("To a cup of water add a tablespoon of vinegar, a bay leaf, pepper, salt; put in a whole mullet and cover" [1953]).

Other Geechee dishes included mullet mull (a mull with no milk), mullet and okra stew, and mullet and yam stew. Both of the latter stews employ bacon or fatback in the preparation. The okra stew adds onions and tomatoes, the mullet and yam stew only onions and yams with the proportion of one mullet per one sweet potato. Both should be prepared with skinned boned mullets cut into chunks. While many fish could be used in the classic Lowcountry fish and grits, mullet stood at the top of the list among coastal residents. Tourists opt for flounder, residents for mullet and whiting.

Mullet spawn in mid-November and December (the period when they are protected from harvest), so the processing of roe-laden females by fishermen takes place primarily in October and early November. Because mullet roe requires time to salt cure, a season's cured roe did not appear in the market until mid-January. The roe sacks were harvested, the split fish usually salted. Salted and set in barrels, the roes cured for two months. White roes were sold as "white mullet roe." If the roes went through an additional step of sun drying like bottarga, they turned orange and were sold as "red mullet roe." In the latter half of the twentieth century the harvest of roe declined, until it became a specialty item available at a few outlets such as Burgess's Fresh Seafood Place and City Market and Georgia Fry House at Brunswick and at the Lenox Square Colonial in Atlanta. In the twenty-first century, however, fine-dining chefs discovered the Sardinian form of cured mullet roe, bottarga, and made it a gourmet treasure. Gulf coast fishermen saw the light and began practicing the art that their grandfathers cherished making cured mullet roe once again. Clearwater, Florida, has become the center of production and Caviar Star Company retails a set of roe from $40 to $60 depending on weight. It is sold as "Medimid-terranean caviar" or "bottarga," not by its traditional Georgia name of mullet roe.

Mustard Greens

Some folks are particular about greens. They favor one variety over the miscellaneous "mess o' greens" that traditionally simmered on the back burner of the stove. Of course many of the greens in the pot hailed from the same broad family: Collards, turnips, kale, and mustard are all brassicas, the European-Asian plant family that also gave us the kohlrabi, cabbage, radish, and rutabaga. Every green in this family is nutritious and worthy of consumption, but sometimes collards take too long to cook to become toothsome, and turnip greens seem gritty no matter how carefully you wash them. Those that wish some bite to their greens favor mustard. And discerning Georgia appreciators of mustard prefer the tender green curly mustard to the old southern Florida broad-leaved type or the small round-leaved white mustard.

Capable of growing to substantial size, seed for the giant curled mustard was broadcast in a corner of the kitchen garden in autumn and the sprouts culled when thumb high so that the healthiest were spaced widely enough (eighteen to twenty-four inches) to let the plants have room to expand. Mustard seeds are small and distinctively black, differing in color from the white and yellow seed mustard varieties used in pickling and making prepared mustard. California, not Georgia, is where yellow seed mustard has been grown. Augusta, Georgia, however, was where the old scalloped-edged curly mustard plant was bred into its most spectacular, ornamental, and tender form, the "ostrich plume" curled mustard. In 1896 the Howard & Willet Drug & Seed Company of Augusta launched this variety: "Only listed by us. New. Leaves are long, exquisitely crimped, ruffled and frilled, that move and look like beautiful green crimped ostrich plumes. Originated here. Limited amounts for sale next fall. Better eating than the Curled Mustard. Pretty enough for a centre table ornament. A field of it is the prettiest of all vegetables. One plant this season weighted five pounds." It was from ostrich plume strain of curled mustard that the Dutch horticulturist Abraham Sluis bred the southern giant curled mustard variety that won in 1935 the rarely awarded gold medal for vegetables by the All-American Selections. He bred in cold tolerance, speed to maturity (full grown in forty-five days), and uniformity of configuration. The old ostrich plume would sometimes grow overlarge. The gold medal winner topped out at a convenient twenty-four inches in height. Since 1935 the southern giant curled has

Giant southern curled mustard, a gaudy and flavorful green, perfected in Augusta during the 1890s. Photograph © David S. Shields.

been the standard greens mustard of the region and the first choice for cooks. You can buy seed at Burpee, Park Seed, Ferry-Morse, Harris Seed, Osborne, and Willhite Seed.

The culinary uses of mustard greens were varied. Since it was substantially more tender than collards or kale, it could be used as a fresh salad plant. "Baby" plants—twenty-four days old or thereabouts—could be picked, ripped, and served with one's favorite dressing. Like all greens, it could be boiled, usually with a piece of fatback, a hock, or a chunk of jowl. Because turnip greens could taste rather innocuously mellow, many Georgians cooked the half turnip-half mustard greens pot described by Mrs. H. A. Price of Thomson, Georgia, in the *Fayetteville Favorite Foods Cookbook* (133). Traditionally the formula for preparing mustard as a pot green was simple—so simple that instructions did not appear in cookbooks or newspaper recipe columns. Greens + jowl + salt and pepper in water. Boil one half hour. In the 1920s adding a chicken bouillon cube to the pot, thyme, marjoram, or some other aromatic herb became standard practice in many households. Hold the sugar—fine with collards—not good with mustard.

Sautéing or braising mustard greens may have begun on a large scale with the breakfast dish mustard greens and eggs. Originally cooked down in oleomargarine or bacon grease, this 1930s southern dish changed in the late twentieth century when olive oil became a default for sautéing vegetables. Some add garlic for punch. There are two ways to make it. The baked version detailed in a December 15, 1976, issue of *The Atlanta Journal* has you cook down the greens, form nests out of them, crack an egg for each nest, and bake the dish until the eggs are firm. The other method has you cook the greens with chopped spring onions, and when they are well rendered in the skillet, add the eggs and seasonings in a scramble. Now, sautéed/braised mustard greens are a common side in meat and three establishments.

Bourbon Braised Mustard Greens and Potatoes

KEVIN MITCHELL

This dish brings back memories of being in the kitchen with my grandmother Doris. I am a huge fan of keeping things simple. I wanted to find a way to cook greens that were vibrant green. Instead of stewing them for an extended period, I blanch them in boiling water with salt and baking soda. Blanching the greens maintains the bright green color. Adding baking soda will help remove some of the bitter flavor of mustard greens. Here, most of your time with this dish is the prep work. Once blanched and your potatoes are parcooked, you only need to cook them briefly in the bacon-onion mixture with an added bourbon kick.

Serves 6 to 8

(continued)

3 pounds mustard greens (see Note)	1 cup diced onion
1 tablespoon baking soda	2 teaspoons minced garlic
1 pound Yukon Gold potatoes, peeled and diced	1 teaspoon red pepper flakes
	1 cup good quality bourbon
4 cups chicken stock	1 teaspoon sugar
8 ounces thick-sliced bacon, diced	Salt and pepper to taste

Bring a pot of heavily salted water with the baking soda to a boil.

Rinse greens well. Remove stems and thick veins; tear leaves into 4- or 5-inch pieces. Add greens in batches until the leaves wilt and the color brightens for 1 to 2 minutes. Drain greens and immediately place them in ice water to stop cooking. Once cooled, remove the greens and squeeze out as much moisture as possible. Reserve.

In a separate pot, boil potatoes in salted water until fork tender. Drain and reserve.

Over low heat, cook bacon in a large braising pan until the fat renders and the bacon begins to brown. Add onion and garlic and cook until onions are translucent, about 5 minutes. Add red pepper flakes and cook for 1 minute. Add bourbon and cook for 2 minutes. Add boiled potatoes and stock. Cook for 5 minutes, long enough to warm through. Add blanched greens and sugar and cook until they are warmed. Adjust seasonings with salt and pepper. Serve.

Note: To save time, purchase washed and precut greens from your local grocery store.

Bourbon braised mustard greens and potatoes by Kevin Mitchell. Photograph © Rhonda Mitchell.

Ogeechee Limes

Georgia is home to a unique fruit preserve. Harriet Ross Colquitt supplied a recipe for Ogeechee lime preserves in her classic *The Savannah Cook Book* (1933). Unfortunately her headnote to the recipe, suggesting that the Ogeechee lime was "a local variety of the Spanish Lime—*Melicoco Bijaga*," was misinformed. The olive-shaped dark red fruits were called "Ogeechee limes" because of their tart taste and because naturalist William Bartram, who first described the fruit, encountered them on the banks of the Ogeechee River at the end of the eighteenth century. The limes are fruit borne by female trees of the tupelo, the *Nyssa ogeche*. Because the nectar that bees draw from the blossoms of the tupelo tree and transformed into the famous tupelo honey, popular notice focusses on that splendid food and less so on the acidic fruit to which the blossoms give rise. But the inch-long fruit found its champions too. Colquitt observed that "The negroes can always find a ready market for 'Geechee limes during their short season, for they are considered a great delicacy, preserved, with meat and game."

Colquitt celebrated the preserved Ogeechee lime as a relish accompanying meat. But the Gullah Geechee people who foraged the wild fruits and sold them in market, had a different understanding of their merits. Planter Gugie Bourquin, who had extensive orchards of grapes and tupelo trees on his lands along the Ogeechee road, supplied the *Savannah Morning News* with some observations about how the saltwater Geechee used the fruit in 1890: "[They] eat them in the raw state, as they say the fruit has virtues of an anti-malarious character, which physicians corroborate, and during the month of September, when the malaria rises from the rank vegetation of swamp regions, it looks as if the Ogeechee lime fruit is one of the wise provisions of nature to ward off malarious attacks." The pungency of the flavor signaled its efficacy as medicine, for "a lemon is sweet by comparison to an Ogeechee lime."

The mouth-puckering acidity of the lime suggests why cooks intending to make use of

Nyssa ogeche fruits. Watercolor by Deborah Passmore, 1902. Courtesy of the USDA Pomological Watercolor Collection, Beltsville, Maryland.

[117]

the fruit paired it with sugar. Bourquin allowed that "the fruit, although quite sour, is considered the most desirable for preserving, and commands good prices in the market." Colquitt instructed boiling the fruits before submerging them in simple syrup as whole fruit preserves. Because her recipe called for alum (an aluminum sulfate salt) in the processing of the fruits, and because of alum's known toxicity in large amounts, we will not reproduce her recipe here. Instead we will take an older Lowcountry recipe (1880s) preserved in manuscript signed "Mrs. Thomson."

Ogeechee Limes

Mrs. Thomson (1880s)

Cut the sharp ends off, prick each one with a fork, pour boiling water upon them one night & repeat it in the morning. To each lb of fruit put [1½] lbs of sugar & to each pound of sugar, 1 pint of water. Boil until the limes are clear & begin to break, then take them out of the syrup and continue boiling the syrup until it can stand on your nail.

The proportion of sugar to fruit indicates precisely how sour the limes were. It was said that the best state to pick the limes for preserving was just prior to their being fully ripe. The tendency of the fruit when cooked to turn translucent made them a candidate for being made into a clear jelly as well. In 1935 when the Joseph Habersham Chapter of the Daughters of the American Revolution (DAR) held its twenty-ninth anniversary Georgia Products Feast in Atlanta, it included Ogeechee lime jelly to accompany its course of corn bread and hot rolls.

Large tupelo trees can grow to forty feet high. The limbs of female trees tend to grow out horizontally from the trunk, and males perpendicularly. Mature trees often have flat crowns. The oval-oblong deep green inch leaves are noteworthy for their whitish undersides, giving the tree the nickname of "white tupelo." The blossoms (March to May) are white and profuse, the fruit pale to reddish, and the autumn foliage gaudy and parti-colored from yellow to purple red. The tree has a decided preference for wet—and it grows most densely in and around the margins of swamps.

Oils

A lot of frying goes on in southern cooking. Chickens, fish, oysters, okra, fritters, potatoes, pies. Rendered lard reigned as the medium in which all these foods cooked for the first two centuries of southern cookery. There is a problem with that. Lard is expensive. You have to raise a pig to get it (see our entry on lard). Because a lot of things were fried, the making of food could be costly. Early in the nineteenth century people were looking for cheap alternatives. People knew that certain plants produced lipids that could be used as both a frying medium and lubricant for salads.

Spanish colonizers brought the olive with them to Florida, and, if the archaeological record is to be trusted, to Georgia, at Tolomato near Darien in 1587. Anglo-American colonists imported olive oil and olive trees. In 1787 Thomas Jefferson memorably announced, "The olive is the tree least known in America, and yet is the most worthy of being known." He secured five hundred for distribution to planters throughout the Southeast. But the effort to established olive groves in the American South was one long tragicomedy. Experimental farmers planted trees in Virginia, North Carolina, South Carolina, Georgia, Florida, and Louisiana. High humidity, cold snaps, and a host of other problems did the plantings in. Georgia proved the single most successful locale for olive planting in the Southeast. James Hamilton Couper planted two hundred trees on St. Simons in the antebellum period. These matured and produced sufficient fruit for small-scale oil production and brining, but were decimated by periodic freezes. Thomas Spalding, the pioneer sugar planter on Sapelo Island, maintained a grove of imported Italian trees that also produced table olives and oil. The oil was advertised in the Darien newspapers. Saltwater inundation from tropical storms did in the trees. The longest-lived olive planting occurred on Cumberland Island. When General Nathaniel Greene obtained the island in the 1780s, he found mature olives planted, survivors from Spanish plantings from the settlement of San Pedro de Macamo. His widow, Catherine, planted a substantial donation of olive trees from Thomas Jefferson, supplementing the surviving Spanish trees. The grove at Dungeness Plantation was famous and trees survived well into the twentieth century. Coastal nurseries sell scion wood from "Jefferson Olive Trees" that descend from the Cumberland plantings, even though Dungeness House has long been in ruins, and the lands have become a nature preserve. The dream of Georgia olives has been kept alive. Georgia Olive Farms in Lakeland since 2011 has offered oil pressed from Arbequina olive, a reputable Spanish oil variety. The product has a tropical note, an undertone of banana along with the classic pepper, butter, and tomato leaf flavors.

Olive oil produced in the 1800s was local, intermittent, and variable in quality. California quickly eclipsed Georgia's efforts. The difficulty of growing olives early turned Georgians attentions elsewhere. Governor Milledge thought the oil from the benne plant (sesame) would be the answer—that tale is told in our entry on benne. Yet during the decades during the nineteenth century when benne oil and peanut oil were being pressed for culinary use, the great desire of Georgia planters was not to grow more benne or peanuts, but to take the foremost cash crop in the state, cotton, and turn its oily seeds into money. There was a problem, cottonseed oil had a harsh flavor—so harsh that cattle would not eat the crushed seed as fodder. Its unsuitability for culinary employment was recognized from the first. An 1820 article touted it as lubricant for shoe leather and possibly machines. In 1829 two Virginians designed the first hulling machine designed for hulling cottonseed to ease oil expression. However it did not trigger an explosion of production. In 1833 Lancelot Johnston coated his house in Madison, Georgia, with paint using cottonseed oil as a base, inviting every curious member of the public to visit and "see for themselves." J. Hamilton Couper, having experienced the limits of olive oil production, began pondering the possibilities of cottonseed oil in the 1840s. Again he thinks its utility lies as a lamp oil or as a paint base, not as a frying medium or salad oil (1845). The first commercial seller of cottonseed oil in Georgia was John Oliver of Savannah in 1861. The need for lubricants by the Confederate forces in the Civil War kickstarted the cottonseed oil industry in Georgia. But the expansion of the uses of the oil to culinary applications had to await the ministrations of food chemist David Wesson, who refined the stink out of the substance, made it taste neutral, and hydrogenated it to serve as a lard substitute. Cottonseed oil factories began to sprout across the state, in Augusta, Rome, Savannah, Atlanta, Brunswick. It quickly became fixed in the center of Georgia's cookery. In the Georgia Products feasts, Dublin stipulated that the Oconee channel catfish be fried in cottonseed oil. The Wesleyan College menu submitted as one of Macon's entries indicated that the Bibb County tomatoes be served with a mayonnaise made from cottonseed oil. Milledgeville, Rome, and Waycross did the same. When the boll weevil arrived in 1915, having spread through the Cotton Belt from Mexico, 5.2 million acres in the state grew cotton. The destruction by the weevil caused acreage to decline precipitously with each passing year. Soon cottonseed oil plants stood vacant. It was then that George Washington Carver counseled farmers to look to the peanut. Cottonseed oil plants became peanut oil plants. The rise of peanut oil is described in our entry on peanuts.

One of the curiosities of the history of culinary oil was that from the time of David Wesson in the 1890s until the 1990s was that the manufacturing ideal was to make an oil as bland or as taste neutral as possible. Wesson's insight—a key principle of modern food processing—is that tastelessness is a virtue since it permits the incorporation of an ingredient in any food without provoking disgust. People object to things with decided flavors.

Immediately after World War II food chemist Herman Kresse of Texas suggested eating the immature pod of the okra plant was unintelligent. He counseled, "We should let the pods mature, extract the maximum nutriment from the soil, and consume the seeds extracted from the dried pods." He was one of the "scientifically-created food" visionaries of the postwar era. The scientists at Louisiana State University (LSU) heard what Kresse preached. Horticulturist Dr. Julian C. Miller of LSU began extracting oil from okra seeds for use by the Wesson Oil

Co. of New Orleans. The oil Miller secured was made on the Wesson model—odorless, colorless, and nearly tasteless. This ultimately doomed the Louisiana experiment because in the northern United States large-scale planting of canola (rapeseed in the early twentieth-century literature) supplied an easily processed prolific source of culinary oil. Since there was no flavor difference between tasteless okra seed oil and tasteless canola oil, the cheaper canola prevailed.

But what if okra seed oil was permitted to have its original, distinctive flavor? This is the question that Clay Oliver asked a decade ago. In 2012 he converted his farm in Pitts, Georgia, into a manufactory for culinary-grade oil. He began first with sunflower oil, since the plant grew readily in his section of Georgia, and the oil had a high smoke point making it useful for frying. He looked at other locally produced plants that could serve as the basis for oil and immediately began pressing pecan oil, a sumptuous finishing oil. Peanuts were next. His reading in Georgia's history with oil inspired him to revive benne oil. He found a steadily

Oliver Farms, the pride of Pitts, Georgia. Photograph © David S. Shields.

growing clientele with his products, a gratifying press notice of his work, and recognition in the form of American Food Awards. This emboldened him to his most daring experiment, reviving okra seed oil in 2016, but in its twenty-first-century version, allowing it to have its intrinsic flavor. Chefs were stunned by its lusciousness. Problems sourcing sufficient stocks of okra seed have forced Clay Oliver to keep his production at the small-batch level. But the resultant scarcity has made it that much more desirable among the chefs who are his chief advocates.

Prize-winning oils from Oliver Farms, left to right: benne seed oil, green peanut oil, okra seed oil, and pecan oil. Photograph © David S. Shields.

Okra

> Actually, of course, okra is one of the most heroic of all vegetables. It has done far more for mankind than mankind generally realizes.
>
> —Dick West, "The Okra Papers," 1964

Okra was brought to the New World with enslaved Africans on the Middle Passage. Native both to Africa and parts of Asia, the okra possesses a variety of ancient forms; it is not simply the green finger-shaped pod growing heavenward on a six-foot stalk. Jon Jackson, of Comfort Farms in Milledgeville, Georgia, grows motherland okra from seed secured in West Africa. This is a different species, *Abelmoschus callei*, not the common *Abelmoschus esculantes* commonly grown in the United States. Motherland okra's pods are like squat swollen barrels; its stalk towers twelve feet high; its dark green leaves are ruffled and vast. How different the leaves are from the smaller, rougher, less numerous leaves of the American-grown okra plants. This is because Africans in the South stopped eating the leaves as greens. European settlers had brought over a plentitude of greens from the Brassica family—cabbage, collard, mustard, turnip, beets—that more than filled the place of their West African potherbs, amaranth, benne, *Adansonia digitata*, and okra. Okra leaves did not preserve as well as the pods did when dried. They tended to crumble into powder. The dried pods could be reconstituted in the stewpot with hot water. In the South the okra became all about the pod.

Okra belongs to the mallow family, and is kin to the cotton and the hibiscus plant. Africans regarded it as one of the most important ingredients they took in the African diaspora, that movement of not only people, but culture from one space to another. With this movement of people, we see that the existence of okra not only is in Africa, but in Brazil, Asia, Australia, the Middle East, Europe, South and Central America and of course in the American South as well.

Being a member of the mallow family, okra's texture matters as much as its flavor. Its texture is "slippery" or mucilaginous. People not from Africa or the South sometimes object to this quality, saying okra is "slimy." But we agree with African diaspora expert and author Jessica Harris who advises, "Let's stop fighting the mucilaginous vegetable. Let okra do its own magnificent thing, after all it's only doing what comes naturally." The flavor is vegetal, agreeable, and distinctive. It resides primarily in the oils in the seed and pod. When Clay Oliver of Oliver Farms in Pitts, Georgia, began pressing okra seed oil for culinary use several years ago, the oil's lovely "okra intensity" won instant converts. Chefs purchased all he could manufacture as a finishing oil for salads and vegetables.

Okra's texture and flavor enable it to be paired with an array of other ingredients, specifically tomatoes, as seen by the recipe included below. No matter the variety, and there are many, okra has mucilaginous property, which makes it highly prized for its thickening capability. This could be why the most popular way to cook okra would be in either soups or stews.

The okra's mucilage can be used in one's beauty regimen. The "slime" contained in okra resembles the texture of aloe. There are beauty products that have okra as a base ingredient, such as Jayjun Okra Phyto Mucin Deep Enhancing Cream or Nabia Okra Balancing Facial Moisturizer and Toner. As author of the *Passport to Beauty*, Shalini Vadhera, states, it is a Zimbabwean tradition to used boiled and mashed okra pods as skin hydrating face mask.

In the nineteenth century okra seed was something people got and saved on a home-by-home basis, and there were lots of diversity in coloration and shape—red, yellow, white, orange, barrel, long skinny, cowhorn shape. At the end of the nineteenth century commercial seed companies decided on certain shapes. The Perkins mammoth pod, bred by M. Perkins, a truck farmer in New Jersey, became the standard long green. White velvet, originally an Alabama landrace, was developed at about the same time. This variety became one the most popular during that time. It is now included on the Slow Food's Ark of Taste. (The Ark of Taste is a living catalog of delicious and distinctive foods facing extinction. By identifying and championing these foods, they are kept in production and on our plates.) An early green dwarf okra was the third biggest seller and dominated the market until the Clemson spineless in 1939.

Chris Smith's book *The Whole Okra: A Seed to Stem Celebration* lists four varieties developed in Georgia. These would be the survivors of old nineteenth-century varieties. The first variety is the Mama Payton, a Georgia/Alabama heirloom varietal. It was grown by Arthur and Carrie Payton when they were given the seed in 1917; they grew this variety exclusively. Second is the old German. This variety has been grown by the Jones family since 1862 in Macon. Third is the Sea Island variety. This is said to be a traditional variety of the Gullah Geechee community, which was labeled as the Ethiopian red okra. This variety is growing at the University of Georgia Center for Research and Education at Wormsloe in Savannah. Sarah Ross, executive director of the center, was given seed from Cornelia Bailey, who was a seed-saving matriarch on Sapelo Island. Last is the UGA red, developed by the University of Georgia in Athens (UGA) in 1985. This variety is a cross between the red wonder and the dwarf green long pod.

Pods growing heavenward, this heirloom Perkins variety of smooth, tender okra is ready to pick. Photograph © David S. Shields.

The saltwater Geechee on the Sea Islands of Georgia gave rise to a distinctive way of processing okra in the nineteenth century. To ensure that they would have a stock available for making okra soup during the winter months, when fresh pods were not available, they would string fresh pods in the summer and dry them on the roofs of their houses. After they had dried crisp, the okra strings came off the roof into the cabin and would be reconstituted in hot water when making a stew or soup. Frozen okra supplanted this old method of preparation, but in the twenty-first century, freeze-dried okra has become a snack food offered in chain grocers under the name Okra Chips. They are delicious.

Okra soup stood at the heart of the antebellum repertoire of recipes for the vegetables. In 1846 a writer to the *Augusta Chronicle* urged that "a large mess of okra soup (called gumbo) should be served on every plantation at least four days in the week, while the vegetable is in season. The pods are gathered while still tender enough to be cut with the thumb nail; cut into thin slices, and with tomatoes, peppers, &c, added to the rations of meat, forms a rich mucilaginous soup." Lowcountry okra soup always has some sort of meat in it. One feature of nineteenth-century preparation of the soup was the length of time cooking—five hours or until the consistency of the soup was "like rags" with no intact okra slices. It remains central to the Gullah Geechee food culture and exemplifies the creativity of African people in a new land, melding the okra of the motherland with the tomatoes and peppers of the Americas.

Fried Okra Fingers

KEVIN MITCHELL

Who doesn't like fried okra? Most fried okra recipes contain cornmeal. This recipe contains rice flour and cornstarch, which makes it lighter and gives you a great crunch. I love the flavor the berbere spice gives the okra, and the addition of tomato powder and onion powder reminds me of my grandmother's stewed okra and tomatoes.

4 cups vegetable oil for frying
1 pound okra pods, sliced lengthwise
1 egg, beaten
¾ cup rice flour (see Notes)
¾ cup cornstarch

1 teaspoon berbere seasoning (see Notes)
1 teaspoon tomato powder (see Notes)
1 teaspoon onion powder
¼ teaspoon salt, plus more

Heat oil in a Dutch oven or fryer to 350°F.

Put the okra in a large bowl and toss with the beaten egg. Let the okra stand for 5 minutes to absorb the egg.

Whisk the rice flour, cornstarch, berbere, tomato powder, onion powder, and ¼ teaspoon salt in a separate medium bowl.

Remove the okra from the large bowl, allowing the excess egg to drip back into the bowl, then transfer the okra to the flour mixture. Toss the okra to dredge evenly. Lift from the flour and shake off the excess.

Cook the okra in batches in hot oil until golden and crunchy, 3 to 5 minutes, depending on size. Remove with a slotted spoon and place on a paper towel-lined plate. Season with salt immediately. Repeat with the remaining okra.

Notes: If you don't have rice flour, all-purpose flour works well. Berbere, a spice mixture from Ethiopia, usually includes chili peppers, coriander, garlic, ginger, and fenugreek. It can be purchased in most specialty grocery stores in the spice aisle. You can also use Cajun spice or barbecue spice in place of berbere.

Tomato powder may also be found in specialty grocery stores or purchased online.

Fried Okra Fingers by Kevin Mitchell. Photograph © Rhonda Mitchell.

Oysters

You've heard it said that it must have been a brave fellow who first ate an oyster. It ain't necessarily so. Surely the first peoples who lived on the Atlantic coast, the ancestors of the Guale, Yamasee, and Timucua peoples saw raccoons stuffing bivalves in their mouths down on the margins of coastal creeks during low tide. Anything relished so enthusiastically was and is worth a try. The huge shell rings on St. Simons and Sapelo Islands attest to the importance of oysters to the diet of the woodland population in the Late Archaic period, from three to four thousand years ago. The bladelike shells found in the middens resemble those of the oysters now found along the Georgia coast, soft-lipped *Crassostrao virginica* growing in clusters along the tidal estuaries and bays. Fortunately, given the pristine character of much of the water along the hundred-mile coastline, the flavor of the present-day oyster—with its brininess, meaty mellowness, and hint of acid (lemongrass? citrus?)—hews close to those savored by the first islanders.

Oyster eating originally was an outdoor affair. Shell fishermen and women pried apart the creatures in the open air eating them raw, or roasted them on heated flat rocks. These oyster feasts began in autumn and continued until May, when the shellfish's reproductive cycle made the oysters get skinny and odd flavored. The outdoor oyster feast revived in the 1880s and 1890s, when the Chesapeake-style oyster feast began to be emulated in South Carolina and Georgia. Held in the open air, a metal sheet was laid over the fire and oysters were placed on the heated surface until they opened. Each guest had a napkin and an oyster knife to assist in extracting the oysters. The host provided beverages and several sides.

Coincidently with the new popularity of the oyster feast, a brand of Georgia oyster appeared—Thunderbolt oysters. Thunderbolt, on the tidal Wilmington River in Chatham County, became the first important brand name of oysters in Georgia. Alfred Haywood, dealer in fine comestibles, sold it in his Savannah store in 1849. Benjamin H. Crandal, Savannah policeman and avocational waterman, began forwarding samples of the salty and fat Thunderbolt oysters to newspapermen in 1851. The editor of the *Savannah Morning News* observed, "The fame of the Thunderbolt Oyster has never been sung. It should be, and if we were in favor with the celestial Nine, we would invoke their aid that we might immortalize our friend Crandal and the oysters of Thunderbolt in the same verse." In the economic disarray after the Civil War, Thunderbolt oysters proved, along with watermelons, to be a vendible commodity with a ready sale in northern markets. J. H. Gould, a Savannah broker, organized the distribution of Thunderbolt oysters northward and into Georgia's interior. Bresnan's Hotel and Restaurant at 100 Bryan Street in Savannah became the headquarters of Georgia's oyster lovers. It served the famous Long Island varieties and alongside them, Thunderbolts! Demand ignited and vast quantities were harvested at Thunderbolt and shipped from Savannah.

The story then becomes the usual tale of everyone trying to cash in on the success. Two hundred boats tonged for Chatham County oysters. Dr. Arminius Oemler in 1889 announced "the fact that the oyster beds of Chatham and Bryan Counties are being rapidly depleted." Unsustainable harvest was crisis enough, but in 1888 extraordinary rainfall caused the salty and brackish rivers to flood with fresh water, disrupting oyster reproduction. Oemler drafted a law to restrict harvesting until the population became reestablished. His efforts failed. Instead of conservation, Henry Ambos built a large oyster plant, and dispatched a fleet of a dozen sloops to systematically dredge the grounds.

Ambos's enterprise, development, the use of the Wilmington River as an outlet for Savannah's domestic sewage in 1896, and poor management of the grounds (no rebuilding of oyster rocks) led to the exhaustion of the beds. The Casino Restaurant in Savannah still advertised Thunderbolt oysters as its draw in 1904 and 1905. But people were sending the restaurant seaside oysters from Daufuskie and Sapelo Islands and labeling them Thunderbolt oysters. When the chamber of commerce of Chatham County forwarded their menu in November 1913 to the Georgia Products campaign listing Thunderbolt oysters as a featured course, the famous oysters were more memory than actuality. Those served by the Hotel Ansley came from a private oyster ground in Tifton, Georgia, one of the few patches of Thunderbolts that hadn't been picked clean.

If oyster harvesting faltered in Wilmington and adjacent rivers early in the twentieth century, it thrived in other parts of the coastal waterways. Eight million pounds of shellfish were landed and processed annually in Georgia at the dawn of the twentieth century. But the problems plaguing the Thunderbolt oyster eventually spread southward along the coast. Overharvesting caused a crash of the oyster industry generally in the 1940s. The last shucking house closed in the 1960s. Small-scale commercial harvesters persisted, but in 2016, they landed only thirty-two thousand pounds of oysters. Farming oysters in cages—the technique that revived the Virginia oyster industry in the twenty-first century—was prohibited until 2019 in Georgia. Only the UGA oyster hatchery on Skidaway Island supplied spat to enable the rebuilding of coastal oyster populations. Its output was insufficient to stock the nineteen leased areas that commercial oyster farmers attempted to develop. Getting spat from out of state required approval of sources, and only two hatcheries were preapproved by Georgia regulators. So as you are reading this, the odds are that the oysters you are being served in Georgia restaurants and raw bars come from out of state. A shame, because the flavor of Georgia-grown oysters is quite distinctive, combining the salt of a Virginia seaside oyster with the mellow wholesomeness of pre-Hurricane Michael gulf and a unique lemongrass tinge.

Georgia's oyster cookery borrows from old English classics such as oyster pie and oyster soup (both dishes not prepared now as much as once were), pickled oysters, french-scalloped oysters and oyster omelet, and then the trio of classic coastal favorites: fried oysters, oyster fritters, and pigs in blankets. Fried oysters and oyster fritters differed primarily in the coating enveloping the oyster before dunking in boiling fat. Fritters used a flour-based batter, fried oysters an egg wash and cracker-crumb coating. Sister Mary, the Jazz Age Georgia food columnist, gives the primordial versions of these classic dishes. Reading these, remember that washing and draining the shucked oysters is now considered a practice sacrificing their intrinsic flavor.

Fried Oysters

Sister Mary, *Americus Recorder* (November 24, 1924)

Eighteen large oysters, one lemon, cracker dust, cracker crumbs, one egg, salt and pepper. Wash and drain and pick over oysters. Sprinkle with the strained juice of the lemon. Season the cracker dust with salt and pepper. Roll each oyster carefully in the cracker dust and let stand a few minutes to absorb. Roll again in the cracker dust, dip in the egg slightly beaten with one tablespoonful of water and roll in the coarser crumbs. Fry about three minutes in deep hot fat. Drain on brown paper and serve at once. It is a saving of time and money to fry oysters in deep fat rather than in a small amount of fat in a frying pan.

Oyster Fritters

Sister Mary, *Americus Recorder* (November 24, 1924)

Twelve large oysters, one egg, one teaspoon salt, three-quarters cup flour, one-half cup milk, pepper. Beat yolk of egg till thick. Add milk and continue beating. Add flour and beat to a smooth batter. Add salt and pepper and fold in white of egg beaten stiff. Wash, drain, and pick over oysters. Dip each in batter and fry in deep hot fat. These fritters may be served with tomato sauce [cocktail sauce].

Pigs in Blankets

Sister Mary, *Americus Recorder* (November 24, 1924)

Twelve large oysters, twelve thin slices of bacon, tooth picks, lemon juice. Wash, drain and pick over oysters. Sprinkle with lemon juice. Roll each oyster in a slice of bacon and fasten with toothpick. Heat a frying pan very hot and put in the prepared oysters. Cook, turning frequently until the bacon is crisp and brown all over.

Peaches

If Georgia is the Peach State, then Fort Valley is the reputational capital for this is where the bulk of Georgia's peaches grow. A spur line of the Macon Railroad opened there in 1851, permitting the large-scale shipping of produce from the fertile groves planted in Fort Valley during the nineteenth century. The seemingly unlimited demand for peaches and nectarines in the United States during their sixteen-week season from mid-May into August emboldened growers to plant huge orchards in the 1870s and 1880s. Georgia became nationally significant in peach production in the 1870s. From 1870 to 1875, Samuel Henry Rumph developed what would become the nation's most popular peach, the Elberta (Mrs. Samuel Rumph's name) at his Willow Lake Plantation near Marshallsville. This peach had exceptional size, color, and texture. It could withstand the travails of shipping. The tree fruited profusely. But most importantly, it ripened early. It was the first showy peach of the year to appear in the produce section. The Elberta had yellow flesh. The Belle of Georgia peach, developed by Rumph's uncle Lewis, had white flesh and was less acid. Two other important commercial peaches originated in Fort Valley: the Hiley variety and the Hale. These were also early and also gaudy.

Travel by train entailed much time and handling. Mass shipment of Fort Valley

Elberta peach. Watercolor by Deborah Passmore, 1898. Courtesy of the USDA Pomological Watercolor Collection, Beltsville, Maryland.

Belle of Georgia white peach. Watercolor by Amanda Newton, 1913. Courtesy of the USDA Pomological Watercolor Collection, Beltsville, Maryland.

peaches dated from 1889. Substantial portions of the crop would spoil during the four-day voyage until the development of refrigerated shipping—first the ice chest box, then the refrigerated boxcar. The availability of first quality fruit in New York City's markets did much to amplify demand. The Elberta's reign as boss peach in the American market would last nearly six decades.

Fortunately, the history of Georgia's peach industry has been well served with an excellent book, William Thomas Okie's *The Georgia Peach* (2016). Okie emphasized the role that pioneering pomologist and horticulturist P. J. Berckmans of Augusta played in promoting the idea that one could plant trees on the scale that one planted cotton, establishing a commodity during the Reconstruction Era. Berckmans's conviction that alternatives might be had to the pernicious soil-killing culture of cotton in southern agriculture made him look to the nascent antebellum citrus industry in Florida for organized planting, shipping, and plant propagation models. Berckmans saw stone fruits as a set of paths forward. He introduced the heat-tolerant peento peach (what we now call a Saturn, donut, or flying saucer peach) in cultivation. He made Augusta the first center of peach farming in the state, before Fort Valley. In the nursery catalogs of Berckmans's Fruitlands Plantation, Berckmans's vision came to fruition. By 1920 there were eighteen million peach and nectarine trees planted in Georgia. While nectarines were a secondary crop in Georgia, from the 1850s when Coleman Farm made them a specialty to the present day, select growers made them a priority.

A problem with concentrated plantings of a single fruit variety is that such monoculture cropping proves an ideal place for pathogens to thrive. Viruses mutate to exploit the available biological hosts. Consequently, Georgia's peach orchards have had to wrestle with disease for the last several decades. A grower must contend with brown spot, peach scab, bacterial spot, leaf curl, gummosis, powdery mildew, phytophthora, plum pox, and "short life." All peach orchards of any size in the state undergo regimes of spraying with fungicides and germicides. Because of the vulnerabilities of the Elberta and the belle of Georgia to diseases, their cultivation has been suspended for the most part in favor of new highly productive disease-resistant varieties that are adapted to the changing climate.

Another problem with mass plantings is that at a certain point your supply exceeds demand. By 1926 the peach boom in Georgia reached a critical point. Too many farmers had gotten into the business. The market glutted with fruit. The prices dropped. Persons who had bought into the business on credit couldn't make debt payments. Two years before the Great Depression hit the nation, Georgia's agricultural sector tanked. Only the oldest established planters with strong commercial ties continued to be solvent. When the peach industry emerged from the Great Depression and the redirection of the economy by the war effort for World War II, Georgia found itself no longer the great power in the peach world. California grew more fruit. Indeed, South Carolina, using Georgia as a model, had built a more robust and productive peach sector. So, since the mid-twentieth century Georgia has been the third-ranked producer.

Still, during its supremacy, Georgia conceived of splendid things to do with peaches.

The trinity of peach ice cream, peach cobbler, and peach pie have made many a summer bearable. Peach cobbler being the state dish inspires vehemence among its champions. It *must* have a biscuit crust; that crust *must* have a tinge of sugar in it; the peach filling *must* be given an extra tang with lemon juice. Yet we've never heard anyone argue about which variety of peach to use, aside from the observation that white peaches won't do. "It's gotta be a yellow peach."

Beginning in the late 1990s a dessert contest was held in Peach County, Georgia. Its results document the creativity of bakers wishing to get beyond the ice cream, cobbler, pie standards. At first the exploration was modest: In 1998 cheesy peach pie and peach-strawberry cobbler won. But innovation quickly appeared. The following year rewarded peach bread pudding with peach sauce and EZ peach cheesecake pie. The millennial year crowned peaches and cream dessert squares. In 2001 rolled peach dumplings and peach bread prevailed. Then in 2002, frozen peach parfait and peach poundcake with peach schnapps frosting. But it may not have been in the realm of desserts that the peach has made its most striking culinary advances. Peach Salsa has developed a strong following in a very short period of time, and peach and hot pepper sauces for meat and game have proven winning. Peach barbecue sauce became "a thing" in the first decade of this century and appeared as an accompaniment to pork chops. The smoke of mesquite coloring peach barbecue does magical things.

Peach Barbecue Sauce

Fort Valley Leader-Tribune
(October 29, 2008)

2 tablespoons olive oil
1 small red onion, peeled, sliced thin
3 peaches, pitted, cut into medium sized cubes
2 medium ripe tomatoes, cut into medium sized cubes
½ cup cider vinegar
½ cup orange juice
⅓ cup light or dark brown sugar
Salt and fresh ground black pepper

In a large skillet over medium-high heat, heat the oil until hot, but not smoking. Add the onions and cook, stirring occasionally, until golden brown, about 11 to 13 minutes. Add the peaches and tomatoes and cook, stirring frequently for 2 minutes. Stir in the vinegar, orange juice, sugar, salt and pepper, to taste. Bring the mixture to a boil, then reduce the heat and simmer until the mixture is reduced by about ½ and thickened slightly, about 20 minutes. Taste and adjust for the seasoning, then transfer the sauce to a blender or food processor and puree until smooth.

Peanuts

Boiled peanuts. Peanut oil. Peanut butter. Peanut candy. And peanut hay for cattle. Even in these days when peanut allergies frighten parents and imperil children, the vast majority of Georgians hold these humble "nuts" (Do we really need to tell you they are a legume and not a nut?) in their hearts. Georgia sent one of its peanut farmers to the White House.

Time was when boiled peanuts were a seasonal treat. The first green peanuts became available to the public in the last weeks of August. From then until the end of October scoops of green peanuts in the shell were dumped into cauldrons or vats of salted water (sea water on the islands) and simmered until they "got slippery." Boiling peanuts was more southern than American, more country than city, more outdoor than indoor, and some would say more male than female. The kind of peanut changed over time. In the 1800s the small Carolina African runner peanut prevailed. Then in the early twentieth century, when the four-peanuts-in-a-pod Valencian Tennessee red skin peanut began to be grown widely as hog food in Georgia, that variety supplanted the Carolina. Later in the twentieth century the highly productive modern runner peanut varieties dominated. No one boiled the big Virginia peanut, or its relative, the jumbo—you roasted those.

Green peanuts went into the vat of boiling brine in their shells. The soil in which one grew the peanuts influenced the porosity of the shell, so no set time existed for boiling the pods. You "boiled them a while" and often let them sit in the brine thereafter to make sure salt seeped into the nuts. When old time Georgians invited neighbors to gather in the backyard around the peanut kettle the event was called a "pindar boiling," after the archaic nickname for the peanut.

Green peanuts are undried raw peanuts freshly dug from the soil. They contain a good deal of moisture (above 30 percent) and cook quickly. Most raw peanuts are cured and dried (down to 10 percent moisture). Until the 1960s these were not generally used for boiling because of the longer cooking time they required. Augusta media personality and peanut entrepreneur John Vance pioneered the use of dry raw peanuts in the brine pot in order to make boiled peanuts a year-round treat. He found a thin-walled runner peanut variety that reduced the long cooking time somewhat and inaugurated the era of the year-round boiled peanut. The advances in freezer technology in the last quarter of the twentieth century enabled processors to freeze green peanuts. When May comes, the peanuts are thawed and shipped to grocers for public sale. So nowadays we have green peanuts available in stores for half a year—a technologically protracted "season."

We regret to say that John Vance's other great innovation in peanut processing failed. The french-fried peanut, a crispy fried raw peanut, salted and flash fried in green peanut oil. It premiered in 1961, and quickly passed into history. There was something about the woodiness of the fried pods that prevented them from seeming fully crispy.

Green peanuts start appearing in grocery stores in late May, because freezing has permitted the in-shell cured peanuts to be preserved over winter. When the season begins to hint of the end of the school year, green peanuts "for boiling" are thawed for sale. Photograph © David S. Shields.

One can roughly date the origin of a peanut candy recipe by the sweet element involved. Molasses—cheaper and more plentiful—dominated antebellum formulae. Cane syrup, brown sugar, and white sugar are hallmarks of candy recipes from 1870 on. There were two classic peanut candies: pea-nut cakes and ground nut cakes. Two April 1882 newspapers give recipes to these two ancestral peanut candies.

Pea-Nut Cakes

Sandersville Herald (April 27, 1882)

Pound one pint of roasted pea-nuts to a paste in a mortar; mix in one pint of light brown sugar and the whites of five eggs beaten to a stiff froth. Put the mixture into small buttered pans and [bake] the cakes light brown in a moderate oven.

San Domingo Ground Nut Cake

Atlanta Weekly Constitution
(April 25, 1882)

Put half a cup of cold water in a sugar boiler; add two pounds of light brown sugar; set it over the fire and boil until a little of it dropped in cold water becomes brittle. Meantime, shell roasted pea-nuts sufficient to make two quarts; when the sugar reaches the point above indicated at once remove it from the fire, stir in the nuts, and drop by the tablespoon on an oil or wet marble slab, slightly flattening each cake with the spoon. Cool and use.

Ground nut cake here sounds like a form of peanut brittle, and not much like the patties sold on the street corners of Savannah, Charleston, and Philadelphia by Black confectioner-vendors until the late 1910s. The identification of the cake with San Domingo derives from Philadelphia commentary on the street candies. No one in Charleston or Savannah believed they hailed from anywhere other than the city in which they were being sold. It was an old candy—the first recipes calling for molasses—and the later nineteenth-century versions indicating sugar or cane syrup as the sweetening, lemon as a flavoring, and cream as something to provide smoothness.

But peanut confections became something of a public obsession around 1916. Georgia had invested heavily in the creation of cottonseed oil plants across the state, turning waste seeds into Wesson Oil. Then the boll weevil came, wiping out the cotton crop. Oil factories stood idle in numbers of Georgia towns until George Washington Carver declared that southern farmers better look to the peanut for their economic salvation after cotton failed. Peanuts produced excellent oil, and they began being planted on an industrial scale in Houston County. Local citizens were encouraged to think creatively about what might be done with the peanut. From 1916 on we see newspapers documenting experiments with peanut fudge, peanut bread, peanut dressing for turkeys, peanut pie, and peanut ice cream. Yet the most consequential innovation in foodways would be what was done to the mash—the leftover matter after the oil had been extracted. A little sugar, a little salt . . . voila! Peanut butter.

Fascination with peanut butter exploded. The Acme Sanitary Market in Americus, Georgia, began manufacturing it in late July of 1916. When the consumption austerities were imposed during World War I, peanut butter found itself listed by USDA bulletin 332 as a meat substitute, boosting its public profile. Peanut butter manufacturers organized. In Atlanta the Sunshine Peanut Company and Savannah's Dixie Peanut Company competed for customers. The wartime propaganda about peanut butter being a protein equivalent to meat became fixed doctrine in the public. In 1921 Mrs. S. R. Dull, Georgia's cooking oracle, declared "Peanut butter is rich in protein, which everyone should know is equal to meat in rebuilding or making tissue, and can be classed as a concentrated food." This is how you claimed something was a superfood a century ago. Perhaps the most trenchant advice she gave to housewives who were contemplating adding peanut butter to the pantry is "peanut butter is better not kept in the ice box."

Joseph Kellogg, the pure grains physical culturist, patented peanut butter in 1895 as a substitute for cow's milk butter. Two years earlier a panic over the possibility of milk-borne tuberculosis scared the vegetarian wing of the physical culture movement into believing that butter would kill. So a campaign for lipid substitutes for butter drew attention to nuts as an answer. Kellogg created peanut butter and served it to the well-heeled clients who made use of his sanitarian for body cleansing. The problem of his peanut butter is that it presented an inch of oil sitting on an inch of roasted peanut mash. It was minimally salted. In Georgia, peanut oil factories syphoned off the oil, leaving only the mash. Companies that set themselves up as peanut butter companies, crushing, roasting, and pressing their own peanuts, sold off their excess oil to manufacturers of peanut oil.

From the first peanut butter as a sandwich spread won favor. Other ideas had less traction. Steamed rice with a topping of peanut butter was offered on some hotel menus of the 1918–1925 period. Few Georgians now doubt that the most consequential culinary development of this period was the peanut butter cookie. The first forms of this cookie, however, did not greatly foreshadow the glorious confection to come. They were created during World War I's austerities, using rye flour, molasses (no sugar), and sour milk. The classic peanut butter cookie appeared in print in 1928.

Peanut Butter Cookies

Atlanta Journal (October 14, 1928)

1 cup sugar
¾ cup peanut butter
3 teaspoons baking powder
2 eggs
½ cup sweet milk
1 teaspoon vanilla
½ teaspoon salt
Flour to make dough stiff enough to handle and roll out (about 4 cups)

Beat eggs together till light, add sugar and peanut butter, mix well, then add milk, salt, vanilla and part of flour with baking powder, stir into the mixture, adding enough flour to make stiff enough to handle; sift flour on rolling board and knead till smooth, roll out one-fourth in thick, cut and bake in moderate oven about ten minutes. This will make about fifty cookies.

The future of Georgia's peanuts may depend on medical science's ability to ascertain why peanut allergies have risen in the population since the middle of the twentieth century. Are the chemicals sprayed on peanut fields to thwart mosaic virus to blame? Has the treatment of soil triggered changes in the peanut plant that in turn trigger somatic responses in children? At this juncture the answer is not clear, and the public trepidation about peanuts as food grows.

Pears

Pear chutney and pear relish have long been Georgia pantry staples. Both featured the hard "sand pears" grown in peoples' backyards. Fire blight prevented home growers from planting trees for the buttery textured French pears that could be eaten fresh plucked from the tree. This terrible bacterial disease caused oozing cankers to appear on trunks and branches and could kill trees outright. It plagued apple and pear groves throughout the region. Asian pears, however, had disease resistance to fire blight. Their fruits were roundish, hard, and ugly looking—mottled brownish green. But they would mellow in storage and cooked with sugar they made toothsome preserves. If you didn't call them sand pears you tended to called them "cooking pears".

Fire blight is native to the American Southeast and comes in waves over the landscape wreaking havoc. Infested trees wither blossoms and foliage looking scorched and blackened. From the antebellum period onward fruit breeders have attempted to cross European pears with Asian pears in order to secure the latter's disease resistance with the flavor and texture of French beurre pears. The LeConte, pear, a natural cross between a European and a hard Asian pear, was a bell-shaped custard yellow pear promoted by Major John Eatton LeConte after its initial fruiting in Liberty County Georgia in 1856. Major LeConte's father, the naturalist Louis LeConte, had planted numbers of pear varieties at Woodmasten Plantation before his death in 1838. Two of these varieties gave rise to the tree from which all LeConte pears derived. The greatest virtue of the variety was its adaptability to nearly every climate zone in the United States, from North Florida to Michigan. Propagated by cuttings, the LeConte pear requires a pollinator partner of another pear variety to set fruit. It proved somewhat blight resistant, and prolific in most settings. When properly ripened it proved a strong market variety in the South. Less grainy and hard than Asian pears, the LeConte could be eaten fresh, but its great virtue was as a cooking and canning variety.

The LeConte pear enjoyed a boom in popularity in the period after the Civil War with many hundreds of acres cultivated in Georgia, Alabama, Mississippi, North Florida, South and North Carolina (1882). Commercial pear culture in the South can be said to date to the general embrace of this variety during the Reconstruction era. Indeed, the hunger for cuttings became so pronounced that some carelessness attended the selection of plant material and certain trees were found to be inferior bearers (1884). The variety's resistance to blight proved to be moderate, and the Kieffer pear, another Asian-European cross, supplanted it in numbers of southern orchards in the 1890s because of its greater blight resistance.

In every part of Georgia, orchards of Asian pears, LeConte pears, and Kieffer pears were planted throughout the nineteenth century. Now we have varieties that are better at melding Asian blight resistance and European flavor and texture—the Orient pear, the Baldwin, and to a lesser extent the Spalding. But the habit of turning backyard pears into chutney, gingered pears, and relish had deeply fixed. Old pear trees full of cooking pears and LeConte's remain for the experiments of the home canner.

When it came to cooking pears there were several dishes that mattered, each having a period of popularity before receding and giving way to the next important preparation. Early in the twentieth century gingered pears ruled. In the 1950s pear chutney came into vogue. Now, one of the oldest preparations, pear relish reigns.

Gingered Pears

Savannah Tribune (August 24, 1918)

Take coarse and firm pears, peel, core and cut into thin strips. To 8 lbs of pears chipped very thin, allow 8 lbs. of sugar. 1 cup of water, juice (and rind) of 4 lemons, cut in thin strips and ⅛ lb of ginger root cut into pieces. Simmer until transparent. Pack into jars and seal at once.

Pear Relish

Marietta Journal (August 29, 1935)

1 peck pears
6 large onions
6 green peppers
1 bunch celery
6 red peppers
Put through food chopper
3 cups sugar
1 tablespoon salt
5 cups vinegar
1 tablespoon allspice

Mix and let stand overnight. Put in jars and process 20 minutes in water-bath at simmering temperature.

A peck is 8 dry quarts of something. Current canning safety instruction would counsel a higher temperature water bath and sterilized jars.

Ginger Spiced Poached Pears

KEVIN MITCHELL

My son Kevin Jr. loves pears of any variety. His favorite way to eat is right out of the bag from the grocery store. I convinced him to try them another way, and he loved it, especially with a scoop of his favorite vanilla ice cream. Try it for yourself!
Makes 12 pears

(continued)

3 cups sugar
2 quarts (8 cups) water
1 quart (4 cups) pear brandy
1 12-ounce can of ginger beer
1 teaspoon ginger paste (see Notes)

3 cinnamon sticks
3 star anise pods
1 teaspoon fresh lemon juice
12 pears, peeled, stem left intact (see Notes)

In a deep 4-quart Dutch oven, combine all ingredients except the pears. Bring the mixture to a boil. Reduce heat slightly. Simmer for 10 minutes. Add pears. Place an inverted ceramic plate over them to ensure pears are entirely submerged in poaching liquid. Cook covered for 15 to 20 minutes. Remove pears from heat and let stand until completely cooled.

Once cooled, cut pears in half lengthwise and remove the core with a melon baller or spoon. Place pear halves in a one or a few glass jars and fill with poaching liquid (see Notes). They can be served at room temperature with your favorite vanilla ice cream. If not serving right away, place in the refrigerator for later use.

Notes: Ginger paste can be found in most grocery stores. If not, use a small piece of fresh ginger.

I used Bartlett pears. You also can use Bosc or Anjou pears. Cooking times may vary.

The extra poaching liquid can be placed in a sauce pot and cooked until a syrup consistency has been achieved and served as a sauce or a simple syrup for cocktails.

Ginger spiced poached pears by Kevin Mitchell. Photograph © Rhonda Mitchell.

Pecans

The pecan is Georgia's favorite nut. Yet for all the fervor of Georgians' love for the pecan, it shocks many to learn that it is not native to the state. The range of the wild pecan extends from East Texas to Mississippi, skirting the Mississippi River up to Illinois and along the Ohio River into Indiana. Every pecan grown in Georgia is an "improved pecan," a variety bred by humans for nut production. By 1924 Georgia led the nation in production of "improved pecans" as a nut crop.

Most Georgians had never tasted a pecan prior to their importation into the state in the late 1840s by W. W. Goodrich of Savannah. These were wild-harvested nuts shipped from Galveston or New Orleans. According to legend, Captain Samuel F. Flood found nuts floating at sea and his wife planted them in St. Marys in Camden County, Georgia. His seedling trees bore abundantly, and he undertook small-scale trade in the nuts along the southeastern seaboard. The centennial was the first "improved pecan" distributed for commercial orchards, released in 1876. Willie Taylor of Frederica was the first experimental grower of pecans, having begun his grove with a Flood seedling. He successfully budded pecans on hickory rootstocks in the 1880s.

Serious cultivation of the pecan only began in the late 1880s. Nurseryman P. J. Berkmans of Augusta explained why he began offering trees after initial reluctance in 1891: "Pecan culture is rapidly increasing, there being few trees that yield as regular and larger income after they attain the bearing age, which is at 8 to 10 years after planting. . . . The Pecan tree is difficult to graft, but as the sub-varieties, of which there are many, reproduce themselves at the rate of 60 to 70 percent, and thus the variation being small, we offer mainly seedling trees grown from the largest Paper-Shell nut obtainable in Louisiana. These vary in number from 60 to 70 nuts to the pound." Perhaps the most active early promoter of nut cultivation was W. D. Beatie of Atlanta Nurseries. Beatie sold almonds, chestnuts (Spanish and American), filberts, pecans, and walnuts—in the 1880s and 1890s, the pecan was the novelty among his listings. By the end of the nineteenth century it dominated

Nearly ripe, these Schley pecans should be dropping in two weeks. Photograph © David S. Shields.

his sales. Small-scale growers, such as Dr. J. D. Reed of Savannah, began appearing in the mid-1880s. G. W. Bacon of DeWitt, Georgia, was the first large-scale commercial grower in the state, with fifty acres of paper shell pecans that he vended through the S. W. Bacon Fruit Company of Atlanta beginning in 1896.

Early vendors of pecans shelled and roasted the nuts, sometimes salted them. The use of pecans in confections didn't occur on any scale until the 1920s. Pecan candy (sugared and spiced) was a San Antonio signature, pralines a New Orleans emblem, and pecan pie a Texas invention. All made their way to Georgia and became naturalized in local foodways during the Jazz Age. The Christmas season became particularly associated with pecan confections. The earliest pecan candymaker in Georgia was M. T. Elam of Americus, who offered homemade pecan candies at his store in 1911. Kamper's Store in Atlanta offered Lillian's Orange Pecan Candy and Bob's Pe-Kons through the 1920s. When the National Nut Growers Association met in Cuthbert, Georgia, in 1924, the exhibition of pecan treats "attracted much attention. Pecan cakes, all kinds of pecan candy, pecan butter, preserved pecan meats in jars and cans, salted pecans and sugared pecans were some of the attractions." What kinds of candy? Pecan pralines, pecan divinity, pecan caramels, pecan rolls, pecan fudge, chocolate-covered pecans, and pecan and coconut candy. The sugared pecans recipe below reflects the old practice of cutting the pecans into brick-like clusters. Now the preference is for individually sugar-coated nut meats—this is achieved by breaking the amalgam apart.

Sugared Pecans

Atlanta Journal (January 11, 1925)

2 cups of pecan nuts
3 cups sugar
1 teaspoon butter
1 cup water
½ teaspoon vanilla
Pinch of salt

Cook sugar and water until it threads; remove from fire. Stir until it becomes creamy; add vanilla, salt and nuts; pour into a buttered dish to harden; cut into squares. Use butter to grease dish.

The formula for pralines did not differ greatly. Vanilla was eliminated, maple flavoring added, and brown sugar was substituted for white sugar.

Pecan cake has evolved into myriad forms—orange pecan cake, butter pecan cake, honey pecan cake. In many of these cakes, pecans are more an ornament than the heart of the confection. The following recipe from autumn of 1940 makes finely chopped pecans the body of the cake.

Pecan Cake

Atlanta Journal (November 10, 1940)

3 cups pecans, chopped to the fineness of coarse corn meal
1 ½ cups sugar
6 eggs
2 tablespoons cake flour
2 teaspoons baking powder

2 cups whipped cream
1 teaspoon vanilla
¼ cup powdered sugar

Beat egg yolks and sugar together until they bubble. Mix baking powder, flour and chopped nuts lights with the stiffly beaten eggs whites and fold this carefully into the egg mixture. Bake in two layers in pans lined with waxed paper and well greased. Cook in moderate oven for 15 or 20 minutes. Let cool in pans. Put together with whipped cream, powdered sugar and vanilla. Cover top with same.

One of Georgia's most significant encounters with the pecan occur in the late 1930s when W. S. Stuckey Sr., added Ethel Stuckey's pecan roll to the line of offerings at his roadside pecan stand in Eastman, Georgia. Demand grew and Stuckey built a candy factory and distribution center in Eastman, servicing a growing number of branch stores. The range of pecan offerings expanded in 1952 when Stuckey's introduced flavored pecans in vacuum-sealed metal tins. Flavors included maple, cinnamon, salted (now sea salt), and orange. Over time, kettle-cooked joined the lineup, orange dropped away, and a separate line of chocolate-covered nuts premiered. Packaging morphed from tins to plastic bags. Famed for their billboards placed on well-traveled highways of the eastern seaboard, Stuckey's expanded in the 1960s, reaching a maximum of 368 outlets in over thirty states. This sort of growth required capital, and consequently Stuckey's merged with Pet Milk Company in 1964. The acquisition of Pet Milk by Illinois Central Industries and the death of W. S. Stuckey Sr., in 1977 triggered the decline of the brand. The new owners shuttered stores, threatening the existence of the chain. In 1984 W. S. Stuckey Jr., intervened, buying the brand back and sought to rebuild. Fortunately, it had a product that still exerted a pull on the hearts of consumers: the pecan log roll—a tube of nougat tinged with maraschino cherry, wrapped in caramel and coated with chunks of pecan. Currently Stephanie Stuckey is CEO and has made numbers of acquisitions of other pecan producers, secured a new manufacturing facility, and has built a strong online presence. As of this writing there are sixty-eight locations and more than two hundred retail outlets. Eastman, Georgia, remains the distribution center for Stuckey's products.

Pecan orchards remain vibrantly in production across Georgia, and some of the larger producers maintain roadside retail outlets, identifying pecans by variety and offering a range of in-shell and shelled products. Some of the regionally respected outlets include Georgia Pecan Farms, Pearson Farm, and Lane Southern Orchards in Fort Valley; Ellis Brothers Pecans in Vienna; and Merritt Pecan Company on Highway 520, between Columbus and Albany.

Persimmon Beer

Not all of Georgia is apple country—only that region north and west of a line drawn from Augusta through Macon to Columbus. Nearly all of Georgia is home to the American persimmon. When it came to country beverages in the era before convenience stores, cider was the home brew for a minority of citizens; more drank persimmon beer. It remains a country treat among lovers of old-time beverages.

Fermented, yet nonalcoholic, persimmon beer was the cherished refreshment at barbecues, catfish fries, oyster roasts, and all outdoor events in the Georgia countryside. Made of the ripened fruit of American persimmons, honey locust pods, water, and sometimes sugar, this cloudy liquid was both tangy and sweet, fresh, yet mellow. It was Kombucha before Kombucha—a ferment whose microbial content was an aid to digestion and full of antioxidants. Adding sugar or syrup will boost alcohol creation. Numbers of the most old-school brewers of persimmon beer do without, but the coming of Prohibition made sugaring the mix a popular path, pushing the beverage over the 3.2 percent alcohol threshold that laws held as the intoxication line.

Recipes abound for persimmon beer. As with most DIY home-brewing favorites, a great deal of variety crept into formulations as individuals tried impressing their own vision on the beverage. Some added cornmeal, others molasses, chunks of sweet potato, some sassafras roots or twigs. Yet the core recipe was simple, effective, and flavorful. H. P. Stuckey, director of the Georgia Agricultural Experiment Station, provided this recipe in 1921, at the height of the interest in manufacturing persimmon beer.

Persimmon Beer

H. P. Stuckey, *Americus Times-Recorder* (September 28, 1921)

Persimmons, 2 bushels
Honey Locust, 5 pounds
Bread yeast, ¼ cake
Water, 10 to 12 gallons

Select a good clean barrel that has one head, and will hold water. Bore a hole for a faucet in the side of the barrel, down at the bottom next to the head. Set the barrel on a table in a room that will be kept moderately warm, that is one having a temperature ranging from 60 to 70 degrees F. Put a layer of clean wheat or oat straw in the bottom of the barrel thick enough to come a few inches above the faucet hole to serve as a filter. Next mash up and thoroughly mix the persimmons, locust and yeast cake in some convenient receptacle. Put the mixture in the barrel, pour the water on top of the mixture, and tie a cloth over the top of the barrel to exclude insects. The beer will be ready for use from six to ten days later, and should be examined from time to time to determine this point. After the beer becomes ready for use, if the barrel is set in a cool place, the beer will remain good several days longer.

Golden hued, a touch effervescent, sharp and fresh tasting with an undernote of honey and caramel apple, persimmon beer has nothing crude about it. Some served it iced, but the vast majority sipped it at room temperature. Some persons gained a large reputation for their persimmon beer. Mrs. E. E. Watson of Atlanta garnered national notice when she supplied a hundred gallons for president-elect William Howard Taft's Georgia banquet given in 1909. Her fame grew so great that thieves would nick the barrels of fresh brewed persimmon beer she kept on her back porch on Richardson Street.

In feasts honoring Georgia food, persimmon beer is the inevitable accompaniment of possum 'n taters. As the editor of the *Tifton Weekly News and Sun* said in 1909 when commenting on the proper beverage to accompany possum, "Persimmon beer, by all means, on the score of 'eternal fitness of things,' the ''possum' being a meat peculiar to the land of 'taters,' and 'simmons' would be an incongruity alongside champagne or the farcical beer substitute. Might as well serve turkey minus cranberries as 'possum minus 'simmon beer.'" Persimmon beer was also thought an ideal partner to ginger cakes.

Persimmons grow on every type of soil in Georgia. Corn farmers used to plant persimmons on the perimeter of their fields to distract deer who preferred the fruit to the ripe ears. There are male and female trees, so they thrive only when they grow in communities. Wise brewers wait until the persimmon tree has dropped its leaves, leaving the ripe fruit exposed and dangling on the branches. Then the fruit will have lost its acrid quality and ripened into a sweet substance somewhere between "a baked apple and soft custard" (1945). Florida fruit nurseries introduced Asian kaki persimmons into southern cultivation in the 1890s, but these, despite their excellent qualities, were not used for making persimmon beer. Only the native American variety was used.

Honey locust (*Gelditsia triacanthos*) is a native tree, famed for its thorns and its sweet pods of seeds. The pulp of the pods when ripe were eaten by Native Americans. And the pulp was combined with persimmons in brewing beer. There were commercial attempts to extract sugar from the pods in the nineteenth century, suspended because it was so much easier to secure it from sorghum; but the chemistry of the honey locust is interestingly complex—indeed it is a natural vehicle for stenocarpine, cocaine, and atropine, hence its extensive use by shamans and homeopathic folk doctors in eastern America. Despite its plush chemistry, it has never been reckoned poisonous (the fate of its close relative the Kentucky coffee tree) and has had extensive culinary employment. The pods were used as fodder for pigs and goats and, when broken up, for chickens. But the pulpy pods were beloved by thirsty humans who used them as a base for brewing honey locust beer, a mildly alcoholic brew, or persimmon beer.

While honey locust pods were the other major component besides persimmons in the brew for the nineteenth and early twentieth century, the sweet potato began to supplant it in recipes in mid century. Harvesting locust pods (they were knocked down with a bamboo pole) was more difficult, because of the locust tree's many thorns, than digging a few sweet potatoes from a nearby field. Convenience won out.

Persimmon beer has throughout its history always seemed antique, imperiled, rare, and deep country. Someone is always lamenting that it is vanishing. But there are always people making it. Today it remains a kind of cult favorite DIY beverage among homesteaders. An 1871 newspaper snippet from Savannah announced, "Persimmon Beer, a relic of the past, has turned up in Columbus." Like crackling bread it is one of those traditional foods that is always fooling people into believing that it is not around or that it is on its way out the door. Don't believe it.

Pickles

Summer's bounty does not last long. The plentitude of vegetables and fruits—the okra, tomatoes, green beans, cucumbers, cauliflowers, peaches, and cherries—have their seasons of harvest and are gone, unless one uses one of the ancient methods of preserving them: drying, salting, sugaring, fermenting, or pickling. Pickling preserves vegetables, fruits, and some meats by bathing them in brine or vinegar in a sterile container. Lacto-fermented preparations such as sauerkraut are classified by some as pickles. And in older cookbooks (think of Savannah resident Mary L. Edgeworth's 1860 *Southern Gardener and Receipt Book*) catsups fall under this category.

Georgia did not commercially brew vinegar. People purchased it at the grocery store—usually apple cider vinegar, usually manufactured in the North (except for during the Civil War). When sugar became cheap in 1825, people could make home-fermented berry wines using sugar as the alcohol engine. Some of their fruit wines turned to vinegar, and this was of course used.

Pickling in the eighteenth and nineteenth centuries was not like that of our grandmothers and great-grandmothers in the twentieth century. In the nineteenth century, alum (hydrated double sulfate of aluminum) was frequently added to vegetable pickles to keep cucumbers, shredded cabbage, and green beans crisp and bright green. Now that it is known to be toxic in larger doses, it is usually not employed in pickling. Then too, there were categories of items once popular in Georgia pickles that do not make it into the mason jar today. Our great-grandmothers stopped pickling grapes, green walnuts, immature musk melons, radish pods, nasturtium leaves, and green peaches. Finally they decided there was too much labor for payoff in making a compound pickle, called a mango. A mango pickle called for an unripe cantaloupe or peach, boiled in hot brine, sliced on one side, from which you removed the seeds/pit. Then you filled the cavity with chow-chow and immersed the whole thing in flavored vinegar. This complicated pickle was a favorite until the Great Depression and then disappeared.

Many popular pickles are not particularly Georgian: dill pickles, sweet cucumber pickles, chowchow, piccalilli, pickled peppers, pickled cabbage, pickled beets, pickled eggs, and pickled oysters are part of a broad southern, if not American, kitchen repertoire. We will, however, treat Georgia's favorite tomato pickle in the entry on Green Tomatoes. If you wish a classic chowchow recipe, refer to that found in Nathalie Dupree's *Cooking of the South*—you'll find it on page 39.

We have suggested the important changes in pickling over the last century. Now we turn too the enduring features. The formula for spiced vinegar has hardly changed in two centuries. If we look at Mary Edgeworth's spiced vinegar recipes we find the full range of spices to be used in vinegar in her Higdon pickle: "To each gallon a quarter of pound each of black pepper and black mustard-seed, one ounce each of turmeric and mace, three ounces of cinnamon, one tablespoonful of ground mustard, three cloves garlic, some horseradish, and a few onions." Ewell & Cooke, druggists in

Savannah, supplied Georgia's towns and cities with "Long pepper, turmeric, ginger, Cinnamon, Cloves, Nutmegs and mace" from the turn of the nineteenth century. Pharmacists since the colony's founding in 1732 had some of these spices in stock, given their quasi-medicinal status. The spice formulation for pickling vinegar was not wholly or even primarily driven by a quest for novel flavor; it was restorative and tonic, compensating in some measure for the loss of nutritive potential in the pickled ingredients by reason of no longer being fresh. Perhaps the most remarkable ingredient added to some vinegar formulas after the turn of the nineteenth century was brown sugar. You can see the changes in pickle formulas wrought by the availability of cheap sugar from Sapelo Island in the transformation of brine-and-spice pickles to sweet-vinegar-and-spice pickles. Take Georgia's iconic pickled peaches. First the brine-spice version, then the sweet version.

To Pickle Peaches

Mrs. Mary L. Edgeworth,
The Southern Gardener and Receipt Book (1860)

Take your peaches when they are at their full growth, just before they begin to turn ripe; be sure they are not bruised; then take spring-water as much as you think will cover them, make it salt enough to bear an egg, then put in your peaches, and lay a thin board over them, to keep them under water; let them stand three days, and then take them out and wipe them very carefully with a fine soft cloth, and lay them in your glass jar; then take as much good vinegar as will fill the jar; to every gallon put two or three heads of garlic, a good deal of ginger cut fine, half an ounce of cloves, mace, and nutmeg; mix your pickle well together, and pour over your peaches. Cover them. They will keep for three months.

In the early twentieth century when USDA instructors began educating home canners on sanitation, this recipe would be altered to ensure that the vinegar and spice mixture would be boiled before being poured into the sanitized jars.

Pickled Peaches

Marion Harland, *Atlanta Journal*
(August 22, 1915)

Peel firm white freestone peaches, dropping each into cold water as it is pared. Take the fruit from the water, weigh it: allow three pounds of sugar and two cups of vinegar to six pounds of fruit. Stick a whole clove in each peach, arrange the fruit and sugar in layers in a preserving kettle, and put the vinegar on to heat in another vessel with two tablespoons each of cloves, cinnamon, and mace to the six pounds of fruit. The spices must be tied up in a muslin bag and left in the vinegar for five minutes after it comes to a boil. When the sugar and peaches have stewed together for five minutes after boiling, the vinegar may be added to them and all boiled gently until the peaches are tender, but not broken. Take them out with a skimmer, spread on flat plates, and boil the syrup until thick. This will require about fifteen minutes. Put the peaches in jars, turn in the syrup, and seal while boiling hot.

T. H. Shaw of Amelia Island, Florida, across the sound from Georgia's Cumberland Island, successfully developed lemon culture in the United States early in the nineteenth century. From the 1830s onward, lemons from the coastal islands and Cuba were available in quantity in Georgia. Consequently, many coastal Georgians developed a taste for the salty Lemon Pickle that the English had adopted from Indian cuisine during the colonial era. The pickle went particularly well with rice-based dishes and enjoyed popularity in coastal Georgia.

Lemon Pickle

Mrs. Mary L. Edgeworth,
The Southern Gardener and Receipt Book (1860)

Slice six lemons; Rub them with salt; lay them in a stone jar, with two ounces each of allspice and white pepper, and one fourth ounce each of mace, cloves, and cayenne, and two ounces each of horse-radish and mustard seed, pour over them two quarts of hot distilled vinegar; after standing for a few days, strain. Some add garlic or shallots.

Despite the claims of a San Antonio, Texas, housewife, Mrs. P. Koclanes, to have invented okra pickle in 1934, and despite the commercialization of okra pickle by Texas companies in the 1950s, the first okra pickle ever offered for sale took place in Savannah in 1851 by G. M. Willett & Company. Well before Texans laid claim to it, jars of pickled okra appeared in state and county fairs all over the South. The earliest award, an honorable mention in the 4th Annual Anderson, South Carolina, Farmer's Association Fair, took place in 1871. Nevertheless, the first national distribution of okra pickles took place in the 1950s by a Texas company from San Angelo. The innovation of the Texas style of okra pickle was the hot pepper in the mix. In Georgia the default was for okra pickles without red peppers, either sweet or salty and spiced. A classic Georgia okra pickle recipe employs dill as its primary flavor complement.

Dilled Okra

Atlanta Journal (August 17, 1961)

3 pounds young uncut okra
Celery Leaves
Garlic
Fresh Dill
Brine:
1 quart water
1 pint vinegar
½ cup salt

Pack washed and dried okra in pint jars with celery leaves, 1 clove of garlic and flower and stem of dill. Make brine and bring to boil and pour on okra and seal. Let stand 3-4 weeks before using.

Pimento Cheese

Many southern cooks claim pimento cheese as a specialty, and many southern states insist that the kind they produce is superlatively fine, quintessentially local, and strikingly distinctive. South Carolina boasts its pimento cheeseburger. Louisiana touts its creole pimento cheese. North Carolina insists that its Queen Charlotte pimento cheese hews closest to the original formula for pimento cheese, having a cream-cheese base. But Georgia has the strongest case of all, for the pimento pepper used by every southern state in the twentieth century—the perfection pimento—was bred in Griffin.

A pimento pepper is a "sweet pepper," as red, but sweeter, fleshier, and more aromatic than its relative, the red bell pepper. Spanish in origin, the imported pimiento first captured American taste buds as the stuffing for green olives in the decades after the Civil War. Attempts to breed a cheaper American version of the pepper that still preserved the smooth skin, three- to four-inch length, and volcanic red color did not succeed, until S. D. Reigel of Spalding County, Georgia, in 1911 secured seed for the Valencian variety and successfully grew a copy that reproduced all of the Spanish pepper's original virtues. Sometime in 1912, Reigel found a sport (mutant plant) growing among his Valencia pimentos, a plant bearing a fruit with decidedly thicker walls. He called the line he propagated from this sole plant the "perfection pimento." Almost immediately the Reigel family established a canning plant for roasting, peeling, and preserving the peppers, since most users of pimentos preferred using the canned peppers with their skins removed. Their product proved such a success that the countryside around Macon became covered with perfection pimentos.

Pimento cheese, alas, was not invented in Georgia, or anywhere else in the South. It came into being in New York early in the 1870s and used cream cheese as its base, along with imported canned Spanish pimiento. It became Georgian after the Reigel family supplied perfection pimento peppers and neighboring South Carolina provided Duke's Mayonnaise. The standard southern formula combined Cheddar, pimento, and Duke's Mayonnaise. Whatever tweaks beyond that marked out individual cooks' house styles.

J. L. Kraft & Brothers introduced its Kraft Pimento Spread sometime in 1915. It was a cream-cheese-based spread, decidedly blander than the "Cheddary" version that Georgians embraced in the 1920s. Kamper's Grocery on Peachtree Street in Atlanta stocked Kraft Pimento Spread in winter of 1918. Elkhorn Pimento Cheese was Kraft's chief rival on grocery shelves during this period. The majority of the pimento cheese provided filling for sandwiches, and it was also spread on fresh slices of apple as a snack.

The first recipe supplying directions for household cooks appeared in the "Haskin's Question Box" column of the *Augusta Chronicle* on November 23, 1919.

How to Make Pimento Cheese

Augusta Chronicle (November 23, 1919)

This can be done by mixing once cup of finely chopped pimento with one cup of grated cheese. Add as much salt, paprika and onion juice as desired.

Already Georgians were stepping away from the northern cream-cheese base for pimento cheese. Home cooks would not propose mayonnaise as the moisture base and binder for the preparation until this Savannah recipe of 1921. It is noteworthy for specifying a grating cheese to be used: "good, snappy American cheese."

Pimento Cheese

Savannah Tribune (September 15, 1921)

A most delicious cheese may be prepared at home in a small fraction of the cost usually paid for such an article. Take one-fourth of a pound of good, snappy American cheese, put through the meat chopper, also grind with three hard-cooked eggs, three or four canned pimentos. Alternate the egg and peppers through the grinder to save the juice of the pepper, season with salt and cayenne, add mayonnaise dressing to moisten, and put away to chill.

For a dish that didn't exist at the dawn of the century, it had assumed tremendous prominence by the end of the century. There was no corner of the state that didn't consider it their own. Every home cook had a tweak: a drop of tabasco sauce, sour cream, garlic, cayenne, olive fragments, a teaspoon of sugar, Vidalia onion juice, Dijon mustard, Worcestershire sauce, bacon, or jalapeños. When the *Atlanta Journal-Constitution* ran a recipe contest for pimento cheese in 1996, readers submitted more than 150 entries . . . for a dish largely made up of three ingredients. Must the cheese be Cheddar? No—Monterey Jack has a strong following. But we will say right now that a version using goat cheese we experienced two years ago violated the sense of the dish.

In the 1990s controversy erupted about those persons who used red bell peppers instead of pimentos and had the audacity to call their preparations pimento cheese. There should be no controversy: The answer is no. Some of the greatest plant breeders in the United States—S. D. Reigel, Georgia's Dr. H. L. Cochran, South Carolina's Dr. Richard Fery—exerted extraordinary genetic expertise to ensure that the finest of all pimento peppers would endure in the face of increasing disease pressure in southern fields. The Truhard perfection pimento pepper kept the pepper available through the latter half of the twentieth century, and in the twenty-first century the Truhard-NR pimento gives the vegetable nematode resistance. What stands as the greatest threat to the Georgia pimento? The closure of pepper canning plants in the state as this sort of food processing migrates overseas.

While pimento cheese is easy to make at home, many people for whom convenience is a priority buy it prepared at the grocery. Several southern-made brands have won followings, albeit labeling laws require most retail chains to characterize the products as "spread" rather than "cheese." Queen Charlotte's Original Pimento Cheese Royale comes from North Carolina and uses Monterey Jack as its base, with other cheese varieties added. Callie's Hot Little Biscuit Traditional Pimento Cheese from Charleston contains Worcestershire sauce in its formula. More traditional is Price's Rich and Savory Pimento Cheese Spread from Texas—a true Cheddar, mayo, and pimento mixture. Publix Cheese Spread with Pimentos (Florida) contains a tincture of sugar and a creamy consistency that hearkens back to the cream-cheese-based spreads of the early twentieth century. Most homemade pimento cheese opts for a chunky texture, and from Greensboro, North Carolina, Emmy's Original Pimento Cheese could be mistaken for fresh-made, home-prepared cheese, so if you are trying to fool your guests. . . . There is also one small-batch commercial Pimento Cheese from Georgia that deserves your attention. Proper Pepper Small Batch Pimento Cheese, founded in 2015, won an American Cheese Society award in 2019. Demand is great, so sometimes there is a wait upon supply. Jalapeños give this cheese its edge.

Creative minds have thought about how to use pimento cheese beyond its classic employment between two pieces of bread. One brilliant inspiration was to incorporate it into the bread itself. Pimento cheese corn bread, like that served by the Honey Café in Millen, Georgia, is a revelation. Grilled pimento cheese on slices of sourdough bread combine bold flavor with homey charm. Still, classics are classics for a reason. When one thinks of food experiences that speak of Georgia, having a Cheddary pimento cheese sandwich at Augusta National Golf Course must rank near the top.

Poke Salad

In late March foragers begin hiking the Georgia countryside seeking wild food: cressy greens, dandelion, poke salad (aka "poke sallet"), and ramps. The spring harvest is one of the oldest of Georgia's foodways. Its persistence this deep into the age of mass-produced vegetables reveals how strongly the tonic flavor of first growth greens has imprinted itself on the imaginations of an enduring group of seekers.

Not everyone is a believer. There are, sad to say, several kinds of detractors. Among foodies the ramp, scarcer, and more pungently flavored enjoys fashionability, while the milder poke salad, because it grows more generally, has become déclassé. As early as May 1955 commentators in the *Atlanta Journal* noted a divide in public feeling about *Phytolacca Americana*/poke salad: "This is poke salad season in Georgia—a time for renewal of the controversy between those who side against, and those who defend the lowly pokeweed. (Proponents recoil at the use of the word 'weed,' choosing to call it the poke salad plant). A sparkle lights the eyes of those with affirmative notions as they dwell on the taste wonder of poke leaves from shoots short and tender parboiled with sidemeat . . . the cynics are many and articulate. They insist poke salad tastes like mustard and smells of Sulphur." Let's be clear from the get-go: It does not taste peppery like cooked mustard greens, rather something between spinach and asparagus. There is no sulphur stench.

Besides detractors, there exists a contingent of consumers worried about poke salad being toxic. It is . . . if eaten raw, but so are lima beans and rhubarb plants. If you know your plants you can quickly cancel the peril by your preparation. By parboiling poke salad greens in two changes of water and draining them thoroughly you eliminate any toxin. Old country people know that, the Cherokee and the Muskogee know that.

Foraging requires knowledge. As with mushroom hunting, your knowledge of plants keeps you from poisoning, from hours of futile searching, and from ruining populations of rare and flavorful plants. The Cherokee and the Muskogee studied the effects of every plant that grew in their domains. The Cherokee nineteenth-century medical books are troves of Native American pharmacology. They knew that raw poke was poisonous—but that ingested in small quantities it operated as a purgative and dilator of one's lungs. Boiling poke cleared the poisons from the plant, making a green as tender as spinach. Botanists have identified phytolaccine, a gastrointestinal irritant, as the principal toxin in the plant.

Georgians cherished poke salad as a tonic, a food that overthrew winter anemia and imparted energy and a sense of well-being. Poke salad was reckoned a medicine. That folk wisdom has been ratified by nutrition science, for molecular biologists discovered that poke contains loads of vitamin A, C, calcium, and iron. Native Americans knew its beneficial effects centuries before the first vitamin (B isolated by chemists in 1910.

You want to harvest the poke when it is still a splay of leaves freshly jutting from the ground. It is most commonly found on the verge of forests, the margins of fields, in fallow meadows, and in the corners of yards. The leaves show two tones, rich green on the top, grayer and duller on the bottom. They alternate around the stem and grow from seven inches to fourteen inches in length, though the sprouts tend to be less sizeable than the leaves on the mature plant. Rule of thumb: Don't harvest the plant if the top is much over your knees—and please don't wait until it is fully grown bearing the famous ink berries. Those berries are quite poisonous to humans. Older poke plants can chemically irritate skin of some sensitive people if one should grab the stalks and leaves bare-handed, so wearing gloves is recommended. When the plant is newly sprung, this irritation should not occur. Cut the greens an inch off the ground, leaving the roots intact in the soil. Much toxic chemistry concentrates in those roots.

Foragers should harvest the poke plant when it is this stature or smaller. Photograph © David S. Shields.

At various times southern processors tried making poke a commercial vegetable. In the mid-1980s the Bush brothers (famous for their beans) of Blytheville, Arkansas, launched a line of canned poke salad. But another Arkansas canning company—Allen's—became the most dependable supplier with their Allen's Poke Sallet. But their last can came off the line in 2000. They did not suspend because of lack of demand, but lack of persons interested in foraging the plant for them around Siloam Springs, Arkansas.

Poke salad is mild tasting when cooked. There have been three traditional ways of preparing the green. The oldest, reputedly Native American, had the cook soaking leaves in water, then braising them in hot, bear grease originally, bacon renderings nowadays. The most common method of preparation resembled the old ways of cooking spinach: parboiling the greens in two waters, draining the moisture, then dressing the greens in butter and salt or vinegar, salt, and pepper. Some combined methods one and two by quickly sautéing the greens in bacon grease after parboiling. An old Georgia breakfast took braised or boiled poke salad and incorporating it into a skillet of scrambled eggs. We've never sampled pickled poke but know that the stems in particular were prepared this way by kitchen canners. Is the flavor worth a May morning traversing the Georgia hills? Without a doubt.

Possum and Taters

Surely the cosmopolitan foodies of Georgia's cities and suburbs—that group that has made duck confit, kombucha, kale salad, and bubble chai contemporary landmarks of "good eating"—would be scandalized to learn that from the Civil War to World War II Georgians regarded the state's signature dish as possum and taters. It appeared as a main dish in more than half the Georgia Products menus of 1913. It was consumed by Native Americans and white and Black people. Then in the decades after the World War II it fell from favor, almost vanishing from the table. By "taters" Georgians meant sweet potatoes. By "possum" was meant the opossum, the sole marsupial mammal found in the Western Hemisphere.

What does the white flesh of this marsupial taste like? Imagine something halfway between pork and chicken, agreeable in texture, modest in flavor, and as fatty as a Boston butt. When roasted crisp, it can be quite sumptuous. Once the excess grease has been poured from the roasting pan, and a bed of roasted sweet potatoes prepared, possum achieves a balance of flavor that is inviting. Sufficiently inviting for strangers to overcome the liability of its appearance. An epicurean Virginian stated the defect cogently: What should one think when encountering at the center of the banquet table a creature "reminding one of a roasted rat sodden in castor-oil" (1866). Georgians judged persons from elsewhere by their ability to overcome the shock and take pleasure in the possum's sumptuousness. Indeed, the serving of possum and taters to an outsider became a test, a trial to which even the highest and brightest in the land were subjected.

When president-elect William Howard Taft, an ample man from Ohio, toured through the South in 1909 drumming up support before he took office, he ate the local fare in every southern state he visited—pine bark stew in South Carolina, burgoo in Kentucky, catfish stew in Mississippi, and Georgians watched curiously wondering whether the president's broad appetite had room for Georgia's luscious marsupial. At the banquet given in his honor, the conventional first courses were dispatched without comment. Then the moment of drama:

> A plentiful helping of Georgia 'possum and potatoes was given Mr. Taft, then from every side appeared waiters with 'possum and potatoes, and the dish that only Georgia can boast in its height of perfection was served to everyone. . . . Then the serious work of dispatching the dish of all dishes was begin. And then it was that the Taft smile made its first complete appearance. . . . With the first savor of possum, the first evidence of the grin appeared. The savor was most reassuring and promising, but the president-elect had had no past experience with the delicacy that smoked before him. He took a gingerly nibble. The smile broadened. He tried again. The sparkle in his eyes fairly lit up his face. He settled himself more

comfortably in his chair, grasped his knife and fork, and the 'possum and potatoes fell as swiftly before his attack as political opposition did in the election just past. Leaning over to Governor Smith, he said: "Fine!" and the smile then was at its apex—a perfect masterpiece.

Taft's welcome feast can easily be recognized as a ritual, and all rituals have symbolisms that convey meaning. Scholar Stephanie Bryan has shown how the possum banquets became exercises in a kind of white male community depending on an adoption of African American foodways and musical culture (Black entertainers featured conspicuously in these feasts) to signal identity. But the flavor of roasted possum and taters invoked a broader community, not limited just to visitors at Georgia political feasts. It featured in African American hospitality. And it stands at the center of the decidedly mixed-sex hospitality of the Georgia Products Feasts. It isn't white supremacist politics that caused it to be included, along with ham and turkey, on the bulk of the Georgia Products menus. It was because by 1913 it had become installed as a key food by Georgians of every class and color.

When persimmons hung sugary on the trees and oak trees shed their leaves, holiday feasting began haunting people's imaginations. Men formed parties for night hunts, loosing dogs in the local woods to tree a fat possum, preferably on a slender young tree. When the tone of the hounds' warble changed into a frenzied ululation, the men took off into night, shining lights, chopping down the tree and bagging the critter. It would be taken to a farm and penned, fed sweet potatoes and all manner of things to fatten and sweeten it. It was killed and dressed on the eve of one of the great holiday feasts, for it was reckoned sumptuous. It appeared on many a Thanksgiving or Christmas table, always accompanied by sugary baked yams. It was often served in preference to turkey or ham. As an ode of 1913 sang:

> Talk o' turkey breast so white
> Goose baked brown an' served up
>   right;
> Smokehouse ham an' likes o' that—
> Streak o' lean and steak o' fat;
> Juice backbone, steak on toas'
> Mutton chops 'at some likes mos'—
> Sakes! They ain't a simmon blossom
> To a big fat Georgy 'possum
> Had one! You jest can bet!
> (Pears like I kin taste 'im yet!)
> Sarved up in old fashion's style
> 'Nough to make a parson smile!
> Thar he lay an' graced the feast!
> Sides jest gleaming with the grease.
> Brown an' juicy, crisp and crackin'—
> (Sally's lips was jest a-smakin'!)
> How they stared—them hotel
>   waiters!
> At that 'possum, dressed in taters!

We should be surprised that hotel waiters witness the revelation of the baked possum in all its glory, for beginning in the mid-1880s Atlanta restaurants began serving possum on its menus from October through February. Folsom's Restaurant in Atlanta became the mecca for holiday diners craving possum and taters, prepping one hundred a month all season long in 1888. By the turn of the twentieth century, New York restaurants catering to southern expats began shipping possums from Georgia in quantity.

How to cook possum was an art not often captured in print. African American cooks were reckoned the masters of possum cookery, and the few recipes that made their way into print before the 1920s with African American sources appear in newspaper oral transcripts that now seem caricatured in their presentation of dialect. This following narration from 1897 is one that least sounds like a minstrel show monologue:

> You cleans him fust. Den you puts him into de pot with cold water, and put de pot over a hot fire an' den you parbiles him—not too much—fur you don't want to lose any of his nice sweet fat. Den you takes him out of de pot an' you dries him in a clean towel. Den you puts him in a big frying-pan; den you scrapes de skin off you sweet potatoes an' you puts dem into de same pan wid de 'possum. Den you has you stove red, and den you puts de pan an' 'possum an' potatoes into de oven and den go away for a little while, but not too long. Den when you come back you puts in a little hot water, an' den you begins and bastes de 'possum an' de sweet potatoes an' you keeps on a-basting and a-basting till de 'possum is a good brown . . . an' de sweet potatoes is soft and juicy an' de gravy is almost black, and plenty of it. Den you takes it out ob de oven an' den you sots de table, and den—well den, you bars de doors, fo' the smell of cooked 'possum goes a long ways,

an' when you have only one 'possum you doesn't want much company besides yourself.

Still, there is a good deal of presumed knowledge about butchering and preparation, so a more detailed account by Virginia-born Marion Harland, published in the *Atlanta Journal* in 1914, is welcome for its practical wisdom and its precision. This is a recipe for baked possum without potatoes, a dish that can be served hot or cold, though in Harland's recipe she requests cold.

> Dip the 'possum in scalding water, scrape and clean it thoroughly—do not skin—cut off the tail and head—cut it down the middle—the flesh is fine and white. It should then be frozen for a week. I packed mine in a bed of ice in an old clothes basket, putting crushed ice inside of them and covering them with ice, also sprinkling the ice and 'possum well with rock salt. This basket I put over a drain in the garage, where it was kept in a frozen condition for a week. The day before Christmas I had them brought in, washed thoroughly, put in a pot, covered well with cold water, and let boil until tender. Then remove from the pot, cover well with salt, red pepper, and flour and put them in a pan to bake. I covered them with a blanket of dough made of flour and water rolled out in a thin sheet, made large enough to cover them thoroughly and tuck well in around to keep the steam from escaping. Put a small amount of water

in the pan and let them steam in a moderate over until nearly done—then remove the blanket, add quite a bit of water in the pan, and let them brown slowly, basting often until they are thoroughly done and you see the meat beginning to separate from the bone. Now take the possum out again and put in a cold place over night—if you have it, cover with snow, as it will not hurt to freeze again—and serve cold. I pour off the heavy grease from the pan and make a brown gravy by adding flour and chopped parsley—no butter—and serve this gravy hot.

The year of the Georgia Products Dinners—1913—might be said to inaugurate the golden age of possum dining. At about that time a group of devotees in Coweta County, southwest of Atlanta, formed into the Coweta Possum Eaters Association, a body that would endure for half a century. But in the final years of the association's existence, in the early 1960s, it had become an anachronism. Possum had become something retrograde.

The generation of African American veterans who fought in World War II turned its back on the obsequious ways of prewar culture. For them eating possum seemed emblematic of poverty, country backwardness, and dislocation from the market culture that supplied fashion, music, name-brand food, and automobiles. These men opted for urbanity and rejected do-it-yourself traditional foodways and culture.

As early as 1900 a contingent of people located around Marietta thought to make fortunes by supplying the market by hunting or raising possums. They banked on northern cities discovering possum as a cheap alternative to pork and beef. They soon discovered that dreams of America discovering the "other, other white meat" were thwarted by numbers of unanticipated problems. Though a wild animal, people declined to view it as "game" or pay premium prices for it, in part because hunting possum possessed the least mystique of any American wild creature. Possums are slow, dim witted, prolific, easily treed, caught, and consumed. Even the raccoon (a southern creature vested with an even greater load of race baggage than the possum) was a superior prey—ingenious, quick, able to move through water, treetops, marsh, and brush at a pace that challenged hounds. Several hound varieties were bred for raccoon hunting, none for possum. Raccoon remained a camp dish when possum and taters fell by the wayside. Market hunters disdained the creature because there was no market for possum pelts, as there was for raccoon. Finally, possum did not taste like game; in fact it was not sufficiently distinctive from pork or chicken to create a following, and rabbits, another alternative meat with little flavor distinction, were easier to breed, farm, and harvest. While a Possum Breeders Association did organize in 1971, it never created a genetics program that produced a more saleable possum. It ceased issuing annual reports in 1990.

The spread of highways and paved roads throughout Georgia in the mid-twentieth century made the slow-moving possums a conspicuous victim of road kill. Indeed, a contingent of Georgians reckoned that night hunting the creature was no longer necessary, since one could readily find fresh meat on the roadside. "Highway suppers" became in the 1970s an amusement of citizens of Morgan County particularly. For the past fifty years too many Georgians primary visual experience of possums has been glimpses of mangled carcasses—not an appetizing view.

More intangible in its influence was the renovation in the public image of the possum after 1948 caused by the extraordinary success of Walt Kelly's comic strip, *Pogo*. Set in the Okefenokee Swamp, near Waycross, Georgia, this immensely popular and beloved strip presented a comic commentary on human foibles in the persons of a host of swamp animals. The central figure, Pogo the Opossum, embodied heart, common sense, modesty, and an instinct for morality. If anything could be said to have made people want not to eat possums, in much the same way that *Charlotte's Web* made persons not want to whack spiders, Pogo made ordinary people want to protect America's marsupial.

The possum's flight from the table can be registered in its scarce presence in cookbooks composed in the last quarter of the twentieth century. It does not appear in *Fayetteville Favorite Foods*, *Gems from Georgia Kitchens*, *From Savannah Kitchens*, *Old and New Recipes* by Augusta's junior league, or *Coastal Cooking*. Its sole appearance is in Newnan Junior Service League's *Taste of Georgia*. And Newnan was the town where the Coweta Possum Eaters Association convened for its annual feasts for much of the twentieth century. Where else? In the pages of Ernest Mathew Mickler's 1986 *White Trash Cooking*? A rather steep status fall from the gentlemen's banquets that greeted President Taft in 1909.

Rattlesnake Watermelon

We live in the age of the convenience melon. No seeds. Minimal rind. Boosted sugar. Round shape, small enough to fit on the bottom shelf of a refrigerator. The legendary family picnic melons of yore—the twenty-pound seeded cylinders with nuanced sweetness and a rind you could pickle—well they still lurk at certain country produce stands, but rarely appear at the grocery these days. Yet when families were ample and neighbors came to partake in summer meals, the legendary melons of the South—the rattlesnake, the Bradford, the Ravenscroft, the Odell's white, the Kleckley sweet, the Florida's favorite—inspired profound devotion.

The first famous Georgia watermelon was the rattlesnake, so called because of the wavy green lines crawling down the length of the melon. To some they looked like wriggling snakes. Developed in Richmond County, Georgia, just before the Civil War, the rattlesnake emerged by crossing the tasty but unproductive Lawson watermelon and the prolific perfectly shaped striped mountain sprout watermelon. The first persons to offer seed for sale were Plumb & Leitner, druggists, in Augusta. The first published characteristic description was by pomologist P. J. Berckmans in 1866, and its reputation as a market melon was made by the inaugural shipment northward of truck farmed melons in 1867 from Augusta. [Truck farming is the cultivation of vegetables specifically for produce markets; it stood in distinction to row crop farming of commodity grains and small fruits.] The shipment of rattlesnake watermelons inspired instant demand in northern markets, a demand that Georgia farmers were willing to satisfy. Newspapers as far north as Providence, Rhode Island, announced its virtues: "The well-known striped and speckled melon of Augusta is known as the 'Rattlesnake,' and has been found to be the most productive of all the varieties grown. This particular seed is cultivated almost entirely to the exclusion of all other varieties, although in a day's travel some five or six other kinds are to be met with. But the 'Rattlesnake' is the universal favorite."

Why was it the universal favorite? It was a sizeable melon in an age of sizeable families. It was a consistently flavorful, sweet melon with a crisp flesh at a time when many melon varieties had soggy flesh, bland

You can, perhaps, see the rattlesnakes crawling over the side of the melons as stripes. Photograph © David S. Shields.

cucumber flavor, lack of sugar, and too many seeds. It had an inch-thick rind ideal for pickling. (On the Georgia Products Menus it is the rind pickle that appears, since November is too late for fresh watermelon.) In the decades after the Civil War there were two categories of melons. The shipping melons such as the Kolb's gem, the scaly bark, the Tom Watson, and the black Spanish wouldn't crush in a railroad boxcar but tasted only so-so. The tasty melons such as the rattlesnake, sugar loaf, blue gem, Bradford, Ravenscroft, Kleckley sweet all had fine flavor but were not so robust in transport. Of this last category the rattlesnake was deemed the one that held up best in shipping. For this reason a nationwide demand for rattlesnake watermelon seed emerged at the turn of the twentieth century from home gardeners who wanted a fine-tasting Georgia melon to grow in the back patch. Mel I. Branch of Berzilia, Georgia, undertook the task of supplying seed to the nation. In 1902 he grew 48,500 watermelons in various sites across Columbia County for seed and for truck. He was Georgia's watermelon king from the dawn of the twentieth century until the Great Depression.

One peculiar testament to the reverence the rattlesnake watermelon inspired was the fact that after the Civil War the unreconstructed Confederates—the Confederados—who left the South and settled in Americana, Brazil, took two crops with them: Carolina Gold rice and rattlesnake watermelons. They cultivated and sold the melons for decades, establishing their popularity in that country.

Georgia's rattlesnake watermelon inspired a faur number of songs—from "A Watermelon Song" of the 1890s to Lefty Frizzel's "It's Watermelon Time in Georgia." You can be sure that it was the rattlesnake they were singing about in 1893 from the lyrics:

A Watermelon Song

O, the Georgia watermelon—it's a-growin' cool an' green
An'll soon be pullin' heavy at the stem:
An' the knife—it needs a whettin', an' the blade is gittin' keen,
OP, the Georgia watermelon is a gem!

Melons cool an' green—
Jes' the best you ever seen?
See the sweet juice drippin'
From them melons cool an' green!

O, the Georgia watermelon—with the purtiest sort o' stripe!
It ain't a streak o' fat an' streak o' lean;
You thump her with yer fingers, an' you hear her answer: "Ripe!"
O, the Georgia watermelon cool an' green!

Melons cool an' green—
Jes' the best you ever seen?
See the sweet juice drippin'
From them melons cool an' green!

Watermelons were grown in all parts of Georgia, though the rattlesnake's greatest concentration was Columbia County. Problems arise when you cover a countryside with just one crop. Sooner or later the pest or pathogen that loves that crop more than anything else will show up and trigger a general infestation. This happened with fusarium wilt and other diseases to which the rattlesnake was vulnerable. In the twentieth century, watermelon growers were increasingly forced to grow other varieties, despite the love for the rattlesnake. Now it is kept as a specialty crop by farmers with a love of food tradition, such as Geechee farmer Matthew Raiford of Brunswick. For Raiford it's the flavor and the cultural traditions that outweigh the risk of possible crop loss from disease.

Of all the old preparations made from the rattlesnake watermelon, rind pickle is the one that carries the richest kitchen traditions. It came in sweet and savory versions. Our sweet version was contributed by Mrs. Joel Hunter for 1921's *Atlanta Women's Club Cookbook*.

Watermelon Rind Pickle No.1 (sweet)

Mrs. Joel Hunter,
Atlanta Women's Club Cookbook (1921)

1 medium size melon
4 lbs sugar
3 pots vinegar [approximately 1 quart]
2 lemons
1 t-spoon ginger
1 t-spoon whole cloves

Cut ring in small squares and peel. Soak overnight in weak salt water in a stone jar. Rinse in cold water and let rind come to a boil in cold water containing a piece of rock alum the size of a pigeon's egg. Drain off alum water and discard. Put in cold water the ginger and let rind come to a boil. Cook until rind can be pierced by a straw. Take rind from ginger water and drain. Make a syrup of sugar and vinegar. Let boil and add lemons sliced thin (removing seed), and cloves. Drain rind and add it to syrup. Let cook until transparent. Put in jars hot. Glass top jars with new rubbers are best for pickles.

The later twentieth century saw a rise in popularity of a spicy form of rind pickle with less sugar, hot pepper, and more pungent mixes of spice. None probably had as much clove in it as Mrs. Joel Hunter's version.

Rice and Gravy

Mrs. Dull said it best, "Rice and gravy seem like one word, much like ham an' eggs." Because milled white rice was an ingredient available year-round, rice and gravy became a standard side. It was the inevitable accompaniment of fried chicken when served for company. It appeared at breakfast, brunch, lunch, dinner, and supper. There was no protein it didn't complement. "Rice served with beef, lamb, pork, veal or chicken is a most satisfying foundation for a dinner menu. Of all the delicious rice combinations none is more appetizing or satisfying than rice and gravy. This might well be termed the favored dish of the southland." So . . . what kind of rice . . . and what kind of gravy? How favored? It was the signature dish of Atlanta's YWCA Café early in the twentieth century. In the 1970s, the Converted Rice Company began adding a packet of gravy fixings to Uncle Ben's (now Ben's) Rice.

Nowadays many sorts of rice can be purchased readily—aromatic basmati or perfumed jasmine, brown rice, black rice, sushi rice, Arborio for risotto. But the rice that Georgia grew on a commodity scale in the nineteenth century, the rice that contributed the base to so many classic Lowcountry dishes, was a medium grained nonaromatic white rice with a yellow hull called "Carolina Gold." Fields of "gold seed" rice blanketed Chatham County. Famed for its wholesome mouth feel, delicate hazelnut flavor, and excellence as a base for mixing flavor, Carolina Gold was the first great American rice, and was generally available until World War I. Dr. Richard Schulze of Savannah revived the rice in the 1980s, the first restoration of the current effort to recover all of the heirloom ingredients that made traditional southern cookery so flavorful.

In the nineteenth century Carolina Gold rice was grown in the plantations on the Sea Islands and along the Savannah River in the "overflow lands." These were tidal water impoundment fields with substantial drainage. In central Georgia numbers of people grew upland rice varieties (gopher, upland white, red bearded) as garden crops. In the 1880s the Georgia Rice Association had formed to oversee crop standards, seed quality, and lobby for protection from foreign rice imports. But cultivation halted in the early twentieth century as cheaper rice from Texas, Arkansas, Louisiana, and Honduras made rice planting uneconomical. After 1910 groceries sold long- or medium-grain white brought in from out of state. Georgia's classic crop rice would not be available to make the classic rice dishes—red rice, duck pilau, sausage pilau, shrimp pilau—until the twenty-first century when the Carolina Gold Rice Foundation brought the crop back.

Classic Georgia cookbooks used the terms boiled rice and steamed rice interchangeably. They offered detailed instructions on how to wash, boil, and dress rice for the table. The traditional ideal end result was fluffy rice with each grain separate. Fortunately, we live in the age of the electric cookpot, a device that can produce perfect rice every time, if you put two cups of water in for one cup of rice. So there is little need to reproduce one of the detailed cookbook instructions. Rather, we print this recipe from 1911 that is more a testament to our subject than an instruction for making rice.

Savory Rice No. 1

Marion Harland, *Atlanta Journal* (January 15, 1911)

Boil the rice in plenty of boiling water until the grains are soft, although still retaining their shape. Turn into a hot dish and pour over it a big cupful of well-seasoned gravy, lifting the rice with a fork that the sauce may go all through it. This is especially nice when made with giblet gravy.

As this "recipe" indicates there exists a taste preference for giblet gravy as the adornment for rice, but brown gravy made from the deglazed pan juices of roasts and steaks is not preluded. Giblet gravy uses stock made from boiling the extraneous parts of chickens, ducks, or turkeys. It was de rigueur at Thanksgiving: "We southerners would hardly leave off rice—the dry fluffy rice for the giblet gravy that seems so important on our table" (1938). Sometimes the gravy was made using the pan juices of frying chicken was called "chicken gravy" rather than "giblet gravy," particularly when milk rather than chicken stock moistened the roux. Food technologists have not yet devised a gadget that makes professional-level gravy without fail. So we do well in following the advice of an expert.

Chicken Gravy

Atlanta Journal (July 26, 1936)

You want your gravy to be a rich light brown in color, creamy and smooth with a bit of grease coming to the top. Surely one never enjoys it if white and thick with a curdled look about it, and lots of grease showing. You remember when we started the frying there was lots of grease in the pan. If you fried it quickly there will still be lots of grease. This is poured off, leaving about two tablespoons in the skillet along with the brown crumbs which have dropped from the pieces of chicken, and should be a golden brown (never black or burned). These browned crumbs are going to add flavor to the gravy.

Add to the skillet two tablespoons of butter and four of flour, rub together until smooth and cook all together until a deep brown, using a gentle heat so as not to burn. When smooth and free of lumps have ready one cup milk and one cup boiling water, mixed together, pour into the skillet and blend. If too thick add more milk or water until the right consistency. Add salt and pepper to taste. If any flour is left in which the chicken was rolled, that may be used for the gravy, and remember it already has some salt and pepper. If the gravy is allowed to cook too long it becomes thick and pasty looking. More liquid should be added.

All milk may be used, but milk and water, with some butter, makes a good gravy. Be careful when browning the flour, not to scorch or burn, for scorched gravy is impossible.

Use a gentle heat. Season well with salt and black pepper.

In the Lowcountry, seasoning chicken gravy with mace as well as salt and pepper has long been traditional. Lemon juice too may be added by persons wishing a counter to the chicken fat in the gravy.

Roast Turkey

The eastern wild turkey (*Meleagris gallopavo silvestris*) is the largest game bird native to Georgia. A food source for Georgia's Native Americans, it became the feasting bird of European settlers after 1732. As the largest and most conspicuous forest fowl, it became the focus of every subsistence hunter and sportsman in the state. Intensive hunting would plague all thirty-nine states where the six types of American turkey reside. So relentless was the harvesting that the wild population declined from an estimated seven to ten million birds in North America at the time of European contact to thirty thousand individuals in 1930. Wild birds had been eliminated completely from eighteen of the original states where they had once roamed.

Passage of the Pittman–Robertson Wildlife Restoration Act of 1937 proved key to preventing the disappearance of the wild turkey in America. It funded the conservation of habitat. Excise taxes on gun sales went to secure protection for breeding territories and manage populations. One hindrance to population increase was the absolute failure of pen-raised wild turkey to naturalize in locales where they were released. Only by capturing and relocating wild birds from areas where they thrived to uninhabited ranges would the population expand into regions where they had gone extinct. This didn't happen until 1951, "when the wildlife biologists in South Carolina's Francis Marion National Forest successfully trapped wild turkeys with a cannon net. The net, propelled over feeding turkeys by black powder cannons, made it possible for state game officials to capture birds from healthy populations and release them in suitable habitat that contained few, if any, wild turkeys" (2000). The National Wild Turkey Federation, founded in 1973, would become an energetic private sector partner to federal management efforts. Nearly 150,000 turkeys were relocated in the last quarter of the twentieth century and more than a hundred thousand square miles of habitat identified and populated. By 2020 the national estimate for wild turkey population in the continental United States was between six and seven million with as many as 350,000 in Georgia. Scarcely seen during a drive through rural roads of Georgia in 1950, wild turkeys are now a common sight.

A decline in hunting pressure on the wild population proved critical to the success of conservation. The domestication of the Bronze turkey, the White Holland, and the Bourbon Red turkey in the 1870s and 1880s supplied turkey meat at reasonable cost, cutting the number of persons depending on wild turkeys as a food source. In particular, development of the Broad-Breasted Bronze and the Broad-Breasted White Holland created varieties that carried substantially more meat than wild birds. When turkey farming became an industry in the period between the two world wars, Georgians joined in. Molena became the center of large-scale turkey farming in the state. By 1940, turkey farms dotted the Chattahoochee River Valley growing 150,000 birds annually. The twentieth-century creation of the factory-raised turkey, while inhumane on its own terms because of the lamentable conditions in which the turkeys existed, enabled the wild population to rebound as demand for it was directed to the domestic product.

Georgian turkey cookery, except for the deep-fried turkey borrowed from late-twentieth-century Cajun cooking, formed at the time when seasonally hunted wild birds supplied the feast. Indeed at least three of the standard turkey preparations, roast, smoked, and stewed, can be traced to Muscogee and Cherokee foodways. Roast turkey began as an open-air preparation, with the bird being suspended before the fire on spits. Since the 1870s oven roasting has supplanted spit roasting the birds. Since before the American Revolution, roast turkey appeared as the standard "main" of the holiday table. In the 1913 Georgia Products Feasts, roast turkey appeared on twenty-eight of the menus. One specified baked turkey. Only seven localities did not list it as a main course.

Native Americans smoked and jerked many of the meats in their larder. Settlers during the great era of smokehouse building (1810s–1840s) may have hung birds in the rafters along with sausages and venison, mutton, and pork hams. Yet smoked turkey did not become a holiday presence until its sudden popularity in the late 1930s. A fashion for colonial foods ignited by the opening of Colonial Williamsburg spread up and down the eastern seaboard. Smoked Turkey appeared in articles as a "colonial" specialty. Fashionable hosts seeking an eye-catching novelty created a sudden demand in Atlanta, Savannah, and Augusta. By 1939 it had become a commercial product. The *Augusta Chronicle* of November 15, 1940, gave the first published newspaper recipe for "Roasted Stuffed Smoked Turkey." It remained a fixture of Georgia turkey cookery when barbecue specialists took up smoking turkeys.

For a century the vast majority of Georgians have secured their turkeys at the butchers and grocers, pre-plucked, with giblets and often the neck stored in the chest cavity of the bird. Since the 1950s an increasing percentage of turkeys are purchased frozen several days before the holiday and defrosted at home. Two approaches have dominated in the treatment of the carcass prior to roasting. Since 1993, when *Cooks Illustrated* published a greatly influential essay on perfecting the flavor of turkey by brining it before cooking, many have taken to immersing the bird in a salt solution for several hours to impart moistness and savor to the cooked bird. The traditional way of prepping the bird was simple. It called for a fresh bird. Here are directions from a century ago: "Remove the giblets and place them in cold salted water. Rub well inside the turkey with salt. Then thoroughly wash it with cold water. Be sure every trace of the salt is gone. Scrape the outside of the bird with the blunt edge of a case-knife, keeping the turkey under water and taking care not to break the skin. Scrub it well with the palm of the hand and wash it through many waters. Rinse the giblets in clear cold water and put the turkey in a cold place until needed" (1924).

The final dressing of the turkey prior to placing it in a heated oven follows one of two approaches. Some coat the exterior of the bird with a flour, butter, and seasoning paste. Others simply butter and strew herbs on the exterior, basting the skin as it browns. If one follows the latter method, one usually roasts the bird at a high temperature (425°F to 450°F) for an hour, then turns the oven down to 250 degrees for the remaining cooking. If you coat the turkey, you don't want to scorch the sheath of the bird by exposing it to high temperatures for an hour. Instead you cook the turkey at a constant 350 degrees for the duration of the roast. Given the difference in oven temperature of everyone's stoves, the best way to judge doneness in turkey is by internal temperature using an oven thermometer. It is done when the center breast meat registers 175 degrees.

Traditionally the turkey was stuffed with chestnut dressing, peanut dressing, or oyster dressing. Because of the peril of the liquids from the baking turkey turning the stuffing into a soggy mass, a sect of modern roasters prepares the dressing in a separate ceramic dish, not putting it into the bird. Prior to the annihilation of Georgia's native chestnut forest by blight from 1917 to 1920, chestnut dressing was the most popular throughout the state. There were two styles: In one, peeled chestnuts were boiled soft, mashed into spoon meat, seasoned, and stuffed into the bird. Here is a pre-blight recipe for the second style.

Chestnut Dressing

Atlanta Journal (November 23, 1915)

Split with knife two pounds of chestnuts and roast them in an oven not too hot. Peel them, and finish cooking in a large saucepan. Cover the chestnuts with white stock add a piece of raw celery, and cook again, slowly to keep them as whole as possible. Drain and cool off. Have one pound of fat sausage meat seasoned with salt, pepper and sage; mix with the chestnuts and stuff the turkey.

In the northern and western areas of the state where chestnut dressing ruled, corn bread stuffing replaced chestnut in diners' affections after the blight. In the coastal counties and along the Savannah River, oyster dressing held sway.

Oyster Dressing for Turkey

Athens Daily Herald
(November 19, 1915)

One pound of bread crumbled fine, add two stalks of celery chopped fine, one half cupful of butter melted, salt and pepper to taste. Add to this one quart of the best oysters, strained from their liquor, and carefully picked over for bits of shell. When oysters are mixed with bread, add enough of their liquor to moisten stuffing well. Fill the Turkey, and baste with hot water to which has been added the remainder of the oyster liquor and a lump of butter.

Rutabagas

Sometimes the taste buds of hogs, cows, and sheep matter more than those of humans. Southerners wouldn't be eating rutabagas if it weren't for the fact that livestock thrive on them. Here's the story.

When the rutabaga (*Brassica napobrassica*) came into America from Europe it was immediately classified as a turnip, but soon took on an identity of its own. The name "rutabaga" literally means round root. It had been a fixture of Swedish agriculture since the seventeenth century and first attracted attention in England in the 1740s from reformers interested in improving animal husbandry. The English political economist William Cobbett publicized the virtues of the plant during his 1816–1818 sojourn in the United States. American experimentalists began working intensively with the plant in the late 1810s with the intention of determining which was the most profitable and advantageous crop for a diversified farm—potatoes, sugar beets, mangel-wurzels (German cattle beets), carrots, turnips, or rutabagas? As with most comparative explorations, the results varied depending on local circumstances. Rutabagas had certain advantages in cultivation: Its growing season was shorter than the other roots; it could be manured by plowing in a clover field after the clover hay had been cut (most other roots required a major application of animal dung); it remained vital in the heat of midsummer; and it harvested more easily than mangel-wurzel. Its disadvantages lay in its poor productivity in clay soils, its susceptibility to the insect pests that afflicted turnips, particularly the turnip fly, and its occasional toughness.

In Georgia rutabaga's first promoters were the "feed boys," farmers looking for a root vegetable that provided ample and good winter feed for livestock. First of all it was big—not as big as a mangel-wurzel, but a whole lot better tasting. You can examine the old cookbooks—aside for a formula for mangel beer, you won't find any widely republished recipes for this old German cattle beet. The real question among farmers was rutabaga or sugar beet? Neither "stranged" the flavor of milk in cows that fed on them over winter. In the South there was no contest—rutabaga hands down, particularly if the variety being planted was locally adapted such as the Ben Air Rutabaga promoted by the Alexander Seed Company of Augusta in the 1910s.

Yet every variety that came out—the Aberdeen, the purple top, the gold cabbage turnip—found takers. They were an autumn-winter crop, and spring-planted fields were rare indeed south of Virginia. The repertoire of dishes is rather broad: Rutabaga appeared in many a beef or venison stew, it was braised, it was mashed with cream or buttermilk, sometimes with butter and garlic, it was cooked au gratin.

Raw, the roots do not look handsome. The pale orange-grey-green skin is nondescript, sometimes homely. Food processors often sheet them with a protective layer of wax before dispatching them to groceries. Cutting the root raw takes your best knife and your gym-trained muscles. There is an odor when it is cooked. Not quite "goose farts on a muggy day," but old European kitchen.

The simplest way of preparing them, described in Theresa Brown's *Modern Domestic Cookery* published after the Civil War, was to boil them whole, slice them, arrange them on a plate and pour salad dressing over them. More popular today is Brown's formula for mashed rutabagas.

Rutabaga Turnips No. 2

Theresa C. Brown,
Modern Domestic Cookery (1871)

Pare off the rind; throw them into boiling water, sliced; boil them gently until tender; lift them out; press the water with a plate; then mash, and return them to a clean hot sauce-pan; stir in a large tablespoonful of butter; season with pepper and salt according to your taste.

This template gave rise to many variations. Garlic became a favorite additive in the mid-twentieth century. Some added buttermilk to the butter to give the mass more tang. Leftover mashed rutabagas were rolled into balls and deep fried as fritters. Edna Lewis made the consistency ultrasmooth in her recipe for "whipped rutabagas." They remain a favorite root vegetable, cherished by some, liked by others. It has a minority of detractors as well. Southern chefs and food processors have become interested in fermenting the raw shredded root to make rutabaga kraut. They appeared on two of the Georgia Products dinner menus—from Rome and Sandersville.

Rutabaga and Turnip Soup

KEVIN MITCHELL

I love this recipe because it reminds me of home. When I was growing up, my grandmother would make a pot of rutabagas from time to time. I wanted to take that flavor into my kitchen and upgrade it. This is a recipe that brings together rutabagas and turnips. I also wanted to move away from pork in the recipe. Here I introduce smoked paprika to give you the smokey flavor of smoked pork products and fortify the smoke flavor with beef sausage. I am a fan of Roger Wood Sausage, which is based in Savannah.

Serves 8 to 10

¼ cup olive oil

2 large onions, diced small

4 cloves garlic, minced

2 tablespoons smoked paprika

1½ pounds beef sausage, sliced

3 quarts water, vegetable broth, or chicken broth

3 pounds large rutabagas, peeled, cut into medium dice

1-pound turnips, peeled, cut into medium dice

1 bunch (5 cups) kale or collard greens, thick stems removed, leaves halved lengthwise and cut crosswise into ¼-inch strips (see Note)

1½ teaspoon fresh lemon juice

Salt to taste

½ teaspoon sugar

½ teaspoon cayenne pepper

In a large Dutch oven or stockpot over medium heat, sweat the onions and garlic in the oil until translucent, 5 to 8 minutes. Add smoked paprika and cook until fragrant. Add sausage and cook for about 5 minutes. Add water or broth. Add the rutabagas and turnips, bring to a boil, then lower the heat to medium-low to simmer gently until everything is tender, 30 to 35 minutes. Add kale, lemon juice, salt, sugar, and cayenne pepper and cook for 10 minutes. Adjust seasoning as needed. Serve in a soup bowl.

Note: You can use prewashed and cut kale, which can be found in your local grocery store.

Rutabaga and turnip soup by Kevin Mitchell. Photograph © Rhonda Mitchell.

Savannah Red Rice

Tomato Pilau

Red rice belongs to a family of rice dishes called "pilaus." Pilau, a one-pot dish with a deep ancestry in the Middle East, became European "pilaff," and Lowcountry "perloo." It has a basic formula: Rice cooks with an ingredient that forms and flavors a stock in which the grains steam. There is usually a fat added to the pot—butter, a strip of bacon, a tablespoon of culinary oil. The ingredient can be a protein or a vegetable—meat, poultry, fish; eggplant, squash, okra, butter beans, field peas, onions. Nineteenth- and twentieth-century newspaper recipes present more than thirty forms of pilau in the South; We've documented all of them in a chapter in our book on South Carolina. In Georgia, the most important pilaus have been hopping John and red rice. The latter has collected many names over the years: tomato pilau, Savannah red rice, Gullah red rice, Lowcountry red rice, Charleston red rice. The most common alternative name, in the 1800s, was tomatoes and rice. This is the name superscribed over the first recipe printed in Georgia. It appeared in several papers in the summer of 1876.

Tomatoes and Rice

Brunswick Advertiser (July 26, 1876)

Scald a teacup of good rice; scald a peel five or six nice ripe tomatoes, put both together in a stew pan, and a tablespoonful of sugar, salt and pepper to taste, and water enough to bring the rice, when done to the consistency of plain-boiled rice; before taking up add a teaspoonful of butter.

The spoonful of sugar may raise eyebrows, but we should remember that tomatoes in the mid-1800s were substantially more acid tasting than they are today. An 1861 description of the dish omits the sugar and characterizes it as "bacon and tomatoes and rice boiled together." This would become the standard formula for much of the dish's subsequent history.

The tomatoes are the key to the dish. Native to the Western Hemisphere, they were planted in Europe and North America as ornamental plants, not becoming nationally popular as a culinary resource until 1834 when Dr. John Bennett published an article extolling their pharmacological virtues. Yet southerners had begun planting and using tomatoes as food in the early 1820s. Tomato catsup recipes appeared as early as 1827 in the *Savannah Daily Georgian*. The earliness with which the tomato was adopted in southern cuisine raises the question whether tomato pilau predates West African jollof. The difficulty of making a judgment about priority rests on two matters: The tomato was an American ingredient introduced into Africa; there is little concrete record about when the tomato was adopted in West Af-

Red rice can have a range of textures in terms of its tomato content. Some prefer a chunky tomato presence, others a smooth thin coating of tomato sauce turning the rice pinkish red. Photograph © David S. Shields.

rican cuisines. There is a general belief that the tomato came to Senegal sometime in the 1820s—precisely the time that African American cooks incorporated it into Lowcountry cookery. What can be stated without hesitation is that both red rice and jollof rice proceed from the same African recipe template, with a grain base, a lipid, and another ingredient. Red rice resembles two popular dishes: thieboudienne, from Senegambia; and jollof, which has ties to Nigeria, Ghana, Senegal, Mali, and Liberia. One distinction about red rice is that, in most cases, pork is added, whether it be bacon or smoked sausage. This suggests a great deal of creolization or the mixture of elements of several cultures brought together to create one singular dish.

The rice in classic red rice was Carolina Gold. In the mid-twentieth century, when Carolina Gold was virtually extinct, one of the nonaromatic American long-grain tropical japonica white rices was used (often possessing a genetic legacy of Carolina Gold). Since the return of Carolina Gold in the first decade of this century, restaurants have returned to using gold seed rice in making red rice. Because the production of Carolina Gold is not yet returned to the commodity level, it cannot be purchased in many grocery stores. Hence cookbooks aimed at home cooks still specify "long grained white rice" in their recipes for red rice. But those in the know, know.

There were several versions of the dish. A quick and dirty breakfast version under the name "tomato pilau" appeared in the *Atlanta Sunny South* in April 1896. It used a pint of precooked or leftover steamed rice that was dumped into a skillet of canned crushed tomatoes simmering in bacon strips and bacon fat. This is the version recorded in Harriet Ross Colquitt's *The Savannah Cook Book* (1933). Another version employed chicken meat as well as bacon. In the 1950s the tomato pilau name was eclipsed by red rice, primarily due to the influence of Mrs. Sema Wilkes, whose boarding house dining room featured the dish under that name in Savannah. It fixed itself in the local imagination under that name, so when the Savannah Chamber of Commerce in the late 1960s sought a hook with which to draw in tourists from other states, it hit upon the motto, "Some People Come 500 Miles for our Red Rice." Print ads appeared in northern and Midwestern metropolitan papers. After that campaign Georgia writers have invariably called the dish "Savannah red rice."

Cookpot versions of Savannah Red Rice have proven singularly convenient and tasty. The formula is easy: 2 strips bacon, one cup Carolina Gold rice, 2 cups chicken stock, a little salt, a little pepper, a tablespoon of Worcestershire sauce, ½ can crushed tomatoes, 2 tablespoons tomato paste, and chopped sweet peppers (if you like them). Cook it on the "Steamed Rice" cycle. Perfect every time!

Anson Mills Savannah Red Rice

ANSON MILLS

This is one of my [Kevin's] favorite pilaus. I first experienced this dish when I moved to the Charleston area. I love the flavor the tomato gives to the rice along with the smokiness of the bacon. At home I like to use smoked sausage in place of bacon. Either way this is a great dish to serve as a main course or side dish.

Serves 4 to 6, as a side dish

- 1 cup rich homemade chicken stock or low-sodium boxed broth (see Notes)
- 1 cup Bionaturae Organic Strained Tomatoes or tomato juice (see Notes)
- 2 teaspoons red wine vinegar
- 1 Turkish bay leaf, crumbled
- 2 small whole chipotle chiles in adobo sauce
- 2 slices of smoked bacon, diced fine (¼ cup)
- 1 small yellow onion, minced (½ cup)
- ¾ teaspoon dried thyme
- 1 teaspoon sea salt
- ½ teaspoon freshly ground black pepper
- 1 celery rib, diced small (⅓ cup)
- 4 ounces small button mushrooms, diced fine (1 cup)
- 1 garlic clove, minced
- 7 ounces (1 cup) Anson Mills Carolina Gold Rice, rinsed and drained

Pour the stock and tomatoes or juice into a small nonreactive saucepan. Add the vinegar and bay leaf. Drop the chiles (and any adobo sauce clinging to them) into the pan and mash them against the sides with a wooden spoon. Cover and bring to a simmer on low heat to infuse the flavors, then remove from the heat.

Set a well-seasoned 8- or 9-inch cast-iron skillet over medium heat. Add the bacon to the cold pan and sauté, stirring, until crisp, about 5 minutes. Add the onion and thyme and sauté until golden, stirring frequently, about 5 minutes. Stir in the salt and pepper. Stir in the celery and cook until barely tender, and then increase the heat. Add the mushrooms and cook until they release their juices and the juices have evaporated, about 2 minutes. While the mushrooms are cooking, bring the stock mixture back up to a simmer. Have a stainless steel, medium-fine-mesh conical strainer and a 9-inch lid wrapped with aluminum foil—to assist with the seal—at the ready. Stir the garlic into the vegetable mixture and sauté until its aroma blooms, about 10 seconds.

Stir the rice into the vegetables and sauté until the grains are opaque, about 30 seconds. Pour the hot stock through the strainer into the skillet, pushing with the back of a wooden spoon to get every bit of liquid into the rice. Stir the rice, cover tightly with the foil-wrapped lid, and turn down the heat to low. Cook for 20 minutes without lifting the lid, and then remove the skillet from the heat. Let rest for 10 minutes before uncovering and serving.

Notes: Anson Mills provides a recipe for rich homemade chicken stock at ansonmills.com. You can also use your preferred stock recipe or substitute store-bought chicken broth. Bionaturae Organic Strained Tomatoes can be found in most specialty grocery stores or online.

The "do not disturb" period at the end of cooking, known in the nineteenth century as "soaking," is designed to give the rice grains a few minutes to compose themselves and help them resist breakage when they're spooned and served. Don't skip this step.

Sea Island Red Peas

Peas could mean two things in early Georgia—it could mean garden pea (*Pisum savitum*), the climbing vines that bore pods of spheroidal green seeds, which were cherished as spring's greatest blessing—or it could be field peas (*Vigna unguiculata*), the summer-grown annual legumes that crossed the Atlantic with the enslaved African people. The latter became a fixture of southern fields and particularly important on the rice plantations of the Lowcountry. Several varieties became beloved, indeed became fixtures of Gullah cookery and later Lowcountry cuisine: the red pea, the rice pea, and black-eyed pea.

In West Africa a variety of red field pea landraces have been nurtured for centuries. The Haricot Rouge de Burkina Faso has the deep red surface of the Sapelo Island red pea, but not the shape and eye configuration. The Dadjime cowpea of Benin has the shape and eye configuration but is a shade smaller than southern red peas. A lineage of the sea island red pea awaits the genetic analysis needed to determine the exact West African patrimony. Both the Benin and Burkina Faso landraces have the good taste (both cooked seeds and leaves), productivity, and ability to withstand extremes of rain or drought that characterize the sea island red peas.

The red pea went everywhere the African diaspora touched—Brazil, Jamaica, Cuba. Its first mention in Lowcountry newspapers occurred in Charleston advertisements as "Bahama red pease" in winter 1786. Francis Courvoisie advertised quantities of "red pease" available at his plantation in Chatham County in February of 1810. Early advertisements indicated that the Lowcountry's early cultivators valued the field peas as fodder for livestock even more than they savored them as human food. A November 1812 newsletter from the Lowcountry reported, "The crop of field peas, or red and back-eyed peas, was never known to be so productive, and many planters think they will not be able to gather above one half the crop of that useful and valuable provision for cattle and sheep." It is a fully established commodity by the 1820s appearing regularly in the lists of products available at Lee & Palmes mercantile warehouse on the Savannah waterfront. By 1830 they were so widely cultivated and so prolific that there was no need for importing seed. Co-cropped with corn in the field, or in a pea row in a Gullah huck patch, it was the most common legume encountered in the Lowcountry. While the black-eyed pea, pods and vines, graced the feed trough in the cattle yard or hog pen, the red pea was found on the human table. The former had a rather chalky texture, the latter a deep meaty richness.

Sarah Rutledge supplied a recipe for red peas soup in *The Carolina Housewife*, the first recorded of a repertoire of red pea recipes ultimately of African origin that would include "hoppin' john, red pea likker, red pea gravy, red peas and snaps, fried red pea cakes, and peas & greens."

Red Peas Soup

Sarah Rutledge, *The Carolina Housewife* (1847)

One quart of peas, one pound of bacon, (or ham bone,) two quarts of water, and some celery chopped; boil the peas, and when half done, put in the bacon; when the peas are thoroughly boiled, take them out, and rub them through a cullender or coarse sieve, then put the pulp back into the pot with the bacon and season with a little pepper, and salt if necessary. If the soup should not be thick enough, a little wheat flour may be stirred in.

The addition of a bird or cayenne pepper was frequent in Gullah versions of the soup.

The red pea's reign began to diminish in the 1880s and 1890s when agricultural experimental stations touted other field pea varieties for their productivity, their disease resistance, and their speed in maturation. It survived where it had installed itself in the traditional foodways of the African diaspora: in the Sea Islands of Georgia and of course in Jamaica and other islands where it thrived and maintained its symbolic significance. Over the centuries the widely grown pea had become so attuned to the growing conditions of the Lowcountry that it naturalized and self-reproducing populations skirted old cornfields and ditches. In Geechee enclaves such as Sapelo Island it had never gone out of cultivation, so when the revival of Lowcountry ingredients occurred, the red pea became one of the signal African diaspora components of soul food and southern food.

Cornelia Bailey, the visionary matriarch of Sapelo Island, before her death in 2020, sought the revival of the economic fortunes of the saltwater Geechee population of the island by selling the island's signature agricultural products: red peas, purple ribbon sugar cane, and bitter oranges. The red peas found immediate favor, with chef Linton Hopkins in Atlanta spearheading their adoption in the culinary community. Now available from several sources—SICARS on Sapelo Island, Georgia Coastal Gourmet Farm, Gilliard Farms in Brunswick, Rollen's Raw Grains, and from Anson Mills—the sea island red pea has become an ingredient that has demonstrated the ability of traditional African diaspora foods to find new appreciators in the twenty-first century.

The late Cornelia Bailey, matriarch of Sapelo Island, her daughter, and her red peas. Photograph © David S. Shields.

Anson Mills Red Pea Gravy

ANSON MILLS

This is a favorite of my [Kevin] daughter, Jordynn. She loves the flavor curry gives the gravy. It must always be served with rice, or things are not right with the world. This hearty gravy served with rice can be a great dinner for "Meatless Mondays" if made with vegetable stock.
Serves 4 to 6, makes about 4 cups

- 1-quart smoked ham and chicken stock, defatted and ham bits reserved (see Note)
- 7 ounces (1 cup) Anson Mills Sea Island Red Peas, covered with water, soaked overnight in the refrigerator, then drained
- ½ yellow onion, peeled and cut through root end
- ½ carrot, peeled
- 2 small inner celery ribs, leaves attached
- 2 cloves garlic, peeled
- 1 small Turkish bay leaf
- 1 teaspoon curry powder
- ½ teaspoon red pepper flakes, or to taste
- Fine sea salt

Bring the stock to a simmer over medium-high heat in a heavy-bottomed 3-quart saucepan. Stir in the soaked and drained peas, onion, carrot, celery, garlic, bay leaf, and curry powder. Return the liquid to a simmer, then reduce the heat to low. Cover the pan partially and simmer gently, stirring occasionally, until the peas are tender, 60 to 75 minutes.

Remove and discard the vegetables and bay leaf. Season with red pepper flakes and salt to taste. Remove ¼ cup or so of peas and broth and puree them in a blender or food processor or using an immersion blender. Return the puree to the pot with the peas. (Alternatively, you can mash the peas directly in the pan with a potato masher or fork.) If the gravy is too thick, thin it with a bit of water. Stir in the reserved ham, if desired. Cook just until heated through. Taste for seasoning and serve hot over simple buttered Carolina Gold Rice grits or Carolina Gold Rice.

Note: Anson Mills provides a recipe for smoked ham and chicken stock at ansonmills.com. You can also use your preferred stock recipe or substitute store-bought chicken broth.

Shrimp

Shrimp stood foremost among the rich list of seafoods harvested along Georgia's Atlantic coast. Its primacy stands revealed in the order of subjects in the "Sea Food" section of Harriet Ross Colquitt's *The Savannah Cook Book*. Shrimp first, crab second, oysters third, terrapin fourth, then fish. Today shrimp remains the most valuable crop harvested by Georgia's fishermen. The bulk of the catch is white shrimp (mid-June through December) or brown shrimp (taken from June through August), with deep-water royal red shrimp a high-paying specialty crop. The harvest is well regulated, and the Georgia Department of Natural Resources notifies the fleet when populations can be sustainably taken.

As for preparation, shrimp were boiled/steamed, peeled and batter fried, stewed with tomatoes, baked with a coating of breadcrumbs in a butter and Worcestershire sauce mixture. Shrimp salad and bell peppers stuffed with shrimp became popular in the twentieth century. Some borrowed dishes developed avid followings: Louisiana's shrimp creole and shrimp gumbo, and Anglo-Indian shrimp curry. Lowcountry Georgia shared with Lowcountry South Carolina an inexhaustible taste for shrimp paste, a fixture on the hospitable table. There were a trio of shrimp dishes, however, that were "old Georgia," and present some of the most vibrant signatures of the region's cookery: shrimp fritters, shrimp pie, and shrimp mull.

Shrimp fritters were saltwater Geechee inspirations and took two forms: the batterless fritter and shrimp and rice croquette. The term croquette was synonymous with fritter, employed on banquet menus and women's club bills of fare from the 1890s onward to impart a French classiness to the food. During the anniversary banquets of the Savannah Rifles during the Gilded Age, shrimp croquettes invariably appeared on the menus—listings employing a liberal amount of menu "franglish." Because of the Howard Johnson Company's adoption of "shrimp croquette" as a mass-produced frozen convenience food in the mid-1960s, we opt for "shrimp fritter" to name these preparations. The first dates from the mid-nineteenth century, soon after the introduction of Worcestershire sauce into the southern pantry.

Shrimp Croquettes Fritters (Very Old)

Harriet Ross Colquitt,
The Savannah Cook Book (1933)

2 quarts shrimp
½ Wineglass Vinegar
1 Tablespoon Butter
A little grated Nutmeg
1 Tablespoon Worcestershire Sauce

Run [boiled and peeled] shrimp through grinder, mix with butter, vinegar, Worcestershire and nutmeg. Form into little cakes and fry in deep fat.

Traditionally the fat that cooks used to fry fritters was lard. But in the late 1880s vegetable based shortenings because of their cheapness began to supplant lard in Georgia's pantry. One of the companies producing vegetable shortening was the Plantene Company that touted its product by placing a recipe for shrimp fritters in the *Augusta Chronicle* in 1906.

Shrimp Fritters

Augusta Chronicle (November 13, 1906)

Boil one pint of shrimps in salted water, remove the shells and chop fine. Make a batter of three eggs, one teaspoonful of melted butter, one of melted Plantene, and grated bread crumbs or cracker crumbs. Beat to a stiff batter. Stir in the shrimps and fry in rolls of boiling Plantene. Serve on a napkin.

Savory rice fritters were standard Lowcountry food items, and combining chopped shrimp with rice seemed a natural improvement on the dish. Colquitt's recipe has the balls coated in bread crumbs, but this was an affectation. Both shrimp and rice caramelize well.

Shrimp and Rice Croquettes Fritters

Harriet Ross Colquitt,
The Savannah Cook Book (1933)

1 Cup Rice
2 Eggs
1 Tablespoon Butter
2 Quarts Shrimp

Cook rice and add butter while hot, then eggs, slightly beaten, and the finely minced shrimp. Season with salt and pepper, roll into shapes, dip in bread crumbs and egg, and fry in deep fat.

Lowcountry diners love the combination of shrimp and rice, so there is little surprise that when exposed to tempura fried shrimp in the latter half of the twentieth century, they embraced it. Tempura batter made of rice flour, egg, and beer seemed a very intuitive and right preparation. If one is tired of the heaviness and granularity of a cornmeal coating in seafood, the delicacy and fineness of a rice flour batter is an answer to one's desire for a new take on frying.

Shrimp and rice are married in the second of our trio of signature shrimp dishes—shrimp pie. At one time shrimp pie rivaled chicken pie as good home eats in Georgia. In Chatham County and the other rice-growing regions of the state, a shrimp and rice pie held sway. In the Midlands and Uplands of Georgia, Shrimp pie was cooked in a pot in a buttery tomato gravy and baked for an hour. No shrimp dishes appeared on the Georgia Products dinner menus from 1913. Unlike the oyster, which could be packed in barrels covered with straw or seaweed and cold shipped wherever you please, the shrimp spoiled in shipping barrels, so it would not be until the refinement of a cold bulk freezing that boxes of frozen shrimp began to circulate in some numbers in 1950. Yet in sections near the coast the shrimp was available from June until December.

Colquitt's shrimp pie is a direct parallel with her rice and chicken pie.

Shrimp or Prawn Pie

Harriet Ross Colquitt,
The Savannah Cook Book (1933)

2 Quarts Shrimp
1 Pint Milk
Mace, Salt, Pepper
1 Teaspoon Butter
1 Quart Rice
1 Egg

Boil rice in salted water until grainy. While hot add the butter, milk and seasoning. Put alternate layers of rice and shrimp in a deep dish, ending up with rice on top. Pour well-beaten egg over top, and bake in moderate oven.

Colquitt does not mention a top crust in her recipe. It was considered optional. The chief variant of the Savannah-style pie was a shrimp and rice pie flavored with curry.

Mrs. Hill in the 1870s pursued the other path of shrimp pie, eschewing rice, and flavoring the shrimp with tomatoes. Tomato catsup was the great innovation of sauce cooking in the mid-nineteenth century South. It was a thick, rich substance, usually depending upon the natural sweetness of tomatoes for flavor rather than adding sugar. This pot pie sometimes took the form of a casserole with mashed potatoes crowning it, rather than a crust or a thick layer of toasted bread crumbs.

Shrimp Pie

Annabella P. Hill,
Mrs. Hill's Southern Practical Cookery and Receipt Book (1872)

To two quarts of peeled shrimps add two tablespoonfuls of butter, half a pint of tomato catsup, half a tumbler of vinegar; season high with black and cayenne pepper; salt to taste; put into an earthen dish; strew grated biscuit or light bread crumbs very thickly over the top; bake slowly half an hour.

Since catsup these days tends to be liberally sugared ketchup, it may be wise to go with the version of this type of pie found in the *Atlanta Semi-Weekly Journal* in 1902. The recipe is said to be that in use in Charleston.

Shrimp Pie

Elle Goode,
Atlanta Semi-Weekly Journal
(January 16, 1902)

One plate tomatoes Take off the skin, and cut out the hard core; put on fire with one tablespoon butter and red pepper to taste; when it begins to boil put shrimps on for a little while; pour in a baking dish; add a large glass of wine, a little mustard and nutmeg; put a thick layer of bread crumbs on topo with little pats of butter; bake, garnish with parsley.

This recipe dates from an era before the Livingston-style tomatoes became standard in the South. Large tomatoes often did not ripen in the center at the same time most of the body of the tomato ripened. This is no longer a worry.

If Georgia shared its taste for shrimp pie with South Carolina, one wonders whether that other Charleston dish of fame, shrimp and grits, appeared on Georgia tables prior to the 1980s southern boom. Alas, neither shrimp and grits, or its older name, shrimp and hominy appear on menus, in cookbooks, or in newspaper recipe columns. Georgia came late to the table, but when it came, it consumed with relish.

Shrimp mull is the third signature shrimp dish in Georgia, and its character and history are detailed in the entry on mulls.

Shrimp and Crab Fritters

KEVIN MITCHELL

My wife, Rhonda, and son Jeremiah love shrimp marinated in buttermilk, dipped in cornmeal, and dropped in a deep fryer. Here I wanted to give them another way to enjoy fried shrimp. Next time you have some shrimp around, try this recipe. I'm sure you will love it.

Makes about 30 1-ounce fritters

- ¾ cup unbleached all-purpose flour
- ½ teaspoon baking powder
- 1 tablespoon salt
- 1 teaspoon smoked paprika
- ⅛ teaspoon cayenne pepper
- 1 egg
- 6 tablespoons water
- 2 tablespoons fresh parsley, chopped
- 1½ pound shrimp, chopped
- 6 ounces lump crabmeat
- ½ cup yellow onion, minced
- Vegetable oil for frying

Whisk together the flour, baking powder, salt, and spices in a bowl. Add the egg, water, and parsley and whisk together. Add the shrimp and onion. Mix until the batter is smooth.

Preheat the oil in a deep fryer to 350°F. Line a baking sheet with paper towels.

Using an ice cream scoop, drop a few balls of batter at a time into the hot oil. Watch out for splattering. Cook for about 8 minutes or until golden, turning halfway through. Drain on a paper towel. Let cool for 5 minutes. Serve with your favorite dipping sauce (e.g., cocktail, remoulade, creole remoulade, tartar sauce).

Shrimp and crab fritters by Kevin Mitchell. Photograph © Rhonda Wilson.

Snap Beans

Once there was a bean pod that had a string sealing the suture along its side. You had to pull the string off when processing the beans for cooking because it would not get tender when boiled and got stuck in your teeth. Older lazy folks know. But plant breeders remedied the problem of strings, breeding pole beans, wax beans, and green beans without strings. The first premiered in 1894—Burpee's stringless green pod bean. There was no turning back. These no fuss beans, as you might imagine, inspired great enthusiasm among those who labored in kitchens. One less task. Oh, there were still types of beans you had to shuck. And some people demanded that the tips of the pods be trimmed off. But one could avoid the labor of pulling bean strings, provided one chose the proper variety to grow. In the South you will find a contrarian group that resents change. They kept growing string beans (a reason why so many old bean varieties survive), claiming the new stringless beans tasted too sweet, and lacked the "lettucy" kiss of a classic stringed green bean.

At any rate, people had to have a term that encompassed the old string bean, the new stringless bean, the colored wax beans, the bush beans all of which were picked immature for cooking and eating, pod and all. The term that emerged was snap bean. They bear the name because the fresh bean is firm and crisp enough to make a snapping sound when broken into segments by your fingers. Yellow snap beans are sometimes called "wax beans." Green-colored beans either bear a variety name such as Kentucky wonder or blue lake, or are referred to as green beans. There are other sorts with other colors, more about that later. In general southerners tended to divide the realm of beans into three regions: snap beans, butter beans, and shuck beans (those produced for dried beans). Now a complication with this mental map is that snap beans if allowed to mature can become shuck beans; they are only snaps if picked immature and prepared for eating "green."

From the Civil War until World War II, great quantities of snap beans were produced as a truck farming crop shipped to northern markets. Ellijay in north Georgia became a growing hub. North Augusta became famous for the quality of its snaps at the beginning of the twentieth century, particularly its wax beans—the German black wax, the Willett's crystal white wax Bean, yellow wax. These would become fixtures in colorful three bean salads in the final quarter of the twentieth century. The canning industry, and then the frozen food industry made extensive use of snap beans. Canneries drove demand for wax beans. Frozen food companies favored green podded beans, a preference of the 1920s that remains today.

Snap beans are grown in good quantities by home gardeners in Georgia. Consumers little care if the snap bean they seek at the produce stand grew on a bush or formed a vine on a pole. Growers, however, tended to favor the bush bean because of its greater convenience when picking. Some pole beans form vines fifteen feet long. Yet some of the heirloom bean varieties most famous for taste are pole beans, so they live on in the garden. Whether one grows bush or pole varieties, one faces the same challenges.

Mexican bean beetles attack the leaves of your plants and can even kill them if not controlled. Thrips can cause your blossoms to shed. Root rot, bacterial blight, rust, and mildew devil your plants. Your beans need watering, so a protracted dry spell can injure the plants by desiccation. Yet with care, irrigation, and modest pest treatment you should bring in a bountiful harvest.

Most people buy seeds from one or another of the seed companies that maintain good lines of beans. But if you save your own seed, there is an old-time Georgia seed-saving hack that will save you some grief. One problem troubling seed saving in beans is the amount of insect larvae intruded in the seed. If you scrape some bark off a chinaberry tree and boil it to a decoction, soak your seeds in that brew; it will kill all pests.

The great debate in southern cookery is whether you cook the snap out of the snap bean. There was a time . . . and in some places it still is that time . . . when the cook filled a saucepan with water, put in a jowl or chunk of salt pork, turned on the heat, and let that pot simmer until the "dook" had been cooked out of the beans. The idea was that the flavors of beans and pork don't swap until the pods have been tenderized. A hallmark of the modern Georgian approach to vegetables is reducing the cooking time to leave the beans with some crisp texture.

Snap bean cookery evolved over the years. In the nineteenth century boiled beans were dressed with butter, sometimes milk and butter. Parsley was the chief herb adorning the plate, until the national discovery of tarragon in the mid-1880s (1885, the year of green goddess dressing). In the twentieth century it became the inevitable side for ham. When the Corning casserole dish became standard kitchen equipment in the 1950s, the snap beans and ham became a casserole. In August of 1955 newspapers in Augusta and Brunswick printed a syndicated recipe by Cecily Brownstone for fresh snap beans and ham casserole. It was a straightforward dish: layered parboiled snap beans, diced ham, Cheddar sauce, and bread crumbs for a crown. One half hour in

Snap beans enjoy pride of place in a classic pantry full of canned goods. Photograph © David S. Shields.

[183]

the over at 325°F made this a relatively short bake.

Green bean casseroles were one of the key dishes of post-World War II Georgia home cooking. When made with canned "french green beans" and canned celery or cream of mushroom soup, and topped with prepacked chow mein noodles or frozen french-fried onion rings, you had the ultimate convenience vegetable dish. To this base you could add cooked loose hamburger meat, hash, or cheese. Not every green bean casserole was so plain an amalgam of products of the American food industry. Certainly not the green bean casserole your aunt brings to the family Thanksgiving. Surely that is made with a white sauce, fresh steamed blue lake snap beans, sauternes, sour cream, sliced porcini mushrooms, and cashews, with a panko bread crumb topping. Or something like that.

If green bean casserole fed the baby-boomer generation, those that grew up in the Great Depression fed on green bean salad. It begins to appear on dinner menus in Augusta in 1933. Often accompanied by nuggets of bacon, slivered almonds, mushrooms, or tomato wedges, the salad employed cold boiled green beans, and the character was imparted by the dressing. Garlic was a bold add in the 1930s. Dijon mustard became popular in the 1960s. This was standard picnic fare, or a buffet dish for an outdoor event.

Snap beans can also be oiled, salted, and grilled. And of course they can be parboiled and pickled. Of the standard pickles prepared by home canners, dilly beans ranks third after chowchow and pickled peaches in the honor roll of pickles, if we are to judge by entries in state and county fairs.

Squash Casserole

Summer squash in Georgia means one of two things: the yellow crookneck squash or the pattypan or button squash (called "cymling" in other parts of the South). The pattypan was considered a refined squash. Its flying saucer shape and scalloped edge catches the eye. Cooks removed the core of seeds, diced the meat, and boiled the vegetable until tender. It could be seasoned, napped in butter, or nestled in a sauce for a simple, clean tasting hot-weather dish. The yellow crookneck squash enjoyed a much broader popularity, generating an ample repertoire of boiled, baked, sautéed and fried preparations. Yellow summer squash contributed to two of Georgia's signature dishes: squash casserole and squash fritters.

The yellow summer squash (*Cucurbita pepo*) can have either a straight or crooked neck, a warted or a smooth skin. It is an ancient vegetable native to the Western Hemisphere and a central food of Native Americans from New England to the West Indies. It can be seen in the 1621 engraving of Native West Indians in Casper Plautus's *Nova Typis Transacta Navigatio* among the pile of native foods encircling a chieftain. Naturalist William Bartram noted its presence in fields of corn and beans during his travels through Georgia and Florida in the 1770s. Native breeders had created the yellow summer squash out of hard-bodied gourds by seed selection over hundreds of plant generations, refining the squash into a succulent tender fleshed vegetable that retained much water. Colonial Georgians obtained seed for their vegetable gardens and the summer squash became, along with the pumpkin, a widely grown cucurbit by the end of the eighteenth century. All strains

Yellow summer squash, the chief ingredient in squash casserole. Photograph © David S. Shields.

of the yellow crookneck share a waxy outer skin, tender flesh, and pointed lance-shaped edible seeds.

European colonists, for the most part, did not know what to do with squash. They did not eat the blossoms of the male plants as the Creeks and Cherokees did, nor did they dry strips of flesh to reconstitute with water later, providing a summer vegetable in winter. Colonists did not co-crop the squash with corn and beans as Native Americans did. Finally, settlers did not eat the vegetable raw as the Native Americans did; indeed, the Algonquin word that suggested the English name squash, *askutasquash*, means "eaten raw." In early American plantings it was a kitchen garden standalone grown in a section where the vines could carpet the soil.

If the squash vine received too great a watering during the growing season, or if it was planted on too sandy a soil, it would produce relatively tasteless fruit. The only thing you can do with a crookneck lacking flavor is to hollow it, stuff it with sausage or a bread crumb, cheese, and mushroom mixture and bake it. But if your yellow squash has its characteristic delicate flavor, then it is best to boil it to preserve its savor. The squash is cut into transverse disc-like slices, then boiled in salted water. A simple favorite preparation is to boil the squash with onion slices, salt, and butter.

Sometimes the boiled squash was mashed. Squash casserole can be said to be the elevation of mashed squash into something artful and yet homey. It was only later that a "slicer" style squash casserole came into existence. A casserole is a medley of ingredients baked in a casserole dish, a French cooking vessel that became a kitchen fixture in the early nineteenth century. Bertrand Latouche in 1827 advertised the first casserole found in American print at his Market Street Restaurant in Philadelphia. It was amalgam of game, rice, and poultry. By the final quarter of the nineteenth century the casserole had ceased being a professional chef preparation and became home cooking. Mrs. J. B. Wells Jr. of Brunswick provided a classic version of the dish for *Gems from Georgia Kitchens* (1963).

Baked Squash Casserole

Mrs. J. B. Wells Jr.,
Gems from Georgia Kitchens (1963)

2 lbs young tender squash
1 small onion
¼ teaspoon salt
½ teaspoon freshly ground pepper
1 cup grated cheese
3 tablespoons butter
½ cup milk
½ cup breadcrumbs

Cut up squash and onion; add pepper, salt and enough water to cover. Stew until ingredients are tender. Drain remaining water and mash squash. Add cheese, 2 tablespoons butter and milk; mix well. Pour into casserole; top with breadcrumbs and remaining butter. Bake for 12–14 minutes at 350 degrees, until brown.

Perhaps the major alternative to this basic recipe is one that substitutes bacon drippings for some of the butter, and folds in two lightly beaten eggs into the mixture before it is placed in the oven.

The Campbell's Soup Company in the 1970s promoted a squash casserole using sour cream, cream of chicken soup, and Pepperidge Farm corn bread stuffing. In the 1960s and 1970s the can-of-soup casserole was a common enough resort among home cooks. But the path to the future lay with persons keeping to the basic ingredients, resisting the compulsion of later twentieth-century southern cooks to add a teaspoon of sugar to dishes, and seeking seasonings beyond pepper and salt to supplement flavor. Paprika, celery salt, bacon crumbles or drippings. But the most consequential additive was grated cheese. A family of Cheddary casseroles came into being that rivaled the plain squash and onion original. In the late 1960s and early 1970s peanuts were added to the casserole as a textural element. Its popularity was short lived because the fundamental attraction of squash in a casserole was its silky tenderness. This quality was explored in the intermittent efforts at making squash soufflé a fine-dining elaboration of the old home favorite.

Sweet Potatoes

In Georgia the older varieties of red, orange, and yellow sweet potatoes bear the name yam; white-fleshed sweet potatoes are called "sweet potatoes," as are modern varieties with colored flesh that were chartered and issued under proprietary names—for instance the Beauregard and Covington sweet potatoes that now dominate produce sections.

Sweet potatoes originated in South America and came to Georgia during the colonial era. The orange- and yellow-fleshed potatoes arrived first and developed an avid following among both Muskogee people and European settlers. Most white-fleshed sweet potatoes (Hayman, dixie queen, etc.) descend from plants imported into the South from the West Indies during the mid-nineteenth century. Shortly after the founding of the United States, Georgia would become home to a series of distinctive varieties of sweet potato: the long, thin, red-coated Spanish; the yellow-fleshed Georgia yam; the orange-fleshed, red-skinned choker sweets; the sugar yam; and the pumpkin yam.

Early on decided preferences developed about how the tubers should be cooked and which varieties performed best. Northerners boiled sweet potatoes and favored the dry flesh Virginia Nansemond (often renamed "Jersey") potato for eating. Georgians, like most southerners, favored sweet, moist, sugary baking varieties.

Among Georgians, preferences diverged between African Americans, who favored the red-skinned fibrous and sweet choker potatoes, while white Georgians favored the sugar yam or the pumpkin yam (Price, 1896). The split in opinion between the sugar and the pumpkin came down to dollars. A commentator in 1897 bemoaned the fact that both sold for the same price at the produce stand, while the former produced about fifty bushels an acre while the latter nearly twice as much. Too bad that the former was more sumptuous. "If epicures only knew the difference, however, we think they would be willing to pay more for the original sugar yam, the imprisoned sweetness of which, liberated by the heat, exudes through the skin and trickles in syrup down the outside as it cooks" (1897). The laments found an audience. Resorts and hotels in Georgia and Florida began requesting the sugar yam by name and Miss Leola Reid of Blakely, Georgia, began supplying them at $5.00 a barrel, with nearly two and a half bushels of potatoes in a barrel. Some hoteliers balked at the price. (A standard barrel price for the pumpkin yam was $1.25.) She responded, "let the guests decide. They did so, and as a result I sold all my crop before the winter was well begun" (1901). She had a profit of $500 on her first crop. Servicing the luxury market kept a handful of producers cultivating the variety until the World War I. The food campaigns of World War I made economy the requirement of all commodity crops, and so expensive items disappeared from the seed catalogs. N. L. Willet of Augusta last listed the sugar yam in his 1919 seed catalog: "The old-fashioned kind; not prolific, making only 60 to 75 bushels per acre, but the sweetest of all potatoes for home use. Tubers are medium size, oblong, light in color, cook soft and yellowish; leaves are forked with

4 or 5 slits; long vines; earlier than Pumpkin Yams." Their loss was somewhat assuaged by the introduction of the Porto Rico yam, a productive pink-fleshed tuber that immediately gained favor among pie makers.

What of those pumpkin yams? Pink-skinned and red-fleshed, they sometimes went by the name of the Dooley and also the Georgia buck. It was a later season potato, but greatly productive, and good tasting. Coming to Georgia sometime in the eighteenth century, it was one of several varieties grown by pockets of cultivators in the state. Its rise to prominence and its recognition as the most profitable commodity sweet potato was due to John A. Phillips of Sterling Station who nurtured a highly productive strain in the late 1870s and spread the potato to other cultivators. As a nineteenth-century writer in the *Savannah Morning News* commented, the Pumpkin yam "is not to be despised for table use. It is a very fair potato and preferable to most other kinds." They remain a variety in cultivation, as does the Porto Rico.

And the sugar yam? We suspect it too survived. Heavenly Seeds in South Carolina offers a sweet named after retired Clemson botanist David Bradshaw. It has the signature split leaves, the same coloration of skin and flesh, the same penchant of weeping sugar when baked. It's one difference: It is more productive than the old sugar yam.

These old varieties of potatoes with their taste and cooking properties shaped the dishes that made the sweet potato a pillar of southern cooking. Modern cultivars rarely taste as good—both the Georgia jet and the Beauregard pale in comparison. The Covington has a good deal of the sensory appeal of the heirlooms, and the Murasaki, a Japanese import, adds a great deal of visual beauty to a winning sweetness. In the two most basic sweet potato dishes, baked sweet potatoes and candied sweet potatoes, the flavor of the potato stands paramount. When it comes to soufflé or pie, texture becomes as important as flavor. If you want the classic texture and taste of pie, hunt down someone growing Porto Rico, pumpkin yam, or a Bradshaw sweet potato. If you are cooking a classic pone, the modern garnet sweet potato will do admirably.

SWEET POTATO PONE

The oldest sweet potato preparation beside ash-roasted sweet potatoes is potato pone. It migrated from the West Indies to the mainland sometime in the late eighteenth century. Reverand Griffith Hughes first records the dish in the 1750 *Natural History of Barbados*. The most widely reprinted recipes from the 1800s in American newspaper alludes to this West Indian background.

Potato Pone

True Flag (February 22, 1868)

This is a favorite dish in the West Indian Islands. Wash, peel and grate two pounds of potatoes; add four ounces each of sugar and butter (or beef dripping), melted, one teaspoonful each of salt and pepper; mix well together; place it in a baking-dish, and put it into a brisk oven until it is done and becomes nicely browned.

In Georgia, Potato Pone differed from custard in that the potato was not precooked before amalgamating the ingredients. Pone is a baked dish whose base is shredded raw sweet potatoes. Cooks sweetened pone with molasses more often than sugar until the 1950s and spiced with nutmeg, clove, and cinnamon, with a zest of lemon or orange. Some sort of fat (butter, margarine, lard, Crisco) was needed. When the eggs were added to make it more like custard is difficult to determine. A March 14, 1883, issue of *Farmer and Mechanic* (Raleigh, North Carolina) chided recent adulterations: adding eggs, boiling and mashing the sweet potatoes. Fortunately Georgians sought to keep the distinction, and we can see that, despite the addition of eggs into the mixture, the following fancy pone recipe by Mrs. Brian Cumming in the Augusta junior league cookbook, *Old and New Recipes from the South* (1947).

Rosa's Sweet Potato Pone

Mrs. Brian Cumming, *Old and New Recipes from the South* (1947)

You probably do not know Rosa, but she is as much a part of Georgia as the cotton and the pines, and this is her recipe for Sweet Potato Pone—will serve 8 persons.

Grate 3 large sweet potatoes and put in baking pan—pour over this 2 eggs well beaten and mix with ¼ cup sifted flour, ½ cup sugar and 1½ cups sweet milk. Stir in the following in order given. Juice of grated rind of 1 large orange, 1 wine glass of sherry or whiskey, 1 teaspoon vanilla, 1 cup raisins, ½ teaspoon nutmeg, ½ teaspoon cinnamon, 1 tablespoon butter. Bake in moderate oven until potatoes are done (½ hour) then pour over the top ½ cup sugar mixed with 1 tablespoon of butter and ½ cup of chopped nuts. Return to oven and brown.

SWEET POTATO PIE

Georgians make two kinds of pies: custard made of mashed sweet potatoes and slicers made of thin disks of yam mingled with butter and brown sugar. The custard form collected a multitude of names: "Sweet potato pie is a great favorite in the south, and the men come in asking, 'Got any tate pone?' Another name for sweet potato pie is 'poodle pie.' Everything is custard, too, in the pie line. Ordinary custard pie is called 'egg custard;' lemon pie is 'lemon custard,' potato pie is 'potato custard'" (*The State*, 1896). The last name applied exclusively to that species of pie made with mashed sweet potatoes. In old cookbooks you'll find the recipe called "custard" as often as "pie." Any open-faced pie lacking a top crust with a body smoothed by beaten eggs could be called a custard.

Old-school sweet potato custard/pie often contained a shot of sherry or brandy in the filling. With the coming of Prohibition, the alcohol disappeared. The post-1919 template for the pie was roughly this:

> 1 cup of sweet potatoes cooked, mashed, salted, and buttered, beaten and run through a sieve
> 1 ½ cups of whole milk, or sour cream intermixed with the sweet potatoes

Spices—cinnamon, ginger, nutmeg an minimum
4 tablespoons of sugar (brown or white)
2 eggs beaten into the mixture

Depending on the taste of the pie maker, the proportions of ingredients, the dryness of the pie, and the spice level might be altered. This would be poured over a crust in a pie plate and baked. Once finished the top may be sprinkled with sugar.

The slicer pie differed. It had a top crust. It baked in a deep dish and so stood thicker than a custard pie. It demanded a longer time in the over—at least an hour. The classic Georgia recipe appeared in *Mrs. Hill's Southern Practical Cookery and Receipt Book.*

Sliced Potato Pie

Annabella P. Hill,
Mrs. Hill's Southern Practical Cookery and Receipt Book (1872)

For baking this, a plate deeper than the common pie-plate is necessary. Bake medium-sized sweet potatoes not quite done; yams are best. Line the plate with good paste; slice the potatoes; place a layer upon the bottom of the plate; over this sprinkle thickly a layer of good brown sugar; over this place thin slices of butter and sprinkle with flour, seasoning with spices to the taste. A heaped tablespoonful of butter and a heaped teaspoonful of flour will be sufficient for one pie. Put on another of potatoes, piled a little in the middle. Mix equal quantities of wine and water, lemon juice and water, or vinegar and water, and pour in enough to half fill the pie; sprinkle over the potato a little flour, and place on the upper crust, pinching the edges carefully together. Cut a slit in the centre, and bake slowly for one hour."

Particularly noteworthy is Hill's designation of a category of sweet potato to employ: the yam.

SWEET POTATO FRITTERS

One of the contributions of saltwater Geechee cooks to sweet potato cookery was the sweet potato fritter. When one had a sumptuous batter, such as that made of mashed sweets intended for baking as a pie or custard, the matter of time sometimes intruded. Pies took time to bake. Sometimes you did not have time. You could have something as wonderful as a pie by dropping a ball of the egg-enriched raw sweet potato custard into a skillet of boiling lard (or Crisco). Cooking time diminished greatly, and the crispy golden fritter retrieved from the skillet, sweetened with a wine sauce or cane syrup. Here is a 1913 fritter recipe published in the *Atlanta Journal.*

Sweet Potato Fritter

Atlanta Journal (March 11, 1913)

Rub through a colander boiled sweet potatoes to make two cupfuls. Add one tablespoonful of melted butter, two tablespoonsful each of cream and flour, and three eggs, well beaten. Drop by spoonfuls into deep fat and fry brown.

SWEET POTATO BISCUIT

Many wonderful things appear in holiday breadbaskets. Cracklin' corn bread, cat head biscuits, corn muffins, light bread, and johnnycakes. But there is a case to be made that the finest item of all is the sweet potato biscuit. These first appeared on Georgia's tables in the mid-1800s when baking powder became widely available on grocery shelves. A ratio of flour to mashed sweet potato developed early on: three units of flour for every one unit of sweet potato. There was milk, there was fat, there was baking powder. The amount and type of seasoning has long been a free-for-all with each family having its special formulation. The oldest forms of the recipe use yeast instead of backing powder and require five to six hours to prepare. Pat Kilmark, columnist for the *Forsyth County News*, provides the recipe in its purist form in the December 12, 1986, issue.

Sweet Potato Biscuit

Pat Kilmark, *Forsyth County News*
(December 12, 1986)

1½ cups sifted flour
1½ teaspoons baking powder
½ teaspoon salt
3 tablespoons butter or shortening
½ cup cold mashed [sweet] potatoes
6 tablespoons milk

Sift together the dry ingredients, work in the shortening, and cut in the sweet potatoes. Moisten with milk, using only enough to form a soft tender dough. Turn onto a lightly floured board, knead until just smoothe and roll out ½ inch thick. Cut into 1 to 1 ½ inch biscuits. Bake in a hot oven (450 degrees F) until browned.

SWEET POTATO JOHNNYCAKE

Perhaps the greatest service any student of Georgia's food can perform is to bring to attention splendid traditional dishes or foodways that have passed from general memory. We don't need more directions on how to make candied sweet potatoes. But we may need something rare and splendid. In 1921 Mrs. H. M. Davis of Fitzgerald, Georgia—one of the foremost cooks in the south-central region of the state—won a newspaper contest with a recipe for a form of biscuit using cornmeal instead of wheat flour. It captures a type of food once popular, cooked on a hearth. All that category of flat breads called "johnnycakes" were cooked by proximity to flames or embers.

Sweet Potato Johnny Cake

Mrs. H. M. Davis, *Fitzgerald Leader*
(September 21, 1921)

Take one pint of corn meal and sift with half teaspoonful of salt; rub into the meal a large table spoon of lard, next add to it one pint of smoothly mashed [sweet] potatoes. If potatoes are not very sweet add a table spoonful of sugar; mix thoroughly to a rather soft dough but not too soft to handle. Have a middle stave of a barrel head (oak wood) and on this evenly spread the dough not quite out to the edges of the board. Dip a knife blade in cold water and with it smooth the surface of the Johnny cake and stick with fork as you would biscuit.

Set before the fire with a brick or flat iron to support it; let it brown nicely, then loosen it from the board by means of a coarse thread pass between the board and the cake. Turn the board over and lay the brown side of the cake down on it again setting it before the fire to brown the other side. When it is done cut it in three inchwide pieces there will be about five of them. Butter well and serve while hot.

Georgia has had a long and passionate engagement with sweet potatoes. Its relation with fried sweet potatoes deserves its own celebration.

Roasted Sweet Potato Apple Soup with Cardamom Crème Fraîche and Country Ham

KEVIN MITCHELL

A bowl of soup is my go-to meal when the temperature lowers in the fall. Sweet potato soup is one of my favorites. It screams fall with nutmeg, allspice, and cinnamon. The cardamom crème fraîche also adds a kick of spice.
Yields 2 to 2½ quarts (8–10 cups)

- 4 large, sweet potatoes, peeled and diced
- 3 shallots, cut into large dice
- 3 fuji apples or another tart apple, unpeeled, cores removed, and diced (about 3 cups)
- 4 sprigs thyme
- 3½ tablespoons olive oil
- 2 quarts (8 cups) vegetable or chicken broth, divided
- 1 tablespoon kosher salt
- Pinch nutmeg
- Pinch allspice
- Pinch cinnamon
- Cardamom Crème Fraîche, to serve (recipe follows)
- Country Ham Cracklings, to serve (recipe follows)

Preheat oven to 450°F.

Toss the potato, shallot, apple, and thyme in a large bowl with 1½ tablespoon olive oil. Place on a baking sheet and roast in the oven for one hour or until tender. Remove the mixture from the oven. Let cool.

Once cooled, add the remaining oil, sweet potatoes, apples, and shallots to a heavy-bottomed soup pot. Sauté over medium heat for about 1 minute. Add 1½ quarts (6 cups) broth. Bring to a simmer over low heat for 10 minutes. In batches, puree mixture in a blender and blend until smooth. Pour it back into the soup pot. Adjust with ½ quart chicken broth if needed. Warm for 5 minutes. Adjust seasoning with salt. Stir in salt, nutmeg, allspice, and cinnamon. Cook for 3 to 5 minutes. Pour soup into prewarmed bowls. Finish with Crème Fraîche and Country Ham Cracklings.

Cardamom Crème Fraiche

1 cup crème fraîche
1 teaspoon ground cardamom

Combine crème fraîche and ground cardamom. Mix until smooth.

Note: Sour cream can be used if crème fraiche is not available

Country Ham Cracklings

3 ounces thinly sliced country ham

Preheat oven to 350°F. Line a baking sheet with parchment paper. Place ham on the prepared baking sheet. Bake for 15 minutes or until crisp. Cool. Crumble and hold for garnish.

Roasted sweet potato apple soup by Kevin Mitchell. Photograph © Rhonda Mitchell.

Sweet Potato Fries

First there was the age of french-fried sweet potatoes, a dish of great simplicity, modeled on the french-fried potatoes and seasoned with basic salt and pepper. It began in the 1890s and lasted through the 1930s. Then there was the age of sweet potato fries, when factory-produced frozen cut fries were distributed to restaurants and groceries. Seasoned with either spicy seasoning or sugar and cinnamon, sweet potato fries became a popular mass food in the 1990s.

French-fried sweet potatoes first appeared on the Christmas menu of the Aragon Hotel in Atlanta in 1897. Early in the twentieth century it remained a special banquet dish or home occasion preparation served to special guests and honored members of the family. In the 1920s french-fried sweet potatoes began being sprinkled with sugar as well as salt. The first printed recipes date from this era, appearing in 1928.

French Fried Sweet Potatoes

Atlanta Journal (December 14, 1928)

Pare large sweet potatoes, cut in finger shaped pieces 2 inches long and ½ inch thick and steam 5 to 10 minutes or until tender but not soft. Drain on soft paper and fry in hot deep fat five minutes. Sprinkle slightly with salt and powdered sugar and serve immediately.

By 1928 locally produced peanut oil rivaled lard as the fat used to fry the sweet potatoes. Both produced excellent results.

French-fried sweet potatoes were considered excellent complements to certain dishes. In Marietta it accompanied ham. It became a dish served with barbecue in the Midlands. Baked bluefish and a side of french-fried sweet potatoes became standard in the Lowcountry.

The commercial potential of the french-fried sweet potato was not lost on the food scientists and agriculture officials in Georgia. In 1958, Dr. J. G. Woodroof of the Griffin Experimental Station began working on making the precut sweet potato a commodity. Sweet potatoes grow in variable sizes, and oversized tubers do not readily sell at the produce stand or for the restaurant trade. Chopping them up would overcome that problem. Woodroof made a fundamental mistake in his development of his idea. He reasoned that homemakers would have personal preferences about the sizes of the sweet potato batons they put in the boiling oil, so he provided frozen sweet potato slices that a cook could cut into sticks as she or he saw fit. It did not catch on.

So, by an odd historical accident, Dr. Maurice W. Hoover, professor of food science at North Carolina State University invented the sweet potato fry as we now know it in the late 1970s. He did not offer the homemaker any say in the size of the batons. Indeed he didn't target the home cook as the ideal customer. He wanted to establish the sweet potato fry as a southern restaurant side dish. He would provide restaurateurs with precut frozen fries ready for the fry basket. He partnered with a processor and had product in 1979.

When the first fries went on sale, consumer feedback indicated that the fries were too soft. Customers expected the crispness of the classic french fry and weren't getting it. So scientists at North Carolina State, Clemson, and Georgia State began furiously testing the various cultivars of sweet potato to determine which possessed the most gumption after a scalding in deep fat. (The Hannah is perhaps best, but it is too light colored; people expect sweet potato fries to be orange.) It took until 1987 before the public began embracing the sweet potato fry. There were places that pioneered its appearance on menus of public eateries: Daytona, Florida, and Myrtle Beach, South Carolina. But the thing that tipped the restaurant industry in favor of the sweet potato fry was research by North Carolina State published in 1987 that neither flavor nor nutrition degraded in the fries after a year of being frozen. It is a sad comment on the fast-food industry that this was the dealmaker. The USDA jumped on this report and began promoting the fries nationally. By 1990 sweet potato fries, cooked in peanut oil, had become a restaurant fixture.

Sometime in 1988 Skeeter's Mesquite Grill in Duluth, outside Atlanta, added sweet potato fries to its daily chalkboard bill of fare. It would become the first documented Georgia eatery to embrace a food that in the past three decades has become one of the most popular sides in the South and particularly beloved in Georgia. It is perhaps surprising that the sweet potato fry came upon the scene so late in the twentieth century. Regular french fries became popular in the state in the 1920s, and since more sweet potatoes were grown in Georgia than "Irish potatoes," one would think that the preparation method was easily transferable. But Georgians were content with their candied sweet potato, and when they tweaked sweet potato dishes it tended to be in the direction of pies, not fries.

Skeeter's pioneered the most popular method of serving the fries, dusting them with sugar and cinnamon. The geographic associations of the sweet potato were broad enough for different types of restaurants to add them to the list of sides.

One problem deviled cooking sweet potato fries. Because the intrinsic color of the sweet potato chips put into the fry basket was darker than standard french fries, it was difficult to judge from the color of the sweet fries when they had cooked sufficiently. Too often overcooked fries came out of the boiling peanut oil. The problem proved so sticky that when food editors decided it was time to recognize the popular new food, the first recipe supplied—in the January 9, 1997, issue of the *Atlanta Journal*, it was for "Spicy Oven-Baked Sweet Potato 'Fries.'" Instead of sugar and spice the "fries" were dusted with Cajun seasoning.

In the twenty-first century sweet potato fries can be had almost anywhere in the state. In the hands of an expert fry cook with a tactful hand at sweetening and seasoning it can be a sublime accompaniment to a wide variety of dishes.

Trout

While the freshwater sport fishing industry in Georgia is smitten with bass, the important culinary fish throughout history has been the trout. On the 1913 Georgia Products menus one finds trout on menus from across the state—from Americus (baked), Chatham County (cornmeal), Dooly County (stuffed), Douglas (broiled), Milledgeville (baked), Savannah (baked), and Sumter County (broiled with butter parsley sauce). Bass did not appear once. The variety served was invariably the native brook trout (aka "speckled trout"). The rainbow trout would not be introduced into north Georgia streams until 1923, and the European brown trout would arrive in the 1930s. Early in the twentieth century, anglers took brook trout from eight to sixteen inches long. The cutting of forests, erosion, development along the rivers and creeks of north Georgia, and a disinclination to impose conservation limitations have caused the population to decline and the size of the surviving trout to diminish. They hold on in the headwaters of the Upcountry, approximately 150 of the state's four thousand miles of waterways, and regular stocking from the Georgia hatchery is the only thing keeping them from disappearing. Until recently no streams had been designated catch and release waters. Few limits have been placed on the harvest of smaller fish. No live bait can be used in trout fishing; artificial lures are specified for many areas. The universal trout creel limit of seven fish per day pertains. So here for the sake of future generations of southerners, we suggest you not serve the old historical brook trout—make use of the rainbow and brown trout instead.

Are the tastes of the brook, rainbow, and brown similar? There is a surprising difference. The brook trout when filleted has a whiter flesh than either rainbow (pink to salmon) and brown (orange). It has a milder, sweeter taste. The rainbow trout has a more pronounced oiliness, and a meatier flavor when baked. The brown trout has a similarly fatty quality and has a nuttier flavor. But some diners detect a faint muddy aftertaste that renders them less cherishable than the rainbow.

Whole trout ready for dressing. Fillet? Stuff and bake? Poach? Your choice. Photograph © David S. Shields.

Three breeding facilities managed by the Georgia Department of Natural Resources—Burton Trout Hatchery in Rabun County, Summerville Trout Hatchery in Chattooga County, Buford Trout Hatchery north of Atlanta—restock state lakes and streams with catchable rainbow and brown trout over nine inches in length. Juvenile brook trout are supplied to streams sufficiently cold to nurture that species.

Specimens of the lustrous rainbow trout, or California trout, and the European brown trout had been secured by Georgia ichthyologists in the 1880s for study. They did not thrive in the conditions in which the scientists raised them, and questions hung over the possibility of introducing these species into Georgia waters. Georgia fishermen read in 1905 of the extraordinary success New Zealand had in naturalizing Europe's brown trout and the California rainbow trout to its waters. In 1907 they read how rainbow trout eggs were being shipped from western hatcheries to Japan. Why not us? They wondered. When the Georgia Railway and Power Company excavated Lake Rabun in 1915 seven miles north of Tallulah Falls, they stocked it with rainbow trout, the first recorded large-scale introduction recorded in the state. The fish began appearing on Georgia restaurant menus in 1922.

Brown trout began being stocked in Georgia's waterways in the late 1920s. In 1934 the US Fisheries department sent two hundred thousand eggs from its Montana hatchery for development at the Summerville breeding facility. This shipment supercharged large-scale stocking efforts that enable the brown trout to rival the rainbow in numbers in the largest lakes and waterways of Georgia by the outbreak of World War II. The brown trout migrates out to the Atlantic Ocean and becomes adapted to salt water and is referred to as a sea trout when captured there. The brown sea trout does not have the faint muddy aftertaste of the freshwater version.

When seeking out recipes for trout, you do best seeking directions from fishermen from upstate Georgia. They supply time-tested presentations that do not mask the delicate intrinsic flavor of the fishes with elaborate sauces or distracting ingredients. Mike Webber, sports editor for the *Forsyth County News* during the 1980s, published versions of all the trout country classics. His recipes can be used for every variety of trout taken from Georgia waters.

Grilled Trout

Mike Webber, *Forsyth County News*
(March 30, 1988)

4 rainbow trout
⅓ cup butter
2 tablespoons lemon juice
1 teaspoon salt
¼ teaspoon pepper
1 teaspoon Rosemary

Build fire placing grill above coals. Melt butter adding salt, lemon juice, and Rosemary. Grill trout using the butter combination for a baste. Grill trout for seven minutes or longer until the fish flakes easily. Serve and eat.

Fried Trout

Mike Webber, *Forsyth County News*
(March 30, 1988)

6 trout
½ pound sliced bacon
1 teaspoon salt
½ teaspoon pepper
¼ cup corn meal or flour

Split trout and clean. Build a fire and fry bacon until crisp. Season fish with salt and pepper, coating each lightly with corn meal or flour. Fry trout in bacon fat for eight minutes or until golden, turning with pancake turner. Fry for seven minutes longer. Serve with bacon and lemon wedges.

Stuffed Trout

Mike Webber, *Forsyth County News*
(March 30, 1988)

Butterfly 6 trout
1 cup sliced mushrooms
½ cup cherry tomatoes
1 tablespoon chopped green pepper
1 tablespoon chopped onion
1 clove garlic
1 teaspoon salt
Dash of pepper
6 slices of bacon
½ cup of butter

Combine mushrooms, tomatoes, green pepper, onion, garlic, salt and pepper. Divide this filling evening among trout. Tie and wrap a slice of bacon around each trout, securing with wooden tooth picks. Built a hot fire and place trout seven to 10 inches above coals on grill. Brush trout with butter, cooking about seven minutes. Serve with chunky French fried potatoes.

Webber devised all of his recipes for cooking outdoor on embers. The temperature control on a grill is less precise than that on a kitchen range, and so Webber stuffs his trout with vegetables, rather than bread crumbs or other ingredients that may perform poorly if the temperature is not strictly regulated. Classic oven-baked stuffed trout recipes employ stuffings made of (1) cooked rice, herbs, butter, and seasoning; (2) sautéed onion, celery, carrot, bread crumbs, lemon juice, and seasoning; and (3) onions, corn bread, parsley, seasoning, and lemon juice.

One of the innovations in trout cookery in the latter half of the twentieth century was the rise in barbecued trout recipes. The barbecue sauce usually employed tomato catsup, Worcestershire sauce, brown sugar, vinegar, and some hot sauce. The fish was laid in an oven dish, covered with barbecue sauce and baked at a rather high temperature (425°F) for a half an hour.

Trout can be fished year-round in Georgia to persons over the age of sixteen holding both a fishing license and trout license. Each individual must use a solitary pole and line for fishing and cannot employ live fish for bait. There are special regulations for certain waters, particularly those that are the native habitat of the brook trout.

Turnips and Turnip Sallet

The turnip was Europe's great root vegetable—the linchpin of the first crop rotation schemes in the Low Countries in the 1300s. It was the food that nourished sheep through the winter and the vegetable whose every part was edible. England went turnip mad in the 1700s. Agronomist Arthur Young proclaimed that it would sustain Britain's sheep in wintertime and grace the January table for humans. Even before Young evangelized Britain, parts of the kingdom had loved the humble vegetable. Some grew it for the greens, which they called "sallet." The Welsh grew it for fodder. Soon after George Oglethorpe founded the Georgia colony in 1732, colonial cultivators planted beds of sallet. Georgia remains one of the few places in the United States where some residents refer to turnips greens as "turnip salad."

Nearly every variety of turnip developed by European gardeners in the eighteenth and early nineteenth century came into North America before 1830. What exactly were the turnip varieties grown in our region during the early 1800s. And where did farmers procure seed? Here are twenty-tree types present in the Lowcountry in 1830. The second column provides the date of introduction in South Carolina, Georgia, or Florida. The third column lists the seed brokers responsible for bringing the seed into the region. This list first appeared in David Shields's *Southern Provisions*. From 1830 to 1860 an additional 13 varieties joined this foundation stock.

Turnip Type	Date Introduced	Seed Broker
Early Flat Dutch	1830	Wilson Phil
Early Spring	1820	Thornton NY-NE
Fine Early Stone	1830	Wilson Phil
French, or Hanover	1820	Thornton NY-NE
Green Round	1811	Nesbet London
Green Top	1820	Thornton NY-NE
Large Norfolk	1808	Wilson London
Large Silver	1800	Vale SC
Large White Flat	1819	Thornton NY
London White	1804	Wilson London
Long Transparent	1816	Wilson London [Cowhorn]
Norfolk	1800	Vale London
Red Top	1820	Thornton NY-NE
Red Top Tankard	1825	Wilson Liverpool
Short Top	1808	Wilson London
Snowball	1848	Landreth PA
Strap Leaf	1849	Dawson Liverpool

Turnip Type	Date Introduced	Seed Broker
Swan's Egg	1837	Wilson NY
White Scotch Globe	1823	Robb ?
White Top Tankard	1825	Wilson Liverpool
Yellow	1808	Wilson London
Yellow Scotch	Eu1820	Thornton NY-NE
Yellow Stone	1811	Nesbet London

The number of turnip varieties is noteworthy. It had become an important root vegetable and intensive breeding had been undertaken in Britain and Europe

In the twenty-first century we tend to think of turnips being white—in part because the greatest turnips bred in the twentieth century were beautifully white Japanese types (the large round Shogoin; the ball-shaped, snow-white Tennoji; the flat round Tokyo; the delicate, fine-textured white Tokinashi; and the round, sweet, perfectly white Hakurei). So the yellow-fleshed turnips, green turnips, and red-skinned, pink-fleshed turnips seem oddities. But of the list above, only half a dozen mattered over time. For edibility the cowhorn and white egg suited persons seeking a "sweet white fine grained and delicately flavored" turnip. They were not large. This disqualified them as fodder crops. Turnips that grew to gargantuan size—the purple top globe and the Pomeranian white globe (a later nineteenth century introduction) stood foremost in farmer preference (1915). In the twenty-first century we forget that huge turnips were once cherished—indeed it was huge turnips carved into faces for the Irish Samhain festival that provided the model for the new-world jack-o'-lantern cut from a pumpkin. While yellow turnips had some following early in the 1800s, the introduction of the related rutabaga in the 1830s stole away those devotees. (See our entry on Rutabagas.)

There were other criteria for selection. Quick-growing turnips—the White Flat Dutch, the Purple Top Strap Leaf—were important to truck farmers trying to get early vegetable crops to northern markets. The late-season turnips were the keepers, the ones preserved over winter as a reliable food source when little was growing: The White Egg, the Purple Top Globe, the White Norfolk, the Yellow Aberdeen, the Amber Globe, and, in the twentieth century, the Grey Stone (1917).

Most turnip varieties were created to be versatile, to be both animal fodder and human food. One variety, however, was created exclusively for table consumption, the seven-top. Notable for not having a bulbous root, this turnip produced abundant foliage—it was turnip salad in its purest form. Created in the 1820s and 1830s, it became a produce stand staple after the Civil War. After the small, round, pure white Japanese turnips became popular throughout the South in the mid-twentieth century, turnip salad began to be served with chunks of cooked turnip root in it.

Because turnips were cheap, available year-round, and providing both starch and greenery, a rich repertoire of preparations developed around it: turnip salad, turnips roots roasted or braised with game, turnip soup, mashed turnips, and raw turnip salad.

Turnip salad was reckoned a health food, a spring tonic. Generations of Georgians believed that winter sapped iron and other important nutrients from the body. Bitter spring greens—dandelion, mustard, cressy greens, poke, and turnip salad—restored what was missing. Of all the tonic greens, turnip salad stood first in the preference of Georgians and was often prepared as a standalone. It's one disadvantage was that it collected sand and required repeated rinsing to free the leaves from grit. The mode of cooking was simple. Mrs. S. R. Dull laid out the standard proportions of jowl/bacon/hock to greens in a piece on "Southern Turnip Greens": "about one-fourth pound to two pounds of greens." Cooking times varied from one to two hours depending on how much one wished to get the greens slippery.

Turnip soup usually took one of two forms: a hearty turnip soup using a meat stock, and a refined cream of turnip soup. A recipe for the former appeared in the *Augusta Chronicle* on March 12, 1912. This could be made from any variety of turnip.

Turnip Soup

Augusta Chronicle (March 12, 1912)

Any sort of foundation stock will serve as a base for turnip soup; but that result from boiled mutton is the best. Dissolve two ounces of butter in a saucepan, add three or four peeled and sliced turnips, a carrot, onion and a stick of celery, all cut up into small pieces. Fry for a few minutes, add just enough to press easily through a sieve. Return the pulp to the saucepan, add enough boiling stock to cover and simmer until the vegetables are soft. Add enough stock to make the quantity of soup you require, and heat thoroughly. Beat up the yolks of two eggs in the tureen. Pour in the boiling soup, season with pepper and salt and serve at once.

The much-published resort chef Jessup Whitehead, who presided over the kitchen of W. F. Stokes Restaurant in Atlanta in the later 1880s, published a formula for a classic cream of turnip soup in which the roots were pureed. This appeared in his *The Steward's Handbook*.

Turnip Puree Soup [Cream of Turnip Soup]

Jessup Whitehead, *The Steward's Handbook* (1889)

Using young white garden turnips. Peel, boil two minutes, then pour off the water; slice the turnips and allow 1 lb. of the vegetables to a pint of separated milk; 12 whole white peppercorns, one blade of mace. Stew till the turnips turn tender, then puree through a steel wire sieve; add also a couple of bottled or canned mushrooms, ¼ oz. of powdered sugar, and salt to taste. Put the puree into a large stew pan, add good white stock [veal stock] to make it of a proper consistence; stir over the fire till it is quite thick and hot, beat in ½ oz. butter to the pint of soup. Add cream to give it a soft mellow taste; pour into a hot tureen and serve.

Mashed turnips were often eaten with barbecued ribs. Invariably the turnips were peeled before boiling and mashing. Much salt and pepper were applied, as well as a large chunk of butter. This was plain country cooking. A point of controversy was whether to add a teaspoon of sugar into the mix. Putting milk in the mix, or better yet, buttermilk, gave it greater richness. In Savannah in the 1910s the dish was transformed into mashed turnips au gratin by napping it with béchamel sauce, sprinkling the top with bread crumbs, and baking the dish. But most of the state was content with the plain mash with a ladleful of brown gravy.

Turnips and Greens

KEVIN MITCHELL

I have always enjoyed the flavor of greens, whether collard, mustard, or turnip. Over the past few years, I have grown to love turnips. What better way of having both the greens and roots than by throwing them in a pot together? Try this recipe at home; I am sure it will become a favorite. Once the pot is empty, you can do as my grandmother did and dip pieces of corn bread into that delicious pot likker!

Serves 8 to 10

- 3 quarts, chicken broth or water
- 1½ to 2 pounds smoked turkey leg or ham hocks
- ¼ cup vegetable or canola oil
- 2 medium yellow onions, diced (approximately 2½ cups)
- 2 tablespoons minced garlic
- 1 tablespoon kosher salt
- 1 tablespoon granulated sugar
- 1 teaspoon red pepper flakes, plus more as needed
- ½ teaspoon baking soda
- 2 large turnips, peeled and diced
- 3 pounds turnip greens, cut (see Note)

Bring broth and turkey leg to a boil in a large Dutch oven. Once it comes to a boil, lower the heat and simmer for 2 hours or until the meat is tender. Remove the turkey leg and let cool. Reserve cooking broth. It should amount to 2 quarts. 8 cups Once the turkey leg has cooled, remove the meat from the bone, discarding the skin.

Heat vegetable oil in a large pot or Dutch oven over medium heat until shimmering. Add the onion and garlic and cook, stirring occasionally, until the onion is translucent, 3 to 5 minutes. Add the salt, sugar, red pepper flakes, and baking soda. Cook, stirring occasionally, 5 to 8 minutes. Add the turnips and stir to combine. Cook for 5 to 8 minutes. Add 1 quart of broth. Add the turnip greens and cook for about 30 minutes, or until turnips are fork-tender. If need be, you can add additional broth. Adjust seasonings as needed and serve. Leftovers can be refrigerated in an airtight container for up to 4 days.

Note: For convenience, you can use precut, prewashed greens.

Vidalia Onions

Some think "Vidalia" is a variety of onion named after a Georgia place. It is not. The variety of onion is the yellow granex hybrid, a Texas-bred sweet onion. The variety is grown in several parts of the United States. It is the Washington sweets onion, the Texas sweet onion. But only when grown in the low-sulfur soils around Vidalia, Georgia, did its flavor have the sublime mellowness and winning sweetness that made it nationally famous, the most famous onion brand of the twentieth century. "Vidalia onion" names a terroir—a growing locale that imparts a distinctive piquancy of flavor.

Sometimes, splendid things happen by serendipity. Moses Coleman Jr., of Toombs County in the 1930s secured some sweet onions from Texas and planted them in Vidalia. Coleman, a graduate of Georgia State University, was president of the Toombs County Sweet Potato Association, and a scientific farmer always seeking to diversify his plantings beyond the big stem Jersey sweet potatoes he grew for northern markets. He also sought alternatives to the tobacco farming that dominated Toombs County agriculture. The flavor of the onions immediately won it a clientele—they were mild and sweet enough to eat raw in quantity. People would drive two counties over to get Coleman's onions. The prices he demanded for each onion set envious farmers inquiring about the variety and Coleman's growing methods. Soon several growers were cultivating the onion. They were first sold to the general public at a produce stand erected in Vidalia. It took forty years for the mystique to develop around the onion. Its arrival in public consciousness can be witness in an *Atlanta Journal* article of May 1975, "Whose Onion Is It." We learn that the onion—a "rare young thing" and a "Spring delicacy in Georgia"—has been shipped by farmers around Vidalia to a "gourmet underground." Its reputation had grown so great that Glenville, Georgia, began agitating for a name change of the onion to the Glenville onion, because the taste quality was better for onions grown around that town. We all know how this campaign turned out. But the important information in the article was its revelation that this yellow granex hybrid was being grown in a good expanse around Vidalia—indeed, in twelve whole counties, besides Toombs, and parts of seven more with the proper soil type. In the early years the growers had onion sets shipped from Texas, and when the yellow granex was scarce some growers opted for the hotter grano.

In 1938, the Toombs County farmer's market was sited at Vidalia. Because of its excellent highway access, travelers stopped at the market and began referring to the sweet onions as "Vidalias." Piggly Wiggly grocery chain had a processing center in town and the onions began to stock stores in southeast Georgia. Yet production remained small scale, with less than three hundred acres in the region devoted to onions. (Each acre supported seventy thousand plants.) The acreage would not double until the mid-1970s Vidalia onion boom. By the mid-1960s signs were aligning that this crop was more than simply another farm commodity. Demand extended from New York to Florida among grocery chains in the 1960s.

Vidalia onions are short-day alliums that start bulbing when day lengths approximate eleven hours. Because the onions require such a short day to bulb, farmers plant in the fall when the days shorten so that they do not bulb prematurely and the plant has sufficient time to emerge and develop leaves and roots that will later support the vegetable. Accordingly, the vegetable is harvested from early April to early May.

Because the onions require much water, the onion fields in the twenty counties have been outfitted with extensive fixed irrigation systems. A liability of this arrangement is the lack of crop rotation to replenish nutrition and repress soil-borne pathogens. Consequently, Vidalia fields are prepped in February with fertilizer and germicide supplements to limit pink rot, bacterial brown rot, and fusarium basal rot. Despite the disease pressures, the onion has been a crop that has never failed from either weather or disease in the history of its cultivation. That said, truly bumper crops occur only once in six years, despite the uniformity of planting stock, fertilization, and watering.

It was strictly a seasonal product for the first half-century of the Vidalia onion. In the 1980s, the development of cold warehouse storage enabled that season to stretch into fall. The 1980s saw the Vidalia onion grow on six thousand acres. The harvest was retailed nationally. In 1990, its fame had grown so great that the Georgia General Assembly legislated protections for the name and defined a twenty-county area that comprised the onion's terroir. In 1990, it took the further step of designating the Vidalia onion as the Georgia state vegetable. This, along with borrowing storage technology from another Georgia product, the apple, called "controlled atmosphere storage," allowed for more than twenty million onions to be stored for six months, which meant they could be marketed well into the fall and the holiday season. The onion became so popular that the Vidalia Onion Committee created the Vidalia Onion Hall of Fame. Inductees into the hall of fame had to be involved with protecting not only the onion but the name as well. The induction of someone would also need to promote the quality of the onion, the marketing, the sales, creative ways of selling, research, and growth of the Vidalia.

Caramelized Vidalia Onion and Corn Skillet Corn Bread

KEVIN MITCHELL

This is not just an ordinary corn bread recipe. The recipe is jazzed up with Vidalia onions and corn. For purists who love sugar in their corn bread, you may not like this recipe; however, the sweetness of the onions and corn make up for the lack of sugar. The great thing about this recipe is the buttermilk. Buttermilk gives this corn bread a fantastic moistness. Try this corn bread with your favorite butter; it will become a household favorite.
Serves 12 to 14

- 1 cup (2 sticks) unsalted butter
- 5 cups Vidalia onions, (5 small onions) thinly sliced or small diced
- 1 teaspoon salt
- ½ teaspoon black pepper
- 3 cups corn kernels cut from the cob
- 2 tablespoons olive oil

Corn Bread

- 2½ cups coarse yellow cornmeal
- 1 cup flour
- 2 teaspoon salt
- 1½ teaspoon baking powder
- 1 tablespoon fresh sage, chopped
- 1 tablespoon fresh thyme, chopped
- 1 tablespoon fresh flat-leaf parsley, chopped
- 1½ teaspoon fresh rosemary, chopped
- ¾ cup (1½ sticks) cold unsalted butter
- 6 cups buttermilk, at room temperature
- 3 large eggs, at room temperature, beaten

Arrange oven racks in the bottom and top thirds of the oven. Preheat oven to 425°F.

In a 13-inch cast-iron skillet, heat 2 sticks of butter over medium-high heat until bubbly. Add half of the onion; cook, stirring frequently, until softened, 4 to 6 minutes. Add remaining onion; stir frequently until softened, 4 to 6 minutes, or until caramel color is achieved. Reduce heat to medium; cook, stirring frequently, until onions are lightly caramelized, 15 to 20 minutes. Fold in 1 teaspoon salt and the pepper.

Transfer the onion mixture to a bowl. Add oil to the skillet and increase heat to high. Add corn and cook, frequently stirring, until caramelized, approximately 10 minutes. Transfer corn to the bowl and mix with the onions. Let cool. Wipe the skillet clean.

Caramelized Vidalia onion and corn skillet corn bread by Kevin Mitchell. Photograph © Rhonda Mitchell.

For the corn bread:

Place the skillet in the hot oven and heat for 10 minutes while mixing the corn bread. Turn the cornmeal, flour, baking powder, salt, and chopped herbs into a large mixing bowl and whisk to combine.

Melt 1 stick of butter in a medium saucepan. Add the buttermilk and warm it slightly. Remove the pan from the heat. Ladle some milk mixture into the beaten egg and whisk to combine. Pour the egg into the saucepan. Whisk to combine. Pour the wet ingredients into the dry and whisk lightly until smooth. Fold in onion-corn mixture and mix into batter.

Add the remaining ½ stick cold butter to the hot cast iron skillet from the oven and tilt to distribute. Scrape the batter into the skillet with a rubber spatula—it should sizzle.

(continued)

Immediately place the skillet on the very bottom of the oven and bake for 10 to 12 minutes Then, transfer the skillet to the upper rack and continue baking until the corn bread is golden brown and a toothpick inserted into the center comes out clean, approximately 15 to 20 minutes longer. On a wire rack, let cool 10 to 15 minutes. Invert the corn bread onto a cutting board so the crackling side faces up or leave the bread in the skillet for serving.

MENUS OF THE 1913 GEORGIA PRODUCTS FEASTS

On November 16, 1913, the *Atlanta Georgian* published a list of all the localities that would be hosting a Georgia Products Dinner. This did not include the state's hotels and schools that were also staging feasts. The final roster was as follows: Abbeville, Albany, Alberton, Americus, Athens, Atlanta, Bainbridge, Barnesville, Baxley, Bremen, Brunswick, Byromville, Cairo, Calhoun, Canton, Carrollton, Cedartown, Chatsworth, Clarksville, Clayton, Columbus, Dallas, Dalton, Decatur, Douglas, Douglasville, Dublin, Eastman, Ellijay, Fitzgerald, Fort Valley, Greenville, Griffin, Hartwell, Hazlehurst, Jackson, Jefferson, Jesup, Kirkwood, Lafayette, LaGrange, Lavonia, Lawrenceville, Lithonia, Macon, Madison, Manasses, Manchester, McDonough, McRae, Milledgeville, Monroe, Montezuma, Moultrie, Nashville, Newnan, Ocilla, Quitman, Raymond, Reidsville, Rome, Saint Marys, Social Circle, Sparta, Stone Mountain, Sylvester, Talbotton, Tallapoosa, Thomaston, Tifton, Toccoa, Valdosta, Vidalia, Vienna, Waycross, and Windsor. Not every one of these seventy-six feasts published the menu of offerings. Several, for instance, simply staged a barbecue. Yet numbers of cities and counties wished to promote their productiveness and culinary abundance. These forwarded menus to newspapers for publication. These are the menus that went public.

AMERICUS

MENU

Turtle   Terrapin Stew

Baker Trout

Turnips, Collards, Green Peppers, Snap beans, Tomatoes, Cabbage, Butter Beans, Beets

Boiled Onions   Radishes

Eggplants

Opossum   Potatoes

Creamed Potatoes   Baker Kershaw

Turkey   Chestnut Dressing

Hot Rolls

Mayhaw Jelly   Scuppernongs

Rabbit   Slice Country Ham

Green Peas on Lettuce Leaves

Roast Beef   Mushrooms

Lamb   Mutton

Cream Chicken

Baker Goose   Quail

Asparagus on Toast

Sweet Peach Pickle   Cucumber Pickle

Fig Preserves   Watermelon Preserves

Pumpkin and Kershaw Pies

Sumter Syrup Pudding

Americus Weekly Times-Recorder (November 13, 1914), 2

Baker = Baked

Kershaw = Cushaw squash, a large baking and pie squash

Sumter Syrup Pudding = Steamed pudding using 1½ cups flour, 1 cup chopped suet, one cupful of cane syrup, ¼ teaspoon of bicarbonate of soda, and milk. Steamed for several hours.

ATHENS

MENU

Savannah River Oysters on Half Shell.

Hearts of Georgia Celery.

Puree of Georgia Vegetables and Croutons.

Dixie Mixed Pickle.

Broiled Tybee Island Spanish Mackerel a la Chatham.

Potatoes Oglethorpe.

Boiled Smoked Clarke County Ham with Turnip Greens.

Braized Madison County Opossum with Sweet Potatoes.

Isle of Hope Terrapin in Cases.

Elberta Peach Fritters. Red and Black Sauce.

Georgia Huzzar Punch.

Roast Oconee County Young Turkey

stuffed with Habersham County Chestnuts.

Mashed Madison County Potatoes.

Ware County Asparagus.

Green County Brussells Sprouts.

Richmond County Cauliflower.

Athens Lettuce and Tomato Salad.

Mount Airy Apples and Baxaroise.

Georgia Ice Cream.

Home-made Georgia Walnut Cake.

Bludwine, the drink that made Athens famous.

Athens Banner (November 18, 1913), 1

Elberta Peach Fritters = The distinctive freestone Georgia peach bred from the Shanghai honey nectar peach. These are sliced, sugared, and left to sit an hour, dipped in a batter of egg yolk, flour, oil, and beaten egg whites, and fried in boiling fat.

Georgia Huzzar Punch = Apricot brandy, lemon peel, tonic water

Baxaroise = Bavarian cream, a pastry cream thickened with gelatin

Georgia Walnut Cake = Two eggs beaten well, one cup of white sugar and two-thirds of a cup of sweet cream, one heaping teaspoonful of baking powder sifted with one and one-half cups of flour, a pinch of salt. Filling—Two thirds of a cup of walnut meats rolled, half a cup of white sugar, two-thirds of a cup of sour cream. Mix and spread between the layers. *Macon Telegraph*, 2-13-1911, p. 5

Bludwine = Carbonated cherry-flavored soft drink of the early 20th century invented in Watkinsville, Georgia.

ATLANTA

MENU

(Prepared by Lee Barnes of the Chamber of Commerce)

Vegetable Soup

Baked Trout

Chipped Potatoes

Young Onions   Mixed Pickles

Radishes

Jenny Lynn Pan Cakes

Roast Young Pig   Apple Sauce

Baked Opossum with Georgia Yams

Mashed Turnips   Boiled Potatoes

Cornfield Peas   Salt Pork

Cold Slaw

Cold Meats

Roast Beef   Tongue   Ham

Georgia Corn Pone

Buttermilk Biscuit

Boiled Custard   Pumpkin Pie

Cheese   Crackers

Atlanta Journal (November 16, 1913), 1

ATLANTA

REVISED MENU

(1000 plate Feast served at the Auditorium-Armory)

Puree of Tomato

Whipped Cream

White Plume Celery

Mixed Pickles a la Dixie Company

Barnesia Young Onions

Salted Peanuts

Roast Young Turkey, Chestnut Dressing

Creamed Potatoes a la Barnesia

Georgia Yams a la Camp

Baked Cornfield Ham a la White Company

Deviled Eggs

Veal Croquettes

Chicken Salad, Georgia raised

Georgia Beaten Biscuits (Made by Mrs. John Marshall Slaton)

Tip Top Biscuits   Uncle Sam Bread

Georgia Corn Pone

Neapolitan Ice Cream

Georgia Muffin Cakes

Block's Butter Wafers

Habersham Apples

Kamper's Roasted Coffee

Valdes Cigars

Elberton Mineral Water

Norris's Banquet Mints

Atlanta Georgian (November 16, 1913), 15

Barnesia = from Barnes, GA

Mrs. John Marshall Slaton = Wife of Governor John Slaton

Uncle Sam Bread = Mass production bread of Schlesinger-Meyer Baking Co., Atlanta

Tip Top Biscuits = Cracker brand manufactured in Ohio

Block's Butter Wafers = Square cookies baked by Block's Biscuits, Atlanta

Kamper's Roasted Coffee = House brand of Kamper's store on Peach Street

Norris's Banquet Mints = Wafer produced by Norris Candies (est. 1909) of Atlanta

ATLANTA

MENU

(Ansley Hotel Products Dinner)

Brunswick Oysters Cocktail

Bibb County Celery, South Georgia Salted Peanuts

New Rosa Radishes.

Cream of Hubbard Squash with small Egg Puffs

Cheese Waffles.

Baked Savannah River Shad with Tomato and Green Peppers

Potatoes with Parsley and Butter

Beaten Biscuit.

Unfermented Muscadine Grape Juice

Boned Terrapin Cassolette St Marie

Pomme Grennade and Apple Jam.

Corn Pone.

Scuppernong Grape Juice.

Houston County Asparagus on Toast with Melted Butter

Special Baked Small Yams Stuffed with Rice and Corn.

Plantation-fashion Ginger Bread.

Unfermented Cane Juice.

Roast Young Dahlonega Turkey with Chestnut Dressing.

Old Down-state fashion Cranberry Sauce.

Macon Spring Water Cress,

Dalton Artichoke Pickles.

Snap Beans with Brooks County Ham Fat.

Crowder and Black-eye Peas Cooked with Turnip Greens.

Cracklin' Bread.

Or

Young Pig Barbecued Stuffed with Rice

Thunderbolt Oysters and White Bread,

Persimmon Gravy.

Or

'Possum Stuffed with Boiled Gilmer County Chestnuts.

Sumter County Sweet Potatoes Candied.

Lowndes County Paw-Paws,

Sweet Apple Cider.

Corn Bread with Sorghum

Salt Rising Bread.

Hot House Lettuce and Tomatoes with Georgia Dressing

Made with Walnut Sweet Oil and Pepper Vinegar.

Fruits and Nuts.

Rabun County Apples, Decatur County Oranges, Georgia Goobers.

Marshallville Pears,

Ben Hill County Pecans.

"Punkin" and Peach Pie.

Black Walnut Ice Cream.

Molasses and Raisins Cake.

Cottage Cream Cheese.

Toasted Corn Biscuits.

Coffee and Cream.

Atlanta Journal (November 16, 1913), 1

Dalton Artichoke Pickles = Pickled Jerusalem artichokes

Salt Rising Bread = Made from dough using salt and sugar to ferment bread

ATLANTA

MENU

(Athletic Club Products Dinner)

Georgia Appetizer

Salted Paper Shell Pecans

Brunswick Oyster on Shell

Winter Radishes

Green Tomato Pickle

Green Turtle Soup

Fried Channel Cat Fish (Corn Meal)

Potato Shoestrings

Patties of Chicken

Green Peas (canned at Waycross)

Roast Suckling Pig   Baked Apples

Creamed Potatoes

Country Gentleman Corn

Vegetable Salad

Elberta Peach Cream

Assorted Cake

Cottage Cheese   Toasted Sodas

Sassafras Tea in Cup

Atlanta Journal (November 16, 1913), 1

Country Gentleman Corn = Famous sweet corn with very wrinkled white kernels

BARNESVILLE

MENU

(Kemper Hotel Products Dinner)

Dinner.

Georgia Chicken Soup.

Roast Pork and Turnip greens, Country Style.

Roast Beef with Brown Gravy.

Roast Turkey with Old-fashioned Dressing.

Cranberries   Cream of Chicken.

'Possum and 'Tatoes, Old Style.

Shoestring Potatoes, Creamed Potatoes.

Combination salads   White Onions.

Hot Rolls.   Apple Tarts.

Candy Yams.

Ginger Cakes.

Sweet Milk   Butter Milk.

Coffee.   Tea.

Peach Gelatin with Whipped Cream.

Pound Cake.

Pecans and Walnuts.

Cigars.   Cigarettes.

BIBB COUNTY

MENU

Bibb County Pecans.

Butter Radishes.

Bibb County Watercress

Ocmulgee Channel Cat a la Bibb County.

Fried Potatoes, Natural.

Roast Bibb County Turkey. Chestnut Dressing.

Bibb Yams.

Sugar Crowder.   Mashed Potatoes.

Combination Salad.

Bibb County Pie and Sweet Cider.

Bibb County Smearcaises, a la Dutch.

Saltine Crackers.

Special Bibb County Coffee.

Sweet Milk.

Macon Telegraph (November 11, 1913), 1

Sugar Crowder = A brown, sweet-tasting field pea; the pea itself is yellowish and globular.

Smearcaises = Spreadable cheese, such as cream cheese, popular particularly in Germanic cultural areas. [Smearcase]

BRUNSWICK

MENU

Blythe Island Oysters on Half Shell

Mock Turle Soup a la Oglethorpe

Celery   Salted Almonds   Olives

Broiled Blue Fish, Lighthouse,

Glynn Corn Bread

Julienne Potatoes

Baked O'Possum

B for Brunswick Style Sweet Potatoes

Roast Glynn County Turkey

Chestnut Dressing   Cranberry Sauces

Georgia Peas in Cases

Asparagus au Beurre

Shrimp Salad, a la Board of Trade

White Way Ice Cream

Assorted Cake

Roquefort Cheese   Georgia Crackers

Mt. Pleasant Oranges

Turtle River Grape Fruit

Fancy Bluff Bananas

Coffee

Brunswick Cigars   Cigarettes

Brunswick News (November 18, 1913), 1

Georgia Peas in Cases = Edible pod peas steamed

BUTTS COUNTY

MENU

Cream of Tomato Soup

Broiled Towaliga Trout   Potato Croquettes

Bread Sticks

Roast Turkey   Chestnut Stuffing

Muscadine Jelly

Creamed Onions   Candied Yams   Green Peas

Vegetable Salad

Backbone Stew   Apple Cider Sauce

Salt Rising Bread   Beaten Biscuit

Jersey Milk

Elberta Peach Cream   Angel Cake

Blackberry Shrub with Carbonated Water

Rye Coffee

Butts County Progress (November 21, 1913), 5

Backbone Stew = Open air stew made from the backbone of a pig during barbecues

CHARLTON COUNTY

MENU

(Open Air Feast)

Bouillon

Vegetables

Roast Beef   Pork   Chicken

Sweet Potatoes prepared various ways

Irish Potato

Corn bread

Tomato Catsup, Chili Sauce

Pickles

Peaches   Pears

Charlton County Herald (November 20, 1913), 1

CHATHAM COUNTY

MENU

Oysters on Halfshell

Brown Bread Sandwiches

Celery

Tomato Bisque   Oyster Crackers

Dill Pickles or Olives

Cornmealed Trout   Creole Sauce

Potato Chips

Braised Sweetbreads

Georgia Pork Ham, Apple Sauce

Candied Yams   Steamed Rice

Scuppernong Punch

Charlotte Russe   Pumpkin Pie

Sponge Cake   Cheese

Pecan Nuts   Dried Figs

Demi Tasse

Atlanta Constitution (November 7, 1913), 2

Scuppernong Punch = No doubt a nonalcoholic mixture of scuppernong juice and carbonated water.

CHATHAM COUNTY

MENU

(Contest Submission)

Chatham County oyster cocktail or Grapefruit,

Turtle Soup,   Tomato Bouillon,   Terrapin Stew

Sweet Peach Pickles,   Celery,   Mixed Pickles

Baked Trout,   Corn Pone Dressing

[223]

MENUS OF THE 1913 GEORGIA PRODUCTS FEASTS

Salted Peanuts,

Roast Turkey, Chestnut Dressing

Georgia Rice, Giblet Gravy

Boiled (Brooks County) Ham, Prime Rib of Roast Beef

Roast Goose, White Potato Dressing

Possum, Baked Sweet Potatoes

Rabbits, Roast Pork

"Irby" Turnips, mashed (Bartow County);

Roast Chicken, Quail (Lowndes County Mayhaw Jelly)

Creamed Onions, Corn,

Cushaw Baked in Shell,

String Beans

Salads,

Artichokes, Asparagus and Pepper Salads,

Lettuce with Cream Dressing,

Coleslaw, Buttered Beets, Sliced Tomatoes;

Desserts

Apple, Pumpkin, Sweet Potato Pie or Potato Pone

Butter Sauce,

Peach or Strawberry Ice Cream,

Pound Cake, John B. Gordon Cake

Crackers, Pecans, English and Black Walnuts

Apples.

Atlanta Georgian (November 5, 1913), 3

John B. Gordon Cake = White cake associated with General Gordon, longtime head of Confederate Veterans Association

CLAXTON

MENU

(For Homemade Georgia Feast submitted by Claxton Woman)

Fruit Cocktail

Creamed Tomato Soup   Croutons

Baked Fish

Cucumber Baskets   Potato Chowder

Broiled Fish   Sassafras Tea

Bread   Turnips

Baked Turkey with Dressing

Chicken Pie   Beef Loaf

Baked Georgia Yams

Stuffed Peppers   Stuffed Tomatoes

Butter

Southern Corn Bread   Bread

Chicken Salad

Potato Salad   Apple and Peanut Salad

Ham and Egg Sandwiches

Cucumber Pickles

Grape Juice

Caramel Ice Cream   Pound Cake.

Atlanta Georgian (November 6, 1913), 2

This menu includes recipes for all the dishes.

CLIFTON

MENU

(Clifton Hotel)

Soup

Cream of Tomato

Pickles

Sweet Mixed (Ga. Raised)　　Sour Cucumber　　Queen Olives

Green Peppers (Ga. Raised)　　Young Shallots　　White Plume Celery

Possum and Taters (Carroll Co. Special)

Baked Yates Apples (Ga. Raised)

Roast Rib (Ga. Raised) Beef　　Natural Gravy

Baked Young (Ga. Raised) Ham with Sage Dressing & Cranberry Sauce

Salad

Lettuce and Egg (Ga. Raised)

Snowflake Potatoes

White Peas　　Young White Dutch Turnips

Steamed Rice

Georgia Corn Bread　　Tip Top Bread

Georgia Peach Cream and Cake

Georgia Sweet Potato Pie Family Style

Georgia Pumpkin Meringue Custard

Cream Cheese　　Tea Flakes (Ga. Baked)

Coffee (Ga. Roasted)　　Hot Tea　　Ice Tea

Sweet Milk　　Buttermilk

Carroll County Spring Water

The Carroll Free Press (November 20, 1913), 1

COLUMBUS

MENU

(Springer Hotel)

Savannah Oyster Cocktail   Celery

Cream of Chicken, Atlanta

Prime Ribs of Beef, Brown Gravy,

Georgia Raised

Roast Young Georgia Turkey with Oyster Dressing a la Macon

Boiled Turnips, Georgia Style

Spinach with Egg, 'Munro' Farm

'Sho' Nuff' Potato Chips.

Columbus Grown and Made Georgia Candied Yams, Nankapoo

Lettuce and Tomato Salad, Augusta

Georgia Product Ice Cream 'Enough Said'

With Everidge's Mixed Cakes

Coffee Roasted in Columbus by Rutledge

Cheese   Crackers

Atlanta Georgian (November 16, 1913), 2C

Nankapoo—locale near Columbus, GA

Everidge's Mixed Cakes—A variety drawn from the stock of J. B. Everidge's Bakery in Columbus. They were known of chocolate and fruit cakes particularly.

Rutledge—Of the Shield Coffee Company in Columbus.

DALTON

MENU

Georgia Raised Turkey stuffed with Georgia Grown Chestnuts

Oyster Seasoning

Possum surrounded by Georgia Yams

Beaten Biscuits

Browned Gravy

Georgia Celery

Georgia Made Cigars

North Georgia Citizen (November 13, 1913), 1

MENU

(Hardwick Building)

Roast Turkey

Dressing   Cranberries   Celery

Savannah Oysters

"Hog and Hominy"

Possum and 'Taters

Pickles

Rolls   Bread

'Simmon Beer

Georgia Peach Cream

Cakes   Cheese

Coffee   Cigars

Fruits   Nuts

Dalton Citizen (November 13, 1913), 4

DAWSON

MENU

(Women's Club)

Brunswick Oyster Soup

Oyster Cocktail from our Own Coast

Georgia Crackers   Tomato Catsup

Possum and Taters

Stuffed Turkey and Jellies.

Cold Slaw

Fall Turnips   Irish Potatoes

Cake   Rebel Coffee

Dawson Made Cigars

Dawson News (November 18, 1913), 1

DECATUR

MENU

"East Lake" Oyster Cocktail

"Panthersville" Turkey

"Peavine Creek" Celery

"Ingleside" Candied Yams

"Georgia" Lye Hominy

"DeKalb" Persimmon Beer

"Decatur Spirit" Coffee

"Silver Lake" Ice Cream

"Brookhaven" Cake

Atlanta Georgian (November 15, 1913), 8

DECATUR

MENU

(Alternate Version)

DeKalb County Cider

"Panthersville Turkey," Chestnut Dressing

"Peavine Creek" Celery

"Druid Hills" Sauce

"Ingleside" Chipped Ham

"Agnes Scott" Sandwiches

"Donald Fraser" Beaten Biscuit

"East Lake" Cream Oysters in Tymbols

"Silver Lake" Ice cream

"Brookhaven" Cake

"Decatur Spirit" Coffee

Atlanta Journal (November 19, 1913), 11

DOOLY COUNTY

MENU

(Prize Winner-the Product of One Farm)

First Course

Vegetable Soup   Croutons.

Second Course

Stuffed Baked Trout   Potato Balls

Georgia Hoecake.

Third Course

Scuppernong Wine,   Peach Pickle,

Corn Salad   Barbecued Pig

Stuffed peppers,   Candied Dooly Yams,   Cold Slaw,

Roast Turkey

Quince jelly,   Fall Turnip Salad.

Fourth Course

Chicken Salad,   Bread Sticks.

Fifth Course:

Sunderlin [Pudding],   Wine Sauce,

Whipped Cream   Georgia Belle Peaches.

Sixth Course

Rebel Coffee.   Smear Case and Crackers.

Turnip Salad = Turnip Greens
Smear Case = Cream Cheese

American Times-Recorder (November 15, 1913), 7

DOUGLAS

MENU

(Breakfast to Governor Slaton at New Douglas Hotel)

Maraschino Grape Fruit

Fried Spring Chicken   Saratoga Chips

Oyster Omelet

Boiled Pork Chops with Fried Apples

Fried Hominy

Buck Wheat Cakes   New Georgia Syrup

Coffee

Coffee Country Progress (November 21, 1913), 3

Maraschino Grapefruit = alternate name for red grapefruit
Saratoga Chips = Potato Chips

MENU

(New Douglas Hotel)

Savannah Oyster Cocktail

Essence of Tomato   Croutons

Young Onions   Cheese Sticks

Broiled Gaskin Spring Trout.

Potatoes Nellie.

Chicken Pot Pie with Dumplings.

Spareribs and Collards

Corn Pone

Roast Turkey, With Dressing

Roast Leg of Veal

Boiled Potatoes   Steamed Georgia Rice

Turnip Greens   Candied Yams

Old Field Peas

Prohibition Mince Pie

Coffee County Pecans   Grape Jelly

Persimmon Punch

Home-made Pound Cake.

Coffee Country Progress (November 21, 1913), 3

Prohibition Mince Pie = Prohibition came to Georgia in 1907; i.e., no alcohol in pie

DUBLIN

MENU

Okra Gumbo, Harrison.

Radford Radishes and Young Onions.

India Relish and Tomato Catsup, a la Baum.

Oconee Channel Catfish, fried in Cotton Seed Oil.

Pig Jowl with Black-eyed Peas.

Fried Hominy.

Braised Veal, Cornpone Garnish.

Barbecued Shoat and Benny Seed Fritters.

Laurens County Beef, the Ribs Roasted.

Cheek's Farm New Potatoes in Rice Butter.

Young Turkey Roasted, Stuffed with Yellow Yams.

Baum Apple Jelly.

Pope's Mill Corn Bread.

Stinson Buttermilk.

Catlin Waxed Beans. Stewed Tomatoes.

Collard Greens.

Mashed Kershaw.

Lettuce Salad, Home Dressing.

'Possum and 'Taters.

Laurens Squab on Eggbread Toast.

Crackling Bread and Dublin Ginger Ale.

Sweet Potato Pudding, Hooks Fashion.

New Dublin Ice Cream—It's Peach

With Assorted Cakes—Same Brand.

Pope's Graham Crackers and Laurens County Syrup.

Persimmon Beer.

Crack your own Pecans, Black Walnuts and Hickory Nuts.

Preserved Peaches, Melon Rinds, Blackberry Jam.

Anderson Cigars.

Benny Seed Fritters = fried benne seed chips

Melon Rinds = sweet watermelon rind pickle

FITZGERALD AND BEN HILL COUNTY

MENU

Ben Hill County Persimmons

Iced Cane Juice

Salter Paper Shell Pecans-raised in Fitzgerald

Brunswick Oyster Cocktail

Mock-Turtle Soup, with Atlanta Made Crackers

Mother's Mustard pickle   Lettuce Head Fitzgerald Raised

Tenderloin Steak of Ocmulgee Trout, Drawn Butter

Julienne Potatoes

Patties of Chicken-Home Raised

Garden Peas (Canned at Fitzgerald)

Georgia Hoe Cake   Corn Bread

Barbecued Native Pork   Baked Apples

Fitzgerald Yams, Roasted in Ashes

Creamed Potatoes   Country Gentleman Corn

Vegetable Salad

Ben Hill County Wheat Cakes and Butter

New Georgia Cane Syrup

Ben Hill County Pumpkin Pie

Crème Cheese   Toasted Sodas   Black Coffee

Fitzgerald Cakes-presented by the Woman's Club

Fitzgerald Leader-Enterprise (November 17, 1913), 1

FLOYD COUNTY

MENU

Oyster Soup

Salad of Lettuce, Celery, Tomato, Bell Pepper, Radish

Pickled Cucumber, Cabbage, Hot Pepper, Bell Pepper, Melon Rind

Vegetables: Boiled Cabbage, Turnip Greens, Beans,

Peas, Spinach, Butter Beans, Okra, Turnips, Swiss Chard, Collards,

Squash, Rice, Kershaw, Creamed Asparagus,

Beets, Parsnips, Carrots, Onions, Baked Sweet Potatoes.

Irish Potatoes. Egg Plant.

Baked Fish

Barbecued Meats: Beef. Lamb. Kid. Pork. Rabbits. Possum

Mint-Parsley

Pies, Chicken, Squirrel, Squab, Quail

Bread: Boston Brown, Corn Bread, Biscuits

Jelly: Apple, Plum, Maypop, Blackberry.

Dewberry, Huckleberry, Scuppernong, Muscadine

Pies: Apples, Blackberry, Dewberry, Peach, Pumpkin, Sweet Potato, Cherry,

Irish Potato

Preserves: Peach, Apple, Plum Pear, Cherry, Muscadine, Fig, Scuppernong

Watermelon Rind

Soft Gingerbread of Syrup

Brown Bread of Sorghum.

Atlanta Constitution (November 7, 1913), 2

FLOYD COUNTY

MENU

(Submitted by farmer Wat Henning)

Wild Roast Turkey

Turnip Greens   Possum

Brunswick Stew   Persimmon Beer

Hash   Water

Moonshine a la Blue Ridge

Atlanta Georgian (November 16, 1913), 10C

FORT VALLEY

MENU

Thunderbolt Oyster Stew

Block's Oysterette Crackers

Pickles

Houston County Pork

Georgia Barbecue

"Say Red Rock (Atlanta GA), Say it Plain,"

Houston County Baked Turkey with Dressing

Chicken Salad   Cold Slaw

Candied Yellow Yams raised by A. J. Evans Houston County

Cracked Houston County Pecans

Elberta Peaches Canned by W. L. Houser

Beaten Biscuit made from "Lily of the Valley" Flour

Wheat Raised in Houston County by W. H. Harris

And Ground at the Fort Valley Roller Mills

Houston County Sugar Cane Juice

Bread from Houston County Wheat

Raised by A J. Harris and ground at his Mill

Hot Waffles with Country Butter

And Houston County raised Syrup

Atlanta Georgian (November 16, 1913), 6C

FULTON COUNTY

MENU

Vegetable Soup

Baked Trout   Chipped Potatoes

Radishes

Jenny Lynn Pan Cakes

Roast Young Pig

Apple Sauce

Baked O'Possum with Georgia Yams

Mashed Turnips   Boiled Potatoes

Cornfield Peas   Salt Pork

Cold Slaw

Cold Meats: Roast Beef, Tongue, Ham

Georgia Corn Pone

Buttermilk Biscuit

Boiled Custard   Pumpkin Pie

Cheese   Crackers

Coffee

Athens Banner (November 9, 1913), 6

Jenny Lynn Pan Cakes = Jenny Lind pancakes: rolled pancake with jelly filling

GRIFFIN

MENU

Oyster Cocktail with Georgia Crackers

Peach Pickles (sweet)   Mixed Pickles

Spalding County Celery

Roast Turkey with Plum and Scuppernong Jelly

Country Ham with Baked Georgia Apples

Candied Yams   New Lima Beans

Steamed Rice

Egg Bread   Hot Rolls

Caramel Ice Cream

Coffee

Apples from Sunshine Farm

Griffin Pecans

Griffin Daily News (November 17, 1913), 1

JACKSON

HOME MENU

Tomato Soup

Peas, Turnips, Greens, Boiled Bacon,

Irish Potatoes, Corn Pone

O'possum and Sweet Potatoes

Fried Chicken, Cream Gravy

Baked Potatoes,

Biscuit   Chicken Pie

Sweet Potato Pudding

Pears and Cream

Cakes and Milk

Sweet Cider   Buttermilk

Jackson Herald (November 13, 1913), 1

LAVONIA

MENU

Georgia Apple Cider.

Salted Peanuts

Oyster Cocktail   Crackers

Celery   Home Made Pickles

Turkey

Green Peas   Tomatoes

Opossum and Sweet Potatoes Lavonia Style

Franklin County Wheat Biscuits

Lavonia Raised Collards

Corn Bread a la Franklin County

Baked Apples   Boiled Country Ham

Country Corn   Lye Hominy

Stuffed Eggs   Light Bread

Fruit Salad   Chicken Salad

Crackers

Pumpkin Pie and Potato Custard (Like Mother Used to Make)

Cottage Cheese

Elberta Peach Cream   Assorted Cakes

Persimmon Beer (Unfermented)

Sassafras Tea   Rye Coffee

Lye Hominy = Dried corn soaked in lye water made of hickory wood ash then made into whole hominy or ground into grits

Potato Custard = Sweet Potato Pie

Rye Coffee = Civil War holdover using parched grains of black seed rye to brew a cup

MACON

MENU

(Mercer University)

Soup

Barbecue of Screven County Pig

Steamed Rice with Gravy

Candied Yams Georgia Style

Celery   Pickles

Brunswick Stew

Potato Salad   Mayonnaise Dressing

Home Grown Radishes   Young Onions

Sears' Luxury Bread

Canned Elbertas   Assorted Cakes

Coffee

MACON

MENU

(Wesleyan College)

Oysters   Brunswick Stew

Carrol County Baked Oppossum

Served with Jasper Yellow Yams and Steamed Rice from Chatham.

Celery from Houston

Jones County Spareribs, Country Style

Creamed Potatoes, Butts County

White Turnips from Twiggs County

Corn Sticks

Monroe Juliette Meal

Bibb County Tomatoes served with Salad Oil Mayonnaise

Cotton Seed Product, Savannah, Ga.

Crisp Lettuce from Bibb

New Onions and Radishes Stonedge Farm

Spalding County Frost-Bitten Persimmons

and Collards from Jasper

Finger Rolls

Henry County Flour

Butter from Bibb

Sumter, GA., Cane Syrup

Apples from the Hills of North Georgia

Flournoy Dairy Pure Cream

Frozen with Macon Cream

Patty Pan-Cakes

Patty-Pan Cakes = Squash fritters made from Patty Pan Summer Squash

MACON

MENU

(Mayor Bridges Smith's Georgia Feast)

Soups—Vegetable, mixed; potlicker, pealicker; diamond-backed Savannah Terrapin, Brunswick stew; catfish chowder.

Relishes—Hoss radish; Georgia pickles.

Meats—Ribs of wire-grass raised beef; middle Georgia mutton; mint sauce; Kid, billy and nanny; Quitman county ham; roast pig, a la Louis Schelbo; barbecued pig, a la Dill Young; 'possum with taters on the side in gravy; smoked country sausage; spareribs; backbone, with dumplings.

Fish—Ocmulgee channel cats, fried; Ogeechee shad, baked; Satilla river bream; Thunderbolt oysters.

Game—Glynn county deer; south Georgia wild turkeys; down-the-river ducks; partridges; rice birds.

Vegetables—Frost-nipped collards with corndodgers; turnip greens with bacon; Houston county asparagus; Bibb county celery; sliced tomatoes; yaller yams, chokers and Spanish sweet potatoes; Irish potatoes; squashes, snap beans, greasy beans with smoked bacon grease; lady-crowder and black-eyed peas.

Specials—Chicken pie, Mrs. Ben Moore style fried yaller-legged chickens; roast turkey stuffed with Brunswick oysters; souse, with pepper vinegar.

Breads-Salt-rising loaf; beaten biscuits; corn-pone; hoecake; cracklin' bread.

Pastry—'Tater custard pie, like mother used to make; apple turnovers, rights and lefts; blackberry dumplings, with butter sauce; old style ice cream, in big saucers.

Drinks—El-beer, Georgia style; persimmon beer; blackberry wine; unfermented cane juice; syllabub; waters of all kinds.

Fruits-Rabun county paw paws; Decatur county oranges, Subers variety; persimmons.

Nuts—South Georgia pecans; black walnuts; hickory nuts; scaly barks; chestnuts; chinquapins; pinders; chufas.

Nibblers—Georgia crackers; hot head cheese; salted peanuts.

El-beer = Elderberry beer

Pinders = Peanuts, the small Carolina African runner peanuts

Scaly barks = Watermelons famous for their tough skin

Chufas = Tubers from the nut sedge

MILLEDGEVILLE

MENU

(Georgia Normal & Industrial College State First Prize)

Planned for any Georgia family of ordinary means.

Breakfast

Baked apples with cream

Country sausage   Hominy

Toasted light bread or buttermilk biscuit

Waffles with Georgia cane syrup

Milk or Coffee

Dinner

Savannah oyster soup

Fried chicken, Apple jelly, Rice with gravy, Candied sweet potatoes,

Celery, Scalloped tomatoes,

Light rolls,   Crackling bread,

Elberta peach pie,   Whipped cream,

Coffee,   Buttermilk.

Supper

Country ham,   Hominy,

Georgia fried potatoes (Irish),

Chili sauce,

Hot soda biscuit,   Blackberry jam or fig preserves,

Tea.

BANQUET MENU

Clear Soup,   Croutons,   Salted pecans,   Celery,

Baked trout with Tartar sauce,

Saratoga Chips.

Roast turkey garnished with parsley, Oyster stuffing,

Rice,   Candied sweet potatoes,

Creamed Asparagus (Grown and canned in Georgia),

Hot rolls,   Beaten biscuit,   Crabapple jelly,   Peach pickle,

Rabun county apple salad on lettuce,

Mayonnaise made with cottonseed oil,

Frozen custard,   Small Angel cakes iced.

Nuts—Pecans, Black walnuts, Scaly Barks, Salted Peanuts, Chestnuts.

Fruits—Oranges, Pears, Apples, Pomegranates, Persimmons.

Black coffee,   Home-made Candies.

Americus Times Recorder (November 18, 1913), 3

Scaly Barks = Scaly Bark Walnuts in this context

PHELPS

HOME MENU

(Submitted by Mrs. Buell Starke)

Beef Soup

Pickles   Celery

Roast Turkey, Chestnut stuffing, giblets Gravy

Brown Sweet Potatoes

Mashed or Creamed Irish Potatoes

Onions with White Sauce

Plum Sauce

Potato Custard Pie   Pumpkin Pie

Apples   Salted Peanuts

Rye Coffee   Buttermilk

RAYMOND

MENU

Barbecued Pork, Rabbit, & Possum.

Rabbit Hash

Brunswick Stew

Home-made Pickles

Fruits   Salads   Preserves

Home Made Light Bread

Cakes, Pies, & Pastries

Newnan Herald & Advertiser (November 14, 1913), 1

ROME

MENU

(For Home Preparation submitted by Mrs. Max Meyerhardt)

Soups

Bouillon, Vegetable, Clam

Crackers, Mixed Pickles

Broiled Trout or Red Snapper

Meats

Roast Beef, Barbecue Lamb, Roast Turkey with chestnut dressing,

Giblet Gravy, Southern Fried Chicken,

Cold Boiled Ham, Georgia Smoked Beef

Salads

Green Peppers, Onions, Celery,

Tomatoes with French Dressing, using Refined Cottonseed Oil

Vegetables

Lima Beans, Duchess Cabbage, Baked Kershaw,

Fried Egg-Plants, Mashed Irish Potatoes,

Candied Yams, Boiled Rice, Fried Corn,

Carrots with Cream Dressing,

Rutabagas.

Breads

Thin slices homemade white and Brown Bread,

Southern Egg Bread, Corn Pones

Home Made Butter

Desserts

Pumpkin Pie, Mince Pie using candied figs and grape preserves instead of raisins.

Sweet Potato Custard Pie, Ice Cream

Old-fashioned Pound Cake

Fruit Cake, using preserved figs, grape, cherry and watermelon rind preserves

Instead of raisins and citron.

Drinks

Buttermilk, Sweet Milk, Lithia Water

Mixed Nuts, Georgia Cane Kisses.

Atlanta Journal (November 16, 1913), 2

ROME

MENU

Vegetable Soup

Home grown beef and vegetables

Endive and green pepper Salad and mayonnaise dressing

Roast beef, au jus

O'possum roti

Baked Sweet potatoes

Irish potatoes au natural

Turnip greens with corn dumplings

Home raised smoked bacon

Pone corn bread

Sweet pickled peaches

Green corn   Butterbeans

Lettuce   Young Onions

Young radish

Ginger cake stuffed with black walnut goodies

Salted peanuts

Grated sweet potato custard front

Butter Milk   Sweet Milk

Persimmon beer au possem

O'possum roti = Roast O'Possum

Green corn = Ears of field corn in the milk stage

SANDERSVILLE

MENU

(Prepared by Mrs. S. M. Moye)

Grapefruit with Cherries

Pork Ham   Sweet Potatoes

Rutabaga   Pork   Pickles

Eggplant

Tomatoes Sliced   Creamed Potatoes

Celery   Fruit Salad

Turkey

Bread   Pumpkin Pie

Apple Rolls   Butter Sauce

Hot Coffee   Whipped Cream.

MORE ELABORATE MENU

Oysters on Half Shell

Cream of Chicken

White Plume Celery   Young Onions

Hastings Radishes

Broiled Savannah River Shad

Shoestring Potatoes

Braised Sweet Breads

Prime Ribs of Georgia Raised Beef

Brown Gravy

Roast Young Turkey, Chestnut Dressing

Mashed Potatoes   Steamed Rice

Asparagus on Toast

Lettuce and Tomato Salad

Hot Rolls   Egg Bread

Neopolitan Cream   Assorted Cakes

Peach Pie

Cream Cheese   Tea Flake Crackers

Kamper's Roasted Coffee

Barnesia Farm Sweet and Buttermilk

Mixed Nuts

Cigars   Cigarettes.

SAVANNAH

MENU

Chatham County Oyster Cocktail, or Grape Fruit

Turtle Soup   Tomato Bouillon   Terrapin Stew

Sweet Peach Pickles, Celery, Mixed Pickles

Baked Trout, (Georgia) Corn Pone Dressed

Salted Peanuts

Roast Turkey (Georgia) Chestnut Stuffing

Georgia Rice   Giblet Gravy

Boiled (Brooks County) Ham Prime Rib of Roast Beef

Roast Goose, White Potato Dressing

Opossum, Baked Sweet Potatoes,

Rabbits   Roast Pork

Irby Turnips, Mashed (Bartow County)

Roast Chicken   Quail

(Lowndes County Mayhaw Jelly)

Creamed Onions Corn Kershaw, Baked in Shell

String Beans   Artichokes, Asparagus and Peppers

Salads: Lettuce with Cream Dressing   Cold Slaw Buttered Beets

Sliced Tomatoes

Apple, Pumpkin, and Sweet Potato Pie or Potato Pone

Butter Sauce

Peach of Strawberry Ice Cream

Pound Cake   John B. Gordon Cake

Nunnally's or Block's Crackers

Pecans   English and Black Walnuts   Apples

Augusta Chronicle (November 7, 1913), 2

SUMTER COUNTY

MENU

(First Prize for County Submission Mrs. E. E. Allen)

Soup

Clear Amber Soup, Croutons, Celery

Fish

Broiled Brook Trout, Drawn Butter, Parsley Sauce,

Corn Meal Muffins,

Scalloped Irish Potatoes, Radishes.

Entree

Baked bell peppers, stuffed with minced veal,

Relish

Salted Pecans.

Meats

Roast turkey   Mayhaw Jelly

Giblet Gravy,

Braised Beef with Carrots.

Green tomatoes   Cabbage and Onions,

Chow Chow,   Candied Yams

Hominy Puff.   Egg Plant Fritters,

Cauliflower with Cream Sauce.

Game

Smothered Wild Duck,   Apple Sauce,

Hot biscuit.

Salads

Lettuce and Tomato Salad,

French dressing made with Sumter County Oil and Apple Vinegar,

Desserts

Pumpkin Pie,   Canned Elberta peaches

Filled with Frozen Whipped Cream.

Layer Cake—Caramel and Black Walnut Filling

Fruit

Apples,   Japanese Persimmons,

Buttermilk,   Sweet Milk,   Adam's Ale

Americus Weekly Times-Recorder (November 13, 1913), 2

SUMTER COUNTY

MENU

(Second Prize for County Submission Mrs. John P. Butt)

Water – a la Artesian

Turtle Soup, Terrapin Stew, Baked Trout,

Turnips, Collards, Green Peppers

Snap Beans, Tomatoes, Cabbage,

Butterbeans, Beets (pickled),

Scalloped Corn,

Boiled Onions, Radishes, Egg Bread

Possum, Potatoes, Persimmons,

Cream Irish Potatoes,

Baked Curshaw,

Pecans.   Salted Peanuts.

Turkey,   Chestnut Dressing,

Hot Rolls.

May-haw, Apple and Blackberry Jelly,

Scuppernong, Plum and Apple Sauce

Rabbit.

Sliced Country Ham.

Green Peas in Lettuce Leaf.

Roast Beef, Mushrooms,

Lamb, Mutton, Cream Chicken

Baked Goose,   Quail

Asparagus on Toast.

Artichoke, Cucumber, Peach and Pear Pickle.

Fig and Watermelon Preserves,

Pumpkin and Cushaw Pie.

Sumter Syrup Pudding

Butter and Sweet Milk, Ameri-cola

Grape juice—Plain

Buckalee, Lee Council, or Georgia Belle Cigar.

Americus Weekly Times-Recorder (November 13, 1913), 2

SUMTER COUNTY

MENU

(Third Prize for County Submission Mrs. Emmett Murray)

Vegetable Soup

Bread Sticks

Roast Turkey   Chestnut Dressing

Sausage

Candied Yams.   Stuffed Peppers

Creamed Potatoes   Sliced Tomatoes

Cold Sliced Ham

Chicken Salad on Lettuce

Radishes   Artichoke Pickles

Pear Pickles   Peach Pickles

Hot Rolls   Sumter County Butter

Salted Peanuts

Pound Cake

Elberta Peaches (Canned) Whipped Cream

Artesian Water   Sweet Milk

Buttermilk

Americus-Made Cigars

Americus Times-Recorder (November 13, 1913), 1

TATTNALL COUNTY

MENU

Fruit Cocktail

Creamed Tomato Soup   Croutons

Cucumber Baskets   Sassafras Teas

Bread Turnips

Baked Turkey with Dressing

Chicken Pie   Beef Loaf

Baked Georgia Yams

Stuffed Peppers   Stuffed Tomatoes

Butter

Southern Corn Bread   Bread

Chicken Salad

Potato Salad   Apple and Peanut Salad

Ham and Egg Sandwiches

Cucumber Pickles

Grape Juice

Creamed Ice Cream   Pound Cake

THOMSON

MENU

Oyster Stew   Crackers

Pickles

Broiled Country Ham, Home Made

Bread

Turkey   Giblet Gravy   Dressing

Candied Potatoes

Floating Island   Layer Cake   Pound Cake.

Crackers   Cheese

Coffee

McDuffie Progress (November 14, 1913), 5

TIFTON

MENU

(Myon Hotel)

Salted Peanuts

Tifton County Tomatoes   Home Raised Radishes

Lettuce

Chow Chow Pickles   Sweet Cucumber Pickles

Boiled Blue-Stem Collards, smoke Bacon

Hoe Cake   Corn Bread   Butter Milk

Roast Country Turkey, Sage Stuffing, Blackberry Jelly

Cut of Native Beef with brown potatoes and gravy

Backbone Stew with bread dumplings

Watermelon Rind Preserves

New Irish Potatoes   Roasted Yams in Ashes

Home-raised String Beans White-eyed Peas

Old Fashion Potato Salad

Boiled Custard Ice Cream

Grandmother's Pound Cake

Fruit Cake

Pumpkin Custard Pie   Peach Cobbler

Home-baked Light Bread   Spider-cooked Biscuits

Cream Cheese   Crackers

Mint Tea   Black Tea

Sweet Milk

Tifton Gazette (November 14, 1913)

TOOMBS COUNTY

MENU

Corn Bread

Turnip Greens and Hog Jole

Collards and Back Bone

Turkey and Dressing

Fried Chicken   Spare Ribs   Roast Beef or Steak

Roast 'Possum and Yams

Toasted Quail

Fried Squirrels

Baked Duck

Fig Preserves   Scuppernong Jelly

Plum & Blackberry Preserves

Stewed Peaches and Sugar-Cane Syrup

Lyons Progress (November 14, 1913), 1

Hog Jole = Hog jowl

MENUS OF THE 1913 GEORGIA PRODUCTS FEASTS

WAYCROSS

MENU

(Home Dinner Submitted by Mrs. Will Haralson)

Soups

Vegetable   Creamed Tomatoes

Fish

Fried Potato Balls

Meats

Roast Beef   Fried Chicken   Sliced Tongue

Salads

Coleslaw, Irish Potato with Mayonnaise made of Georgia Cotton Oil

Pickles

Bell Pepper Stuffed Mangoes   Artichokes

Entrees

Salted Peanuts   Celery

Bread

Corn Muffins, Pone or Cornbread

Beaten Biscuits   Light Bread

Vegetables

Rice, Steamed,   Cream Irish Potatoes

Turnips with fresh pork,   Boiled Cabbage

Fried Egg Plant,   Field Peas

Baked Sweet Potatoes, Georgia Collards with Dumplings

Fried Corn Fritters

Stewed Tomatoes (canned)

Desserts

Apple Dumplings, Hard Sauce

Sweet Potato Pudding

Spice Cake, Pumpkin Pie, Sponge Cake

Drinks

Sweet Milk, Buttermilk, Sweet Cider, Persimmon Beer

Fruits and Nuts

Apples, Pears, Pecans, Walnuts, Hickory Nuts, Georgia Goobers

Atlanta Georgian (November 7, 1913), 2

SOURCES

Preface
"Atlanta Will Eat Only Georgia Dainties on Nov. 18th," *Atlanta Journal* (November 16, 1913), 34.

Apples
"Apple Sauce Pie," *Sunny South* (December 29, 1879), 7. "Compote of Apples," *Savannah Tribune* (November 25, 1911). "The Georgia Apple," *Clayton Tribune* (September 26, 1918), 1. "Georgia Apples Given Boost," *Athens Banner-Herald* (January 6, 1927), 6. "Georgia Apples Gain in Popularity," *Early County News* (September 19, 1929), 6. Hugh McMillan, "Georgia Apples Are Pick of the Fruit," *Forsyth County News* (January 15, 1986), 12B. "Apples, Born in Asia, Are a Good Source of Nutrition," *Forsyth County News* (October 1, 2000), 5B. "Pick of the Week: Yates Apple," *Atlanta Journal* (November 30, 2000), 68. Catherine G. Lind, "Apples," *New Georgia Encyclopedia* (May 18, 2004): www.georgiaencyclopedia.org/articles/business-economy/apples/. Robert Westerfield, "Home Garden Apples," University of Georgia Extension (June 1, 2006): https://extension.uga.edu/publications/detail.html?number=C740. Creighton Lee Calhoun, *Old Southern Apples: A Comprehensive History and Description of Varieties for Collectors, Growers, and Fruit Enthusiasts*, 2nd ed. (White River Junction, VT: Chelsea Green Publishing, 2011). "Heritage Orchard Reclaiming Georgia's Forgotten Apples," *UGA Today* (March 9, 2021): https://news.uga.edu/heritage-orchard-reclaiming-georgias-forgotten-apples/.

Barbecue
"Fellow Citizens," *Augusta Chronicle* (May 31, 1794), 1. "Myrtle Springs," *Americus Times-Recorder* (July 9, 1923), 3. John T. Boifeuillet, "A Story of the Barbecue," *Atlanta Journal* (August 17, 1933), 10. "Hot Barbecue Sauce," *Augusta Chronicle* (February 2, 1967), 41. John N. White, *A Taste of Georgia* (Newnan Junior League, 1977). Timothy W. Patridge, "Barbecue," *New Georgia Encyclopedia* (April 6, 2005): www.georgiaencyclopedia.org/articles/arts-culture/barbecue/. Robert F. Moss, "The Great Barbecue Men of Augusta," BBQ Hub (October 31, 2016): www.bbqhub.net/features/The-Great-Barbecue-Men-of-Augusta. Mike Jordan, "Is There Such a Thing as Georgia Barbecue?" Eater Atlanta (November 20, 2020): atlanta.eater.com/21523544/georgia-style-barbecue-explainer-fox-bros-bar-b-q-atlanta. Robert F. Moss, *Barbecue: The History of an American Institution*, 2nd ed., (Tuscaloosa: University of Alabama Press, 2020).

Benne
"Bene Oil," *Augusta Chronicle* (June 24, 1809), 3. "Darien Cold Press Castor and Benne Oil," *Darien Gazette* (May 29, 1823), 3. "Benne Oil," *Savannah Daily Republican* (January 11, 1845), 2. "Sesame Culture in the South: New and Lucrative Crop for the Planters," *Dalton Argus* (May 12, 1900), 6. "Castor Bean and Benne Seed," *Washington Gazette* (April 1, 1870), 1. "Bene Oil," *Savannah Morning News* (February 25, 1878), 1. M. Sheron & Company, "We Never Rest on our Laurels," *Augusta Herald* (April 26, 1907), 3.

Biscuits

"Southern Biscuits. How to Make Them" *Telegram-Herald* (September 30, 1889), 8. "Sweet Potato Biscuit," *Jeffersonian* (February 6, 1913), 3. Mr. S. R. Dull, "Southern Biscuits," *Atlanta Journal* (June 20, 1926), 104. "Cheese Biscuits," Snowdrift ad, *Atlanta Journal* (November 2, 1926), 20. "Fixt," *Atlanta Journal* (February 16, 1939), 37. "Cheese Biscuits," *Dallas Morning News* (January 31, 1950), 4. "Spicy Cheese Biscuits," *Dallas Morning News* (April 17, 1964), 2.

Brunswick Stew

"How to Make a Brunswick Stew," *Charleston Southern Patriot* (August 13, 1845), 1. "A Brunswick Stew," *Alexandria Gazette* (June 26, 1855), 4. "Lunch," *Savannah Advertiser* (July 1, 1871), 2. "The Georgia Barbecue," *Atlanta Journal* (May 1, 1894). "The Midway's Barbecue," *Atlanta Journal* (August 24, 1895). I. E. Spatig, ed., "The Brunswick Stew," *Brunswick County, Virginia* (Richmond, VA: Williams Printing, 1907), 22–23. Mrs. S. R. Dull, "Georgia Barbecue and Brunswick Stew," *Atlanta Journal* (July 1, 1923), 27. Mrs. Dull's Cooking Lessons, *Atlanta Journal* (29 May 1938), 73. "The Real Brunswick Stew," *Atlanta Journal* (May 29, 1938), © 1938 *Atlanta Journal-Constitution*. All rights reserved. Used under license. Joe Lambright, Jr., "Origin of Brunswick Stew Located—in Many Places," *Brunswick News* (April 12, 1946), 8. O. Kay Jackson, "Stew Wars: Origins of Succulent Pottage Hotly Contested, *Brunswick News Extra* (January 6, 1988), 10. "Honor of Brunswick Stew Defended during Main Street Jubilee Cook Off," *Brunswick News* (November 21, 1988), 16. Matt Lee and Ted Lee, *The Lee Brothers Southern Cookbook: Stories and Recipes for Southerners and Would-Be Southerners* (New York: W. W. Norton, 2006). Jessica Dupuy, *United Tastes of the South: Authentic Dishes from Appalachia to the Bayou and Beyond* (Birmingham, AL: Oxmoor House, 2018). Michale Rivera, photograph, in Linton West, "Brunswick Stew Monument, Brunswick Georgia," *Atlas Obscura* (September 24, 2021): https://www.atlasobscura.com/places/brunswick-stew-monument.

Butter Beans

"The Lima or 'Butter' Bean," *Savannah Morning News* (February 3, 1884), 7. W. Atlee Burpee, "Jackson Wonder Bean," *Burpee's Farm Annual* (Philadelphia, 1893), 18. N. L. Willet, "Jackson Wonder Bean," *Catalog of Sound Seeds for the South* (Augusta: N. L. Willet Seed Company, 1917), 8. Connie Dougherty, "Butterbeans with Pecans," *Augusta Chronicle* (October 19, 1986), 118.

Cane Syrup

"Cognac, Brandy," *New York Mercantile Advertiser* (April 14, 1819), 2. J. B. Avequin, "The Red or Purple Ribbon Cane," *Louisiana Planter* (October 24, 1891). "Merchants of the North and West: It Is Rousing Time for You Also," *Cairo Messenger* (December 16, 1921), 1. "Speaking of Syrup," *Cairo Messenger* (July 25, 1924), 1. Dylan E. Mulligan, "The Original Progressive Farmer: The Agricultural Legacy of Thomas Spaulding of Sapelo" (honors thesis, Georgia Southern University, 2015): https://digitalcommons.georgiasouthern.edu/cgi/viewcontent.cgi?article=1102&context=honors-theses.

Catfish

Henry William Herbert, *Frank Forester's Fish and Fishing of the United States, and British Provinces of North America* (London: Richard Bentley, 1849), 193. "Catfish in Cornfield," *Augusta Chronicle* (August 5, 1887), 8. "Catfish and its Habits," *Savannah Morning News* (October 10, 1903), 7.

"Fried Catfish," *Savannah Morning News* (March 20, 1904), 26. "Catfish Chowder," *Atlanta Journal* (August 13, 1905), 6. "Things Found in a Catfish's Stomach," *Atlanta Journal* (August 24, 1930), 69. David M. Newell, *The Fishing and Hunting Answer Book* (Garden City, NY: Doubleday, 1948), 33. Don Biggers, "New Farm Commodity—Catfish," *Atlanta Journal and Constitution* (June 25, 1961), 20. Vlad Evanoff, *The Freshwater Fisherman's Bible* (New York: Doubleday, 1964), 170. Virgil Adams, "Acres of Catfish," *Atlanta Journal* (August 24, 1969), 185.

Chatham Artillery Punch

Charles C. Jones, Jr., *Historical Sketch of the Chatham Artillery* (Albany, NY: J. Munsell, 1867), 25. "Mike! The Ne Plus Ultra of Barkeepers," *Savannah Daily Republican* (April 13, 1868), 2. "A Reunion," *Savannah Republican* (July 25, 1868), 3. "Mayor's Court," *Savannah Daily Republican* (August 11, 1868), 3. "Entertainment of the Press Associations in Savannah," *Savannah Morning News* (May 7, 1870), 1. A. R. Watson, "Ode to Artillery Punch," *Savannah Morning News* (February 27, 1873), 3. "Artillery Punch," *Savannah Daily Times* (May 12, 1885), 1. "A New Drink," *Atlanta Evening Capitol* (September 5, 1885), 2. "Admiral Dewey Artillery Punch," *Augusta Chronicle* (March 23, 1900), 6. Archibald Henderson, *Washington's Southern Tour* (New York: Houghton Mifflin, 1923), 227–28. "Chatham Artillery Punch," *Christ Church Savannah Cook Book* (Savannah, GA: Christ Church Episcopal, 1933), 10. Harriet Ross Colquitt, "Chatham Artillery Punch," *The Savannah Cook Book* (New York: Farrar & Reinhart, 1933), 167. "Famous Old Punch," *New Orleans Item* (January 5, 1934), 4. "Chatham Artillery Punch," *From Savannah Kitchens* (Savannah, GA: Christ Church Episcopal, 1962), 11. Drew Podo, "Drink This: Chatham Artillery Punch," *Atlanta* (June 8, 2016): https://www.atlantamagazine.com/dining-news/drink-chatham-artillery-punch/. Beth McKibben, "Chatham Artillery Punch: Maybe the Strongest Drink in American History," *Paste* (July 8, 2016): https://www.pastemagazine.com/drink/chatham-artillery-punch-maybe-the-strongest-drink. Marleigh Riggins Miller, "Chatham Artillery Punch Recipe," Serious Eats (updated August 30, 2018): https://www.seriouseats.com/drink-the-book-chatham-artillery-punch-original-recipe-wondrich.

Cheese Straws

"London Entertaining," *Baltimore Bulletin* (January 22, 1876), 2. "Cheese Straws Good," *Jeffersonian* (August 11, 1910), 2. Mrs. Jewel Burks, "Cheese Straws," *Fayetteville's Favorite Foods* (Fayetteville, GA: Women's Civic Club, 1949), 6. Cecily Brownstone, "Cheese Straws Melt in Your Mouth," *Brunswick News* (December 10, 1963).

Chicken Pie

Mrs. S. R. Dull, "Ye Goode Olde Chicken Pie," *Atlanta Journal* (June 30, 1929), 101. Lee Stanley, "Smithville, A Town Rich in History," *Lee County Ledger* (January 15, 2004), 5. "Leah McCrary Wins Chicken Pie Festival Contest," *Lee County Ledger* (November 2, 2005), 8.

Coca-Cola Cake

Atlanta Journal (June 21, 1990), 78. Anne Byrn, *American Cake: From Colonial Gingerbread to Classic Layer, the Stories and Recipes behind More than 125 of Our Best-Loved Cakes* (New York: Rodale, 2016). "The History of Coca-Cola Cake," *Quaint Cooking* (November 7, 2022): quaintcooking.com/2022/08/26/the-history-of-coca-cola-cake/.

Coleslaw

"Cold Slaw," *Woman's Work* (October 1, 1893), 14. "Cold Slaw with Mustard," *Rome Tribune* (November 9, 1896), 2. "Folsom's Restaurant Closes Doors," *Atlanta Semi-Weekly Journal* (August 27, 1909), 1. "Cold Slaw," *Atlanta Golden Age* (December 29, 1910), 15. "Household Hints," *Griffin Daily News* (March 6, 1925), 6. Elizabeth Wood, "Homemaker News–Hot and Cold Dressing," *Jackson Progress-Argus* (September 27, 1945), 3. Louise Doak, "Dutch Slaw," *Gems from Georgia Kitchens* (Athens: Garden Clubs of Georgia, 1963), 118. Newnan Junior Service League, *A Taste of Georgia* (Newnan, GA: 1977).

Collards

H. P. Stuckey, "Sow Collard Seeds Late in Season," *Leader-Tribune and Peachland Journal* (June 16, 1921), 8. Emily Johnstone, "Coast Line News Features Article on Grady Collard Seed Industry," *Cairo Messenger* (October 18, 1946), 5. "Wintertime Is Collard Time in Middle Georgia," *Houston Home Journal* (January 10, 2002), C1. David S. Shields, *Southern Provisions* (Chicago: University of Chicago Press, 2015), 42.

Condiments
Tomato Catsup

"Tamata Catsup," *Easton Gazette* (October 4, 1823), 1. "Tomato Catsup," *Augusta Daily Constitutionalist* (September 18, 1861), 1. "Tomato Catsup," *Columbus Sun* (May 23, 1862), 3. David S. Shields, "Tomato Catsup," *Foodlore and More*, Issue 27: Sauces, Part 3 (Substack, July 20, 2021): https://davidsanfordshields.substack.com/p/issue-27-sauces-part-3-tomato-catsup.

Worcestershire Sauce

Dickson & Miles, "Rich Meat and Fish Sauces," *Charleston Courier* (November 3, 1843), 3. Hone & Connery, "Worcestershire Sauce," *Savannah Daily Republican* (November 2, 1850), 3. J. A. Millen & Co., "Worcestershire Sauce and French Mustard," *Augusta Chronicle* (January 1, 1852), 1. "Worcester Sauce," *Augusta Daily Constitutionalist* (July 14, 1866), 23. William Shurtlief and Akiko Ayoyagi, *History of Worcestershire Sauce 1837–2012* (Lafayette, CA: Soyinfo Center, 2012).

Pepper Vinegar

"Peter Catonnet," *Savannah Columbia Museum* (November 21, 1797), 2. "Just Received and For Sale by James Belcher," *Georgia Gazette* (August 30, 1798), 1. "John I. Sluyter," *Georgia Gazette* (January 10, 1799), 1. "Charles McKenna," *Savannah Republican & Evening Ledger* (March 24, 1807), 4. "Every Soldier His Own Physician," *Southern Recorder* (June 10, 1862), 1. Marion Harland, "Pepper Vinegar," *Common Sense in the Household* (New York: Scribner's Sons, 1871), 200. Annabella P. Hill, *Mrs. Hill's Southern Practical Cookery and Receipt Book*, Damon Fowler, ed. (Columbia: University of South Carolina Press, 1995 reprint of 1872 ed.), 207. "Pepper Vinegar," *Afro-American Advance* (October 7, 1899), 4.

Corn Bread

"Best Corn Bread," *Daily Constitutionalist* (September 21, 1886), 3. "Decline and Fall of Corn Bread," *Augusta Chronicle* (July 23, 1899), 4. "Corn Bread vs. Biscuit," *Augusta Chronicle* (July 17, 1901), 5. "The Days of Corn Bread," *Augusta Chronicle* (February 10, 1918), 6. "It's Birdsey's Flour, the Best," *Augusta Chronicle* (June 21, 1930), 10. "Southerners Make a Cornucopia of Corn," *Marietta Daily Journal* (September 21, 1989), 34.

Country Captain

"Henry Ellison," *Charleston City Gazette* (October 13, 1797), 1. "John J. Sluyter," *Savannah*

Columbian Museum (December 26, 1800), 2. "Dr. Hunter's Imitation of India Curry Powder," *Magazine of Domestic Economy*, Volume 1 (London: W. S. Orr, 1836), 219. Maria Louisa Poyas Gibbs, recipe book (ca. 1844; South Carolina Historical Society manuscripts 34/702). Hadji Nicka Bauker Khan, "Indian Sketches XLV," *Boston Commercial Bulletin* (March 17, 1877), 1. Mary J. Lincoln, "Chicken Curry," *Philadelphia Inquirer* (January 20, 1900), 11. Morrison Wood, "Readers Submit Their Recipes for Chicken Country Captain," *Dallas Morning News* (March 9, 1958), 3. Grace Hartley, "Country Captain," *Atlanta Journal and Constitution* (September 22, 1968), 235. Ben Green Cooper, "On 'Receipt' Controversy," *Marietta Daily Journal* (May 19, 1971), 21. Molly O'Neill, "Long Ago Smitten, She Remains True to the Country Captain," *New York Times* (April 17, 1991), C6. Edwin S. Grosvenor, "FDR's Favorite Dish: Country Captain," *American Heritage* (July/August 2020): https://www.americanheritage.com/fdrs-favorite-dish-country-captain.

Country Ham

"For Curing Hams," *Covington Enterprise* (March 22, 1907), 4. A. C. Wharton, "Curing Hams and Bacon," *Bainbridge Search Light* (February 16, 1912), 2. Mrs. S. R. Dull, "To Bake a Ham," *Atlanta Journal* (September 10, 1922), 78. Harriet Ross Colquitt, "Baked Ham," *The Savannah Cook Book* (New York: Farrar & Reinhart, 1933), 69–70. "Smith House Cooks Share Country Ham Secrets," *Forsyth County News* (March 20, 1985), B3. Catherine Collier Rentz, "Glazed Country Ham," *Houston Home Journal* (December 27, 2001), 2B.

Crab

"The Delmonico," *Augusta Chronicle* (September 27, 1890), 5. Mrs. Grant Wilkins, "Deviled Crabs," *Atlanta Journal* (April 4, 1891), 5. "Soft Shell Crabs," *Savannah Morning News* (June 7, 1894), 3. "Hick's Restaurant & Soft Shell Crab", *Savannah Morning News* (March 21, 1897), 9. Harriet Ross Colquitt, "Crab Stew," *The Savannah Cook Book* (New York: Farrar & Rinehart, 1933), 42. "Crab Salad," *Atlanta Journal* (March 10, 1935), 85. "Crab Dishes," *Marietta Journal* (December 18, 1958), 16. Kaye Jones, "Cooking for the Cool Nights of Fall," *Leader-Tribune* (October 20, 2004), 13.

Crowder Peas

"Crowder Pea," *Augusta Chronicle* (November 16, 1859), 2. Hugh N. Starnes, "Cow Peas," *Jackson Argosy* (May 24, 1895), 2. Joseph Montelaro, "Field Peas Have Many Values to Farm Folks," *Baton Rouge State Times Advocate* (April 18, 1951), 12. Hugh Gibson, "Gullah Folk Remedies," *Charleston News and Courier* (June 17, 1962), 25.

Deviled Eggs

"Deviled Eggs," *Savannah Morning News* (July 26, 1888), 4. Mildred Huff, "Eggcellent Ideas," *Houston Home Journal* (March 30, 1972), B3. "Why Don't You Bring the Deviled Eggs," *Atlanta Journal* (June 6, 1973), 139. Hines V. Causey, interview by D. S. Shields, October 6, 2003. Nancy R. McArthur, "The Deviled Egg: History and Present," *Eggs in Cookery: Proceedings of the Oxford Symposium of Food and Cookery 2006*, Richard Hosking, ed., (Oxford, UK: Prospect Books, 2007), 125–28.

Doves

W. W. Sprague, "Dove Pie," *From Savannah Kitchens* (Savannah, GA: Christ Church Episcopal, 1962). Mildred E. Warren, "Smothered Doves," *Houston Home Journal* (October 19, 1972), 22. "Georgia Dove Season Opened September 3rd," *Lee County Ledger* (September 7, 2022), B1.

Duck
"Wild Ducks (Stewed)," *The Unrivaled Cook-Book and Housekeeper's Guide* (New York: Harper and Brothers, 1886), 157. "The Ducks," *Savannah Morning News* (July 2, 1900), 7. "Ducks," *Atlanta Journal* (February 7, 1913), 20. "Duck Hunting is a Great Sport," *Augusta Chronicle* (September 23, 1917), 2. Mrs. Darwood Holm, "Mallard or French Duck," *Gems from Georgia Kitchens* (Athens: Garden Club of Georgia, 1963), 98. Used by permission.

Figs
"August Epicures Feast on Fine Figs," *Augusta Chronicle* (August 14, 1910), 2. "Fig Marmalade," *Augusta Chronicle* (December 29, 1911), 8. Mrs. S. R. Dull, "Jellies, Jams, and Preserves," *Atlanta Journal* (September 7, 1924), 95. "Fig Preserve Cake," *Atlanta Journal and Atlanta Constitution* (November 27, 1976), 20. © 1976 The Atlanta Journal-Constitution. All rights reserved. Used under license.

Fried Bologna
"Bologna Sausage," *Augusta Chronicle & Georgia Advertiser* (March 3, 1827), 3. "Fulton Market Beef &c," *Savannah Daily Georgian* (November 16, 1827), 1. "Some of Joyce's Specialties," *Savannah Morning News* (October 25, 1903), 21. "Fried Bologna Sausage," *Wayne County News* (December 7, 1904), 4. "Swift & Company Atlanta," *Atlanta Journal* (July 20, 1928), 15. "Bologna Scramble," *Atlanta Journal* (August 22, 1930), 24. Glynn Moore, "I Ought to Be Thin Because I Can't Eat Anything," *Augusta Chronicle* (April 10, 2003), 88.

Fried Pie
"Cheap Diet," *Edgefield (SC) Advertiser* (February 26, 1852), 2. "To Make a Nightmare," *Philadelphia Sunday Dispatch* (February 29, 1852), 4. Caroline Coe, "Fried Pie Crust," *Augusta Chronicle* (November 30, 1913), 3. William Orten Carleton, "Eyes on the Pies," *Athens Flagpole* (July 22, 1998), 18. "In the Kitchen with Lucile Kirk," *Pickens County Progress* (September 23, 2004), 19. "Soup's Still in Season," *Houston Home Chronicle* (March 15, 2006), 6. "Mulberry Works on Church Building," *Braselton News* (May 1, 2019), 12. "Mary Vinson-Obituaries," *Pickens County Progress* (January 24, 2019), 13.

Green Tomatoes
"Green Tomato Pickle," *Augusta Daily Constitutionalist* (February 1 1863), 4. "To Drive Away Bedbugs," *Marietta Journal and Courier* (May 5, 1871), 3. "Fried Green Tomatoes," *Charleston Evening Post* (June 22, 1899), 7. "Green Tomatoes," *Atlanta Journal* (October 4, 1903), 1. Emma Paddock Telford, "Green Tomato Catsup," *Augusta Chronicle* (September 18, 1904), 9. Mrs. C. G. M. "Green Tomato Mince Pie," *Atlanta Journal* (December 18, 1904), 43.

Grits
Marjorie Kinnen Rawlings, *Cross Creek Cookery* (New York: Scribner's Sons, 1942), 73. Grace Hartley, "Down South Menu for Home Ec Guests," *Atlanta Journal* (March 28, 1963), 73. Ann Byrn Phillips, [Sautéed Grits Cake] "Tribute to a Dixieland Delight," *Atlanta Constitution* (July 10, 1983), 311. "Grits are Mysterious," *Athens Flagpole* (May 3, 1995), 9. "Sofkee (Corn Drink)," *Southeast Native Food* (November 9, 2012): https://nas415.wordpress.com/2012/11/09/sofkee-a-traditional-muskogee-corn-drink/.

Grouper
"Gulf Stream Home of Giants," *Augusta Chronicle* (September 24, 1967), 20. "Red Grouper is Versatile, Plentiful Fish," *Atlanta Journal* (June 14, 1990), 104. "Pan Fried Grouper on a Bun," *Augusta Chronicle* (March 31, 1996), 73. "Restrictions

Might Protect Dwindling Fish," *The [SC] State* (October 27, 2002), 5. "Fake Fish Steams Buyers," *Baton Rouge Advocate* (January 4, 2008), 44. "Grouper Ban Strains SC Seafood Industry," *The [SC] State* (January 28, 2010), 14. Kiyoshi Soyano, et al., "Endrocrine Regulation of Maturation and Sex Change in Groupers," *Cells* (February 27, 2022), 825: https://www.ncbi.nlm.nih.gov/pmc/articles/PMC8909327/.

Guinea Fowl

Marian Harland, *Common Sense in the Household* (New York: Scribner, Armstrong, 1873), 95. "A Word for the Guinea Fowl," *Schley County News* (December 4, 1890), 7. "Guinea Fowls," *Schley County News* (March 4, 1892), 7. C. F. Langworthy, *The Guinea Fowl and Its Use as Food: USDA Farmers' Bulletin No. 234* (Washington, DC: Government Printing Office, 1905), 19–20. "Guinea Fowl Destroy Boll Weevils," *Newnan Herald* (June 30, 1916), 1. "Guinea Fowl of Value in Lieu of Game Birds," *Atlanta Georgian* (September 23, 1917), C2. "Guinea Gumbo," *Atlanta Journal* (June 22, 1944), 102. "Fricassee of Guinea, You Asked for It," *Atlanta Journal* (September 15, 1960), F2. Mrs. A. P. Mulkey, "Breast of Guinea Hen au Sherry," *Gems from Georgia Kitchens* (Athens: Garden Club of Georgia, 1963), 98.

Guinea Squash

Sarah Josepha Hale, *Mrs. Hale's New Book of Cookery* (New York: H. Long & Brother, 1852), 234. William Nathaniel White, *Gardening for the South; or the Kitchen and Fruit Garden* (New York: C. M. Saxton, 1857), 265, 267–68. Jules Arthur Harder, "Egg Plant Salad," *Physiology of Taste: Harder's Book of Practical American Cookery* (San Francisco, 1885), 155. "Eggplant Fritters," *Evening News* (August 10, 1914), 2. "Guinea Squash," Carolina Gold Rice Foundation (August 25, 2016): www.thecarolinagoldricefoundation.org/news/2016/6/4/guinea-squash. Melanie Fincher, "11 Types of Eggplants to Know (and Grow) This Summer," *Allrecipes* (April 28, 2021): www.allrecipes.com/article/types-of-eggplants/.

Honey

J. J. Wilder, "Beekeeping in West Florida," *Gleanings in Bee Culture* (January 15, 1913), 53. "Sweetening the World," *Cairo Messenger* (August 20, 1926), 2. "Honey Cake," *Augusta Chronicle* (May 28, 1952), 14. "Bogus Honey Not Sweet to Tourists," *Forsyth County News* (September 4, 1985), 12. "Disappearing Honeybees in the Wild," *Forsyth County News* (January 13, 2002), B5. Kelly S. Hockersmith, "Apalachicola's Gold: Archaeology and the History of Tupelo Honey Production in Northwest Florida" (master's thesis, University of South Florida, 2004): https://scholarcommons.usf.edu/etd/1080, 25–32. Samantha Rachelle Gardiner, "Physicochemical and Flavor Characterization of Tupelo Honey" (master's thesis, University of Illinois at Urbana-Champaign, 2015), iii, 24–30. Kim Severson, "On the Trail of Tupelo Honey, Liquid Gold from the Swamps," *New York Times* (May 28, 2019), https://www.nytimes.com/2019/05/28/dining/tupelo-honey.html.

Lard

"Rendering Lard," *Savannah Tribune* (March 23, 1889), 4. "Compound Lard Bill," *Savannah Morning News* (April 2, 1890), 5. "Get Rid of the Lard Habit," Cottonlene ad, *Augusta Chronicle* (March 13, 1908), 2. Anne Kingsley, "Plain Pastry," *Augusta Chronicle* (January 28, 1934), 3. "Try New Tastes for Tired Palates," *Atlanta Journal* (April 24, 1958), 77. T. A. Wilson, M. McIntyre, and R. J Nicolosi, "Trans Fatty Acids and Cardiovascular Risk," *Journal of Nutrition Health Aging* (May 2001), 184–7. Josh Ozersky,

"Lardcore: Southern Food with Hard-Core Attitude," *Time* (October 27, 2010), https://content.time.com/time/nation/article/0,8599,2027672,00.html. Nancy Shute, "Lard Is Back," *The Salt* (May 2, 2012): https://www.npr.org/sections/thesalt/2012/05/02/151868208/. "Ossabaw Island Hog," *The Livestock Conservancy* (2023): https://livestockconservancy.org/heritage-breeds/heritage-breeds-list/ossabaw-island-hog/.

Mull

"Chicken Mull Promotes Peace," *Atlanta Journal* (August 30, 1945), 12. Clementine Paddleford, "Sea Island Picnic," *Chicago Tribune* (March 10, 1951), 99. "Chef Shares Old Recipe for Coastal Shrimp Mull," *Atlanta Journal* (November 20, 1964), 35. "Many Do Mull over This One," *Augusta Chronicle* (October 10, 1965), C6. "Famous Shrimp Mull Tops Restaurant Menu," *Atlanta Journal* (January 10, 1968), 81. "Turtles Go to Roscoe's," *Augusta Chronicle* (August 31, 1970), 24. Louise Thrash, "Dove Mull," *Augusta Chronicle* (May 24, 1979), 8. "Burke County Chefs," *Augusta Chronicle* (May 24, 1979), F1. Jim Christian, "Southern Foods Are Distinctive," *Augusta Chronicle* (October 13, 1983), 9. "Chase Street Café," *Anderson Independent Mail* (October 5, 1986), 43. Nancy Roquemore, "Answer to Chicken Mull Request Is Heaven-Sent," *Atlanta Journal* (February 8, 1996), H2. © 1996 The Atlanta Journal-Constitution. All rights reserved. Used under license. Sallie Anne Robinson, "Daufuskie Catfish and Shrimp Mull," *Gullah Home Cooking the Daufuskie Way* (Chapel Hill: University of North Carolina Press, 2003), 64–65. John Garst, "Mull," *New Georgia Encyclopedia* (edited May 2, 2013): http://www.georgiaencyclopedia.org/articles/arts-culture/mull. "Chicken Mull," *boonie foodie* (February 1, 2011): http://wanderluck.wordpress.com/2011/02/01/chicken-mull/.

Mullet

"With the Quaint Mullet-Men in the Gulf of Mexico," *Sunny South* (April 9, 1904), 3. "Four Cars of Mullet," *Dawson News* (September 16, 1908), 10. Alex W. Bealer, "The Mullet or the Child," *Golden Age* (June 1, 1911), 6. "A Florida Law that Pinches," *Cairo Messenger* (December 11, 1925), 2. Chalmers S. Murray, "Edisto Islanders Have Sea Food Dishes of Their Own," *Charleston News and Courier* (January 28, 1953), 8. Joe Blake, "Mullet Stew [with Yams]," *Favorite Recipes* (Kansas City, KS: Bev-Ron, 1956), 67. Oscar Vick, "Mullet and Okra Stew," *Gullah Cooking: Fish Cooking* (pub. by author, 1991), 99. Jim Rooney, "Fried Mullet," *Jim Rooney's Edisto Eatin'* (Lenexa, KS: Cookbook Publishers, 1996), 19.

Mustard Greens

"Ostrich Plume Mustard," *Seed Catalogue of the Howard & Willet Drug Co.* (Augusta, 1896), 1. "In a Mustard Field," *Savannah Morning News* (March 10, 1900), 8. "Mustard Southern Giant Curled L.S.," *AAS Winners*: https://all-americaselections.org/product/mustard-southern-giant-curled-l-s/. "Pot Herb," *Atlanta Journal* (December 15, 1976), 140.

Ogeechee Limes

Mrs. Thomson, "Ogeechee Limes," Parker Family Papers, South Carolina Historical Society Manuscripts 28/604/1–3, ca. 1880–1900. "The Ogeechee Lime Fruit," *Savannah Morning News* (September 12, 1890), 9. Harriet Ross Colquitt, "The Ogeechee Lime," *The Savannah Cook Book* (New York: Farrar & Rinehart, 133), 151. "Annual Georgia Products Feast for D.A.R.," *Atlanta Journal* (November 10, 1935), 29.

Oils

"Cotton Seed Oil," *Columbian Museum and Savannah Gazette* (November 18, 1820), 2. Lancelot

Johnston, "Cotton Seed Oil," *Southern Banner* (October 19, 1833), 3. J. Hamilton Couper, "Cotton Seed Oil," *Augusta Chronicle* (July 9, 1845), 1. "Cotton Seed Oil," *Savannah Republican* (June 29, 1861), 5. "Cotton Hulling Machine," *Augusta Chronicle* (December 12, 1929), 77. "Okra Seed Oil Is New Product in Louisiana," *Cairo Messenger* (September 10, 1948), 10. "About Us," *Georgia Olive Farms*: https://georgiaolivefarms.com/gof/about-us/. David S. Shields, "Prospecting for Oil," *Gastronomica* (Fall 2010), 25–34.

Okra

"Okra," *Augusta Chronicle* (February 11, 1846), 2. "Some Useful Hints," *Milledgeville Union Recorder* (April 6, 1886), 8. "Okra," *Savannah Morning News* (July 6, 1891), 6. Shalini Vadhera, *Passport to Beauty* (New York: St. Martin's Griffin, 2006). National Research Council of the National Academies, *Lost Crops of Africa: Vegetables, Vol. 2* (Washington, DC: National Academies Press, 2006). Jessica B. Harris, "Okra," *Africooks* (March 1, 2017): https://africooks.com/wordpress/p-81/. Chris Smith, *The Whole Okra: A Seed to Stem Celebration* (New York: Chelsea Green, 2019). Jill Neimark, "This Southern-Crafted Oil Is a Secret Weapon in the Arsenals of Atlanta Chefs," *Atlanta* (November 12, 2019): https://www.atlantamagazine.com/dining-news/this-southern-crafted-oil-is-a-secret-weapon-in-the-arsenals-of-atlanta-chefs/.

Oysters

"Alfred Haywood," *Savannah Daily Morning News* (September 6, 1849), 3. "Thunderbolt Oysters," *Savannah Daily Morning News* (October 17, 1851), 2. "Oysters! Oysters!" *Savannah Morning News* (December 15, 1868), 2. "Oysters Disappearing," *Charleston News and Courier* (May 13, 1889), 5. "The Oyster Season Well In," *Savannah Morning News* (November 11, 1889), 8. "May Mean a Fight in Court," *Savannah Morning News* (October 19, 1896), 8. Sister Mary, "Menus for a Family," *Americus Recorder* (November 24, 1924), 3. Tyler H. Jones, "Reviving Coastal Georgia's Oyster Industry," *Pickens County Progress* (July 5, 2018), A6.

Peaches

Sue Leslie, "Peach Historical Society's Spotlight," *Fort Valley Leader-Tribune* (May 27, 1987), 8. Billy Dick, "Peach History from a Peach Grower," *Fort Valley Leader-Tribune* (June 19, 1991), 2. Billy Power, "Fort Valley, Peach Capital of Georgia," *Fort Valley Leader-Tribune* (June 9, 2004), 2. "Peach Barbecue Sauce," *Fort Valley Leader-Tribune* (October 29, 2008). William Thomas Okie, *The Georgia Peach* (Cambridge, UK: Cambridge University Press, 2016). Kevin Mitchell and David S. Shields, *Taste the State: South Carolina's Signature Foods, Recipes & Their Stories* (Columbia: University of South Carolina Press, 2021), 112-14. "7 Types of Peaches: A Guide to Popular Peach Varieties," *MasterClass* (December 14, 2021), www.masterclass.com/articles/types-of-peaches.

Peanuts

"San Domingo Ground Nut Cake," *Atlanta Weekly Constitution* (April 25, 1882), 3. "Pea-Nut Cakes," *Sandersville Herald* (April 27, 1882), 4. "Acme Sanity Market to Make Peanut Butter," *Americus Times-Recorder* (July 26, 1916), 5. "F. D. Terry Buys New Machinery," *Atlanta Georgian* (August 4, 1918), C6. "Patriotic Recipes," *Cordele Dispatch* (July 2, 1918), 4. Mrs. S. R. Dull, "New Uses for Peanut Butter," *Atlanta Journal* (January 16, 1921), 57. "Peanut Butter Cookies," *Atlanta Journal* (October 14, 1928), 11. "Pindar Boilin' Time," *Atlanta Journal* (August 27, 1944), 12. "French Fried Peanuts New Vance Specialty," *Augusta Chronicle* (March 27, 1961), 5.

Pears

William Parry, *Forty Years in Pear Growing* (Cinnaminson: New Jersey State Horticultural Society, 1876), 10–11. "The LeConte Pear Boom," *Southern Agriculturist* (December 1, 1882), 7. "A New Race of Pears—the Oriental," *American Agriculturist* (November 1884), 501–02. *Cherokee Nursery Catalogue* (Waycross, GA, 1893), 11. "The Kieffer Pear: Conflicting Opinions," *Rural New Yorker*, Issue 42, no. 1766 (December 1, 1883), 22. "Gingered Pears," *Savannah Tribune* (August 24, 1918), 7. "Pear Relish," *Marietta Journal* (August 29, 1935), 3. Charlotte Walker, "Pear Chutney," *Charleston News and Courier* (July 10, 1961), 5.

Pecans

"Pecans," *Savannah Daily Republican* (January 27 1849), 3. "The Brunswick Advertiser Remarks," *Marietta Journal* (April 6, 1881), 3. "Savannah Grown Pecans," *Savannah Morning News* (October 27, 1886), 9. W. D. Beatie, "Pecans," *Atlanta Nurseries* (Atlanta: Beatie, 1891), 22. Herbert Post, "The Pecan Industry," *Savannah Morning News* (May 16, 1892), 6. "Paper Shell Pecans—New Industry Started by G. W. Bacon," *Augusta Chronicle* (October 27, 1898), 7. "Famous Pecan Tree Interested Visitors," *Dawson News* (October 7, 1924), 2. "Sugared Pecans," *Atlanta Journal* (January 11, 1925). "Pecan Cake," *Atlanta Journal* (November 10, 1940). © 1940 The Atlanta Journal-Constitution. All rights reserved. Used under license. "First Pecan Trees Grown Here in 1840," historical marker, *Georgia Historical Society:* https://georgiahistory.com/ghmi_marker_updated/first-pecan-trees-grown-here-about-1840/. "Stuckey's History," *Stuckey's:* https://stuckeys.com/history/.

Persimmon Beer

"Georgia News," *Savannah Morning News* (December 30, 1871), 2. "The Proper Thing to Serve with Possum," *Tifton Weekly News and Sun* (January 8, 1909), 4. "Thief Takes Beer and 'Possums' Too," *Atlanta Journal* (March 4, 1909), 10. "Page Says Persimmon Beer," *Augusta Chronicle* (January 6, 1909), 6. H. P. Stuckey, "Persimmon Beer," *Americus Times-Recorder* (September 28, 1921), 6. Herbert Wilcox, "Persimmon Beer," *Atlanta Journal* (December 23, 1945), 68. Earl L. Bell, "Do Any Farmers in Augusta Area Still Produce 'Persimmon Beer'?" *Augusta Chronicle* (January 11, 1959), 30.

Pickles

"Drugs, Medicines, Etc., Ewell & Cooke," *Columbian Museum and Savannah Advertiser* (July 13, 1802), 1. "G. M. Willett," *Savannah Daily Republican* (February 22, 1851), 3. Mrs. Mary L. Edgeworth, "To Pickle Peaches," "Higdon Pickle," "Lemon Pickle," *The Southern Gardener & Receipt Book*, (Philadelphia: Lippincott, 1860), 143–46. "Premiums Awarded at the 4th Annual Anderson Farmers Association Fair," *Anderson Intelligencer* (November 16, 1871), 3. Marion Harland, "Pickled Peaches," *Atlanta Journal* (August 22, 1915), 39. "Pickled Okra, New Edible Invented by S. A. Housewife," *San Antonio Light* (July 18, 1934), 11. "Pickled Okra," *San Angelo Standard-Times* (October 6, 1953), 7. "Dilled Okra," *Atlanta Journal* (August 17, 1961), 78. Nathalie Dupree, "Chow Chow," *Cooking of the South* (New York: Irena Chalmers Cookbooks, 1984), 39.

Pimento Cheese

"Kamper's," *Atlanta Journal* (February 22, 1918), 2. "How to Make Pimento Cheese," *Augusta Chronicle* (November 23, 1919), 6. "Pimento Cheese," *Savannah Tribune* (September 15, 1921), 8. "Georgia's Great Pepper Industry," *Augusta Chronicle* (October 31, 1921), 3. J. D. Jones, "Georgia Excels Spain in Growing Peppers," *Atlanta Journal* (January 6, 1924), 77. Miriam Longino, "Very

P. C. Pimento Puts the Punch in the South's Preferred Spread," *Atlanta Journal* (May 9, 1996), 108. "Northerner Discovers Pimento Cheese," *Brunswick News* (June 1, 1996), 2.

Poke Salad

"Poke Salad Battle Is On," *Atlanta Journal* (May 22, 1955), 76. "Granma Watts's Poke Salad—Recipes Guide Good Cooks to New Taste Horizons," *Marietta Journal* (March 17, 1982), 40. Ernest Hodgson, "Toxins and Venoms: Pokeweed 2.5.17, Toxicology and Human Environments," *Progress in Molecular Biology and Translational Science* (Elsevier, 2012), 373–417. David Taylor, "American Pokeweed (Phytolacca americana L.)," Plant of the Week, *USDA, U.S. Forest Service:* https://www.fs.usda.gov/wildflowers/plant-of-the-week/phytolacca_americana.shtml.

Possum and Taters

A Virginian, "Personal Recollections of the War," *Harper's Magazine* 33 (1866), 55. "'Possum and 'Tater," Folsom's Restaurant, *Marietta Journal* (December 20, 1888), 7. "Possum and Taters," *Augusta Chronicle* (November 21, 1897), 16. "Most Notable and Unique Banquet is Given Judge Taft," *Atlanta Journal* (January 16, 1909), 1. "Atlanta Will Eat Only Georgia Dainties on November 18," *Atlanta Journal* (November 16, 1913), 10. Marion Harland, "How to Cook 'Possum," *Atlanta Journal* (February 15, 1914), 40. "The Highway's Wildlife Toll," *Greensboro Daily News* (June 26, 1966), 47. Newnan Junior Service League, *A Taste of Georgia* (Newnan, GA: 1977), 269. Charles Salter, "Playing Possum is Hot Dish at Highway Supper," *Atlanta Journal* (March 22, 1978), 66. Stephen Winick, "A Possum Crisp and Brown: The Opossum and American Foodways," Folklife Today, *Library of Congress Blogs* (August 15, 2019): https://blogs.loc.gov/folklife/2019/08/a-possum-crisp-and-brown-the-opossum-and-american-foodways/. Stephanie Bryan, "The Emblem of North American Fraternity: Opossums and Jim Crow Politics," *Southern Spaces* (October 21, 2022): https://southernspaces.org/2022/emblem-north-american-fraternity-opossums-and-jim-crow-politics/. "Possum Breeders Association," Alabama Company Director (n.d.): https://al.ltddir.com/companies/possum-growers-and-breeders-association-of-america-inc/.

Rattlesnake Watermelon

P. J. Berckmans, "Notes on Melons, Fruitland, April 3d, 1866," *Southern Cultivator* 24, no. 5 (May 1866), 124. "Where Thousands upon Thousands of Georgia Watermelons Grow," *Providence Evening Press* (August 3, 1876), 4; reprint from the *Augusta Chronicle*. N. L W., "The Augusta Territory for Watermelon Growing," *Augusta Chronicle* (January 3, 1898), 4. "Mr. Branch's Rattlesnakes," *Augusta Chronicle* (September 2, 1902), 7. Mrs. Joel Hunter, "Watermelon Rind Pickle No. 1 (sweet)," *Atlanta Women's Club Cookbook* (1921), 92. "The Glory of the Georgia Peach," *Augusta Chronicle* (July 6, 1930), 14. "Old Confederacy in Exile Thrives in Brazil," *Atlanta Journal and Constitution* (January 30, 1966), 62.

Rice and Gravy

Marion Harland, "Savory Rice No. 1," *Atlanta Journal* (January 15, 1911), 41. "Y.W.C.A. Dining Room," *Atlanta Journal* (April 26, 1912), 15. "Mrs. Dull Today Discusses Rice," *Atlanta Journal* (January 31, 1936), 22. "Chicken Gravy," *Atlanta Journal* (July 26, 1936), 82. Grace Hartley, "Housewives Find Versatility of Rice Makes It a Pleasing Dish for Any Meal," *Atlanta Journal* (February 5, 1937), 29. "How About That Turkey," *Atlanta Journal* (November 13, 1938), 104.

Roast Turkey

"Chestnut Dressing," *Atlanta Journal* (November 23, 1915), 15. "Oyster Dressing for Turkey," *Athens Daily Herald* (November 19, 1915), 6. Sister Mary, "Planning Thanksgiving Dinner," *Americus Recorder* (November 24, 1924), 2. "Roasted Stuffed Smoked Turkey," *Augusta Chronicle* (November 15, 1940), 15. "Many Turkeys Grown in Georgia This Year," *Butler Herald* (December 29, 1949), 5. "Brined Bird a Crispy Succulent Wonder," *Atlanta Journal* (November 20, 2000), 22. "Turkey Federation: Preservation Goals Being Attained," *Forsyth County News* (November 23, 2000), A29.

Rutabagas

"Ruta-Baga," *Southern Agriculturist and Register of Rural Affairs* 10 (March 1837), 120. "Sugar Beet versus Rutabaga," *Farmer's Cabinet* (April 1840), 275. "Root Culture," *American Farmer* (December 13, 1843), 238. Theresa C. Brown, "Rutabaga Turnips No. 2," *Modern Domestic Cookery* (Charleston: Edward Perry, 1871), 77. "Rutabagas for Milch Cows," *Southern Cultivator* (July 1892), 334. "Rutabagas," *Southern Cultivator* (July 15, 1905), 7. "How to Plant Rutabagas," *Southern Cultivator* (August 15, 1905), 17. Edna Lewis and Scott Peacock, "Whipped Rutabaga," *The Gift of Southern Cooking* (New York; Alfred A. Knopf, 2003), 129.

Savannah Red Rice

"Messrs. Editors," *Savannah Daily Georgian* (September 18, 1827), 2. "A Cheerful View," *Columbus Daily Times* (October 12, 1861), 2. "Tomatoes and Rice," *Brunswick Advertiser* (July 26, 1876), 3. "Tomato Pilau," *Sunny South* (April 11, 1896), 6. "Carolina Gold: Pearls from Long Ago Plantations," *Atlanta Journal-Constitution* (March 8, 2008), 44. Terrance Zepke, *Lowcountry Voodoo: Beginner's Guide to Tales, Spells and Boo Hags* (Sarasota: Pineapple Press, 2009). Jessica B. Harris, *High on the Hog: A Culinary Journey from Africa to America* (New York: Bloomsbury USA, 2011). Kevin Mitchell and David S. Shields, *Taste the State: South Carolina's Signature Foods, Recipes & Their Stories* (Columbia: University of South Carolina Press, 2021), 133. Blair Lonergan, "Charleston Red Rice," The Seasoned Mom (March 21, 2023): https://www.theseasonedmom.com/red-rice/.

Sea Island Red Peas

"Bahama Red Pease," *Charleston Morning Post* (January 27, 1786), 2. "For Sale," *Republican and Savannah Evening Ledger* (February 20, 1810), 3. "Crop Report Field Peas," *Trenton Federalist* (November 23, 1812), 1. Sarah Rutledge, "Red Pea Soup," *The Carolina Housewife* (Charleston: W. R. Babcock, 1847), 44. "Christmas Time at Hog Hammock," *Atlanta Journal* (December 22, 1994), 31. Jingle Davis, "The Haven of Hog Hammock," *Atlanta Journal and Constitution* (June 25, 1995), 25. "How One Georgia Island Is Fighting to Keep a Small Red Pea Alive," *Cornelia Walker Bailey Program on Land and Agriculture, University of Georgia* (n.d.): https://cwbp.uga.edu/how-one-georgia-island-is-fighting-to-keep-a-small-red-pea-alive/.

Shrimp

"The Rifle Association's Anniversary Dinner at Hotel Tybee," *Savannah Morning News* (May 21, 1890), 9. Elle Goode, "Shrimp Pie," *Atlanta Semi-Weekly Journal* (January 16, 1902), 6. "Shrimp Fritters," *Augusta Chronicle* (November 13, 1906), 5. Harriet Ross Colquitt, "Another Receipt for Shrimp Croquettes," "Shrimp and Rice Croquettes Fritters," "Shrimp or Prawn Pie," *The Savannah Cook Book* (New York: Farrar & Reinhart, 1933), 36. Annabella P. Hill, *Mrs. Hill's Southern Practical Cookery and Receipt*

Book, Damon Fowler, ed. (Columbia: University of South Carolina Press, 1995 reprint of 1872 ed.), 44.

Snap Beans

"To Save Snap Beans for Seed," *Milledgeville Southern Recorder* (October 7, 1851), 465. Patricia Bruschini, "Snap Beans Vary in Name, Color," *Marietta Daily Journal* (April 15, 1984), 26. "Beans an Important Food in All Wars of U.S.A.," *Marietta Journal and Courier* (April 20, 1943), 5. "French Green Bean Casserole," *Atlanta Journal* (June 14, 1962), 74.

Squash Casserole

Casper Plautus, *Nova Typis Transacta Navigatio, Nova Orbis Indiae Occidentalis* (Linz Austria: Honorio Philophono, 1621), plate 6. William Bartram, *Travels through North and South Carolina, Georgia, East and West Florida, the Cherokee Country, etc.* (Philadelphia, James & Johson, 1791), 509. Mrs. J. B. Wells Jr., "Squash Casserole No. 1," *Gems from Georgia Kitchens* (Athens: Garden Club of Georgia, 1963), 132. Used by permission. Linda Murray Berzok, *American Indian Food* (Westport, CT: Greenwood Press, 2005), 57. Alan Davidson, *The Oxford Companion to Food* (Oxford, UK: Oxford University Press, 1999), 749.

Sweet Potatoes

"Potato Pone," *True Flag* (February 22, 1868), 3. "Pumpkin Yams," *Brunswick Advertiser* (January 22, 1881), 3. "Notes on Sweet Potato Culture," *Savannah Morning News* (April 11, 1882), 5. "Cape Fear versus Neuse 'Scissors!'," *Raleigh Farmer and Mechanic* (March 14, 1883). "Southern Lunch Counter Slang," *The State* (SC) (April 25, 1896), 5. Pat Kilmark, "Sweet Potato Biscuit," *Forsyth County News* (December 12, 1986), A9. R. H. Price, *Sweet Potato Culture for Profit* (Dallas: Texas Farm and Ranch, 1896), 57–59. "The Old-Fashioned Yam," *Newnan Herald & Advertiser* (January 1, 1897), 1. "The Sugar Yam," *Early County News* (February 21, 1901), 1. Martin V. Calvin, "Sweet Potatoes," *Jeffersonian* (February 27, 1911), 5. "Sweet Potato Fritters—Sweet Potatoes in New Dresses," *Atlanta Journal* (March 11, 1913), 5. "Sweet Potatoes," *Willet's 1919 Spring Catalog* (Augusta: N. L. Willet Seed, 1919), 20–21. Mrs. H. M. Davis, "Sweet Potato Johnny Cake," *Fitzgerald Leader* (September 21, 1921), 1. Mrs. Brian Cumming, "Rosa's Sweet Potato Pone," *Old and New Recipes from the South* (1947), 51. Annabella P. Hill, *Mrs. Hill's Southern Practical Cookery and Receipt Book*, Damon Fowler, ed. (Columbia: University of South Carolina Press, 1995 reprint of 1872 ed.), 225.

Sweet Potato Fries

"The Aragon," *Atlanta Journal* (December 23, 1897), 8. "French Fried Sweet Potatoes," *Atlanta Journal* (December 14, 1928), 20. "Sweet Potatoes Create Sensation at Exhibit," *Atlanta Journal* (October 13, 1958), 29. "Sweet Potato Fries to Go on Sale Soon," *Greensboro Daily News* (January 15, 1979), 19. "Sweet Potato Fries," *Grand Island Daily Independent* (September 25, 1987), 6. "Smoky Flavor of Mesquite Permeates Skeeter's Menu," *Atlanta Constitution* (March 4, 1989), 111. "School Menus," *Brunswick News Extra* (September 7, 1996), 7. "From Soup to Fries, This Quartet Really Cooks," *Atlanta Journal* (January 9, 1997), 22.

Trout

"Paradise for Sports; What Propagation Has Done for New Zealand," *Augusta Chronicle* (March 19, 1905), 10. "Lake Rabun, at Tallulah, Is New Jewel in Georgia's Crown of Mountain Views," *Atlanta Journal* (May 23, 1915), 19. "Dick Smith's Rules for Fishing," *Atlanta*

Journal (June 26, 1921), 65. "Georgia Obtains a Large Amount of Fame Fish Eggs," *Augusta Chronicle* (December 17, 1934), 8. "Corn Bread Stuffs Trout," *Augusta Chronicle* (April 11, 1968), 55. "His Fish Farm Means Family Fun," *Atlanta Journal* (September 12, 1969), 30. "Baked Stuffed Trout," *Atlanta Journal* (September 2, 1970), 15. "Trout Fever," *Forsyth County News* (March 30, 1988), B1. Mike Webber, "Trout Can Provide Tasty Dinners for Table," *Forsyth County News* (March 30, 1988), B1.

Turnips and Turnip Sallet

Jessup Whitehead, "Turnip Puree Soup," *The Steward's Handbook* (Chicago, Whitehead, 1889), 449. "Turnip Soup," *Augusta Chronicle* (March 12, 1912), 10. N. L. Willet, "An All the Year Dish," *Augusta Chronicle* (August 9, 1915), 4. N. L. Willet, "The All-Important Turnips," *Augusta Chronicle* (July 7, 1917), 4. Mrs. S. R. Dull, "Southern Turnip Greens," *Atlanta Journal* (December 6, 1936), 90. David S. Shields, *Southern Provisions* (Chicago: University of Chicago Press, 2015), 42–43.

Vidalia Onions

"Toombs County Starts Shipping Sweet Potatoes," *Vidalia Advance* (July 7, 1927), 1. "Toombs County Is Georgia's Leading Producer of Onions," *Atlanta Journal and Atlanta Constitution* (April 20, 1958), 113. "Onions Make Good Eating," *Atlanta Journal* (May 26, 1965), 76. "Whose Onion Is It?" *Atlanta Journal* (May 14, 1975), F2. Juanita Garrison, "Solved: The Mystery of the Vidalia Onion," *Anderson Daily Mail* (August 13, 1975), 15. "History of the Vidalia Onion," *Atlanta Constitution Sunday* (March 26, 1995), 398. Reid Torrance, "Vidalia Onions," *New Georgia Encyclopedia* (August 15, 2003, edited September 17, 2019): https://www.georgiaencyclopedia.org/articles/business-economy/vidalia-onions/. George E. Boyhan, et al., "Onions: UGA Cooperative Extension," University of Georgia Extension (June 1, 2006). "10 Things You Didn't Know about Vidalia Onions," *Explore Georgia* (April 2018): www.exploregeorgia.org/blog/10-things-you-didnt-know-about-vidalia-onions. "Vegetables: Vidalia Onions," *College of Agricultural and Environmental Science, University of Georgia:* https://vegetables.caes.uga.edu/trial-results/vidalia-onions.html.

GENERAL INDEX

Acheson, Hugh, 105
Africa, ix–xii, 92, 98–100, 122; cookery, ix–xii, 100, 124, 170–71; ingredients, 8, 18, 48, 64, 98–99, 122–24, 132, 170–71, 174–76
African American, 6–8, 15, 49, 55, 59–61, 64–66, 154–56; gardens, 8, 98; Gullah-Geechee, 22–23, 25, 52, 59–60, 65, 98, 107–8, 124, 174–76; medicine, 66; party, 111–12; vegetables, 98–99, 122–24, 170–71, 174–76
Afro-American Advance, 50
Albany, GA, 78; W. W. Rawlins Sausage Co., 78
Alderman, Sydney, 101
Alexander Seed Co. (Augusta), 167
All, Ernest, 26
All-American Selection, 114
Altamaha River, 24
alum, 145
Ambos, Henry, 127
Amelia Island, 147
American Cakes, 37
American Farmer, 46
Americus, 128, 140, 198, 211, 212; *Recorder*, 128; *Times-Recorder*, 142–43
anchovy, 47–48
Anson Mills, 172–73; "Anson Mills Red Pea Gravy," 176; "Anson Mills Savannah Red Rice," 172–73
Apalachicola River, 101–2
apple, 1–4; seasons 1–2; cider, 1, 4; cideries, 4; compote, 3; diseases, 4; flavor, 2–3; fried pie, 81; Georgia Apple Association, 2; healthfulness, 2; production, 3–4; "Roasted Sweet Potato Apple Soup," 194–95; sauce, 2; sauce pie, 2; varieties, 1–2; Yates cider apple, 4
Athens, 41, 106; Bowhunter's Club, 106; *Daily Herald*, 166; Five and Ten Restaurant, 79; Georgia Products Feast, 213–14; *Woman's Work*, 41
Atlanta, 6, 13, 16; *Atlanta Constitution*, 6, 134; Atlanta Food Processors Cagle Inc. 28; Atlanta Nurseries, 139; Georgia Products Feasts, 214–19; *Golden Age*, 40; *Journal,* 11, 13, 16, 24–26, 35, 61, 63, 76–77, 85, 115, 135, 140–41, 147, 151, 155–56, 162, 197; Midway's Saloon, 16; *Semi-Weekly Journal,* 179; *Sunny South,* 172; *Women's Club Cookbook,* 160
Augusta, 6, 9, 16, 18, 46, 62, 78, 114, 130, 158–59, 184; Augusta National Golf Course, 150; *Chronicle,* 51, 77, 79, 80, 84, 102, 104, 107, 148–49, 178, 203; *Daily Constitutionalist,* 48, 52, 83; Delmonico Restaurant, 62; Jansen's Restaurant, 6; Junior League cookbook, 157; *Weekly Constitutionalis*t, 134

bacon, 19, 52, 56, 61, 67, 108, 112, 128, 170–73; grease, 103, 115, 152
Bacon, G. W., 140
Bailey, Cornelia, xiv, 22–23, 123, 175; Maurice, 23
Bailey, Mashama, vii–viii
baking, 10–14, 35–36, 59, 61–62, 85; powder, 10–11, 52; soda, 10, 52
bar, 30, 33
barbecue, 5–7, 16, 40; African American, 6–7; contests, 7; grouper, 90–91; "King of," 6; outdoor event, 5–6; "Peach Barbecue Sauce," 131; politics, 6–7; pork, 7; restaurant, 6–7; sauce, 7, 102; Slaton Barbecue, 6; stands, 7
Barnesville, 219; Georgia Products Feast, 219
batter, 25, 39, 52, 80, 90–91, 98, 128, 191
beans, [see also butter beans] xi, 18–19, 64; bush, 18–19; casserole, 183; cooking, 182; pole, 18–19, 182; snap, 174, 182–84
Beatie, W. D., 139
benne [heirloom sesame seed], 8–9; biscuit, 12; candy, 9; feed for fowls, 9; medicinal uses, 8; oil, 8–9, 25, 86; processing, 8; Savannah Benne Candy Company, 9; seed cake, 8
Bennett, John, 170
Berckmans, P. J., 130, 158
Berzilia, 159

[273]

Bibb County, 220; Georgia Products Feast, 220
biscuit, 10–14, 57, 103–4; baking powder, 11; Ballard's Oven Ready, 12; beaten, 10; buttermilk, 11; cheese, 13; dough, 80; ham, 57; Pillsbury Grands, 10, 12; sweet potato, 14, 191–92
black walnuts, 41
Blairsville, 53
Bluffton, 57; White Oak Pastures, 57
boiling, 58, 61, 67–68, 77
bologna, 78–79; Mortadella, 78; "Scramble," 78
Bonner, Daisy, 55
Boston, 43; *Commercial Bulletin,* 55; Cooking School, 55; Hovey Seed Co., 43
bourbon, 38; "Bourbon Braised Mustard Greens and Potatoes," 115–16
Branch, Mel I., 159
bread, 51–53; "Caramalized Vidalia Onion and Corn Skillet Corn Bread," 208–9; corn, 51–53; crackling, 144; crumbs, 61; pimento cheese corn bread, 150; rye, 79
breakfast, 10, 20, 32, 53, 78, 87, 101–2, 172–73
Bridges, Smith, 65
brining, 165
Brock, Sean, 105
Brown, Theressa C., 168; *Modern Domestic Cookery,* 168
Brownstone, Cecily, 33, 183
Brunswick, GA, 15, 17, 60, 90, 113, 160; *Advertiser,* 170–71; Georgia Products Feast, 220–21; Main Street Jubilee Festival, 17
Brunswick, VA, 15–17
Brunswick stew, 15–17, 65; origin, 15–17; "How to Make a Brunswick Stew," 10

Bryan, Stephanie, 154
Burnt Mountain, 82
Burpee, W. Atlee, 19
butchers, 78, 103–4; Pinetucky Country Meats (Swainsboro), 98
butter, 51, 62, 67, 80, 165, 183
butter beans, 15, 18–19; flavor, 18–19; Jackson Wonder, 18–19; speckled, 18–19; willow leaf, 18
buttermilk, 10–14, 27–28, 52, 77, 180, 208–9; biscuit, 12
Butts County, 57; Georgia Products Feast, 221–22
Byrn, Anne, 37; *American Cakes,* 37

cabbage, 25, 40–44, 114, 122, 145, 167; Charleston Wakefield, 40
Cairo GA, 111; *Messenger,* 111
cake, 37–39; fig preserve, 77; "Pecan Cake," 140–41
Callaway, John, 6
Camden County, 139
camp cooking, 71, 73, 156, 200
Campbell's Soup, 187
candy, 9, 133–34; "Pea-Nut Cakes," 133; pecan, 140; "San Domingo Ground Nut Cakes," 134
cane syrup, xiv, 20–23, 133
canning, 76–77, 136–37, 146, 148–49, 152, 182, 184
cantaloupe, 102, 145; pickle (mango), 145
Carolina Gold Rice Foundation, xiv, 23
Carver, George Washington, 120
Catawba wine, 30
catfish, 24–28; bait, 24; chowder, 26, 65; farming, 26; fried, 25. 27–28; stew 25–26; varieties, 26
catsup, 45–48, 83–85, 145, 170, 179; varieties, 45

cayenne, 15, 46–47, 49–50, 55, 61–62, 67–68, 116
celery, 41, 61, 63, 69, 107–8, 137, 176; leaves, 147; salt, 187; seed, 35, 40
Charleston, 10, 21, 45, 54, 174; *News and Courier,* 66; *Southern Patriot,* 10
Charlton, 222; Georgia Products Feast, 222
Chatham Artillery Punch, 29–31; Company 29–30; Gouda, potency, 30–31; recipe, 30
Chatham County, 126–27, 174, 178; Georgia Products Feast, 223–24
Chattooga County, 199
cheese, 13, 186–87; cheddar, 32, 34, 149; 183; goat, 32; Gouda, 34; Monterey-Jack, 149; pimento, 148–50; straws, 32–34
chestnut, 166; dressing, 165
chicken, 15, 54–56; "Chicken Gravy," 162; cream of chicken coup, 187; curried, 54–56; fried, 56; mull, 109–10; pie, ix, 35–36
Child, Julia, 69; *Julia's Kitchen Wisdom,* 69
chowder, 25–26, 48; catfish, 26, 65
Christ Church Savannah, 30, 71; *Cook Book,* 30; *From Savannah Kitchens,* 71
Christmas, 53, 57, 80, 140, 154, 196
Civil War, 21, 32, 35, 45–46, 48–49, 52, 83, 92, 120, 126, 145, 159
Claiborne, Craig, 53, 88
Clarke County, 108
Claxton, 225; Georgia Products Feast, 225
Clifton, 226; Georgia Products Feast, 226
Cobb County, 18, 53

Cobbett, William, 167
Coca-Cola, 22–2, 37, 58; Bourbon and Cherry Coca-Cola Cake, 38–9; Cake, 37–39, Cherry Coke, 38; glaze, 58
Coe, Caroline, 80;" Fried Pie Crust," 80
Coleman, Moses, Jr., 206
collard, 41–42, 43–44; blue stem, 44; coleworts, 43; Collard Green and Cabbage slaw, 42; perennial, 44; salt extraction, 44; seed, 44; slaw, 41; varieties, 43–44; white cabbage, 44
coleslaw, 40–42; cold slaw, 40; hot, 40–41; sugar in, 41
Colonial Williamsburg, 165
Colquitt, Harriet, 31, 58, 60–61, 117–18, 172, 177–78; *The Savannah Cook Book*, 31, 58, 60–61, 117–18, 172, 177–78
Columbus, GA, 46, 55; Georgia Products Feast, 227; *Sun*, 46
Common Sense in the Kitchen, 50
condiments, 45–50; pepper vinegar, 49–50; tomato catsup, 45–47; Worcestershire sauce, 47–49
Conger Compound Lard Bill, 103
contest, 7, 17, 33, 35, 51–52, 67–68, 131, 149, 192
cookie, 135; "Peanut Butter Cookies," 135
cookstove, 52
Cordele, 7, 102
corn, 11, 174; bread, 44, 51–53; bread mix, 52–53; "Caramalized Vidalia Onion and Corn Skillet Corn Bread," 208–9; dent, 51; dodger, 51; flint, 51, 87; flour, 11, 51–52; grits, 87–89; heirloom, 53, 87–

89; hoecake, 51; lye processing (nixtamalization), 87; meal, 25, 51–52, 192; pone, 51; stone ground, 53, 88
cotton, 20, 103, 111; Cottonlene, 103; cottonseed oil, 24–25, 111, 120
Country Captain, 54–56; name, 55
country cooking, 16, 66
country ham, 57–58, 154, 183
COVID-19, 5, 60
Coweta, 156; Possum Eaters Association, 156
crab, 48, 59–63; blue, 59–60; oyster, 59; pie, 59; rice; 59, soft-shelled, 60, 62–63; stew, 48, 59; stone, 59
cracker, 106–10, 128
Cracker Barrel, 37
Cracklings, 196
Crawford, 106
Crawfordville, 19
Cumberland Island, 72, 119–20; Dungeness Plantation, 119; lemon culture, 147
Cumming, Mrs. Brian, 190; "Rosa's Sweet Potato Pone," 190
curry, 54–56, 63; powder, 54
Cuthbert, 140

Dalton, 228; Georgia Products Feast, 228
Darien, 8, 21; "Cold Press Castor & Benne Oil," 8
Davis, Mrs. H. M., 192–93; "Sweet Potato Johnny Cake," 192–93
Dawson, 229; Georgia Products Feast, 229
Decatur, 7, 111; Georgia Products Feast, 229–30
"Decline and Fall of Cornbread," 51
Dewey, Admiral George, 31
DeWitt, 140

dill, 147
Dillard, 57
Dixon, Jerome, Sr., 23
Doak, Louise, 41; *Gems from Georgia Kitchens*, 41
Dooly County, 230–31; Georgia Products Feast, 230–31
Douglas, 231–32; Georgia Products Feast, 231–32
dove, 70–71, 107; field dressing, 70; mull, 107; pie, 71; smothered, 71
drought tolerance, 18–19
Dublin, GA, 24; Georgia Products Feast, 232–33
duck, 72–74; black, 72; canvasback, 73; Ducks Unlimited, 72; farmed, 72; hunting, 72; mallard, 73; redhead, 72; scaup, 72; teal, 72, 74; widgeon, 72; wood, 72
Dull, Mrs. S. R., 11–12, 35, 63, 76–77, 134, 161; Chicken Pie, 35; Fig Preserves, 76–77
Duluth, GA, 197
Dupree, Nathalie, xii, 88, 145; *Cooking of the South*, 145
dyspepsia, 41

Eastman, 141
Ebenezer, xi; Salzburgers, xi
Edgeworth, Mary, 145–46; *Southern Gardener and Receipt Book*, 145–47; "To Pickle Peaches," 147; "Lemon Pickle," 147
egg, 25, 40–41, 51; deviled, 67–69; casserole, 69; guinea fowl, 93–94; hard boiled, 36, 68–69; scramble, 115, 152
eggplant, 98–100; African origin, 98; fritter, 100; red, 98
Elam, M. T., 140
Elijay, 3, 81, 182
England, 10, 47–49

Fannin County, 3
Fayette County, 4
Fayetteville, 115; *Fayetteville Favorite Foods Cookbook*, 115, 157
Fery, Richard, 149
festival, 17, 35, 44, 81; Chicken Pie, 35
field peas, 64–66, 174–74; black-eyed, 174; brown sugar crowder, 64–66; pods, 64; sea island red, 174–77; varieties, 64
fig, 75–77; brown turkey, 75; cake, 77; lemon, 75; marmalade, 77; preserving, 76–77; seasons, 75–76; sugar, 75–76; white Adriatic, 75–76
fish, 24–28, 62; black bass, 24, 198; camp cooking, 25, 90; catfish, 24–28; fried, 25, 112, 40; grouper, 90–91; hatchery, 199; mullet, 111–13; perch, 24; trout, 198–99; United States Fish Commission, 24
Fitzgerald, 7; Georgia Products Feast, 234; *Leader*, 192–93
Flint River, 101–2
Flood, Captain Samuel F., 139
Florida, 20, 59, 101, 113
Floyd County, 26; Georgia Products Feast, 235–36
foraging, 151–52
Forsyth County, 199; *News*, 199–200
Fort Benning, 55
Fort Valley, 129; Georgia Products Feast, 236–37; *Leader Tribune*, 131
Fowler, Damon, xii
Frederica, 139
freezing, 132–33, 178, 182
fried, 52, 62; bologna, 78–79; chicken, 52; eggplant, 98; "Fried Okra Fingers," 124–25; "Fried Oysters,"
128; green tomato, 84–85; hominy cakes, 88–89; mullet 111–12; pie, 80–82; soft shell crabs, 62; sweet potato fries, 196–97
fritter, 80; apple, 80; eggplant, 100; oyster, 128; shrimp, 177–78; "Shrimp and Crab," 180–81; "Shrimp and Rice," 178; sweet potato, 191–92
Fulton County, 237; Georgia Products Feast, 237

Gardening for the South (White), 98–99
Gardiner, Samantha Rachelle, 101
garlic, 41, 56, 116, 145; powder, 41
Gems from Georgia Kitchens, 41, 73, 186; "Baked Squash Casserole," 186; "Mallard or French Duck," 73
Georgia, ix–xv; Beekeepers Association, 102; Chamber of Commerce, ix–x; regions, xii; seed companies, xiii
Georgia Products Feast, ix–x, 10, 13, 24, 40, 65, 118, 127, 153, 178, 198, 211–53; Americus, 212; Athens, 213–14; Atlanta, 214–19; Barnesville, 219; Bibb County, 220; Brunswick, 220–21; Butts County, 221–22; Charlton, 222; Chatham County, 223–24; Claxton, 225; Clifton, 226; Columbus, 227; Dalton, 228; Dawson, 229; Decatur, 229–30; Dooly County, 230–31; Douglas, 231–32; Dublin, 232–33; Fitzgerald and Ben Hill County, 234; Floyd County, 235–36; Fort Valley, 236–37; Fulton
County, 237; Griffin, 238; Jackson, 238–39; Lavonia, 239–40; Macon, 240–42; Milledgeville, 243–44; Phelps, 244; Raymond, 245; Rome, 245–47; Sandersville, 247–48; Savannah, 249; Sumter County, 250–53; Tattnal County, 253; Thomson, 254; Tifton, 254–55; Toombs County, 255; Waycross, 256–57
Gibbs, Maria Louisa Poyas, 54–55; recipe book, 54–55
Gibson, Hugh, 66
Gillespie, Kevin, 105
Gilmer County, 3
ginger, 137; "Gingered Pears," 137; "Ginger Spiced Poached Pears," 137–38
glaze, 58
Glynn County, 60
Goode, Elle, 179; "Shrimp Pie," 179
Gould, J. H., 126
Grady County, 22–23, 44; cane syrup, 22–23; collard seed, 44
gravy, 35, 44, 71–74, 161–63, 204; "Chicken Gravy," 162; Madeira, 95–97
greens, x, 8, 43–44, 49–50, 65, 114–16, 122, 151–52, 201–5; "Bourbon Braised Mustard Greens and Potatoes," 115–16; mustard, 114–16; "Turnips & Greens," 205
griddle, 51, 78
Griffin, 41, 44; Agricultural Experimental Station, 44; *Daily News*, 41; Georgia Products Feast, 238; pimento pepper, 148–49
grilling, 74, 99; "Grilled Trout," 199
grits, 51, 87–89; cheese, 88; flint corn, 51, 87; instant, 87; yellow, 52, 88

[276]

GENERAL INDEX

grocery, ix–x, 21, 49, 54; Piggly Wiggly, 206
grouper, 90–91; hermaphroditic, 90; stuffed, 91; varieties, 90
Guerra, Antonia, 82
guinea fowl, 56, 92–94; gumbo, 93–94; roasted, 95–97; *The Guinea Fowl and Its Use as Food,* 93
guinea hog, 105
guinea squash, 98–100; fritter, 100; salad, 100; varieties, 98–99

Habersham County, 3
Hall County, 3
ham [see country ham]
Hansford, Sarah, 108
Haralson County, 3
Harder, Jules Arthur, 100; *Physiology of Taste,* 100
Harland, Marion, 50, 146; *Common Sense in the Kitchen,* 50; "Pickled Peaches," 146–47; possum, 155–56
Harris, Jessica, 122
Harris, Joel Chandler, 31
Hill, Annabella P., 50, 179; "Shrimp Pie," 179; "Sliced Sweet Potato Pie," 191; *Southern Practical Cookery & Receipt Book,* 50
Hog Hammock, 22–23
Holm, Mrs. Darwood, 73; "Mallard or French Duck," 73
home, 33; cooks, 44, 82; entertainment, 33
honey, 101–2; flavor, 101; sourwood, 101; tupelo, 102, 117; cake, 102
honey locust, 142–43
hominy, 51; fried hominy cakes, 88–89; grits, 51, 87–89; whole kernel, 87–88
Hopkins, Linton, 105, 175

Hoschton, 81; Mulberry Baptist Church, 81
hotel dining, 72, 154–55
Houston County, 134
Howard & Willet Drug and Seed (Augusta), 114
Hunter, Mrs. Joel, 160
hunting, 70–71, 106; duck, 72–74; regulations, 70; turkey, 164–65

icing, 38–39
India, 54–55
Indian meal [see corn meal]

Jackson, GA, 40; Georgia Products Feast, 238–39; *Progress-Argus,* 40
Jackson, Thomas, 18
Jasper, 53, 82; Farmers Market, 82
Jefferson, Thomas, 119
Jeffersonian, 14
Jekyll Island, 107
Jews, 24
Jones, Charles C., Jr., 29; *Historical Sketch of the Chatham Artillery,* 29
Jones, Harry "Squab," 108–9

kale, 115
Kellogg, Joseph, 135
Kentucky, 10
ketchup, 25, 108 [see also, catsup]
Khan, Hadji Nicka Bauker, 55; "Indian Sketches," 55
Kingsley, Anne, 104; "Plain Pastry," 104
Kirk, Lucille, 81–82; Fried Pies, 81–82
Kraft Pimento Cheese, 148
Kresovich, Steve, 23
Kresse, Herman, 120

Lake Eufaula, 24
Lakeland, 119
landrace, 44

Langworthy, C. F., 93–94; *The Guinea Fowl and Its Use as Food,* 93
lard, 8, 25, 36, 103–5; Armor Pastry Blend, 104; lardcore movement, 79, 105
Lavonia, 239–40; Georgia Products Feast, 239–40
Lee County, 35–36
lemon, 61, 77, 147; juice, 163; "Lemon Pickle," 147
Lewis's Crab Factory, 60–62
Liberty County, 136
lima beans, 18–19; Burpee's Bush, 18; Henderson's Dwarf, 18
Lincoln, Mary, 55
Long, Roscoe, 106
Louisiana, 20–21, 139; Louisiana State University, 120
Lowcountry, 47, 54, 91, 163, 174–76

McAfee Hotel, 35–36
McDonald's fried pies, 82
McIntosh, Ben, 107–8
Macon, 3, 16, 65, 68, 123; Georgia Products Feast, 240–42; mayor Smith Bridges, 65; *Telegram-Herald,* 10
macaroni and cheese, xi
Madeira, 48, 61, 68–69, 71, 95
Madison, 120
mangel wurtzel, 167
Mann, Roy, 26
Marietta, 61, 83, 156; *Journal,* 137
Maryland, 10, 45, 62; *Easton Gazette,* 45–46
Mayfield, 26
Matthews, Jimmy, 15, 17
mayonnaise, 41, 148–50; Duke's, 41, 63, 79
milk, 59, 106–10, 135, 163; base for stew, 60, 106–10; scalded, 80
Milledge, John, 8, 119
Milledgeville, 30; Georgia Products Feast, 243–44

Millen, 150
milling, xi, 52, 87–89
Mims, J. L., 46
molasses, 21, 47, 57, 133–34, 190
Moore, Glynn, 79
Morgan County, 157
mull, xii, 106–10; chicken, 106, 109–10; dove-106–7; snake, 106; turtle, 106
mullet, 111–13; fried, 112; roe, 113
Mullen, Aire, 55–56; Country Captain, 55–56
Murray County, 3
mustard, 33, 40; curled, 114–15; greens, 114–16; ostrich plume, 114–15; powder, 33, 40, 58, 62; prepared, 40–41, 67; seed, 50, 114, 145

Native American, 18, 59–60, 143, 185–87; contributions to Georgia food, xi; Cherokee, xi, 151, 165; Guale, 59, 126; Muscogee, xi, 87, 151, 165; Sewee, 18; Timucua, 59, 126; Yamasee, 59, 126
Neal, Bill, 53, 88
Neal, Irene, 82
nectarine, 129–31
Neely, Bobby, 107; "Dove Mull," 107
New Georgia Encyclopedia, 106
Newnan, 41; Junior Service League, 41; possum, 157
New Orleans, 29, 54, 89
North Carolina, 44, 190
New York, 130, 148
nutrition, 104–5, 151; lipids, 104

Ocmulgee River, 24
Oconee National Forest, 106
odor, 111–12
Ogeechee lime, 117–19; jelly, 118; pickle, 117–18
Ogeechee River, 101–2, 117
oil, 8–9, 25, 40, 103, 119–21; canola, 103; cottonseed, 24–25, 103, 111, 134; facto-

ries, 134; okra seed, 120–21; olive, 25, 56, 115, 119–20; peanut, 25, 120, 130; smoke point, 25, Wesson, 103
Okie, William Thomas, 130; *The Georgia Peach,* 130
okra, 120–21, 122–25; cosmetic use, 123; dried, 124; "Fried Okra Fingers, 124–25; Perkins Long Pod, 123; pickle, 147; seed oil, 120–21
Old and New Recipes from the South, 190
olive, 119–21; Arbequina, 119; oil, 25, 56, 115, 119–20
Oliver, Clay, 121; Oliver Farms Oils, 121
Oliver, John, 120
onion, 19, 42; Vidalia, 42, 206–9; yellow granex, 206
opossum [see possum]
orange, 72; juice, 131
Ossabaw Island, 105; pig, xiii, 105
oyster, 126–28, 166; "Fried Oysters," 128; "Oyster Dressing for Turkey," 166; roast, 126

Paddleford, Clementine, 107–8; "Shrimp Mull, 108"
pastry, 2, 32, 35–36, 73, 80–82, lard, 104–5
peach, 47, 58, 86, 129–31; Belle of Georgia, 129; cobbler, 131; diseases, 130; Elberta, 129–31; fried pie, 81; jam, 58; leaves, 47; pickled, 146; salad, 86
Peach County, 131
pea likker, 65, 174
peanut, 132–35; allergy, 135; butter, 134; french-fried, 132; green, 132; oil, 25, 120, 134, 197; "Pea-nut Cakes," 133; varieties, 132
pear, 136–38; blight, 136; "Gingered Pears," 137; "Ginger Spiced Poached Pears,"

137–38; Kieffer, 136; LeConte, 136; "Pear Relish," 137; sand, 137
pecan, 139–41; improved, 139; paper shell, 139
pellagra, 51, 87
Pemberton, John, 37
peppers, 41, 54–55, 61, 124; bird, 49, 65; cayenne, 15, 49–50, 65; pimento, 41, 15, 148–50; sweet green, 50; tabasco, 49; Truhard-NR, 149; vinegar, 49–50
Perry, Bob, 105
persimmon, 142–44, 154; "Persimmon Beer," 142
Phelps, 244; Georgia Products Feast, 224
Philadelphia, 43, 80; Landreth Seed Co., 43
Physical culture movement, 103
Pickens County, 81
pickle, 26, 41, 145–47; cantaloupe, 145; green tomato, 83–84; Higdon, 145; juice, 58; Ogeechee lime, 117–18; "Watermelon Rind Pickle," 159–60
picnic, 15–16, 40
pie, 80–82; crust, 80–81, 85; green tomato mince, 85; sweet potato, 190–91
pilau, 170–73
pimento, 34, 41; cheese, ix, 34, 148–50; Elkhorn Pimento Cheese, 148; Kraft Pimento Cheese, 148; peppers, 41; perfection, 148; straws, 34
pineapple, 54
Pitman-Robertson Wildlife Restoration Act of 1937, 164
Plumb & Leitner Drug Store (Augusta), 158
poke salad, 151–52; medicinal qualities, 151; toxicity, 152
Polk County, 3

poetry, 10, 29, 112, 154, 159
poison, 152
pork, 15–17, 78–79, 114–16; fat, 78, 103–5; lard, 103–5
possum and taters, 143, 153–57; cooking, 155; flavor, 153
potato, 25, 115–16, 167, 220; mashed, 44, 52, 179; pancake, 89; salad, 16
potlikker, 43–44, 65
preserving, 76
Price, Mrs. H. H., 115
Prohibition, 31, 61, 68–69
punch, 29–31

Quinan, Michael T., 29–30

rabbit, 15, 106, 109, 156
raccoon, 156
Rabun Gap, 53, 199
Raiford, Matthew, xii, 160
railroad, 35–36, 129–30
Raymond, 245; Georgia Products Feast, 245
Reigel, S. D., 148–49
restaurant, 6–7, 29, 16, 53, 87, 91; Awning Post Saloon (Savannah), 29; Booty's Fish House (Royston), 110; Bresnan's Hotel (Savannah), 126; *Café de la Paix* at the Atlanta Hilton, 91; Chase Street Café (Athens), 108; Crab Trap (Kennesaw), 91; Delmonico (Augusta), 62; Elizabeth on 37th (Savannah), 88; Five and Ten (Athens), 79; Georgia Fry House (Brunswick), 113; Hicks (Savannah), 62; Honey Café (Millen), 150; Kaufman's (Savannah), 61; Leake & McCrae (Marietta), 61; Med Henderson's (Savannah), 16; Midway's Saloon (Atlanta), 16; Miki (Atlanta), 62;

New Hotel (Brunswick), 61; Pickens Café (Savannah), 60; roadside, 7; Roscoe's Kountry Kitchen (Crawford), 106; Skeeter's Mesquite Grill (Dulluth), 197; The Grey (Savannah), vii–viii
rice, 25, 52, 55; and gravy, 161–63; Carolina Gold, 161–62, 170–73; flour, 25, 124–25; instant, 52; jollof, 170; pilau, 170–73; "Savannah Red Rice," 170–73; "Savory Rice #1," 162; steamed, 55, 161; "tomatoes and rice," 170–73; upland, 161
Richmond County, 258
road kill, 156
roasting, 95; guinea fowl, 95
Robinson, Sallie Ann, 108; *Gullah Home Cooking the Daufuskie Way*, 108
roe, 113
Rome, 245–47; Georgia Products Feast, 245–47
Rooney, Jim, 112; *Jim Rooney's Edisto Eatin'*, 112
Roopville, 57; Gum Creek Farm, 57
Roosevelt, Franklin Delano, 55
Roquemore, Nancy, 109; "Chicken Mull," 109
Ross, Sarah, 123
Royston, 110
Rumph, Samuel Henry, 129–30; Elberta Peach, 129–30
rutabagas, 167–69; livestock feed, 167; "Rutabaga and Turnip Soup," 168–69; "Rutabaga Turnips. #2," 168
Rutledge, Sarah, 174–75; *Carolina Housewife*, 174; "Red Peas Soup," 175

salad, 19, 40, 100, 182; butter bean, 19, coleslaw, 40–42;

crab, 59, 63; dressing, 42; eggplant, 100; green tomato and peach, 86; mustard greens, 115
salt, 57–58
Sandersville, 247–48; Georgia Products Feast, 247–48; *Herald*, 133
sandwich, 5, 7, 78, 83, 91, 148, 150; peanut butter, 135
Sapelo Island, xiv, 20–21, 23, 107, 123, 146, 174–76
sardine fat, 66
sauce, 9, 102; garum, 47; John Bull, 47; "Peach Barbecue Sauce," 131; Worcestershire, 46–48
Savannah, 3, 9, 29–31, 45, 49, 54, 60–61, 78, 88, 90, 126–28, 147; Chamber of Commerce, 172; *Daily Georgian*, 170; *Morning News*, 25, 31, 62–63, 67–68, 126; red rice, 170–73; River, 161–62; *Savannah Tribune*, 3, 137, 149
Sea Islands, 59–63, 90–91, 107–9, 161–62; red peas, 174–76
seafood [see also crab, oyster], 48, 59–63; oysters, 126–28; soups, 48
Shaw, T. H., 147
shortening, 36, 103; Cottonlene, 103; Crisco, 103
shrimp, 49, 177–81; and grits, 53; "Croquette Fritters," 177; mull, 107–8; pie, 49, 178–79; "Shrimp and Crab Fritters," 180–81; "Shrimp Fritters," 178; "Shrimp and Rice Croquettes,' 178
sieva bean [see butter bean]
Sister Mary, 128; "Fried Oysters," 128' "Pigs in Blankets," 128
Sluis, Abraham, 114
Slow Food Ark of Taste, 123
Smalls, Robert, 107

Smithville, 35–36
smokehouse, 57, 154, 165
smoking, 57, 165; corn cob, 57; hickory wood, 57
soaking, 58
Social Circle, 106
soup, 48, 59, 187; okra, 124; "Red Peas Soup," 175; "Roasted Sweet Potato Apple Soup," 194–95; "Rutabaga and Turnip Soup," 168; stock, 96, 115–16; "Turnip Puree Soup," 203–4
sour, 47
southern cookery, ix–xi; distinguished from American cookery, x–xi
Spalding County, 148
Spaulding, Thomas, 20–21
spices, 45–46, 54–55, 63, 76–77, 85, 146; allspice, 47; black pepper, 49, 55, 61; cardamom, 54; clove, 46–47; coriander, 54; cumin, 54; curry powder, 45, 48, 54–56, 63; fenugreek, 54; mace 46; medicinal, 49; nutmeg, 47, 55; pickling, 145–47; turmeric, 54
spinach, 152
Sprague, W. W., 71
squash, 185–87; yellow, 185–87; casserole, 186–87; pattypan, 185
squirrel, 15, 106
St. Simon, 17, 20, 107
state signature foods, x
stew, 8, 48, 167; Brunswick, 15–17; catfish, 25–26; fish, 48, 90; mull, 106–10; mullet, 112; "Wild Duck," 73
Stuckey, Stephanie, 141
Stuckey, W. S., Sr., 141
sugar, 20–23, 41, 50, 52, 76–77, 80, 133, 140, 145–47, 170; beet, 22, 167; brown, 21, 46, 57, 85, 133; cane, 20–23; export 21; Louisiana, 21–22; preserving, 76–77; purple ribbon, 20–21, Otahiete, 20; refined, 21; syrup, 20–23

Sumter County, 250–53; Georgia Products Feast, 250–53
Sunny South, 2
Swainsboro, 79
sweet potato, 14, 144, 188–93; biscuit, 14, 192; custard, 189–90; "French Fried Sweet Potatoes," 196; fried pie, 81; fries, ix, 196–97; possum and taters, 154–57; "Roasted Sweet Potato Apple Soup," 194–95; "Rosa's Sweet Potato Pone," 190
Swift & Co. (Atlanta), 78

Taft, William Howard, 6, 31, 143, 153–54; possum, 153–54; tour of Georgia, 6, 31, 143, 153–54
tamarind, 46–47
Taste of Georgia, 41, 157
Taste the State South Carolina, ix, 170
Tattnal County, 253; Georgia Projects Feast, 253
Taylor County, 3
Taylor, June, 45
Taylor, Willie, 139; centennial pecan, 139
tempura, 62
Terry, Elizabeth, 88–89
Texas, 147, 206
Thanksgiving, 53, 154, 162, 184
Thomas, Dr. William, 23
Thomson, 14, 19, 115; Georgia Products Dinner, 254; *Jeffersonian*, 14
Tifton, 127; Georgia Products Dinner, 254
tomato, 19, 55–56, 61, 109, 124, 170–73, 179–80; catsup, 45–47, 84, 170; gravy, 178;

green, 83–86; Livingston Acme, 46, 83; popularity of, 45; "Savannah Red Rice," 170–73
Toombs County, 206; Georgia Products Dinner, 255; Sweet Potato Association, 206
trout, 198–200; brook, 198–99; brown, 199; farmed, 198–99; "Fried Trout," 200; "Grilled Trout," 199; native, 198; rainbow, 198–99; "Stuffed Trout," 200
truck farming, 258
turkey, 164–66; domesticated breeds, 164; roast, 164–65; smoked, 165
turnip, 72, 201–5; fodder, 201–2; greens, 201; Japanese bred, 202; mashed, 204; sallat, 201–4; soup, 203–4; "Turnip's and Greens," 205; varieties, 201–2

University of Georgia, 106–10; Center for Research and Education at Wormsloe, 123

Vadhera, Shalini, 123; *Passport to Beauty*, 123
Vance, John, 132–33
Vidalia, GA, 206–7; onion, 72, 206–9; "Caramelized Vidalia Onion and Corn Skillet Corn Bread," 208–9
vinegar, 19, 40–42, 58, 145–47; apple cider, 58, 145; pepper, 48–50; spice, 49
Virginia, 15–17, 21, 153; *Alexandria Gazette*, 15; Brunswick 15–16

Walker County, 3
Warm Springs, 55
Washington, GA, 19

Washington, Mrs. [pseudonym], 73; *The Unrivaled Cookbook,* 73
watermelon, 258–60; "A Watermelon Song," 159; pickle, 160; Rattlesnake, 258–60; rind, 159–60
Waycross, 256–57; Georgia Products Dinner, 256–57
Wayne County, 78; *News,* 78
Webber, Mike, 199–200
Wells, Mrs. J. B., 186
Wells, Pickens, 6

Wesson oil, 120–21
West Indies, xi, 20
wheat, 36, 51; flour, 61, 71; Timilia durum, xi; white winter, 36, 51
White, William, xii, 98–99; *Gardening for the South,* xii, 98–99
white tupelo, 101–2
Whitehead, Jessup, 203–4; *Steward's Handbook,* 203–4
Wilder, J. J., 102
Wilkes County, 6

Wilkins, Mrs. Grant, 61–62; Deviled Crabs, 61–62
Willet, G. M., 147
Willet, N. L., 18; *Willet's Catalog,* 18
Wilmington River, 126
Wood, Elizabeth, 40
World War I, 51, 134
World War II, 61, 88, 120, 130
Worcestershire sauce, 25, 60–61, 71, 107–8, 172; John Duncan & Sons, 47–49; Lea and Perrins, 48–49

RECIPE INDEX

Apples:
    Compote of, 3
    Apple sauce pie, 2

Barbecue:
    sauce, 7
Biscuits:
    beaten, 10
    buttermilk, 11
    cheese, 13
    sweet potato, 14
Brunswick Stew:
    How to make a, 15
    Real Brunswick stew, 16

Cardamon Crème Fraîche,
    see Roasted Sweet Potato
    Apple Soup, 194
Catfish:
    chowder, 26
    fried, 25, 27–28
Chatham Artillery Punch, 30
Cheese Straws:
    Cheese straws, 32
    pimento, 34
Chicken Pie:
    Chicken pie, 36
Coca-Cola Cake
    Bourbon and cherry
        Coka-Cola cake, 38–39
Coleslaw:
    cold slaw, 40, 41
    collard green and cabbage, 42
Condiments:
    Tomata catsup, 46
    Tomato catsup, 46–47
    Pepper vinegar, 50
    Worcester [Worcestershire]
        sauce, 48

Corn Bread:
    Best corn bread, 52
Country Captain:
    Curry powder, 54–55
    Country captain, 56
Country Ham, *see* Sweet Potato
    cracklings, 195
Crab:
    boiled, soft-shell, 62
    deviled, 61–62
    fried, Maryland style, 63
    stew, 60–61

Deviled Eggs, 69
Doves:
    pie, 71
Duck:
    Mallard, 71
    wild, stewed, 71–72
Dressing, *see* Roast Turkey, 164
    chestnut, 166
    oyster, 166

Figs:
    cake, preserve, 77
    marmalade, 77
    preserves, 76
Fried Bologna:
    scramble, 78
Fried Pies:
    crust, 80
    Kirk, Lucille, 81

Gravy, *see* Guinea Fowl,
    Madeira, 97
Green Tomatoes:
    catsup, 84
    fried, 84
    Green tomato and peach salad, 86

    mince pie, 85
    pickle, 83
Guinea Fowl:
    Carolina gumbo, 93
    cooking of, 93
    roasted, 95–97
Guinea Squash (eggplant):
    fried, 98
    fritters, 100
    salad, 100

Honey:
    cake, 102

Lard:
    Plain pastry, 104

Mull:
    chicken, 109
    dove, 107
    shrimp, 108
Mullet:
    fried, 112
Mustard Greens:
    Bourbon braised mustard
        greens and potatoes, 115–16

Ogeechee Limes, 118
Okra:
    Fried okra fingers, 124–25
Oysters:
    fried, 128
    fritters, 128
    pigs in blankets, 128

Peaches:
    barbecue sauce, 131
Peanuts:
    Pea-nut cakes, 133

[283]

Peanut butter cookies, 135
San Domingo ground nut
    cake, 134
Pears:
    Gingered pears, 136
    Ginger spiced poached
        pears, 137–38
    relish, 137
Pecans:
    cake, 140–41
    sugared pecans, 140
Persimmon beer, 142–43
Pickles:
    Dilled okra, 147
    Lemon pickle, 147
    Pickled peaches, 146
Pimento Cheese, 149

Rattlesnake Watermelon:
    Watermelon rind pickle
        no. 1 (sweet), 160
Rice and Gravy:
    Chicken gravy, 162–63
    Savory rice no. 1, 162
Rutabagas:
    Rutabaga turnips no. 2, 168

Rutabaga and turnip soup,
    168–69

Savannah Red Rice:
    Anson Mills Savannah red
        rice, 172–73
    Tomatoes and rice, 172
Sea Island Red Peas:
    Anson Mills red pea gravy,
        176
    Red peas soup, 175
Shrimp:
    fritters, 178
    pie, 179
    Shrimp and crab fritters,
        180–81
    Shrimp croquettes fritters,
        177
    Shrimp or prawn pie, 179
    Shrimp and rice croquettes
        fritters, 178
Soup, *see* Rutabaga, 167
    rutabaga and turnip, 168–69
Squash:
    casserole, baked, 186
Stock, *see* roasted guinea hen,
    95–97

Sweet Potatoes:
    biscuit, 192
    cake, johnny, 192–93
    fritter, 191–92
    pie, sliced, 191
    pone, 190
    soup with apple and crème
        fraîche, 194–95
Sweet Potato Fries:
    French fried, 196

Trout:
    fried, 200
    grilled, 199
    stuffed, 200
Turnip and Turnip Sallet:
    soup, turnip puree [cream
        of], 203
    soup, turnip, 203
    turnips and greens, 205

Vidalia Onion:
    Caramelized Vidalia onion
        and corn skillet corn
        bread, 209

MENU INDEX

This index accompanies "Menus of the 1913 Georgia Products Feasts."

Breads and Quick Breads
    beaten biscuit, 215, 216, 222, 228, 236, 242, 243
    biscuit, 238, 239, 243, 250
    bread, 225, 228, 237, 240, 246, 253; sticks, 221, 252
    brown bread, 223, 246
    buckwheat cakes, 231
    buttermilk biscuit, 214, 237, 243
    corn bread, 216, 221, 222, 225, 226, 234, 239, 253; dodgers, 242; dumplings, 247; pone, 215, 216, 232, 238, 246, 247, 249; sticks, 241
    crackers, 220, 223, 234, 236, 237, 239, 242, 245, 248
    crackling bread, 233, 242
    egg bread, 238, 246, 248
    hoecake, 230, 234, 242
    hot rolls, 212, 219, 228, 238, 243, 248, 251; finger, 241
    light bread, 239, 243
    pancakes, Jenny Lynn, 214, 237
    salt rising bread, 217, 222, 242
    Tip Top bread, 215, 226
    Uncle Sam bread, 215
    waffles, 237, 243; cheese, 216
    wheat cakes, 234

Desserts
    apple, baked, 213, 215; turnovers, 242
    blackberry dumplings, 242
    butter wafers, 215
    cake, 226, 227, 228, 229, 233, 240, 245, 248; angel food cake, 222, 244; Brookhaven, 229, 230; caramel layer, 251; fruit, 246, 255; John B. Morgan cake, 224, 249; layer, 253; molasses and raisin cake, 218; pound cake, 219, 224, 232, 246, 249, 253, 254
    charlotte russe, 223
    cream. 241, 243
    custard, boiled, 214, 237; frozen, 244; sweet potato, 247
    floating island, 254
    gingerbread, 235, 247
    ice cream, 213, 226, 227, 228, 242, 246, 253; black walnut, 218; caramel, 225, 238; Elberta peach, 218, 222, 224, 233, 243, 249; Neapolitan, 215, 248; Silver Lake, 229, 230; strawberry, 224, 249; white way, 221
    pastry, 245
    peaches and cream, 231, 250, 253; cobbler, 255; gelatin, 219
    pie, 212, 224, 245; apple, 249; blackberry pie, 235; cherry, 235; country pie, 19; cushaw pie, 212, 252; dewberry, 235; peach pie, 218, 248; mince, 232, 246; pumpkin pie, 212, 214, 218, 223, 226, 234, 235, 237, 242, 246, 247, 249, 250, 252, 255; sweet potato pie, 224, 226, 235, 242, 244, 246
    pudding, Sunderland, 231; sweet potato, 233, 238; syrup, 212, 252
    sponge cake, 223
    walnut cake, 213

Fish and Shellfish
    bluefish, broiled, 220
    bream, 242
    catfish, fried channel, 218, 220, 242
    oysters, 213, 218, 220, 223; cocktail, 216, 227, 229, 232; creamed, 230; Thunderbolt, 217, 242
    red snapper, 245
    shad, baked, 216, 242
    Spanish mackerel, 213
    terrapin, 213; cassolette, 216
    trout, baked, 214, 230, 237, 240, 249; broiled, 21, 250, cornmeal fried, 223, 245, steak, 234

Gravies, Sauces, and Preserves
    apple sauce, 214, 251; fried, 231; jelly, 233
    blackberry jam, 233, 235, 243, 251
    butter sauce, 242
    cane syrup, 234

cranberry, 217
fig preserves, 212, 235, 252
grape jelly, 232
mayhaw jelly, 212, 224, 249, 250
peach preserve, 233, 235, 252
pear relish, 252
persimmon gravy, 217
plum jelly, 235, 251; sauce, 244
red and black sauce, 213
sorghum syrup, 217
watermelon preserves, 212, 252; rind pickle, 235, 246, 254

Main Dishes
    beef, 214, 254; and mushrooms, 212, 252; backbone, 241; barbecued, 235; braised, 250; loaf, 225, 253; prime rib, 218, 227, 233, 241, 248, 249; roast, 214, 222, 223, 226, 237, 245, 246, 255; smoked, 245; spareribs, 232, 240, 241, 255
    bacon, smoked, 247
    chicken, 222; creamed, 212, 219, 252; fried, 231, 239, 243, 245, 255; patties, 218, 234; pie, 225, 232, 238, 253; roasted, 224, 249
    duck, 242, 250; baked, 255
    goose, baked, 212, 252; roast, 224, 249
    ham, 215, 223, 237, 241, 247, 252; baked, 215, 226; boiled, 213, 224, 239, 245, 249; chipped, 230; country, 212, 238, 239, 243, 251, 254
    hash, 236
    hog and hominy, 228
    kid, 241; barbecue, 235
    lamb, 212, 252; barbecued, 235, 245

mutton, 212, 241, 252
partridge, 242
pig, roast, 214, 218, 219, 224, 249
pork 222, 236, 247; barbecue, 217, 230, 233, 234, 235, 236, 240, 241, 245; chops with fried apples, 231
possum and sweet potatoes, 212, 213, 214, 219, 224, 226, 228, 229, 233, 237, 238, 239, 240, 241, 249, 251, 255; barbecued, 235, 245; roasted, 246; with chestnuts, 217
quail, 212, 224, 249, 252, 255
rabbit, 212, 224, 249; barbecued, 235, 245; hash, 245
ricebirds, 242
sausage, 243, 252; smoked, 241
squab, 233
squirrels, fried, 255
sweetbreads, 223, 248
tongue, 214, 237
turkey, 213, 229, 236, 239, 254, 255; baked, 225, 236; roasted, 213, 219, 221, 228, 231, 236, 238, 250, 254; with chestnut dressing, 212, 215, 217, 220, 221, 224, 228, 230, 244, 245, 248, 249, 251, 252; with oyster dressing, 227, 244; with sweet potato stuffing, 233
veal, braised, 233; croquettes, 215; roast leg, 232
venison, 242

Salads and Relishes
    apple, 242; and peanut salad, 225, 253
    artichoke pickle, 252; salad, 224, 252

asparagus and pepper salad, 224
beet, 224, 249
cabbage, 236, 250
celery, 220, 223, 228, 229, 230, 236, 238, 239, 240, 243, 244, 247; hearts, 213, 216; white plume, 215, 226, 248
chow chow, 250, 254
chicken salad, 215, 225, 236, 239, 252
coleslaw [cold slaw], 214, 224, 229, 231, 236, 237, 249
combination salad, 219, 220
corn salad, 230
cucumber pickle, 212, 225, 226, 252, 253; dill, 223; dixie mixed pickle, 213, 214, 215, 223, 226, 238, 249
endive, 246
fruit, 239, 247
horseradish, 241
India relish, 232
lettuce, 224, 232, 234, 236, 241, 249; and egg, 226; and tomato, 217, 227, 248, 250
melon rind [mango pickle], 236
mustard pickle, 234
olives, 220, 223, 226
peach pickle, 212, 223, 230, 238, 247, 249, 252
pear pickle, 252
peppers, green, 226, 236, 245, 246; hot, 236
pickles, 222, 236, 239, 240, 241, 244, 245, 247
potato, 225, 240, 253
radishes, 214, 218, 220, 232, 236, 240, 241, 248, 252
shallots, 226
shrimp, pickled, 221
spring onions, 214, 215, 241, 245, 248

tomato pickle 218; green, 218, 250, sliced salad, 224, 236, 241, 245, 247, 249

vegetable salad, 218, 234

watercress, 220

Soups and Stews

backbone stew, 221, 222

beef, 244

Brunswick stew, 236, 240, 241

catfish chowder, 241

chicken, Cream of, 248; Georgia 219

clam, 245

clear amber, 250

mock turtle, 220, 234

okra gumbo, 232

oyster, 243; Brunswick, 229; Thunderbolt stew, 236, 254

pealikker, 241

potato chowder, 225

potlikker, 241

terrapin, soup, 223, 241; stew, 213, 249, 251

turtle, 223, 249, 251; green, 218

tomato, 215, 221, 238; bisque, 223; bouillon, 223, 232, 249, 253; cream of, 221, 225, 226, 256; puree, 215

vegetable, 214, 230, 237, 241, 245, 246, 252, 256

Vegetables

asparagus, 212, 213, 221, 242, 248, 252; creamed, 235, 244

beans, 235; butter [lima], 212, 235, 238, 245, 247, 251; snap, 212, 217, 242, 251; string, 224, 248, 255; wax [greasy], 233, 242

beets, 212, 235, 249, 251

Brussels sprouts, 213

cabbage, 235, 245, 251

carrots, 235, 246, 250

cauliflower, 213, 250

collards, 212, 232, 233, 235, 239, 241, 242, 251, 254, 255

corn, 218, 224, 239, 247, 249; country gentleman, 218, 234; fried, 246; scalloped, 251

cushaw [Kershaw], baked, 212, 224, 235, 245; mashed, 233

eggplant [guinea squash], 212, 235, 247, 249; fried, 246; fritters, 250

greens, 238

hominy, 228, 229, 239, 243; fried, 231, 233

mushroom, 212

okra, 235

onions, boiled 212, 251; creamed, 224, 244, 248

parsnips, 235

peas [field peas], 232; black-eyed, 217, 242; cornfield, 214, 237; crowder, 217, 220, 242; white [lady], 226, 242, 255

peas [green peas], 218, 221, 234, 235, 238, 239; on lettuce leaves, 212; pods, 221

peppers, green, 212, 216, 251; stuffed, 225, 231, 250, 252, 253

potatoes, baked, 238; boiled, 214, 216, 222, 229, 232, 235, 237, 242, 247, 254; chips [Saratoga chips], 223, 227, 231, 237, 243; creamed 212, 215, 218, 219, 221, 234, 242, 247, 252; croquettes, 221, 230; fried, 220, 243; julienne, 221, 234; mashed, 212, 220, 244, 246, 248, 249; scalloped, 250; shoestring, 218, 219, 248; snowflake, 226

rice, 223, 224, 226, 232, 235, 238, 240, 243, 244, 246, 248, 249

rutabagas, 246, 247

squash, 216, 235, 242; hubbard, 216

spinach, 235; with eggs, 227

sweet potato [candied yam], 214, 217, 219, 220, 221, 222, 223, 224, 225, 227, 228, 229, 231, 232, 233, 234, 235, 236, 237, 238, 240, 242, 243, 244, 246, 250, 252, 253, 254

Swiss chard, 235

tomatoes, 212, 216, 239, 242, 247, 252, 254; green, 250; scalloped, 243; stewed, 233; stuffed, 225, 253

turnip, 213, 225, 226, 227, 229, 238, 251, 253; greens [sallet/salad], 213, 217, 219, 231, 232, 236, 242, 255; mashed, 214, 224, 237

vegetables, 222, 246

[287]

MENU INDEX